# Windows® 7

## Step by Step

**Joan Preppernau and Joyce Cox**
**Online Training Solutions, Inc.**

PUBLISHED BY
Microsoft Press
A Division of Microsoft Corporation
One Microsoft Way
Redmond, Washington 98052-6399

Library of Congress Control Number: 2009932323

ISBN: 978-0-7356-2667-6

Printed and bound in the United States of America.

14 15 16 17 18 19 20 21 22  QG  9 8 7 6 5 4

Distributed in Canada by H.B. Fenn and Company Ltd.

A CIP catalogue record for this book is available from the British Library.

Microsoft Press books are available through booksellers and distributors worldwide. For further information about international editions, contact your local Microsoft Corporation office or contact Microsoft Press International by fax at (425) 936-7329. Visit our Web site at www.microsoft.com/mspress/. Send comments to mspinput@microsoft.com.

**Acquisitions Editor:** Juliana Aldous Atkinson
**Developmental Editor:** Sandra Haynes
**Project Editor:** Rosemary Caperton
**Editorial Production:** Online Training Solutions, Inc.

Body Part No. X15-74141

[2014-03-28]

# Contents

---

**What do you think of this book? We want to hear from you!**

Microsoft is interested in hearing your feedback so we can continually improve our books and learning resources for you. To participate in a brief online survey, please visit:

**microsoft.com/learning/booksurvey**

**Part 2    Experiencing the World Wide Web**

## 12    Set Up Hardware Devices    391

**What do you think of this book? We want to hear from you!**

Microsoft is interested in hearing your feedback so we can continually improve our books and learning resources for you. To participate in a brief online survey, please visit:

**microsoft.com/learning/booksurvey**

## About the Authors

**Joan Preppernau** has worked in the training and certification industry for 13 years. As President of Online Training Solutions, Inc. (OTSI), Joan is responsible for guiding the translation of technical information and requirements into useful, relevant, and measurable training and certification tools. Joan is a Microsoft Certified Trainer (MCT) and Microsoft Certified Application Specialist (MCAS) in Microsoft Office 2007 and Windows Vista, a Microsoft Certified Technology Specialist (MCTS) in Windows Vista, and the author of more than two dozen books about Windows and Office (for Windows and Mac). Joan lives in Bartonville, Texas, with her husband, Barry, and their daughter, Trinity.

**Joyce Cox** has 25 years' experience in the development of training materials about technical subjects for non-technical audiences, and is the Vice President of OTSI. She is the author of dozens of books about Office and Windows technologies and developed the *Quick Course* series of computer training books for beginning and intermediate adult learners. She was the first managing editor of Microsoft Press, an editor for Sybex, and an editor for the University of California. Joyce and her husband, Ted, live in downtown Bellevue, Washington.

## The Team

This book would not exist without the support of the entire OTSI publishing team:

- Jean Trenary, who managed the project
- Charles Preppernau and Rob Carr, who reviewed the content for technical accuracy
- Jaime Odell, who copy edited and proofread the text
- Kathy Krause, who acted as a reader advocate and indexed the book
- Lisa Van Every, who laid out the book in InDesign and created the eBook
- Jeanne Craver, who processed the graphics
- Marlene Lambert, who compiled the index and pitched in wherever necessary
- Susie Carr, who created the companion CD

We're especially thankful to the people at home who make it possible for our team members to devote so much of their time and attention to our projects.

Thanks also to the many people at Microsoft Press and Microsoft Learning who supported this book through its inception, creation, and release, including Rosemary Caperton, Sandra Haynes, and Juliana Aldous.

## Online Training Solutions, Inc. (OTSI)

OTSI specializes in the design, creation, and production of Office and Windows training products for information workers and home computer users. For more information about OTSI, visit

www.otsi.com

# Introducing Windows 7

Windows 7 is the computer operating system we've all been waiting for!

This latest version of the Windows operating system provides a deceptively simple computing experience; deceptive because on a Windows 7 computer, you can perform more—and more advanced—computing operations than ever before.

One of the first things you might notice about Windows 7 is the elegant look of the user interface. If you're accustomed to working with Windows Vista, you'll find a refined and enhanced interface with only a few new navigational features to learn. If you have been using an earlier version of Windows, you'll find there have been significant changes, and will quickly appreciate the high-quality visual effects of the Windows 7 interface. Windows 7 includes several new features that utilize the Aero functionality introduced with Windows Vista. Features such as animations, translucent glass window frames, Windows Flip, Windows Flip 3D, Aero Peek, and Aero Shake provide an amazing desktop computing experience.

Beneath the attractive and efficient interface lies a powerful yet unobtrusive operating system. Windows 7 operates very efficiently, so your computing experience is faster than ever before—you'll particularly notice this if you upgrade your computer from Windows Vista. Security features that were introduced with Windows Vista have been refined to maximize usability and minimize interruptions.

A new view of the file storage structure, called a *library*, gives you access to multiple storage locations from one window. Locating files, programs, and utilities has never been easier, and various tools and gadgets make it simple to do the things you want and need to do with your computer. Certain programs that were formerly installed with Windows, such as the e-mail management program known, in its various versions, as Windows Live Mail, Windows Mail, or Outlook Express, have been removed from the operating system to concentrate Windows 7 resources on managing your computer. These programs are now available to all Windows users as part of the Windows Live family of programs.

You might have purchased a new computer with Windows 7 pre-installed or you might have already upgraded your existing computer from another operating system to Windows 7. If Windows 7 is already running on your computer, you can skip most of the information in this section. For readers who are still in the planning stages, this section provides information about the editions of Windows 7 that are available and the process of installing Windows 7 on a computer that is running Windows Vista, Windows XP, or another operating system.

# Windows 7 Editions

Windows 7 is available in six editions, although not all editions are available to all people. Three editions are commercially available for installation on a desktop or notebook computer. These standard consumer editions of Windows 7 are as follows:

- **Windows 7 Home Premium**  This edition is designed for the average home computer user. It contains an impressive set of features, including the following:

  - The stunning Aero user interface, which provides an enhanced visual experience with features such as transparent window frames, extended color schemes, live preview thumbnails, and artistic desktop decoration

    **Tip**  Aero-driven features function only on computers that meet minimum hardware specifications. See "Minimum System Requirements" later in this section.

  - New Aero-driven window-management techniques such as Aero Peek, which turns open windows temporarily invisible so you can see the computer desktop, Aero Shake, which minimizes windows you're not working with so you can concentrate on a specific task, and Snap, which quickly sizes windows to fit specific areas of the desktop

  - New navigation features, including libraries and jump lists

  - Support for simplified home networking with homegroups, and for the secure sharing of files, printers, and media among multiple computers

  - Windows Search technology, with which you can quickly locate files, programs, and messages on your computer

  - Desktop gadgets and familiar applications such as the Calculator, Paint, WordPad, Windows Fax And Scan, and Windows Media Player 12

  - Windows Media Center, with which you can watch television programs (if your system includes a TV tuner) and DVD movies, display and manage pictures, and listen to music from multiple sources

  - Security features, including User Account Control (UAC), Action Center, Windows Update, Windows Defender, Windows Firewall, and Parental Controls

  - Backup for system images and files, and the Previous Versions and System Repair Disc features

  - Support for 32-bit and 64-bit hardware

  **Tip**  With Windows 7, the Home Basic Edition is not the most basic commercially available edition. As confusing as it might sound, the most basic edition of Windows 7 that you can purchase for installation on a desktop computer is Home Premium.

- **Windows 7 Professional** This edition is designed for the average business user. It includes all the features of Windows 7 Home Premium plus support for network domains, automatic backups to network locations, and Remote Desktop. It also includes Windows XP Mode, which you can use to run older programs in a virtual Windows XP session on your Windows 7 computer (if your hardware supports virtualization).

- **Windows 7 Ultimate** This edition is designed for the user who wants to have all the capabilities of Windows 7 available outside of an enterprise installation. It includes all the features of Windows 7 Professional, plus Windows BitLocker Drive Encryption, BitLocker To Go drive, and support for 35 languages.

Three editions of Windows 7 are available only for specific devices or markets. These limited-distribution editions are as follows:

- **Windows 7 Starter** Designed specifically for small portable computers, such as netbooks and mini notebooks. This edition includes all the core Windows 7 features but, by eliminating some of the flashy Aero interface features, it requires less memory.

- **Windows 7 Enterprise** Available only to Microsoft Volume Licensing customers. This edition includes every Windows 7 feature, as well as support for the Microsoft Desktop Optimization Pack (a tool used for central management of computers in very large organizations).

- **Windows 7 Home Basic** Available only in "emerging markets" such as Mexico, India, and the People's Republic of China, and not in countries defined by the World Bank as having high-income economies, such as Canada, Denmark, Sweden, the United Kingdom, and the United States. This edition includes most of the core Windows 7 features, including a subset of the Aero interface features.

    **See Also** For information about World Bank, country classifications, and the countries currently assigned to each classification, visit www.worldbank.org/.

The exercises in this book cover the features of Windows 7 that you are most likely to use at home and at work. Graphics depict the Windows 7 Ultimate user interface.

**Tip** If you want to upgrade to a different edition of Windows 7, the Windows Anytime Upgrade feature makes this an easy process. To learn about the available upgrade options, click the Start button, type *upgrade* in the Start menu Search box, and then in the Programs section of the search results list, click Windows Anytime Upgrade.

# Minimum System Requirements

To install Windows 7 and work your way through the exercises in this book, your computer must meet certain specifications.

## Windows 7

To run Windows 7, including the Aero desktop experience features, your computer needs to meet the following minimum requirements:

- 1 gigahertz (GHz) or faster 32-bit (x86) or 64-bit (x64) processor
- 1 gigabyte (GB) of system memory (RAM) for 32-bit systems; 2 GB for 64-bit systems
- 16 GB of available hard disk drive space for 32-bit systems; 20 GB for 64-bit systems
- Support for DirectX 9 graphics with Windows Display Driver Model (WDDM) 1.0 or higher driver and 128 megabytes (MB) memory (to enable the Aero theme)
- Internal or external DVD drive
- Monitor with minimum 1024 × 768 screen resolution
- Keyboard and mouse or compatible pointing device
- Internet connection for product activation, accessing online Help topics, and any other Internet-dependent processes

Some features of Windows 7 work only if you have the hardware or network connections to support them. For descriptions of the system requirements for specific features of Windows 7, visit windows.microsoft.com/en-us/windows7/products/system-requirements/.

## Step-by-Step Exercises

In addition to the hardware and Internet connection required to run Windows 7, you will need the following to successfully complete the exercises in this book:

- Any version of the Windows 7 operating system
- Access to the following peripheral devices:
    - Printer
    - Speakers
    - Microphone
    - External storage device
- At least 21 MB of available hard disk space for the practice files

If your existing computer runs Windows Vista, it should be able to run Windows 7, and you'll probably notice a significant increase in computing speed. If your existing computer runs Windows XP, it might be able to run Windows 7, but likely won't support Aero.

If you have questions or concerns about whether your existing computer will support Windows 7, you can install the Windows 7 Upgrade Advisor from

www.microsoft.com/windows/windows-7/get/upgrade-advisor.aspx

The Upgrade Advisor generates a list of any known compatibility issues between Windows 7 and your computer, including the peripheral devices connected to it.

---

### Identifying Genuine Windows Software

Counterfeit software floppy disks, CDs, DVDs, and packaging might look the same as or similar to the authentic software. A genuine retail copy of a Microsoft software product (one not acquired with the purchase of a computer or through the Microsoft Volume Licensing program) is distributed on an edge-to-edge hologram disc featuring a holographic image printed directly on the disc rather than on a sticker. Each product has a Certificate of Authenticity sticker on the top of the retail package and an orange product key label on the installation disc case. The front of the disc features

- A copper hologram with a clean, wavy outer edge and/or a feathered edge that transitions smoothly to a silver color at the outer edge of the disc.
- A high-resolution, three-dimensional hologram of the Windows logo, in which the flag appears to wave when you tilt the disc.
- A security patch located at the bottom of the disc, in which the word *Microsoft* changes to the word *GENUINE* when you tilt the disc.

The back of the disc features a detailed hologram on the inner mirror band, containing the words *Microsoft* and *GENUINE*.

**See Also** You can see samples of counterfeited software from around the world at www.microsoft.com/howtotell/. To verify whether your copy of Windows 7 is genuine, run the Windows Genuine Advantage validation tool available from that site.

Pirated software is often distributed preloaded on the hard drive of a used computer, as part of a software bundle; through street vendors; or through auction Web sites, spam e-mail messages, and downloads from Web sites other than those located within the microsoft.com domain. The easiest way to avoid counterfeit software is to purchase it from a reputable reseller, or directly from the Microsoft Store, which you can visit at store.microsoft.com.

# Installing Windows 7

You can convert a computer to the Windows 7 operating system by using either of the following methods:

- Upgrade an existing computer that runs Windows Vista to Windows 7. Upgrading retains your installed programs and stored files.

- Perform a clean installation of Windows 7 on a computer that runs Windows Vista, Windows XP, or another operating system. A clean installation removes all installed programs, files, and settings.

## Performing a Clean Installation of Windows 7

The simplest way to convert an existing computer system to Windows 7 is to perform a clean installation. This process takes about 30 minutes and requires very little interaction. It does, however, remove all programs and files from your computer, and it configures all your settings to the Windows 7 defaults.

If your existing computer runs Windows XP or anything other than Windows Vista, the only way to "upgrade" the computer to Windows 7 is by performing a clean installation.

Before you start the installation process, you can take the following steps to move programs, files, and settings from your existing operating system to Windows 7.

1.  Create a list of the programs that are installed on your computer and decide which programs you'll need on your Windows 7 computer. Ensure that you have the installation discs or installation points and product keys for the necessary programs.

    **Tip** If you use Adobe programs or other programs that limit the number of times you can use a product key, deactivate the program installation to make that instance of the product key available for your Windows 7 computer.

2.  Use Windows Easy Transfer to create a transfer file containing your existing files and settings:

3.  After ensuring that you will have access to the programs, files, and settings you will need to have available on your Windows 7 computer, insert the Windows 7 installation disc into your computer's DVD drive and follow the onscreen directions. Select the Custom installation option to perform a clean installation of Windows 7.

4.  Install the necessary programs, and then use Windows Easy Transfer to transfer the saved files and settings to the Windows 7 computer.

## Using Windows Easy Transfer

You can use Windows Easy Transfer to transfer files and settings to a different computer or to a new operating system installation on the same computer. You can transfer the following types of files and settings from a computer running Windows XP, Windows Vista, or Windows 7 to a computer running Windows 7:

- Folders and files
- E-mail settings, contacts, and messages
- Program settings
- User accounts and settings
- Internet settings and favorites

You can transfer files, but not settings, from a computer running Windows 2000 to a computer running Windows 7.

You can transfer information directly from one computer to another by using an Easy Transfer Cable (a USB cable that connects the two computers). You can create a portable transfer file on a DVD, CD, external hard drive, or USB flash drive; or you can save the file to another computer on your network.

**Tip** While transferring settings to or from a computer, you can't use the computer for other purposes. Because the transfer can take several hours, you can't start the process from a portable computer that is running on battery power; you must first plug it in.

To begin the transfer process:

1. Log on to your computer as an administrator.
2. On the Start menu, click All Programs, click Accessories, click System Tools, and then click Windows Easy Transfer.
3. Follow the instructions in the Windows Easy Transfer wizard to specify the transfer media or method, the information you want to transfer, and the password for recovering that information.
4. If you're transferring files and settings via removable media, start Windows Easy Transfer on the second computer, and click Continue Transfer In Progress.
5. Provide the information requested by the wizard. When prompted to do so, insert the transfer disc into the second computer, select the destination drive, enter the password, and then click Next.

The files and settings transfer to the new computer.

## Upgrading to Windows 7

Upgrading is the process of replacing your computer's operating system with a newer version without disturbing the programs installed on your computer, your personal preferences and settings, or existing information such as documents, spreadsheets, and data files. You can upgrade to Windows 7 only from Windows Vista.

Although upgrading to Windows 7 should not affect your personal files and settings, it is always a good policy to back up important files before upgrading. The time and effort it takes to back up files and settings will likely be far less than the time and effort required to re-create the same information.

**See Also**   For information about backing up files and settings on a computer running an earlier version of Windows, consult *Windows Vista Step by Step*, by Joan Preppernau and Joyce Cox (Microsoft Press, 2007) or *Microsoft Windows XP Step by Step*, by Online Training Solutions, Inc. (Microsoft Press, 2005).

To begin the upgrade process, insert the Windows 7 installation disc into the computer's DVD drive, follow the onscreen directions ,and select the Upgrade installation option.

**Tip**   To ensure that you're getting the latest Windows 7 files, select the option to stay online during the installation.

**See Also**   After you upgrade the operating system, follow the process we describe in "Updating Windows System Files" in Chapter 1, "Explore Windows 7" to ensure that you have any Windows 7 drivers that are available for your computer and peripheral hardware.

## Activating Windows

When you upgrade your computer's operating system to Windows 7, or the first time you start a new computer, you are prompted to activate your copy of Windows.

Each copy of Windows 7 must be activated within 30 days of the first use. After that grace period expires, you will not be able to use all the functions of Windows. You can activate Windows over the Internet or by telephone. Until you activate it, Windows will periodically prompt you to do so. You don't have to give any personal information about yourself or your computer during the activation process.

**Tip**   If you are asked to *register* after activating a product, the information you provide might be used to send you marketing materials. Registration is optional; activation is not.

The goal of Windows Product Activation is to reduce a form of software piracy known as *casual copying* or *softlifting*, which is the sharing of software in a way that infringes on the software's license terms.

You can locate your Windows activation status at the bottom of the System window of Control Panel.

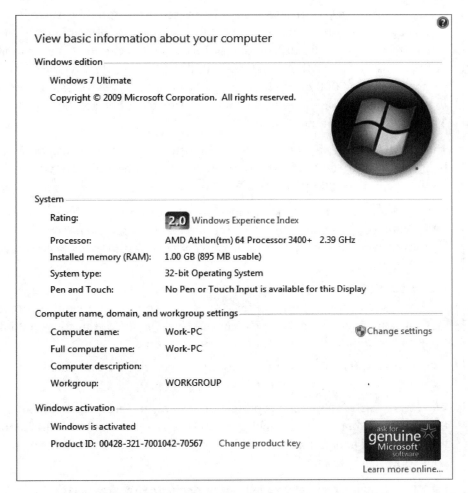

*The System window provides current information about your computer system, including its activation status.*

If your copy of Windows has been activated, *Windows is activated* appears in the Windows Activation area at the bottom of the window. Otherwise, the time remaining in the grace period appears, with a link to complete the activation process.

## The Perils of Piracy

Windows Product Activation is a security measure instituted by Microsoft to help prevent the use of unlicensed copies of Windows. Software piracy—the illegal reproduction and distribution of software applications—is a multibillion dollar industry. The Sixth Annual BSA and IDC Global Software Piracy Study, commissioned in 2008 by the Business Software Alliance (www.bsa.org) concluded that the worldwide software piracy rate had risen to 41 percent, representing over $50 billion in lost revenue.

The counterfeit software manufacturing industry stifles the potential growth of the high-tech industry and contributes to loss of tax revenue. Software piracy is also harmful to its users, for these reasons:

- Unlicensed software is not eligible for technical support or product upgrades. When you attempt to install a product update or service pack from the Microsoft Web site, your system or software is tested to verify whether it's licensed.

- Abuse of software licenses can result in financial penalties and legal costs, as well as a bad reputation for you or your company. Individual company executives can be held criminally and civilly liable for the copyright infringements of individuals within their organizations.

- Pirated software can contain harmful viruses with the potential to damage individual computers or entire networks.

Windows 7 has a built-in piracy protection system—if certain conditions alert it to the possibility that you are running a pirated copy, most Windows 7 functionality will shut down, and you won't be able to create or save any files until you activate your copy of Windows.

**See Also**  For more information about software piracy, visit www.microsoft.com/piracy/.

# Features and Conventions of This Book

This book has been designed to lead you through all the tasks you are most likely to want to perform on your Windows 7 computer. You can also use the book as a reference guide. The following features of this book will help you look up specific information:

- **Detailed table of contents** Get an overview of which topics are discussed in which chapters.

- **Chapter thumb tabs** Easily locate the beginning of the chapter you want.

- **Topic-specific running heads** Within a chapter, quickly locate the topic you want by looking at the running heads at the top of odd-numbered pages.

- **Glossary** Look up the meaning of a word or the definition of a concept.

- **Detailed index** Look up specific tasks and features in the index, which has been carefully crafted with the reader in mind.

- **Companion CD** Install the practice files needed for the step-by-step exercises, and consult the additional resources on the CD, including a fully searchable electronic version of this book.

You can save time when you use this book by understanding how the *Step by Step* series shows exercise instructions, buttons to click, and other information. These conventions are described in the table on the next page.

| Convention | Meaning |
|---|---|
| **SET UP** | This paragraph preceding a step-by-step exercise indicates the practice files that you will use when working through the exercise. It also indicates any requirements you should attend to or actions you should take before beginning the exercise. |
| **CLEAN UP** | This paragraph following a step-by-step exercise provides instructions for restoring your system before moving on to another topic. |
| **1**<br>**2** | Blue numbered steps guide you through step-by-step exercises. |
| 1<br>2 | Black numbered steps present instructions for performing procedures that you might need or want to carry out on your own. These optional procedures are not among the book's exercises. |
| **See Also** | These paragraphs direct you to more information about a given topic in this book or elsewhere. |
| **Troubleshooting** | These paragraphs explain how to fix a common problem that might prevent you from continuing with an exercise. |
| **Tip** | These paragraphs provide a helpful hint or shortcut that makes working through a task easier, or information about other available options. |
| **Important** | These paragraphs point out information that you need to know to complete a procedure. |
| **Keyboard Shortcut** | These paragraphs provide information about keyboard shortcuts that are helpful for carrying out the task at hand or related tasks. |
| Ctrl+Home | A plus sign (+) between two key names means that you must hold down the first key while you press the second key. For example, "press Ctrl+Home" means "hold down the Ctrl key while you press the Home key." |
| | The first time you are told to click a button in an exercise, a picture of the button appears in the left margin. |
| **Program interface elements** | In exercises, the names of keys, such as **Enter**; program elements, such as buttons, commands, windows, and dialog boxes; and files or folders that you interact with are shown in boldface type characters. |
| **User input** | In exercises, anything you should type is shown in blue boldface type. |

# Using the Practice Files

The companion CD included with this book contains the practice files you need to complete the book's exercises. The following table lists these practice files.

| Chapter | Folder | File |
| --- | --- | --- |
| Chapter 1:<br>Explore Windows 7 | None | None |
| Chapter 2:<br>Manage User Accounts | Accounts | Angelic.jpg |
| Chapter 3:<br>Manage Your Network | Networking | Share Me!.txt |
| Chapter 4:<br>Navigate Windows<br>and Folders | Navigation | Apple Spice Junction Menu.pdf<br>FrostKing1.docx<br>FrostKing2.docx<br>FrozenBranch.jpg<br>IceBerries.jpg<br>Iceskatesmed.png<br>IcyLeaves.jpg<br>License.doc<br>License.txt<br>Readme.txt<br>Recipe1.docx<br>Recipe2.docx<br>Scoops.gif<br>Sflakemed.png<br>Skiermed.png<br>SlickStump.jpg<br>Smanmed.png<br>StrausOrganicIceCream.jpg<br>StreetSign.jpg<br>Trinity1.jpg<br>Trinity2.jpg |

| Chapter | Folder | File |
| --- | --- | --- |
| Chapter 5: Manage Folders and Files | Structure | Narrations folder (empty) |
| | | Photographs folder (empty) |
| | | Presentations\Background.jpg |
| | | Presentations\TagTemplate.pptx |
| | | Videos\HouseHome.wmv |
| | | AlbumSlides.pptx |
| | | Bamboo.docx |
| | | Bamboo1.jpg through Bamboo3.jpg |
| | | BookBeat.docx |
| | | BookSales.xlsx |
| | | CakePlate.jpg |
| | | Cat.jpg |
| | | ColorSlides.pptx |
| | | ComparisonShop.docx |
| | | Costs.xlsx |
| | | Crow.jpg |
| | | FabricSpecial.docx |
| | | FengShuiSlides.pptx |
| | | Figurine.jpg |
| | | Frog.jpg |
| | | Introduction.wav |
| | | JournalSlides.pptx |
| | | Lady.jpg |
| | | LoanPayment.xlsx |
| | | MusicBox.jpg |
| | | OrgSlides.pptx |
| | | PlanningSlides.pptx |
| | | Procedures.docx |
| | | RoomMakeover.docx |
| | | SalesMtgSlides.pptx |
| | | TagAnnounce.docx |
| | | TagIntroduce.docx |
| | | TeaPot.jpg |
| | | Welcome.docx |
| | | YinYang.png |

| Chapter | Folder | File |
|---------|--------|------|
| Chapter 6: Connect to the Web | None | None |
| Chapter 7: Work with Web Pages and Sites | None | None |
| Chapter 8: Manage Internet Explorer | None | None |
| Chapter 9: Change Visual Elements | Visual | Arizona01.jpg through Arizona10.jpg |
| Chapter 10: Change System Settings | None | None |
| Chapter 11: Work with Programs | Programs | MakeOver.docx MusicBox.bmp |
| Chapter 12: Set Up Hardware Devices | None | None |

In addition to the practice files, the CD contains resources that will enhance your ability to get the most out of using this book and Windows 7, including the following:

- *Windows 7 Step by Step* (this book) in eBook format
- *Before You Call Tech Support: Windows 7 Troubleshooting Tips* in XPS format and PDF format
- Links to online resources, including Microsoft Learning Snacks, technical support resources, and an online survey
- Links to online installation points for Adobe Reader and the Microsoft XPS viewer

   **Tip** The XPS Viewer is installed with Windows 7, so you will need it only to view XPS-format files on Windows XP and Windows Vista.

**Important** The companion CD for this book does not contain the Windows 7 operating system. You should purchase and install that operating system before using this book.

# Installing the Practice Files

You need to install the practice files in the correct location on your hard disk before you can use them in the exercises. Follow the steps below:

**Note** If for any reason you are unable to install the practice files from the CD, the files can also be downloaded from the Web at *http://go.microsoft.com/FWLink/?Linkid=214135*.

1.  Remove the companion CD from the envelope at the back of this book and insert it into the CD drive of your computer.

    An end-user license agreement appears. To use the practice files, you must accept the terms of the license agreement.

2.  If the end-user license agreement does not appear, click the Start button, click Computer, double-click the icon for your CD drive, and then double-click the StartCD executable file.

3.  Review the end-user license agreement. To accept the terms, click Accept, and then click Next.

    A menu appears with options related to the book.

4.  Click Install Practice Files.

5.  Follow the instructions that appear.

    The practice files are installed to your Documents\Microsoft Press\Windows7SBS folder.

6.  After the practice files are installed, click Finish.

7.  Close the Step By Step Companion CD window, remove the companion CD from the CD drive, and return it to the envelope at the back of the book.

# Locating the Practice Files

When you install the practice files from the companion CD that accompanies this book, the files are stored on your hard disk in chapter-specific subfolders of your Documents\ Microsoft Press\Windows7SBS folder. Each exercise is preceded by a paragraph that lists any files needed for that exercise and any preparations you need to make before you start working through the exercise, like this:

 **SET UP**  You need the Angelic image located in your Documents\Microsoft Press\ Windows7SBS\Accounts folder to complete this exercise. Open Control Panel, display the User Accounts window, and then follow the steps.

You can browse to the practice files in Windows Explorer by following these steps:

1.  Click the Start button, and then click Documents.

2.  In your Documents library, double-click Microsoft Press, double-click Windows7SBS, and then double-click the specific chapter folder.

You can browse to the practice files from a dialog box that includes a Navigation pane by following these steps:

1.  In the Navigation pane, click Documents.

2.  In your Documents library, double-click Microsoft Press, double-click Windows7SBS, and then double-click the specific chapter folder.

# Removing and Uninstalling the Practice Files

After you finish working your way through the exercises in this book, you can free up hard disk space by uninstalling the practice files. The uninstall process deletes the practice files that were installed in your Documents\Microsoft Press\Windows7SBS folder and its chapter-specific subfolders, but it does not delete any additional files you created while working through the exercises.

Follow these steps to uninstall the practice files:

1. Display Control Panel in Category view.

2. In the Programs category, click Uninstall A Program.

   The Programs And Features window opens.

3. In the list of installed programs, click Windows 7 Step By Step, and then on the toolbar at the top of the window, click Uninstall.

4. In the message box asking you to confirm the deletion, click Yes.

To remove files you created while working through the exercises, start Windows Explorer, browse to the files, and select and delete them.

# Information for New Computer Users

Windows 7 is the latest version of the Windows operating system. Windows is the most widely used operating system in the world. (Other operating systems you might have heard of are Linux, UNIX, and Mac OS X.) The operating system basically acts as an intermediary between you and your computer, between the computer and the hardware devices connected to it, and between the computer and the software programs you run on it. For your computer to work, Windows 7 must do the following:

- Translate commands that you provide into code that tells the computer what to do and how to do it.
- Coordinate interactions among its components, such as receiving input from the keyboard and mouse, locating programs and files, and displaying output on the monitor.
- Enable your computer to communicate with other computers and with peripheral devices, such as printers, scanners, and external hard drives.
- Interact with programs installed on your computer.

Windows 7 presents its tools, commands, and information storage structure through a graphical user interface (commonly referred to as a *GUI*). Graphical user interfaces enable you to interact with a computer by clicking items on the screen instead of having to type precise sequences of commands, and include the following types of components:

- **Pointing device** A device such as a mouse that controls a pointer with which you can select objects displayed on the screen.
- **Desktop** The basic display area on top of which you can work with windows, icons, menus, and dialog boxes.
- **Window** A frame, usually resizable, within which the computer runs a program or displays a folder or file.
- **Icon** A visual representation of a program, folder, file, or other object or function.
- **Menu** A list from which you can give an instruction by clicking a command.
- **Dialog box** A fixed-size window in which you refine instructions by typing information or selecting from the available options.

The programs you purchase and install on your computer *run on* Windows 7, meaning that they call on the operating system whenever they need to work with your computer's components or with peripheral devices. They also build on the interface provided by the operating system to communicate with you. This relationship allows the programs to concentrate on their specialized tasks, such as word processing or performing calculations in a spreadsheet or locating and displaying Web sites on the Internet, while the operating system handles the basic behind-the-scenes tasks.

If you are new to computing, or haven't worked on a Windows computer before, you might be unfamiliar with some of the terms that we use in this book, so we'll briefly cover them here to bring you up to speed.

**See Also** For information about terms mentioned in the book but not explained in this section, see the Glossary at the end of this book.

# Your Mouse

A mouse is a pointing device with which you control the location of the on-screen pointer and click, drag, or select on-screen items to carry out tasks. A standard mouse includes two buttons—the primary button and the secondary button—with different functions. By default, the left button is the primary button and the right button is the secondary button, but you can switch them. In this book (other than in the exercise where you switch the button functions), references to the left button mean the primary button, and references to the right button mean the secondary button.

**See Also** For information about switching the primary and secondary mouse buttons, see "Changing the Way Your Mouse Works" in Chapter 12, "Set Up Hardware Devices."

Here's a summary of the standard actions you perform with a mouse:

- **Pointing** Moving the mouse so that the on-screen pointer is over the item you want to work with. Pointing to an on-screen item usually displays a ScreenTip containing information about that item.

- **Clicking** Pointing to an on-screen item and pressing and releasing the primary mouse button once. Clicking an on-screen item usually selects the item. Clicking a hyperlink displays the link target.

- **Double-clicking** Pointing to an on-screen item and pressing and releasing the primary mouse button twice in rapid succession. Double-clicking an on-screen item usually starts or opens the item. Slowly double-clicking a file or folder activates the file or folder name for editing.

- **Right-clicking** Pointing to an on-screen item and clicking the secondary mouse button once. Right-clicking usually displays a menu, called a *shortcut menu* or *context menu*, listing actions you can perform with the item you right-clicked. You invoke an action by clicking it on the shortcut menu.

- **Dragging** Pointing to an on-screen item, holding down the primary mouse button, moving the mouse until the pointer or item is in the location where you want the item to appear, and releasing the mouse button. You can also drag through multiple on-screen items to select them.

- **Right-dragging** Pointing to an on-screen item, holding down the secondary mouse button, moving the mouse until the pointer or item is in the location where you want the item to appear, and releasing the mouse button. Right-dragging displays a menu of actions you can perform with the item you dragged.

Your mouse might also include a third button, scroll wheel, tilt wheel, or roller ball that provides additional methods of moving the pointer around the screen and clicking. On a portable computer, you might use an alternative pointing device, such as a touch pad, a pointing stick (a small rubber button in the center of the keyboard of a portable computer), or a Tablet PC pen.

# Your Keyboard

Most people use a keyboard to input information into their computers by typing letters, numbers, and symbols, or to give commands by pressing function keys or key combinations. Standard U.S. keyboards have 101 keys; there are also smaller keyboards, keyboards with different key configurations, and variations with special-purpose keys for performing such actions as:

- Starting your default Web browser or e-mail program.
- Searching the Internet by using your default search engine.
- Displaying the Windows Help And Support window.
- Playing, pausing, stopping, and otherwise controlling audio and video recordings you play on or through your computer.
- Increasing or decreasing the volume of audio playback.
- Putting the computer into Sleep mode.

These special-purpose keys are very convenient and can save you a lot of thinking and clicking time. Look at your keyboard to ascertain whether it includes any of these extra keys. They're usually located on the left or right side or along the top edge of the keyboard, and they are often labeled with universal symbols, such as an envelope for the e-mail program, a globe or home icon for the Web browser, speakers for volume control, a moon for Sleep mode, and the standard symbols for playing, pausing, skipping, or stopping media playback.

# Windows

Windows 7 displays information in windows. A window can either fill the entire screen or occupy only part of the screen. No matter what its size, each window uses the following components to display information about the window contents and to manage the window:

- **Title bar**  Located at the top of the window. The title bar might tell you the window's purpose, the name of the program running in the window, and/or the name of the file open in the program. You can maximize or reduce the size of a window by double-clicking its title bar. When a window is not maximized, you can move it on the screen by dragging it by its title bar.

- **Window-management buttons**  Located at the right end of the title bar.

  - ○ You click the Minimize button to collapse the window into a button on the Windows Taskbar (called *minimizing* the window).

  - ○ When the window fills the entire screen, you click the Restore Down button so that the window occupies only part of the screen (called *reducing* the window).

    **Tip**  When the window occupies only part of the screen, it is surrounded by a frame. You can drag the edges of the frame to change the size of the window.

  - ○ When the window occupies only part of the screen, you click the Maximize button so that the window fills the screen (called *maximizing* the window).

    The Maximize and Restore Down buttons share a position on the title bar; only one button appears at a time.

  - ○ You click the Close button to close the window. If the window contains a program or file, closing the window might also exit the program or close the file.

    **See Also**  The title bar of a folder window also contains navigation buttons, the Address bar, and the Search box. For information about these title bar elements, see "Understanding Files, Folders, and Libraries" in Chapter 4, "Navigate Windows and Folders."

- **Menu bar and/or toolbar**  Located below the title bar. A menu bar provides drop-down lists, called *menus*, of the commands you click to give instructions regarding the contents of the window. A toolbar displays visual representations of the commands as buttons you click.

   **See Also**  For information about menus and toolbars, see "Understanding Files, Folders, and Libraries" in Chapter 4, "Navigate Windows and Folders."

- **Status bar**  Located at the bottom of the window. This bar provides information about the contents of the window, and sometimes about on-screen elements you point to or click.

- **Vertical and horizontal scroll bars**  Located on the right side and at the bottom of a window when it is not big enough to show all its contents. You use the vertical scroll bar to move the contents up and down within the window, and the horizontal scroll bar to move the contents from side to side, as follows:

   ○ Clicking the arrow at either end of a scroll bar moves the contents one line or column at a time.

   ○ Clicking directly on the scroll bar on either side of the scroll box moves the contents one "windowful" at a time.

   ○ Dragging the scroll box on the scroll bar moves the contents in larger increments.

   The position of the scroll box in relation to the scroll bar tells you where you are in the contents. For example, when the scroll box is in the middle of the scroll bar, the window is displaying the portion of its contents located about halfway through.

   **See Also**  For information about sizing, moving, and arranging windows, see "Working with Windows" in Chapter 4, "Navigate Windows and Folders."

# Commands, Buttons, and Keyboard Shortcuts

You can give instructions to Windows 7 by clicking a command on a menu, clicking a button on a toolbar, or pressing a key or combination of keys on the keyboard. Commands and buttons provide visual clues to tell you how to use them.

● Commands are dimmed if they are unavailable for use under the current circum-stances. Buttons might be dimmed, but in Windows 7, buttons are usually not displayed if you can't use them.

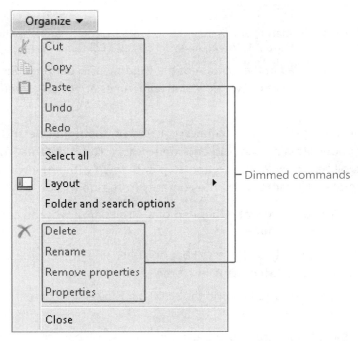

— Dimmed commands

*Commands on menus and in dialog boxes, and buttons on toolbars, are dimmed when they're not available for use.*

● If a command or button name includes an ellipsis (...), clicking the command or button opens a dialog box so that you can provide information Windows needs to perform the task.

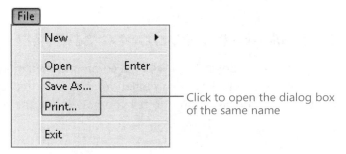

— Click to open the dialog box of the same name

*An ellipsis following a command or button name indicates that you will need to supply additional information to complete the operation.*

● If a command can be turned on or off, a check mark appears to the left of the command name in the menu when it is turned on. Clicking the command then turns it off and removes the check mark.

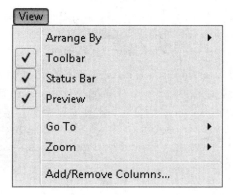

*A check mark indicates that the adjacent command is turned on.*

A small round circle to the left of a menu item indicates the selection of one of a group of mutually exclusive options.

**Tip** On some menus, if a command has a toolbar button equivalent, the button's icon appears to the left of the command name.

● If a command is accompanied by a right-pointing arrow, clicking the command displays a menu of options for refining the command.

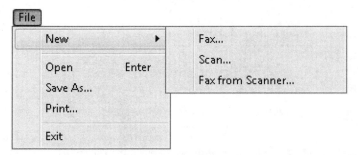

*An arrow to the right of a command name indicates that clicking the command will display a submenu of options.*

- Some buttons include one of two types of downward-pointing arrows:

  ○ If the arrow is part of the button, clicking the button displays a list of options.

  ○ If the arrow is separate from the button, clicking the button invokes the default option and clicking the arrow displays a list of options. Clicking an option in that list makes it the default for the button.

If your hands are on the keyboard, you might find it more convenient to give commands by using keys or key combinations, called *keyboard shortcuts*, than to relocate one hand to the mouse. Keyboard shortcuts are available for many Windows commands (and also for many program-specific commands). Throughout this book, we provide information about keyboard shortcuts related to the topic being discussed. You can also find keyboard shortcuts for commands on some menus.

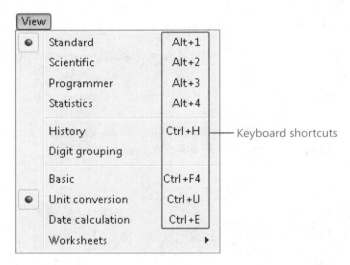

*A key combination to the right of a menu command indicates the keyboard shortcut for the command.*

**Keyboard Shortcut** For a full list of Windows 7 keyboard shortcuts, search the Windows Help And Support Center for "keyboard shortcuts."

# Dialog Boxes and Message Boxes

If Windows 7 or the program you are working with needs information from you in order to carry out the command, it might display a different window or a dialog box to gather that information. The window or dialog box might present only one set of options, or it might include several sets of options presented on tabs.

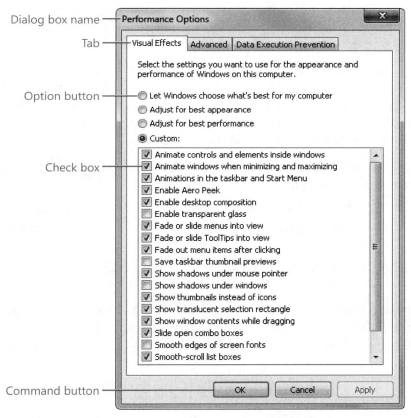

*Clicking a tab below the dialog box title bar displays the corresponding set of options.*

Regardless of whether Windows requests the information in a window or a dialog box, you can provide the information in consistent ways by using these common components:

- **Check box**  A square box representing an independent option or one of a group of non–mutually exclusive options.

  - ○ Clicking an empty check box selects the associated option; a check mark appears inside the box to indicate that the option is *selected* or *turned on*.

  - ○ Clicking a box that contains a check mark removes the check mark to indicate that the option is *deselected*, *cleared*, or *turned off*.

- **Command button**  A button that initiates an action. Most dialog boxes have at least two command buttons: an OK button that carries out the command, and a Cancel button that cancels the command. Clicking either button also closes the dialog box. Other buttons might be available, such as the Apply button that applies changes without closing the dialog box.

  - ○ If a command button label includes an ellipsis (...), clicking the button opens another dialog box.

  - ○ If a button label includes two greater-than signs (>>), also called *chevrons*, clicking the button expands the window or dialog box to reveal more options or information.

  - ○ A dark border indicates the active button; you can press Enter to implement that command.

- **Link**  Hyperlinked text that initiates an action. When you point to a link, it becomes underlined, and the pointer changes to a hand. Clicking a link might open another dialog box or window, or it might take you to information stored on your computer or on the Web.

- **List box** A box containing a list of options.

  - ○ A list box might contain multiple options from which you can select one or more than one.
  - ○ A drop-down list box appears as a single-line box with an arrow at the right end. Clicking the arrow displays a drop-down list from which you can choose one option.
  - ○ A combo box is a text box combined with a drop-down list box. In a combo box, you can either type information or select an option from a list.

  Regardless of the format of a list box, you select an option by clicking it. (To select multiple options in a list box, select the first option, press the Ctrl key, and select the additional options.) In a list box, selected options are highlighted; in a drop-down list box or combo box, the selected option appears in the box.

- **Option button** Sometimes called a *radio button*. A small circle representing an option that can be either selected or not selected. Option buttons represent mutually exclusive values for a setting; one and only one option must be selected. When you click an option or its button, a dot appears in the circle to indicate that the option is selected. Clicking another option or its button removes the dot from the previously selected option.

- **Slider** An indicator on a horizontal or vertical bar representing a range of values for a setting (such as speed, brightness, or volume). To change the setting, you drag the slider or click to either side of it on the bar.

- **Spin box** A box with a pair of up and down arrows at its right end. Clicking an arrow moves through a list of suggested values (usually numbers) for a setting. You change the value either by clicking one of the arrows or by selecting the existing number and typing a new one.

- **Text box** A box in which you can enter text, such as a file name. To replace an existing entry in the text box, drag over or double-click the entry to select it and then delete it, or type new text to replace the selection.

**Tip** You can move between dialog box components by clicking them with the mouse or by pressing the Tab key.

When Windows 7 is performing a lengthy action or cannot carry out a command you have chosen, or if an action is potentially risky (such as deleting files), a message box containing information or a warning appears. You can click OK or Yes to acknowledge the message or confirm that you want to proceed in spite of the warning. Click Cancel or No to close the message box and cancel the operation.

*Windows 7 displays messages and alerts you to the consequences of some commands.*

**See Also** Depending on the type of user account you have, before Windows 7 carries out an action that affects your computer system, it might display a User Account Control (UAC) dialog box. For information about UAC, see the sidebar "Understanding User Account Control" in Chapter 1, "Explore Windows 7."

# Getting Help

Every effort has been made to ensure the accuracy of this book and the contents of its companion CD. If you do run into problems, please contact the sources listed below for assistance.

## Errata & Book Support

If you find an error, please report it on our Microsoft Press site at oreilly.com:

1. Go to *http://microsoftpress.oreilly.com*.
2. In the Search box, enter the book's ISBN or title.
3. Select your book from the search results.
4. On your book's catalog page, under the cover image, you'll see a list of links.
5. Click View/Submit Errata.

You'll find additional information and services for your book on its catalog page. If you need additional support, please e-mail Microsoft Press Book Support at *mspinput@microsoft.com*.

If for any reason you are unable to install the practice files from the CD, the files can also be downloaded from the Web here:

*http://go.microsoft.com/FWLink/?Linkid=214135*

Please note that product support for Microsoft software is not offered through the addresses above. For software assistance, visit *support.microsoft.com*.

# Getting Help with Windows 7

If your question is about Windows 7, and not about the content of this Microsoft Press book, your first recourse is the Windows Help And Support system. This system is a combination of tools and files stored on your computer when the operating system was installed and, if your computer is connected to the Internet, information available from the Windows Web site.

You can find Help information in several ways:

- You can display a ScreenTip containing information about an item on the screen by pointing to the item.
- You can open the Windows Help And Support window by clicking Help And Support on the Start menu.
- You can click links in many dialog boxes and Control Panel windows to display the Windows Help And Support window with the linked topic already displayed.

To practice getting help, you can work through the following exercise.

 **SET UP** You don't need any practice files to complete this exercise; just follow the steps.

1. On the **Start** menu, click **Help and Support**.

   The Windows Help And Support window opens.

 2. In the **Search Help** box at the top of the window, type **libraries**, and then click the **Search Help** button or press **Enter**.

   Help displays a list of topics related to libraries.

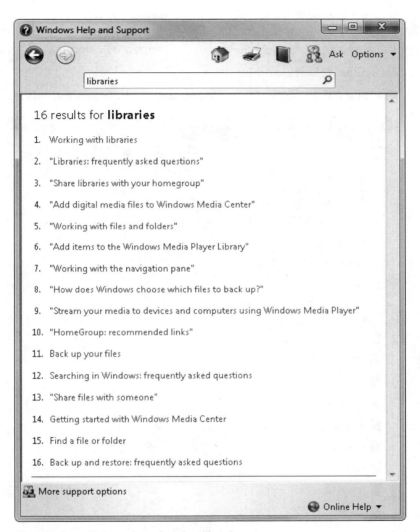

*The Windows Help topics related to libraries.*

You can click any topic to display the corresponding information.

**3.** On the toolbar, click the **Browse Help** button.

The contents of the Help file appear, organized by category.

**4.** Click **Files, folders, and libraries**.

The topics in that category are listed, along with any subcategories.

*The contents of the Files, Folders, And Libraries category.*

**5.** Click the **Working with libraries** topic.

Windows Help And Support displays the topic.

**Tip** Clicking a green word or phrase displays its definition. Click away from the definition box to close it.

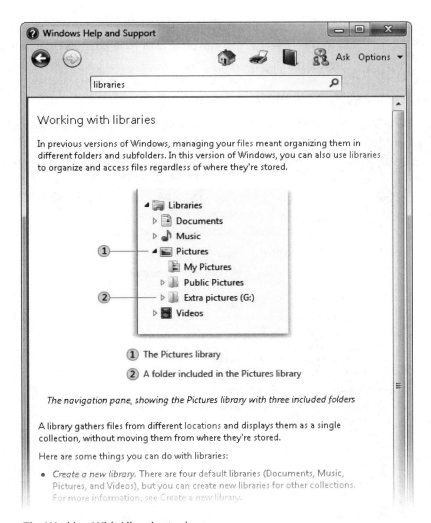

*The Working With Libraries topic.*

6. Read the topic, and click any blue links that interest you to jump to related topics. Then click the **Back** button one or more times to return to the **Files, folders, and libraries** category.

7. Click the **Creating, opening, and saving** category, and then click the **Save a file** topic.

   The title of each of the topic's subtopics is shown in bold text and preceded by an arrow.

8. At the top of the topic, click **Show All**.

The two subtopics expand to display hidden auxiliary information, and the Show All button changes to Hide All. You can display or hide an individual item by clicking it.

**Tip** You can print the displayed topic by clicking the Print button on the toolbar. If the topic contains subtopics, they will be printed only if they are displayed.

9. On the toolbar, click the **Ask** button.

The Windows Help And Support window displays suggestions of other ways to get help.

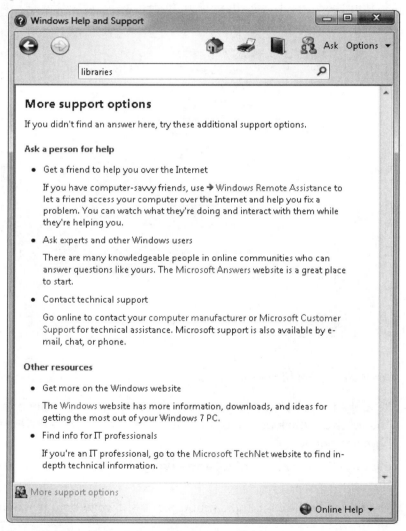

*Several alternative support resources are available.*

10. In the upper-right corner of the **Windows Help And Support** window, click the **Close** button.

# More Information

If your question is about Windows 7 or another Microsoft software product and you cannot find the answer in the product's Help file, please search the appropriate product solution center or the Microsoft Knowledge Base at

support.microsoft.com

In the United States, Microsoft software product support issues not covered by the Microsoft Knowledge Base are addressed by Microsoft Product Support Services. Location-specific software support options are available from

support.microsoft.com/gp/selfoverview/

# We Want to Hear from You

At Microsoft Press, your satisfaction is our top priority, and your feedback our most valuable asset. Please tell us what you think of this book at:

*http://www.microsoft.com/learning/booksurvey*

The survey is short, and we read every one of your comments and ideas. Thanks in advance for your input!

# Stay in Touch

Let's keep the conversation going! We're on Twitter: *http://twitter.com/MicrosoftPress*

# Chapter at a Glance

Explore Control Panel, **page 18**

Update Windows system files, **page 28**

Explore the desktop, **page 5**

Use the Start menu, **page 8**

End a computing session, **page 36**

Use the Windows Taskbar, **page 15**

# 1 Explore Windows 7

This chapter will help you quickly become familiar with the Windows 7 user interface and the tools you'll use to interact with your computer's operating system.

Each time you turn on your computer, it goes through a startup process during which it loads the system files necessary for you to interact with your computer and for your computer to interact with other devices, such as the monitor, keyboard, and mouse. When the startup process is complete, you log on to Windows 7 by providing identification information that uniquely identifies you to the system. After you log on, Windows 7 presents a working environment individually tailored to your preferences. The process might sound somewhat complicated, but in actual practice, it's quite simple.

When you first set up your computer, or if it's been a while since you used it, it's a very good idea to check for and install any updates released by Microsoft to keep your system running smoothly. You can configure Windows 7 to update itself with available updates at regularly scheduled intervals (provided your computer is on). By setting up automatic updating, you can be sure that your computer system always includes the most current features and security tools.

When you finish working with your computer, you can either shut down the computer entirely or leave it running in various ways. For example, you can log off from Windows 7 to end your computing session, lock the computer to restrict access to your session, or put the computer into Sleep mode to conserve power.

In this chapter, you'll learn the basic skills needed to work on a Windows 7 computer and to complete the exercises in this book. You'll learn about logging on to and off from Windows and explore tools you can use to control the computer. You'll practice using these tools to locate your computer's hardware and operating system specifications, and then ensure that your installation of Windows 7 is absolutely up to date.

> **Practice Files**  You won't need any practice files to complete the exercises in this chapter. See "Using the Practice Files" at the beginning of this book for more information.

**Important**  Before you can work through the exercises in this book, you must have Windows 7 already installed on your computer, and you must know your user account name and password (if your user account requires one).

# Logging On to Windows 7

The process of starting a computing session is called *logging on.* After you turn on the computer and it goes through its startup processes, the Windows 7 Welcome screen appears. The appearance of the screen and the exact process to log on to Windows depends on whether more than one user account has been created on your computer, and whether your account is protected by a password.

- If there is only one account, and it is not protected by a password, Windows might bypass the Welcome screen entirely and log you on. If the Welcome screen displays your user account name and picture, click the picture to log on to Windows.

- If there is only one account, and it is protected by a password, the Welcome screen displays your user account name and picture and a password box. You enter your password and then press Enter or click the Go button to log on to Windows.

- If there are multiple accounts, the Welcome screen displays the user account names and pictures for all the active user accounts. You click your user account picture and, if your account is password protected, enter your password to log on to Windows.

**Tip**  When you assign a password to a user account, you can specify a password hint. Then if you enter your user account password incorrectly, Windows displays the password hint to help you correct your error.

After you log on, Windows 7 loads your user profile and then displays your working environment. Known as the *desktop*, this environment reflects settings you make to personalize Windows. The first time you log on to a computer, Windows also sets up a file structure specific to your user account, which might take a few extra seconds.

# Exploring the Desktop

The desktop background you see the first time you log on to Windows 7 might be the default Windows 7 desktop background, which depicts a stylized Windows logo on an organic blue background, or, if you purchased your computer with Windows 7 already installed, the computer manufacturer (also called the original equipment manufacturer, or *OEM*) might have specified a brand-specific desktop background. In either case, you can change the background to one of the many beautiful photographs or artistic renderings that come with Windows 7, to a solid-colored background, or to one of your own photos or graphics. With any background other than a solid color, you can have the background switch to a different image as often as every 10 seconds.

**See Also**  For more information about desktop background options, see "Modifying a Theme" in Chapter 9, "Change Visual Elements."

Desktop icon          Desktop background                    Windows Taskbar

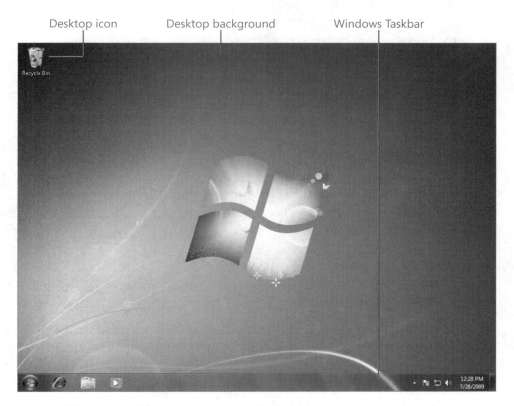

*A typical Windows 7 desktop, with the default background.*

**See Also**  If you're new to computing, refer to "Information for New Computer Users" at the beginning of this book for an explanation of basic terminology you will encounter throughout this book, as well as instructions for working with user interface components.

Depending on your Windows 7 settings and the programs installed on your computer, you might have one or more icons on your desktop. Windows 7 assigns an icon to every type of item on your computer to make it easier to identify files, storage locations, and programs. The icon might represent a file type (such as a document, a text file, or a database) or storage component (such as a folder, hard disk drive, or CD drive); or it might indicate the default program for opening a file. This visual representation can make it easier to find a file or program you're looking for. When an icon represents a link, or shortcut, to an item stored somewhere else, an arrow appears in its lower-left corner.

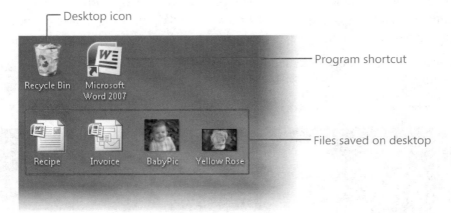

*An icon can represent an item stored in the current location or elsewhere.*

There are six standard desktop icons representing Windows elements; you can turn the display of these on or off. The only desktop icon that is displayed by default on a standard Windows 7 installation is the one that represents the *Recycle Bin*, which is where Windows temporarily stores files you delete. When the Recycle Bin is empty, the icon depicts an empty trash can; after you delete items (and until you empty the Recycle Bin), the icon depicts pieces of paper in the trash can. You can recover deleted files from the Recycle Bin, or you can empty the Recycle Bin and permanently delete the files to free up space on your hard disk.

**See Also** For information about Windows desktop icons, see "Creating Shortcuts" in Chapter 5, "Manage Folders and Files." For information about managing the Recycle Bin, see "Deleting and Recovering Folders and Files" in the same chapter.

The manufacturer of a new computer might have installed programs—either trial or full versions—on it. To bring these programs to your attention, the manufacturer might have placed shortcuts to them on the desktop, along with links to "offers" (advertisements) for products and services you can purchase. It's not unusual to purchase a new computer and find 20 shortcuts already on its desktop the first time you start it up.

Another way icons might appear on your desktop is if you save or move files or folders there. For example, if you download a program or other file from the Internet that you'll need to use only once, you might save it on your desktop so that you can quickly find it, use it, and then delete it. When you install a program on your computer, you often have the option of creating a shortcut to it on the desktop. (Some installation programs automatically create a desktop shortcut, but others give you the courtesy of choice.) If you created desktop shortcuts before upgrading your computer operating system to Windows 7, your existing desktop shortcuts are still available after you upgrade.

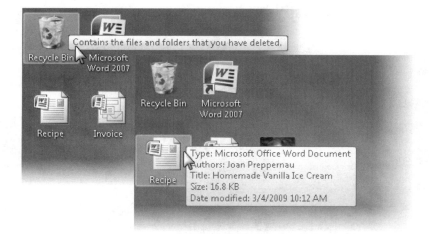

*Pointing to an item on the desktop displays a ScreenTip indicating its function or properties.*

Below each icon on the desktop is the name of the item it represents. If the name is too long to fit onto two lines, it is truncated by an ellipsis (...) when not selected and displayed in full when you click it, or sometimes when you click the desktop. When you point to an icon, a ScreenTip containing identifying information appears. Pointing to a program shortcut, for example, displays the location of the file that starts the program. Pointing to a file displays the file name, type, size, and modification date. You can start a program, open a folder or file, or jump to a network location or Web site by double-clicking the associated icon or shortcut.

**Tip** You can create your own shortcuts to programs, to specific folders or files, to other computers, or to Web sites, on the desktop or in any other folder. You can delete an item from the desktop as you would from any folder. When you delete a shortcut, however, you aren't actually deleting the linked program, folder, or file—only the link to that item.

**See Also** For information about creating desktop shortcuts, see "Creating Shortcuts" in Chapter 5, "Manage Folders and Files."

# Using the Start Menu

The Start menu is your central link to your computer's programs, management tools, and file storage structure. You open the Start menu by clicking the Start button at the left end of the Windows Taskbar, or by pressing the Windows logo key (the keyboard key, usually located to the left of the Spacebar, labeled with the Windows logo). The Windows 7 Start menu looks similar to that of earlier versions, and features the vertical folder expansion introduced in Windows Vista.

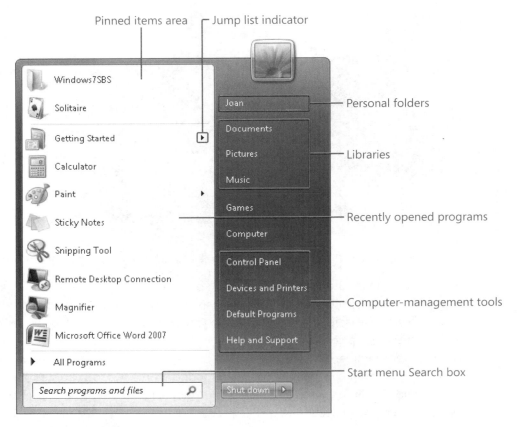

*The Windows 7 Start menu.*

**See Also**  For information about customizing the Start menu, see "Modifying the Start Menu" in Chapter 10, "Change System Settings."

## Quickly Getting Started

Clicking the Getting Started link on the Start menu displays the Getting Started window of Control Panel. (Pointing to the Getting Started link displays a jump list of the same items.)

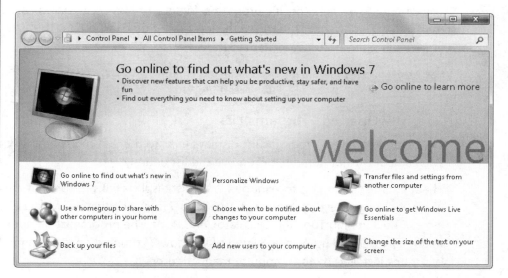

*The Getting Started window of Control Panel contains links to some of the tasks that you are likely to want to perform when setting up a new computer.*

If you're familiar with Windows, you might want to jump right in and start working from this window. If you're uncertain about these tasks, or want to learn more about how the associated functionality works in Windows 7, you might prefer to read about them in this book before taking action.

In this book, we cover the common startup tasks in a logical order and provide step-by-step instructions for completing them in the manner that is appropriate for your situation.

From the Getting Started window, you can also link to online information about Windows 7, and download useful programs from the Windows Live Essentials Web site.

## Exploring the Left Pane of the Start Menu

The left pane of the Start menu provides efficient access to programs and other items installed on your computer.

### Pinned Items Area

You can quickly access specific programs, folders, or files by inserting links to them in the pinned items area at the top of the left side of the Start menu. This area is not visible until the first time you pin an item to it.

**See Also** For information about pinning and unpinning Start menu links, see "Creating Shortcuts" in Chapter 5, "Manage Folders and Files."

### Recently Opened Programs List

The recently opened programs list displays links to the last 10 programs you started. You can adjust that number, or remove the list entirely.

The first time you log on to Windows 7, the list displays links to some of the new and improved programs that come with Windows 7, such as Windows Media Center, Sticky Notes, the Snipping Tool, the Calculator, and Paint. The programs that appear here might vary depending on the edition of Windows 7 running on your computer and any programs installed by the computer manufacturer.

**See Also** For information about the different editions of Windows 7 and how they are addressed in this book, see "Introducing Windows 7" at the beginning of this book.

### All Programs Menu

The All Programs menu provides access to most of the programs and utilities installed on your computer. These include programs installed as part of Windows 7, programs installed by the computer manufacturer, and programs you have installed. (Most program setup utilities add a program link to the Start menu.)

You display the All Programs menu by pointing to or clicking All Programs at the bottom of the left pane of the Start menu. Some programs are available from the menu itself, and some are grouped in folders. Clicking a folder expands it to make its programs accessible. If you want to close the All Programs menu without starting a program, you can point to or click Back to return to the standard Start menu.

In a default installation of Windows 7, the programs and utilities that are not available from the root of the All Programs menu are grouped in these folders:

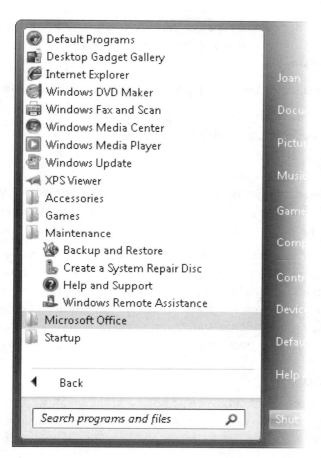

*On the All Programs menu, new programs are highlighted to bring them to your attention.*

- **Accessories** This folder includes links to the following programs and utilities: Calculator, Command Prompt, Connect to a Network Projector, Connect to a Projector, Getting Started, Math Input Panel, Notepad, Paint, Remote Desktop Connection, Run, Snipping Tool, Sound Recorder, Sticky Notes, Sync Center, Windows Explorer, and WordPad. Also included are the Ease Of Access, System Tools, Tablet PC, and Windows PowerShell subfolders.

  **Tip** On a Tablet PC, the *Tablet PC* folder appears directly on the All Programs menu.

- **Games** This folder includes links to the games that come preinstalled with Windows 7, to the Games Explorer window, and to the Game Providers page of the Microsoft Web site, from which you can download additional games.

- **Maintenance** This folder contains links to the following preventive maintenance tools: Backup and Restore, Create a System Repair Disc, Help and Support, and Windows Remote Assistance.

- **Startup** This folder contains links to programs that you want to start automatically with Windows 7.

We'll explore many of these programs and utilities in this book.

## Jump Lists

In earlier versions of Windows, a right-pointing arrow next to a link or menu item indicated that additional options for that entry were available. This functionality has been expanded in Windows 7 to create a very useful feature called *jump lists*.

On the Windows 7 Start menu, pointing to (not clicking) a right-pointing arrow next to a program name in the recently opened programs list or the pinned items area displays a list of files recently opened with that program, of related tasks, or of common actions you can perform within that program. For example, pointing to WordPad in the recently opened programs list displays a list of the WordPad documents you've recently been working with. You can "jump" to a specific file or task by clicking it in the jump list.

## Start Menu Search Box

In the lower-left corner of the Start menu, you'll find one of the greatest treasures of Windows 7—the Start menu Search box. This feature made our Top 3 Favorite Features list when it was introduced in Windows Vista, and it's still right up there—the time savings it provides are just amazing.

The first thing to note about Start menu Search is that it's immediately available regardless of what you're currently doing on your computer. Simply click the Start button—or press the Windows logo key if your keyboard has one—and the Start menu expands with the cursor already active in the Search box. Then type any characters in the Search box, and Windows immediately displays a list of programs, Control Panel items, files, documents, music, videos, and e-mail messages containing that string of characters, grouped by category. As you type more characters, Windows refines the search results almost instantly.

You can open any item that appears in the search results by clicking it, or you can open the folder containing that item by right-clicking the item and then clicking Open File Location. To view more information about documents and messages matching the search term, click See More Results (at the bottom of the list) to open the Search Results In Indexed Locations window. This window displays the file type icon (or, for certain types of graphics, a thumbnail of the actual graphic), name, location, date, and size of each item in the search results. For documents and HTML files, the first 150 or so characters of the file's content appear in the window. The search results remain available in the window until you close it.

**See Also**  For more information about Start menu Search, see "Exploring Control Panel" later in this chapter. For information about efficient search techniques, see "Finding Specific Information" in Chapter 4, "Navigate Windows and Folders."

## Exploring the Right Pane of the Start Menu

The right pane of the Start menu is divided into three sections whose contents can vary depending on the Start menu properties you specify.

- The top section provides quick access to file storage locations. It displays your user account picture and name, and links to the Documents, Pictures, and Music libraries. Clicking your user account picture displays your user account settings. Clicking your user account name displays all your personal folders (the Windows folders specifically associated with your user account). These include the Contacts, Desktop, Downloads, Favorites, Links, Saved Games, and Searches folders as well as your Documents, Music, Pictures, and Videos folders.

- The middle section provides access to games installed with Windows 7 and to the Computer window, from which you can access all the devices attached to your computer or network. This section can also display links to your Internet Explorer Favorites menu, to a list of the 15 files you have most recently worked with, to a window that displays the contents of your computer, and to a window that displays the computers, programs, folders, and files you can access on your network.

- The bottom section provides access to computer-management tools. It can display links to existing network connections, to the Control Panel window from which you can access all the Windows 7 system settings, to the default settings for opening various types of files and media, to the Devices And Printers window, and to Windows Help And Support.

By default, clicking an item in the right pane of the Start menu opens the corresponding folder window. Some items can alternatively be displayed as menus, to give you even faster access to files and commands.

At the bottom of the right pane of the Start menu, the Power button and Shut-down Options menu provide options for ending your computing session.

**See Also**  For information about the Power button and the Windows 7 shut-down options, see "Ending a Computing Session" later in this chapter.  For information about Start menu links and menus, see "Modifying the Start Menu" in Chapter 10, "Change System Settings."

## Quick Access to Windows Functionality

The Windows logo key is located to the left of the Spacebar (between the Ctrl and Alt keys) on most keyboards. It is labeled with the Windows logo, which resembles a waving flag. On currently manufactured keyboards, the Windows logo on the key is inside a recessed circle. This makes the key easier for keyboard users to locate. Similarly, many keyboards incorporate raised bars on the "home keys" (the F and J keys on an English-language keyboard) to enable keyboard users to quickly locate the "home position" (the correct placement of hands on the keyboard) by touch.

Pressing the Windows logo key alone or in combination with other keys enables you to move around and work with Windows without using a mouse or other pointing device. In Windows 7, the Windows logo key enables functionality including that shown in the following table.

| Keyboard shortcut | Function |
| --- | --- |
| Windows logo key | Open or close the Start menu |
| Windows logo key+B | Select the first icon in the notification area of the taskbar |
| Windows logo key+D | Minimize all open windows |
| Windows logo key+E | Open the Computer window |
| Windows logo key+F | Open the Search window |
| Windows logo key+G | Select or move between desktop gadgets |
| Windows logo key+L | Lock the computer |
| Windows logo key+M | Minimize all open windows |
| Windows logo key+Shift+M | Redisplay the windows |
| Windows logo key+P | Display the Projection controls |
| Windows logo key+R | Open the Run dialog box |
| Windows logo key+T | Select or move between taskbar buttons |
| Windows logo key+U | Open the Ease Of Access Center window |
| Windows logo key+X | Open the Windows Mobility Center (portable computers only) |
| Windows logo key+Spacebar | Make all open windows temporarily transparent (Aero-capable computers only) |

**Keyboard Shortcut**  You'll find other keyboard shortcuts throughout this book. For a full list of keyboard shortcuts for Windows 7 and for the Windows 7 programs and utilities, search Windows Help And Support for "keyboard shortcuts."

# Using the Windows Taskbar

The taskbar that appears, by default, across the bottom of your screen is your link to current information about what is happening on your Windows computer. In Windows 7, the taskbar functionality has been significantly upgraded. The default taskbar is twice the height that it was in previous versions of Windows, so you can more clearly see its contents. The Start button still appears at the left end of the taskbar, and the time and date still appear near the right end. However, what appears between them has undergone a transformation. Larger icons, improved grouping, thumbnail window previews from which you can view and work with window content, and the ability to move taskbar buttons where you want them all contribute to the increased usefulness of this feature.

**See Also** For information about changing the size of the taskbar and the taskbar buttons, moving the taskbar to another location, and adding toolbars to the taskbar, see "Modifying the Taskbar" in Chapter 10, "Change System Settings."

The Show Desktop button appears at the far right end of the taskbar. (If you've used previous versions of Windows, you'll notice that the button appearance has changed significantly.) Pointing to the Show Desktop button makes all the open windows transparent so that you can see the desktop. Clicking the button once minimizes all currently open windows; clicking it again redisplays the windows.

**Keyboard Shortcut** Pressing the Windows logo key+D has the same effect as clicking the Show Desktop button.

*The default Windows 7 taskbar.*

**Tip** The Quick Launch toolbar that was available on the taskbar in previous versions of Windows is, by default, not displayed in Windows 7 because you can now pin programs directly to the taskbar. If you miss this feature, you can display the Quick Launch toolbar by adding the hidden AppData\Roaming\Microsoft\Internet Explorer\Quick Launch folder, located in your personal folder structure, to the taskbar.

## Taskbar Buttons

To the right of the Start button, buttons for starting Internet Explorer, Windows Explorer, and Windows Media Player are pinned to the Windows Taskbar. Almost any action, such as starting a program or opening a file, dialog box, or Control Panel window, adds a corresponding, temporary button to the taskbar. These taskbar buttons, which by default are larger in Windows 7 than in previous versions of Windows, are identified by their program icons. When multiple files or windows of the same type are open, they are stacked under one taskbar button.

**Tip** Windows Explorer windows stack under the pinned Windows Explorer button, and Web pages stack under the pinned Internet Explorer button.

**See Also** For information about pinning and unpinning taskbar buttons, see "Creating Shortcuts" in Chapter 5, "Manage Folders and Files." For information about displaying multiple taskbar rows or small taskbar icons, see "Modifying the Taskbar" in Chapter 10, "Change System Settings."

The number of taskbar buttons you can fit on each row of the Windows 7 taskbar varies depending on your screen resolution and whether the taskbar is displaying large icons or small icons. When there are more buttons than the taskbar can display, a scroll bar appears so that you can get to hidden buttons. The following table provides examples of the taskbar capacity:

| Screen resolution | Buttons per row (large icons) | Buttons per row (small icons) |
|---|---|---|
| 800 × 600 | 10 | 15 |
| 1024 × 768 | 15 | 22 |
| 1280 × 1024 | 20 | 29 |
| 1600 × 1200 | 26 | 39 |

Pointing to a taskbar button displays thumbnails of each open window of that type. You can switch to a window by clicking its thumbnail. Pointing to a thumbnail temporarily displays that window and makes all other windows transparent, so you see only the selected window and the desktop. (If the window was minimized, it appears in its most recent location.) Pointing to a thumbnail also causes a Close button to appear in its upper-right corner, so you can close the window without making it active.

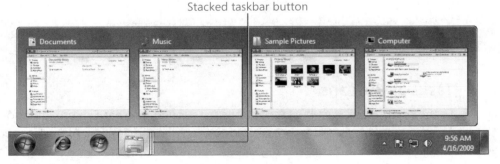

Stacked taskbar button

*Large, grouped thumbnails make it easier to manage multiple open windows.*

**Keyboard Shortcut**  You can use keyboard shortcuts to minimize, maximize, close, and switch between windows. For more information, see "Working with Windows" in Chapter 4, "Navigate Windows and Folders."

Right-clicking a taskbar button displays a shortcut menu of related files and commands. The list varies depending on the type of item the taskbar button represents. For example:

- Right-clicking the Internet Explorer taskbar button displays your Internet Explorer browsing history so that you can access a recently visited Web site directly from the taskbar.

- Right-clicking the Windows Explorer taskbar button displays a list of windows you frequently open.

- Right-clicking the Windows Media Player button displays a list of tasks related to the media that is currently accessible on your computer.

- Right-clicking a running program's taskbar button displays a list of files recently opened with that program, and gives you the options of pinning that program to the taskbar and closing all the open program windows.

The shortcut menu for every taskbar button includes links to start the associated program and to remove the button from the taskbar.

**Tip**  You can rearrange buttons on the taskbar by dragging them.

## Notification Area

The notification area at the right end of the taskbar displays information about the status of programs, including those running in the background (programs you don't need to interact with), as well as links to certain system commands. Some notification icons and system icons are hidden by default, and you can choose to hide others that you don't actively want to monitor.

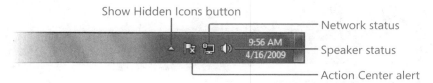

*The notification area displays information about programs and your computer system.*

**See Also**  For information about displaying and hiding notification area icons, see "Modifying the Taskbar" in Chapter 10, "Change System Settings."

# Exploring Control Panel

Control Panel is the central location from which you can manage all the aspects of your Windows 7 operating system: how it looks, how it works, how it communicates, and so on. When you open Control Panel, it's displayed in a unique instance of Windows Explorer; the taskbar button representing Control Panel and the various Control Panel windows appears on the taskbar independent of the Windows Explorer taskbar button.

## Control Panel Categories

In Windows Vista and Windows XP, Control Panel offered two views: Category view and Classic view. To help guide users to the correct Control Panel item, Category view described the tasks you might want to perform. Classic view provided direct access to the Control Panel items, and retained the look and feel of the Windows 2000 Control Panel. (In Classic view, you had to know or guess which item to use.)

In Windows 7, you can choose from three views of the Control Panel window—Category view, Large Icons view, and Small Icons view. Category view is the default. In this view, Control Panel items are divided into eight categories:

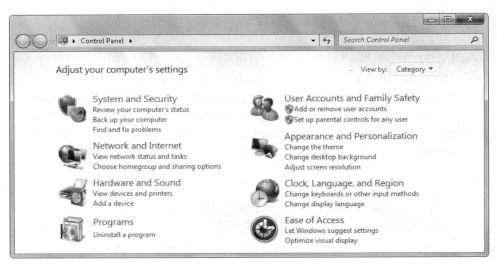

*In Category view, links to the most common tasks are available under the category name.*

The most common tasks within each category are listed below the category name so that you can go directly to the window or dialog box in which to perform that task.

Alternatively, you can browse through a category to the windows, dialog boxes, and tasks related to that category.

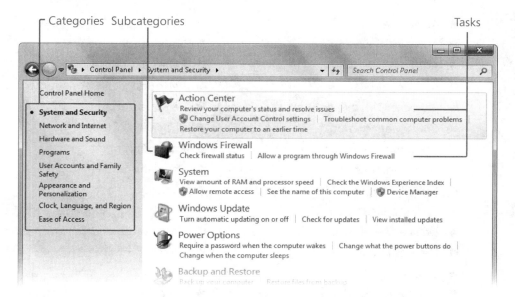

*Within a Control Panel category, clicking a subcategory opens that item's window; clicking a task jumps to a specific command center available from the item's window.*

## Accessing Individual Control Panel Items

From Control Panel, you can access more than 40 individual controls—windows and dialog boxes—with which you manage specific aspects of your computer system. Clicking Small Icons or Large Icons in the View By list displays the All Control Panel Items window.

*Small Icons view of the All Control Panel Items window displays links to every Control Panel window or dialog box.*

In Small Icons view or Large Icons view, the All Control Panel Items window displays the following items, which are common to all Windows 7 installations:

- Action Center
- Administrative Tools
- AutoPlay
- Backup and Restore
- BitLocker Drive Encryption
- Color Management
- Credential Manager
- Date and Time
- Default Programs
- Desktop Gadgets
- Device Manager
- Devices and Printers
- Display
- Ease of Access Center
- Folder Options
- Fonts
- Getting Started
- HomeGroup
- Indexing Options
- Internet Options
- Keyboard
- Location and Other Sensors
- Mouse

- Network and Sharing Center
- Notification Area Icons
- Parental Controls
- Performance Information and Tools
- Personalization
- Phone and Modem
- Power Options
- Programs and Features
- Recovery
- Region and Language
- RemoteApp and Desktop Connections
- Sound
- Speech Recognition
- Sync Center
- System
- Taskbar and Start Menu
- Troubleshooting
- User Accounts
- Windows CardSpace
- Windows Defender
- Windows Firewall
- Windows Update

Other Control Panel items might also be available, including controls with which you manage specific hardware components, software programs, and peripheral devices. Throughout this book, we will discuss many of these controls and how you can use them to manage your computer.

**Tip**  The Control Panel view you choose remains in effect until you choose another, even if you log off of Windows 7.

## Different Ways of Opening Control Panel Items

As you gain experience with Windows 7, you'll learn the Control Panel items to use to perform common management tasks. You can access controls in other ways than navigating
through the Control Panel categories, such as the following:

- If you're not certain of the specific name of a Control Panel item, you can
  browse a list of all the items in the All Control Panel Items window to locate
  the one you want.

  To display individual Control Panel item icons in the All Control Panel Items window,
  click Small Icons or Large Icons in the View By list in the upper-right corner of Control
  Panel. Then simply double-click the Control Panel item you want to open.

  **Tip**  You can return to the original Control Panel view by clicking Category in the View
  By list.

- If you know part of the name of the Control Panel item you want to open, you can
  locate it from Control Panel by entering it in the Search box at the right end of the
  Control Panel window title bar.

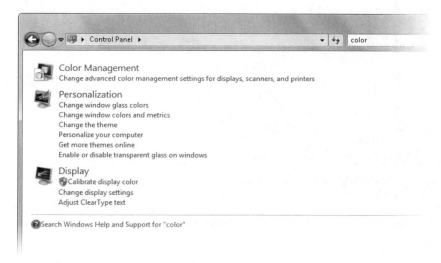

*Typing part of an item name in the Control Panel Search box displays items matching your
entry so that you can choose the one you want.*

● The simplest method of opening a Control Panel item is directly from the Start menu, by typing part of the item name into the Start menu Search box.

*As you enter characters into the Start menu Search box, the Start menu displays a list of matching items.*

**See Also** For more information about searching, see "Finding Specific Information" in Chapter 4, "Navigate Windows and Folders."

## Understanding User Account Control

User Account Control (UAC) is a security feature first introduced with Windows Vista. The intention of UAC is to enable you to log on to and operate the computer with a more secure standard user account. When you want to perform an operation that could pose a security risk, UAC requires that you enter an administrator account password before it proceeds. This system offers a greatly increased level of security, especially to computers that are not protected as part of a network domain.

**Important**  We'll talk about UAC in depth in Chapter 2, "Manage User Accounts." What you need to know now is that your computer responds differently to commands marked with a security icon, depending on whether you are logged on with an administrator or standard user account and which UAC security level is currently selected.

When UAC is turned on, as it is by default, clicking a command that requires administrator approval opens the User Account Control dialog box.

*When you're logged on as an administrator, Windows requests only that you acknowledge the security prompt; you don't need to enter your password.*

To continue with the restricted operation:

- If you're logged on as a standard user, click one of the administrator accounts, enter its password, and then click Yes.
- If you're logged on as an administrator, click Yes.

**Important**  In this book, we assume that you are logged on as a standard user and that User Account Control is set to Default. Under these conditions, the User Account Control message box appears only when a program tries to make changes to your computer, and not when you make changes to Windows settings, as you'll be doing when working through the exercises. If User Account Control is set to Always Notify and a User Account Control message box appears, you'll need to provide the requested credentials or acknowledgment.

# Finding Information About Your Computer System

Sometimes you'll want or need to locate information about your computer system, such as the processor speed, amount of memory, or edition of Windows. The System window of Control Panel displays information about your computer hardware and operating system, in the following categories:

- **Windows edition** This section contains information about your operating system including the version (such as Windows 7), edition (such as Home Premium), the most recently installed service pack (if a service pack for the operating system has been released) and, depending on the installed edition, a link to the section of the Microsoft Web site from which you can upgrade your edition of Windows.

- **System** This section provides the computer's Windows Experience Index base score (a number from 1.0 to 7.9), the processor type (such as Intel Pentium 4) and speed (such as 2.80 GHz), the amount of onboard random access memory (RAM) that is available, the system type (32-bit or 64-bit), and whether pen input or touch input is available through the computer monitor. This section might also provide information about the manufacturer and model of the computer.

- **Computer name, domain, and workgroup settings** This section displays the computer name (and a description if one exists) and the network domain or workgroup the computer belongs to. If your computer belongs to a homegroup, that information is not shown here.

  **See Also** For information about connecting your computer to homegroups, workgroups, and domains, see Chapter 3, "Manage Your Network."

- **Windows activation** The section displays the Windows activation status and product ID, or if Windows hasn't yet been activated, provides an online activation link.

The computer manufacturer may provide additional information, such as support contact information or links to associated hardware and software vendors, in the System window.

**Tip** You can quickly display the System window by right-clicking Computer on the Start menu and then clicking Properties.

The Windows Experience Index base score shown in the System window is not a cumulative rating; it is the lowest of the individual ratings scored by the following five system components:

- Processor speed
- Installed RAM
- General desktop graphics capabilities
- Three-dimensional gaming graphics capabilities
- Primary hard disk data transfer rate

The highest score available for a Windows 7 computer is 7.9 (updated from 5.9 in Windows Vista, to take advantage of improvements in available processor, graphics, and hard disk technologies). Higher scores may be introduced as necessary to keep up with hardware advances.

**See Also** For more information about the Windows Experience Index, see "Rating Your Computer's Hardware" in Chapter 12, "Set Up Hardware Devices."

In this exercise, you'll open Control Panel and locate information about your computer system. In the process, you'll learn different methods of accessing Control Panel items.

**SET UP** You don't need any practice files to complete this exercise. Log on to your Windows 7 computer, and then follow the steps.

1. At the left end of the **Windows Taskbar**, click the **Start** button.

   The Start menu expands.

2. On the right side of the **Start** menu, click **Control Panel**.

   The Control Panel window opens.

   **Troubleshooting** If Control Panel opens in a view other than Category view, click Category in the View By list before continuing.

3. Click the **System and Security** category.

   **See Also** For information about some of the security features of Windows 7, see "Updating Windows System Files" later in this chapter; "Understanding User Accounts and Permissions" in Chapter 2, "Manage User Accounts;" and "Configuring Power Options" in Chapter 10, "Change System Settings."

4. In the **System and Security** window, click the **System** subcategory.

   The System window opens.

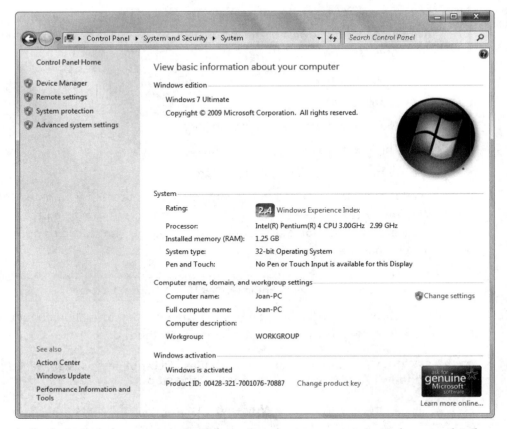

*In the System window, you can view information about your computer and access related tools and Control Panel items.*

5. View the information about your computer that is displayed in the right pane of the **System** window.

The left pane of each Control Panel window contains links to related tools at the top, and to related Control Panel items at the bottom. You can return to Control Panel by clicking the Control Panel Home link at the top of the left pane, but for the purpose of learning how to navigate through Control Panel, we'll use a different method, which involves working with the path displayed in the Address bar above the panes. This path shows the route you have taken to get to the displayed window—in this case, the System window.

6. In the **Address bar**, click the arrow to the right of **System and Security**.

A list of the System And Security subcategories appears, with System (the current window) displayed in bold.

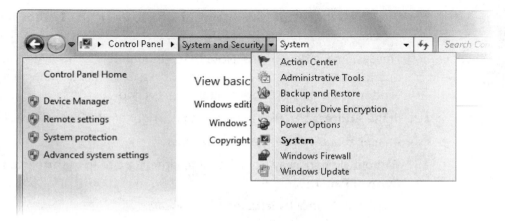

*You can open any subcategory window by clicking it in the list.*

7.  In the list, click **Action Center**.

    The path in the Address bar changes, and the Action Center opens.

8.  In the **Address** bar, click **System and Security**.

    You return to the System And Security window.

9.  If **Control Panel** appears at the left end of the path shown in the **Address** bar, click **Control Panel**. Otherwise, click the left-pointing chevron to the left of the first item in the path, and then in the list that appears, click **Control Panel**.

    You return to the Category view of Control Panel window.

10. In the **View by** list, click **Large Icons**.

    Control Panel displays large icons and names for the individual subcategories.

*In Large Icons view, the icons provide visual clues to the purpose of each control.*

11. Scroll the **All Control Panel Items** window to locate the **System** item, and then click it.

    The System window opens. Note that although this is the same window that opened after step 4, the path in the Address bar reflects that you accessed the window from the All Control Panel Items window.

12. In the **Address** bar, click the arrow to the right of **All Control Panel Items**.

    An alphabetical list of the items appears.

13. Without clicking away from the list to close it, point to the arrow to the right of **Control Panel**.

    The list of Control Panel categories appears.

14. In the **Address** bar, click **Control Panel**.

    You return to the Control Panel home page.

✖ **CLEAN UP** Click the Close button to close the Control Panel window before continuing to the next exercise.

# Updating Windows System Files

When you upgrade to Windows 7 or purchase a Windows 7 computer, the operating system files are the ones available when your Windows 7 installation media was created or when Windows was installed. Whenever necessary, Microsoft releases updates to Windows (and to other products), either to provide additional functionality or to protect your computer from new security threats. It's important to install these updates as soon after their release as possible.

Windows Update is a utility that scans your computer, confers with the Microsoft Update online database, and recommends or installs any updates that are available for your operating system, your Microsoft software programs, or your hardware. Quite apart from knowing that you have the "latest and greatest," by using Windows Update, you can be sure that your computer is updated whenever necessary.

## Types of Updates

During the Windows 7 installation process, your computer is automatically configured to install updates. (If you upgraded to Windows 7 from a previous version of Windows, Windows Update retains your previous settings.) Updates are classified as follows:

- **Important updates**  These increase the security or reliability of the operating system and Microsoft software products.

- **Recommended updates**  These address non-critical problems, and help enhance your computing experience.

- **Optional updates**  These do not address specific Microsoft software problems. They might include software add-ons or drivers for third-party hardware.

With the default settings, Windows Update collects the version numbers of your operating system, Web browser, and other installed software, as well as information about the hardware devices that are connected to your computer, at 3:00 each morning. It then proactively contacts the Microsoft Update site, compiles a list of updates that are available for your system, downloads any available Important or Recommended updates for Windows and Windows programs (even for Windows Update itself), and installs them.

**Tip**  When the update process is complete, Windows Update discards the version and ID information that it collected from your computer.

## Completing an Update

Some updates require that you restart the computer to finish the installation, because files can't be updated while they're in use. If you don't restart the computer immediately after installing an update that requires a restart, Windows Update displays a reminder message. From the message box, you can restart the computer or dismiss the message for 10 minutes, 1 hour, or 4 hours. If you don't postpone the reminder, Windows Update counts down to a restart time. If you don't interrupt the countdown, Windows saves auto-recover copies of open documents, shuts down running programs, performs any other tasks necessary to safely shut down the computer, restarts the computer, and displays a message that it has done so.

## Windows Update Options

The frequency, time, and independence of the Windows Update utility are your choice. You can access Windows Update from the Start menu, from Control Panel, or from Windows Help And Support. The options are to have Windows 7 do one of the following:

- Download and install updates automatically.
- Download updates and notify you when they are ready to be installed.
- Check for updates and notify you when an update is available.
- Check for updates only when you manually initiate the process.

**Important** If your computer is connected to a network domain, your network administrator might control the installation of updates.

The default setting in Windows 7 allows you to install updates whether you're logged on as an administrator or as a standard user. You can choose to restrict the installation of updates to administrators only.

Automatic updating is very convenient if you don't want to bear the responsibility of remembering to manually update your system, or if you want to be sure updates are installed as soon as they become available. The default update settings make the automatic update process reasonably unobtrusive—but they are effective only if your computer is usually on and online at 3:00 in the morning.

**Tip** The default Windows 7 Sleep mode options allow scheduled programs such as Windows Update to bring your computer out of Sleep mode to check for, download, and install available updates according to your Windows Update settings. For more information, see "Configuring Power Options" in Chapter 10, "Change System Settings."

When an update has been downloaded and is ready to be installed, Windows Update alerts you in one or more ways:

- When any type of update is ready, a Windows Update icon appears in the notification area of the taskbar.

- When an Important update is ready, a security icon appears on the Power button on the Start menu. You can't shut down your computer without first installing the update.

In addition to updating Windows system files, you can update other Microsoft products and featured programs through Windows Update. When not already selected, these options are available from the box at the bottom of the Windows Update window:

- **Get updates for other Microsoft products** To have Windows Update monitor availability of updates to Office and other Microsoft programs, click the Find Out More link. This opens the Microsoft Update site. At the bottom of the page, select the I Accept The Terms Of Use check box, and then click Install.

- **Additional Windows Update options are available** Windows Update can notify you when featured updates and programs are available. To invoke this option, click the View Options link and then, in the Windows Update message box, click Turn On This Option.

In this exercise, you'll check update settings, install available updates, and set up the computer to periodically install critical updates.

**SET UP** You don't need any practice files to complete this exercise; just follow the steps.

1. Click the **Start** button, click **All Programs**, and then click **Windows Update**.

   Windows Update displays information about your computer's current update status, when it most recently checked for updates, when it most recently installed updates, and the scope of updates your computer receives from Microsoft Update.

   If your computer is up to date or only optional updates are available, a green bar and security shield appear at the left end of the update status pane. If Important or Recommended updates are available, the bar and shield are yellow or red.

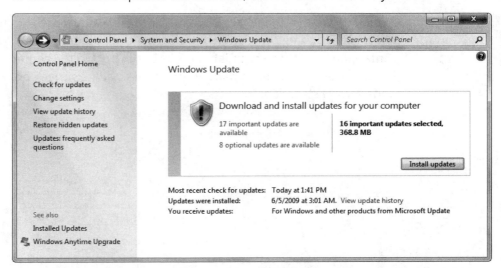

*The color of the bar and shield indicates your Windows Update status: green means that all available Important updates are installed.*

2. If a link to available updates appears in the status box at the top of the **Windows Update** window, click it. (If there are multiple links, click any one.) Otherwise, skip to step 6.

The Select Updates To Install page displays the selected category of updates that are available for your computer.

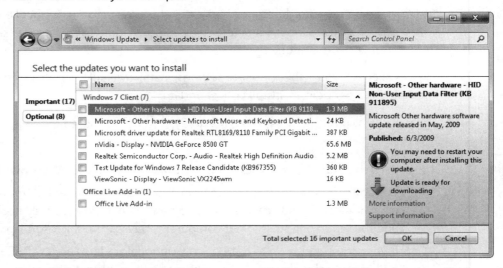

*On the Select Updates To Install page, you can display the description of each available update and select whether to install it.*

In the left pane of the Select Updates To Install window are tabs for each level of available updates. Clicking a tab displays the updates of that type in the center pane. Clicking an update (not its check box) in the center pane displays its description in the right pane. Selecting an update's check box selects that update for installation.

Important updates are automatically selected for installation. You can choose to not install an update by clearing its check box, but unless you have a very good reason to wait, we recommend that you install Important updates as soon as possible.

**Tip** If administrator permission is required to install an update, the Windows security icon appears on the Install Updates button.

**3.** Select the check boxes of the updates you want to install, and then click **OK**.

Windows Update prompts you to begin the installation process.

**Tip** You can select all the updates in the center pane by selecting the check box to the left of the Name column header.

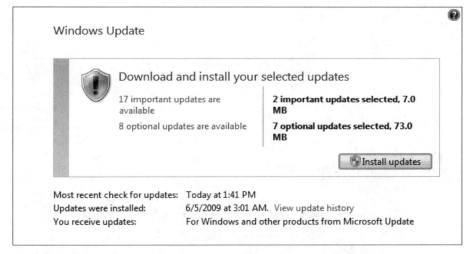

*Windows Update is ready to download and install the selected update.*

**4.** In the **Windows Update** window, click **Install updates**.

**Troubleshooting** Some software program updates require that you agree to the licensing terms and conditions of the program before you can install the update.

A progress bar reports on the update activities as Windows downloads the selected update(s), creates a restore point, and then installs each update.

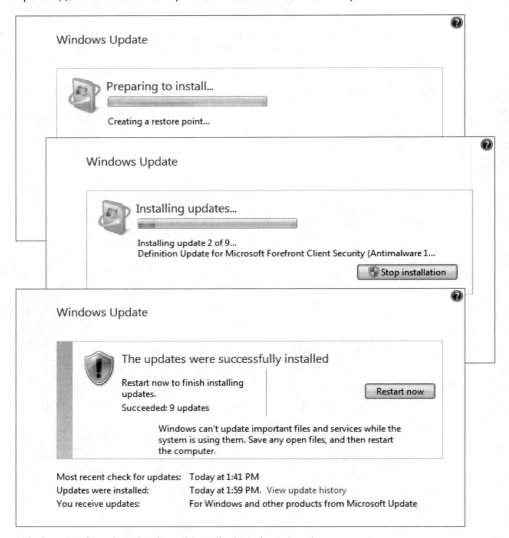

*Windows Update downloads and installs the selected update.*

**5.** If Windows 7 prompts you to restart your computer, close any open files, and then click **Restart now**. Windows will complete the configuration of installed updates before and/or after restarting the computer. After your computer restarts, log on, and then repeat step 1 to return to Windows Update.

**6.** In the left pane, click **Change settings**.

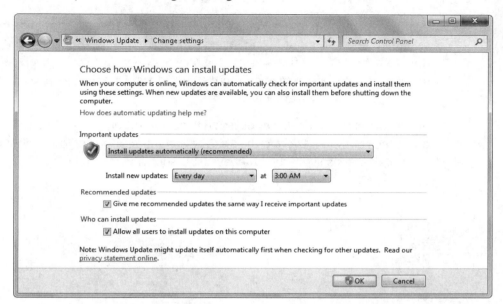

*In the Change Settings window, you can change the frequency, time, type, and scope of automatic updates.*

**7.** In the **Important updates** section of the **Change Settings** window, if **Install updates automatically** is not already selected in the first list, select it now.

**8.** In the two lists to the right of **Install new updates**, click a frequency and a time at which your computer will usually be on and online.

It's best to select a time outside your core work hours—say at the beginning or end of your workday—when connecting to the Internet and installing updates won't impact your ability to work by monopolizing your computer's resources.

**Tip** If you prefer to have more control over the update process but still enjoy the benefit of automatic updates, select the Download Updates But Let Me Choose Whether To Install Them option. With this option, Windows 7 downloads available updates to your computer and displays the Windows Update icon in the notification area. You can click the icon to review and approve or reject the installation of each update.

**9.** Select or clear the check boxes in the **Recommended updates**, **Who can install updates**, and **Featured update notifications** sections to reflect the way you want Windows Update to function on this computer. Then click **OK**.

Windows Update saves your changes.

 **CLEAN UP** Close the Windows Update window.

# Ending a Computing Session

If you are going to stop working with your computer for any length of time, you can safeguard your information and save power in a number of ways. Although not all the options actually turn off the computer, they are referred to collectively as *shut-down options*, and they are available from the Shut-down Options menu located in the lower-right corner of the Start menu.

By default, clicking the Power button (labeled *Shut Down*) starts the process of shutting down the computer. Clicking the Shut-down Options button (to the right of the Power button) displays a list of the other available shut-down options.

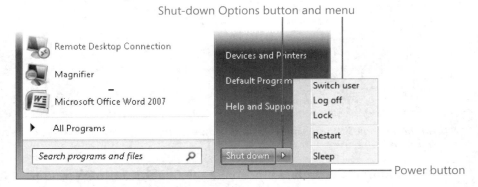

*By default, clicking the Power button invokes the Shut Down command. Click the Shut-down Options button to display other options for ending your computing session.*

**Tip**  The shut-down option currently assigned to the Power button does not appear on the Shut-down Options menu.

**See Also**  For information about changing the Power button behavior, see "Modifying the Start Menu" in Chapter 10, "Change System Settings."

The shut-down options include the following:

● **Log off**  If you're finished working on a computer that you share with other people, you can end your Windows 7 session (but not affect other users' sessions) by logging off. You must save your files and shut down all running programs before you log off; if you don't, Windows 7 will close any open windows and exit programs, possibly losing unsaved data in the process.

  **See Also**  For information about multiple concurrent user sessions, and about the Switch User shut-down option, see the sidebar "Switching Quickly Among Users" in Chapter 2, "Manage User Accounts."

● **Lock**  If you want to prevent passersby from seeing what you're working on, you can lock the computer, which displays the Welcome screen and requires that you log on to your account to resume. Locking is most effective when your user account is protected by a password; otherwise, anyone can click your user account picture on the Welcome screen to unlock the computer and access your information.

**Keyboard Shortcut**  You can lock the computer by pressing the Windows Logo key+L.

**See Also**  For information about configuring a screen saver to lock a computer, see "Implementing a Screen Saver" in Chapter 9, "Change Visual Elements."

● **Restart**  After installing certain programs and program updates, it is necessary to restart the computer to complete the update of system files that are in use. You might also find, at times, that restarting the computer helps to resolve a technical difficulty.

**Troubleshooting**  If your computer seems to be operating unusually slowly, or you're experiencing technical problems that seem related to the operating system rather than to an application, try restarting your computer. Restarting clears the system cache—an area in memory where Windows 7 stores information it might need to access quickly—and frequently resolves minor issues..

● **Sleep**  If you're going to be away from your computer, conserve power and protect your work by putting your computer into Sleep mode. When you do, Windows 7 saves any open files, records their state and the state of any running programs in memory, and then puts your computer into a power-saving mode. When you "wake up" the computer, usually by moving the mouse or by pressing the Enter key or the computer's power button, Windows 7 needs only a few seconds to come out of its power-saving state and retrieve information from memory. Then it does one of the following:

❍ If your user account is not password protected, resumes your previous computing session, exactly as you left it.

❍ If your user account is password protected, displays the Welcome screen.

**Troubleshooting**  Some video card drivers don't support Sleep mode. If the Shut-down Options menu doesn't include the Sleep option, update your video driver. A Hibernate shut-down option is available on computers that don't support Sleep mode. Hibernate is similar to Sleep, except that it saves open files and the state of running programs on your hard disk instead of in memory, and then completely turns off the computer. When you awaken the computer, Windows 7 retrieves information from the hard disk and restores your previous computing session.

Putting your computer into Sleep mode conserves power and keeps your work quickly available. When a desktop computer is sleeping, it uses approximately 10 percent of the power required to run normally. When a mobile computer is sleeping, it uses approximately 2 percent of its battery power per hour.

**See Also** For information about configuring your computer to automatically enter Sleep mode after a period of inactivity, see "Configuring Power Options" in Chapter 10, "Change System Settings."

● **Shut Down** If you need to turn off your computer entirely—for example, to install hardware or to move a desktop computer—you do so by shutting down the computer. Shutting down closes all your open programs and files, ends your computing session, closes network connections, stops system processes, stops the hard disk, and turns off the computer. This option appears by default on the Power button.

**See Also** For information about specifying which shut-down option appears on the Power button, see "Modifying the Start Menu" in Chapter 10, "Change System Settings."

In this exercise, you'll lock and unlock your computer, put it into Sleep mode and wake it up, log off from Windows 7, and then shut down the computer.

 **SET UP** You don't need any practice files to complete this exercise; just follow the steps. Windows will prompt you to save and close any open files during the shut-down process.

1. On the **Start** menu, click the **Shut-down Options button**, and then on the **Shut-down Options menu**, click **Lock**.

   The Windows 7 Welcome screen appears, displaying only your user account. The word *Locked* appears under your user account name.

2. If your account is password protected, enter your password in the **Password** box, and then press the **Enter** key. Otherwise, click your user account picture.

   Your previous computing session resumes.

3. On the **Shut-down Options menu**, click **Sleep**.

   Windows saves your file and program information and then puts your computer into a power-saving state. The hard disk stops spinning, but the power light on the computer itself is still on, either steadily or blinking slowly.

4. Depending on your hardware, either move the mouse, press **Enter**, or press your computer's power button to wake up your computer.

   The Windows 7 Welcome screen appears on the screen.

   **Troubleshooting** If you don't know which method to use to wake up your computer, try them in the order given. If none of these methods work, consult your computer's manual or the manufacturer's Web site.

5. If your account is protected by a password, enter your password in the **Password** box, and then press **Enter**.

   Windows logs you on to your user account.

6. On the **Shut-down Options menu**, click **Log Off**.

   If no programs are running on your computer, Windows 7 logs you off. Otherwise, Windows 7 displays a list of running programs and open files.

7. If you don't have any unsaved work, click **Force log off** to complete the process and display the Welcome screen. Otherwise, click **Cancel** to return to your computing session; then save and close open files, shut down running programs, and click **Log Off** again on the **Shut-down Options menu** to complete the process.

   The Windows Welcome screen appears.

8. In the lower-right corner of the Welcome screen, click the **Power** button.

   **Troubleshooting** If any other user accounts are logged on to the computer, Windows 7 gives you the opportunity to cancel the shut down process. If you shut down a computer while people are logged on to it, they could lose data in open files or running programs.

   Windows 7 shuts down all computer processes and turns off your computer.

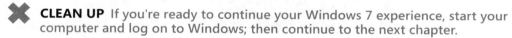

**CLEAN UP** If you're ready to continue your Windows 7 experience, start your computer and log on to Windows; then continue to the next chapter.

# Key Points

- You start a computing session by logging on to Windows.

- Each computer user has an individual user account. Each person using a computer logs on to the computer with his or her own user account.

- To maintain security, log on as a standard user. You'll enjoy the most secure computing experience when you log on to your computer as a standard user and keep the User Account Control feature turned on.

- Your Windows environment preferences are linked to your user account. When you log on to Windows 7, it looks and works the way you want.

- Your primary interactions with the Windows 7 operating system are through the Start menu, the Windows Taskbar, and Control Panel.

- It's important to keep your computer up to date with the most current security updates. Windows Update makes it easy to do this automatically or manually.

- You end a computing session by logging off from Windows. You can log off and leave the computer running, or you can log off as part of the process of shutting down.

- You can save power without closing files and exiting programs by putting your computer into Sleep mode.

# Chapter at a Glance

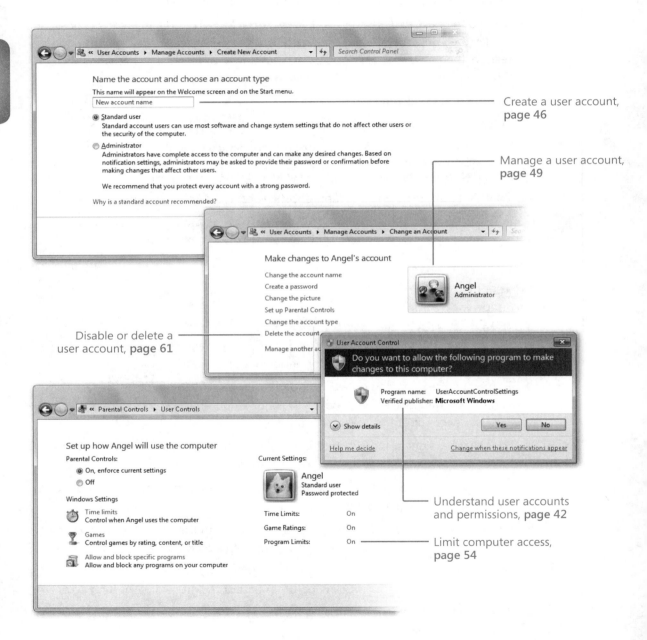

Create a user account,
**page 46**

Manage a user account,
**page 49**

Disable or delete a
user account, **page 61**

Understand user accounts
and permissions, **page 42**

Limit computer access,
**page 54**

# 2 Manage User Accounts

---

**In this chapter, you will learn how to**

✔ Understand user accounts and permissions.

✔ Create a user account.

✔ Manage a user account.

✔ Limit computer access.

✔ Disable or delete a user account.

---

You might be the only person who uses your computer, or you might share it with other people. If more than one person uses the same computer, each person should log on with his or her own user account. By using separate accounts, each person can set up the Windows 7 environment to look and work the way he or she wants it, without interfering with another person's computing experience.

Each user account is associated with a user profile that describes the way the computer environment (the user interface) looks and operates for that particular user. This information includes simple things such as the color scheme and fonts used in windows and dialog boxes, the desktop background, and program shortcuts, as well as personal information that you want to keep confidential, such as saved passwords and your Internet browsing history. Each user profile includes a personal folder not accessible by other people using the computer, in which you can store documents, pictures, media, and other files you want to keep private.

A Windows 7 user account can be either an administrator account or a standard user account. The account type determines the extent of the changes you can make to the computer; when you are logged on with an administrator account, you have more control than when you are logged on with a standard user account. Additional restrictions can be applied to a standard user account to limit the user's access to the computer, to the Internet, and to certain types of programs and content.

In this chapter, you'll first learn about the two types of user accounts supported by Windows 7 and the important role played by User Account Control (UAC) in helping to protect your computer from unwanted changes. Then you'll create a user account, change user account information, place restrictions on an account, and delete an account.

**Important**  The information in this chapter applies to computer user accounts (sometimes referred to as *local user accounts*) and not to domain user accounts. The features we discuss in this chapter are not available on computers that are connected to a network domain.

> **Practice Files**  Before you can complete the exercises in this chapter, you need to install the practice file specified in "Using the Practice Files" at the beginning of this book to its default location. The practice file you will use to complete the exercises in this chapter is in the Accounts practice file folder.

# Understanding User Accounts and Permissions

The Windows 7 system of user accounts and passwords allows more than one person to use the same computer while providing the following safeguards:

● **Each user's information is kept private**  You prevent other users from reading or altering your documents, pictures, music, and other files by storing them in sub-folders automatically set up within your user account folder. For example, if you manage your family's financial records on a home computer that is also used by your children to do their homework, you can set up separate accounts for your children so that they can't view confidential information or change your files.

● **Each user's working environment is protected**  You can personalize your environment in various ways, without worrying about other people making changes to your personal settings.

**See Also**  For information about user account folders, see "Understanding Files, Folders, and Libraries" in Chapter 4, "Navigate Windows and Folders." For information about customizing the Windows environment, see Chapter 9, "Change Visual Elements."

## User Account Types

Windows 7 supports two levels of computer permissions: administrator and standard user. An administrator account has higher-level permissions than a standard user account, which means that an administrator account owner can perform tasks on your computer that a standard user account owner cannot.

Administrator account credentials are necessary to do things such as:

● Create, change, and delete accounts.

● Change settings that affect all computer users.

● Change security-related settings.

● Install and remove programs.

● Access system files and files in other user account profiles.

 Tasks that require administrator permission are indicated in windows and dialog boxes by a Windows security icon.

Standard user account credentials allow a user to do things that affect only his or her account, including:

● Change or remove the password.

● Change the user account picture.

● Change the theme and desktop settings.

● View files he or she created and stored in his or her personal folders, as well as files in the Public folders.

**Tip** Windows creates a special account called *Guest*, which is inactive by default and disabled on computers that are part of a domain. You can activate the Guest account to give someone temporary, limited access to your computer without having to create a user account for that person.

Even if you have an administrator account, it is a good idea to create and use a standard user account for your day-to-day computing. If a malicious person or program infiltrates your computer while you're logged on as an administrator, there is a much higher risk of serious damage to the computer system than if you're logged on as a standard user. Through an administrator account, the person or program has access to all system files and settings, whereas a standard user doesn't have access to certain functions that can permanently damage the system.

# User Account Control

User Account Control (UAC) protects your computer from changes to Windows system settings by requiring that an administrator expressly permit certain types of changes. Each area of the Windows interface that requires administrator permission is labeled with a security icon. When you attempt to access or change protected Windows settings, a User Account Control dialog box appears, asking for confirmation that Windows should continue the operation.

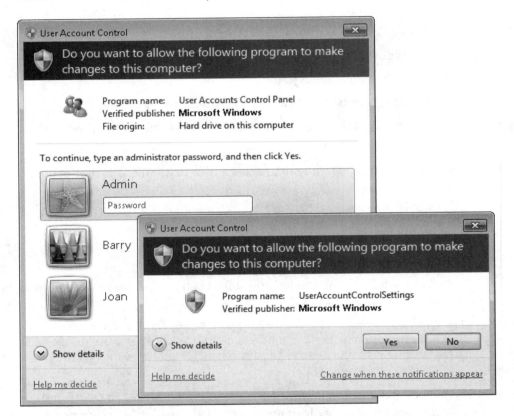

*The appearance of the User Account Control dialog box varies depending on the type of user account you're logged on with and what you are trying to do.*

**See Also** For information about working with UAC while completing the exercises in this book, see the sidebar "Understanding User Account Control" in Chapter 1, "Explore Windows 7."

If you're logged on with an administrator account, you can simply click the Yes button to continue the operation. If you're logged on with a standard user account, the dialog box lists the administrator accounts on the computer. To continue the operation, you click one of the administrator accounts, enter its password in the box that appears, and then click Yes.

**Tip** If an administrator account doesn't have an associated password, you can continue the operation by simply clicking that account and then clicking Yes. For this reason, it's important to assign a password to each administrator account on the computer.

Windows doesn't save the credentials you enter in the User Account Control dialog box; they are valid for this operation only. Anyone who doesn't have access to administrator credentials can't perform the operation, which effectively prevents non-administrators from making changes you haven't authorized.

UAC has four levels of control. Only the first two are available when you're logged on with a standard user account, even if you have access to administrator credentials:

- **Always notify** When a user or program initiates a change that requires administrator credentials, the desktop is dimmed and the User Account Control dialog box opens. You must click Yes or No, or close the dialog box before you can take any other action.

- **Notify for programs and dim the desktop** This is the default setting. Unlike the Always Notify setting, this setting allows any user to make changes. Program changes are still restricted, however. When a program initiates a change that requires administrator credentials, the desktop dims and the User Account Control dialog box opens. You must respond to the dialog box before you can continue.

- **Notify for programs and don't dim the desktop** Any user can make changes. When a program initiates a restricted action, the User Account Control dialog box opens. The restricted action will not be performed until you respond to the dialog box, but you can perform other tasks while the dialog box is open.

- **Never notify** This is the equivalent of turning off UAC. Any user or program can make any changes to the computer without restriction.

To change the UAC setting:

1. Display the System And Security window of Control Panel. In the Action Center subcategory, click Change User Account Control Settings.

   **Tip** The security icon to the left of the command indicates that administrator credentials are required to complete this operation.

The User Account Control Settings window opens.

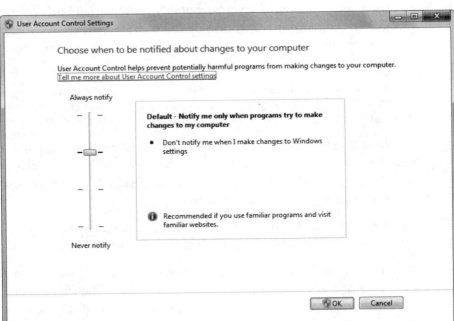

*You can use the slider to select the level of control you want.*

2. Click above or below the slider, or drag it, to set UAC to the level you want, and then click OK.

**Tip** You must be logged on to an administrator account to select either of the two lowest settings. If you select the Never Notify setting, you must restart your computer to complete the process of turning off UAC.

# Creating a User Account

The first user account created on a computer is automatically an administrator account—every computer must have at least one—so if yours is the first or only user account on the computer, you are operating as an administrator. You can create additional accounts for yourself or for other people who will use your computer.

To create a user account, you need to specify only a user account name and the account type. The user account name you choose is displayed on the Welcome screen and at the top of the Start menu. The first time anyone logs on with a new user account, Windows creates a corresponding user profile, including a set of personal folders within the Users folder structure.

Windows assigns a user account picture from its standard set to the new user account. After creating the user account, any administrator or the account owner can change the user account name or picture, or protect the account with a password. Changing the user account name or picture changes the corresponding elements on the Welcome screen and Start menu. After the account has been used to log on to the computer and Windows has created the personal folders, changing the user account name does not change the name of the user's personal folder.

**See Also** For information about changing user account names and pictures, and assigning passwords to user accounts, see "Managing a User Account" later in this chapter.

**Important** If your computer is part of a domain, network permissions are administered through your domain account. You might be able to create a new account on your local computer, but only a network administrator can create or modify a domain user account.

In this exercise, you'll create a user account with administrator permissions.

 **SET UP** You don't need any practice files for this exercise, but you will need administrator account credentials. Display Control Panel in Category view, and then follow the steps.

1.  In **Control Panel**, under **User Accounts and Family Safety**, click **Add or remove user accounts**.

    The Manage Accounts window opens.

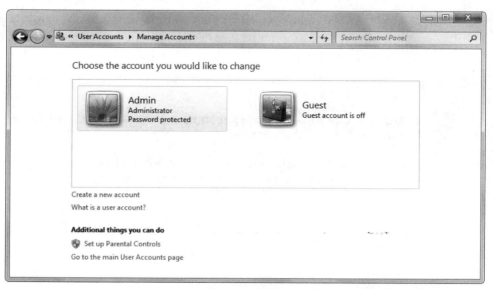

*The Manage Accounts window displays icons for all the accounts set up on your computer.*

2. Click **Create a new account**.

The Create New Account window opens.

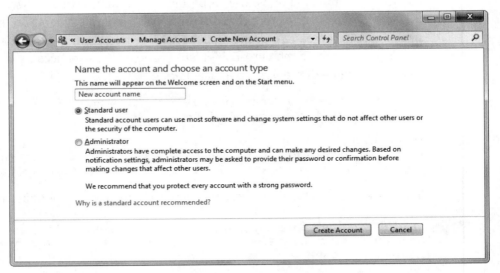

*You can set up either a standard user account or an administrator account.*

3. In the **New account name** box, type **Angel**.

4. Click **Administrator**, and then click **Create Account**.

Windows 7 creates a new account with the user account name *Angel*, and randomly assigns a user account picture to the account, which now appears in the Manage Accounts window.

**See Also** For information about user account pictures, see "Managing a User Account" on the next page.

 **CLEAN UP** Close the Manage Accounts window, retaining the Angel account for use in later exercises in this chapter.

**Tip** You can quickly display your user account settings by clicking your user account picture that appears at the top of the right pane of the Start menu.

### Switching Quickly Among Users

More than one user account can be logged on to the same computer at the same time. For example, if you are working on a shared home computer and your son wants to check e-mail on that computer while you get a snack, he can log on to his user account without disturbing the programs and files you are working with.

To log on to your user account while another account is active:

1. On the Start menu, click the Shut-down Options button, and then click Switch User.

2. On the Welcome screen, click your user account, and then enter the password if one is required.

Repeat the process to switch back to the original user's session or between user accounts.

When you shut down your computer, Windows warns you if another user account is active so that you don't inadvertently lose another user's unsaved work or shut down the computer without appropriately exiting running programs.

# Managing a User Account

Every user account has an associated user account name and a user account picture. The account might also have a password, if one has been assigned.

**Important** If you're going to take the trouble to protect your user account with a password, choose one that no one is likely to guess. A strong password is at least eight characters, does not contain words that might be in the dictionary or names, and contains at least one uppercase character, one lowercase character, one number, and one punctuation mark.

Any user can change the following for his or her account:

- **Account name** You can change the display name that appears on the Welcome screen and Start menu.

- **Account picture** You can change the picture that identifies you on the Welcome screen and Start menu.

- **Password** You can create or change the password.

## Be Safe Now, Not Sorry Later

When you assign a password to your user account, you can also save a password hint. Windows 7 displays the password hint if you enter an incorrect password. If you didn't save a password hint, or can't remember the password even with the help of the hint, you can reset your password—but only if you have created a password reset disk. You can create this disk on a USB flash drive or on a floppy disk, but not on a CD.

Don't think you'll ever forget your password? It might sound unlikely, but it can happen, especially if you are required you to change your password frequently. Creating a password reset disk is a simple precaution to take.

To create a password reset disk:

1. Connect a USB flash drive, or insert a disk into your computer's floppy disk drive.

2. Open the User Accounts window of Control Panel. In the left pane, click Create A Password Reset Disk.

3. On the Welcome page of the Forgotten Password wizard, click Next. On the Create A Password Reset Disk page, select the USB flash drive or floppy disk drive you want to use, and then click Next.

4. On the Current User Account Password page, enter the password you use to log on to Windows 7, and then click Next.

5. When the progress bar displays *100% complete*, click Next. Then on the Completing The Forgotten Password Wizard page, click Finish.

Be sure to store the password reset disk in a safe place, because anyone can use it to reset your password and gain access to your computer.

If you enter an incorrect password on the Welcome screen, a message box informs you that the user account name or password is incorrect. After clicking OK to return to the Welcome screen, you can use your password reset disk as follows:

1. On the Welcome screen, below the password box, click Reset Password.

2. On the Welcome page of the Password Reset wizard, click Next. On the Insert The Password Reset Disk page, select the USB flash drive or floppy disk drive you want to use. Insert the password reset disk into the drive, then click Next.

3. On the Reset The User Account Password page, enter a new password and password hint, and then click Next.

4. On the Completing The Forgotten Password Wizard page, click Finish.

If you have administrator credentials, you can change these properties for any user account. You can also change the account type from administrator to standard user (provided at least one administrator account remains on the computer) or vice versa.

Windows 7 comes with many user account pictures, depicting a variety of animals, sports, and interests. You can personalize your user account by selecting the picture that most closely matches your personality or interests. If you don't like any of the pictures provided, you can use one of your own. You can use .bmp, .gif, .jpg, or .png files as user account pictures. The original graphic can be any size, but the user account picture is always displayed as a square. If you select a graphic whose height and width are not the same, the graphic will be stretched or cropped to a square shape when displayed.

In this exercise, you'll change the type of the account you created in the previous exercise. You'll change the account picture first to one provided by Windows 7 and then to a custom image. Finally, you'll assign a password to the account.

**SET UP**  You need the Angel account you created in the previous exercise and the Angelic image located in your Documents\Microsoft Press\Windows7SBS\Accounts folder to complete this exercise. You also need administrator account credentials. Display the Manage Accounts window of Control Panel, and then follow the steps.

1. In the **Manage Accounts** window, click **Angel**.

   The Change An Account window opens.

   *The Change An Account window displays the options for changing the selected account.*

   **Tip**  The user account picture assigned to your Angel account might be different than ours because pictures are randomly assigned.

2. Click **Change the account type**.

The Change Account Type window opens.

*You can change a user account from Standard User to Administrator and vice versa.*

**3.** With **Standard user** selected, click **Change Account Type**.

In the Change An Account window, Standard user now appears under Angel's user account name.

**4.** Click **Change the picture**.

The Choose Picture window opens.

*The Choose Picture window displays the user account pictures that come with Windows 7, and any custom images you've used.*

**5.** Click any picture that you want, and then click **Change Picture**.

In the Change An Account window, the picture has changed.

**6.** In the **Change an Account** window, click **Change the picture**. Then below the thumbnails in the **Choose Picture** window, click **Browse for more pictures**.

**7.** In the left pane of the **Open** dialog box, click **Libraries**. Then in the center pane, double-click **Documents**, double-click **Microsoft Press**, double-click **Windows7SBS**, and then double-click **Accounts**.

**8.** Click the **Angelic** image, and then click **Open** to switch to that picture.

The Change An Account window displays the selected user account picture for Angel's account.

**9.** Click **Create a password**.

The Create Password window opens.

*You can enter the password and a hint to remind you if you forget it.*

**10.** In the **New password** box, type **wOOfw00f!** (with two capital letter *O*s and two zeros). Then press the **Tab** key to move to the next field.

To ensure the secrecy of the password, the characters are displayed as dots as you type.

11. In the **Confirm new password** box, retype **wOOfw00f!**

12. In the **Type a password hint** box, type **What does Angel say?**

13. Click **Create password** to save the password as part of Angel's user account profile.

    In the Change An Account window, *Password protected* appears under Angel's user account type.

 **CLEAN UP** Close the Change An Account window.

# Limiting Computer Access

Many children have access to computers. Some of these computers, such as those located at a school or library, are regulated by network domain controls or by the oversight of a teacher, librarian, or other concerned adult. Other computers, especially those located in private homes, might not be regulated.

If you have a child in your home, that child has access to your computer. The child's level of interest is a function of his or her age and of the computing behavior you model. The pretty lights on the computer case make it an object of fascination for a very young child. (Note to computer manufacturers: please stop putting pretty lights on the power button! They attract two-year olds who don't care whether you've recently saved your work.) If you are a member of the ever-increasing population of "information workers" and your computer consumes your attention for several hours a day, your child might assume that he or she should also have access to it. Older children are attracted more by what they can do with the computer than by the machine itself. Many excellent computer-based educational programs are available for children of all ages, as are a plethora of entertainment options that are free if you don't count the price of the Internet connection. Unfortunately, there is also a massive amount of easily available content that is inappropriate for children. You can control the functionality and content available to your child by setting up a restricted user account specifically for him or her.

If you want to allow or encourage your child to use the computer but also want to ensure that his or her computer use meets certain criteria, you can create a standard user account for the child's use and apply restrictions to that account. By using the Parental Controls feature of Windows 7, you can limit the computer access of a user account in the following ways:

- **Time limits** You can specify the time period during which the user account can be logged on to the computer. At the end of the designated time period, Parental Controls will cause the account to log off of Windows, and the account will be unavailable until the next designated time period.

- **Game restrictions** You can restrict the user from playing specific games or games with ratings that fall into specific age or content categories.

- **Program restrictions** You can restrict the user from using any installed program other than those you specifically permit access to.

The Parental Controls feature is similar to User Account Control, in that a password can be entered to bypass the limits you set. For example, when a user attempts to start a program that is restricted by Parental Controls, a dialog box appears. You can allow one-time access to the program by clicking a link in the dialog box and entering your password.

You can apply Parental Controls to any standard user account.

**Important** Anyone with an administrator account on your computer can set up, alter, or remove Parental Controls. For the controls to be fully effective, ensure that all administrator accounts are protected with a password.

**See Also** For information about restricting Windows Internet Explorer from displaying certain types of content and limiting access to objectionable Web content, see "Restricting Objectionable Content" in Chapter 8, "Manage Internet Explorer."

In this exercise, you'll specify the hours during which a specific user account can be used to log on to your computer.

**Important** Administrator account credentials are necessary to complete this exercise.

**Troubleshooting** Since the time this book was written, parental controls have become part of Windows Live Family Safety. To set up parental controls, complete step 1 of the following exercise and then sign in to Windows Live Family Safety by using your Microsoft account (previously called a Windows Live account). Then choose the account you want to monitor. This turns on Family Safety monitoring for your computer. You can then return to the User Accounts window and click any account to access Family Safety and configure the types of parental controls that are described in the exercise.

**SET UP** You don't need any practice files to complete this exercise. Use the Angel account you modified in the previous exercise. Display Control Panel in Category view, and then follow the steps.

1. In **Control Panel**, under **User Accounts and Family Safety**, click **Set up parental controls for any user**.

   The Parental Controls window opens.

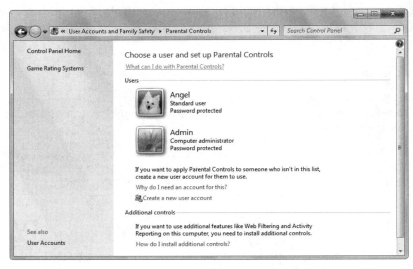

*You can select the user account to which you want to apply Parental Controls.*

   **Tip** To limit a user's computer access in additional ways or to view reports of computer activity, click How Do I Install Additional Controls? at the bottom of the window.

2. Click the **Angel** user account you created earlier in the chapter, and then in the **User Controls** window, click **On, enforce current settings**.

   After you turn on Parental Controls, the restriction options become available in the User Controls window.

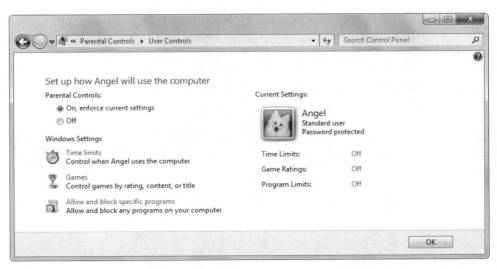

*You can specify the time period in which the computer may be used and whether games and specific programs can be accessed.*

**3.** On the left side of the **User Controls** window, under **Windows Settings**, click **Time limits**. Then in the **Time Restrictions** window, drag diagonally from the **Sunday 12 Midnight** box to the **Saturday 5 PM** box.

The selected time is designated in the window as blocked.

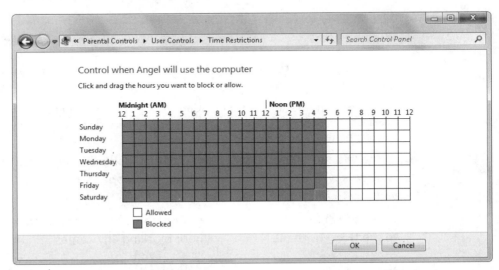

*During the blocked time, Windows 7 will deny access to the account and display a message that the user account is blocked.*

4. Drag from the **Sunday 12 Noon** box to the **Sunday 5 PM** box to unblock those times.

5. In the **Time Restrictions** window, click **OK**.

6. In the **User Controls** window, click **Games**.

   The Game Controls window opens.

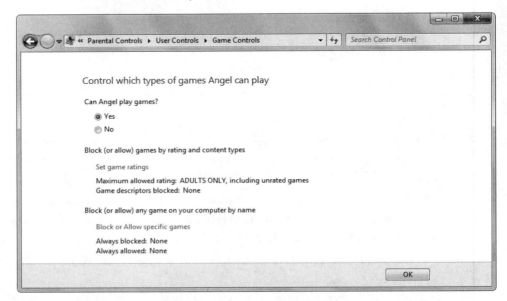

*You can block all games, block games based on their rating, or block specific games.*

7. Click **Set game ratings**, and then scroll the window, noticing that you can select an age/maturity level or select check boxes to block specific types of content.

   **Tip**  By default, the age/maturity ratings of the Entertainment Software Rating Board are used. You can select a different rating system by clicking Game Rating Systems in the left pane of the Parental Controls window.

8. At the left end of the **Address** bar, click the **Back** button to redisplay the **Game Controls** window. Then click **Block or Allow specific games**, and scroll the window to see the status of all the installed games.

9. Click **Cancel** to return to the **Game Controls** window, and then click **OK** to return to the **User Controls** window without blocking any games.

**10.** In the **User Controls** window, click **Allow and block specific programs**. Then in the **Application Restrictions** window, click **Angel can only use the programs I allow**.

Windows searches your computer and displays a list of programs you might want to block.

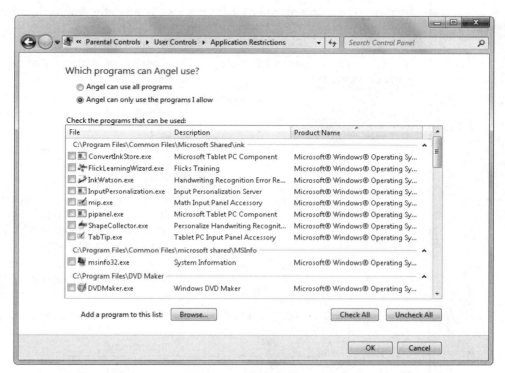

*Windows 7 will deny access to the listed programs unless you select their check boxes.*

**Tip**  You can add programs to the blocked list by clicking Browse and navigating to the program's file.

**11.** Click **Cancel** to return to the **User Controls** window without blocking any programs.

**12.** In the **User Controls** window, click **OK**.

**CLEAN UP**  Turn off the Parental Controls if you don't want to use them, and close the Parental Controls window.

## Playing Safely

Windows 7 recognizes game ratings such as those assigned by the Entertainment Software Rating Board (ESRB), which indicate the minimum age recommendation for the game. Content ratings include those listed in the following table.

| Rating symbol | Recommended for | Description |
| --- | --- | --- |
| EC (Early Childhood) | Ages 3 and older | Contains no material that parents would find inappropriate. |
| E (Everyone) | Ages 6 and older | May contain minimal cartoon, fantasy, or mild violence; and/or infrequent use of mild language. |
| E10+ (Everyone 10+) | Ages 10 and older | May contain more cartoon, fantasy, or mild violence; mild language; and/or minimal suggestive themes. |
| T (Teen) | Ages 13 and older | May contain violence, suggestive themes, crude humor, minimal blood, simulated gambling, and/or infrequent use of strong language. |
| M (Mature) | Ages 17 and older | May contain intense violence, blood and gore, sexual content, and/or strong language. |
| AO (Adults Only) | Ages 18 and older | May include prolonged scenes of intense violence and/or graphic sexual content and nudity. |

**See Also** For more information about software and game ratings, visit www.esrb.org.

Additional content descriptors may indicate the specific reason or reasons for the rating. The ESRB employs many descriptors, including Alcohol And Tobacco Reference, Blood And Gore, Cartoon Violence, Crude Humor, Nudity, Real Gambling, Sexual Violence, and Strong Language. These descriptors can help you to determine whether a specific game is suitable.

# Disabling or Deleting a User Account

If you no longer need one of the user accounts that are set up on your computer, you have two options:

● You can disable the account. A disabled account is not available, but all of its settings, folders, and files remain in place.

**Tip** The ability to disable an account might be unavailable in some versions of Windows 7.

● You can delete the account. All settings are permanently removed and cannot be restored. You can choose during the deletion process whether to retain the account's folders and files.

To disable a user account:

1. On the Start menu, right-click Computer, and then click Manage.
2. In the left pane of the Computer Management window, click Local Users And Groups.
3. In the center pane, double-click the Users folder.
4. Double-click the user name of the account you want to disable.
5. In the Properties dialog box, select the Account Is Disabled check box, and then click OK.
6. Close the Computer Management window.

   The account no longer appears in the Manage Accounts window of Control Panel.

To enable a disabled user account:

1. Perform steps 1 through 4 of the preceding procedure.
2. In the Properties dialog box, clear the Account Is Disabled check box, and then click OK.
3. Close the Computer Management window.

   The account reappears in the Manage Accounts window of Control Panel.

In this exercise, you'll delete a user account and its folders and files from your computer.

**Important** Administrator account credentials are necessary to complete this exercise.

 **SET UP** You don't need any practice files to complete this exercise. Display Control Panel in Category view, and then follow the steps.

1. In **Control Panel**, under **User Accounts and Family Safety**, click **Add or remove user accounts**.

   The Manage Accounts window opens, showing all the accounts set up on your computer.

2. In the **Manage Accounts** window, click **Angel**.

   **Troubleshooting** You cannot delete a user account that is logged on to the computer. You must switch to that account and log off before you can delete it.

3. In the **Change an Account** window, click **Delete the account**.

   The Delete Account window opens.

*When you delete a user account, you can choose to delete or keep the content of the account's personal folders.*

4. Angel has not created any files that you care about, so click **Delete Files**.

5. In the **Confirm Deletion** window, click **Delete Account**.

   Angel's account no longer appears among the active accounts.

 **CLEAN UP** Close the Manage Accounts window.

# Key Points

- User Account Control helps ensure that your computer is protected from unwanted and potentially destructive changes.
- It's a good idea to create a password-protected, standard user account for everyday use so that an administrator password has to be supplied for any actions that affect your computer or Windows settings.
- A standard user can modify certain aspects of his or her account. An administrator can also modify other users' accounts, including using Parental Controls to limit when and what users can access.
- When you no longer need an account, you can delete or disable it.

# Chapter at a Glance

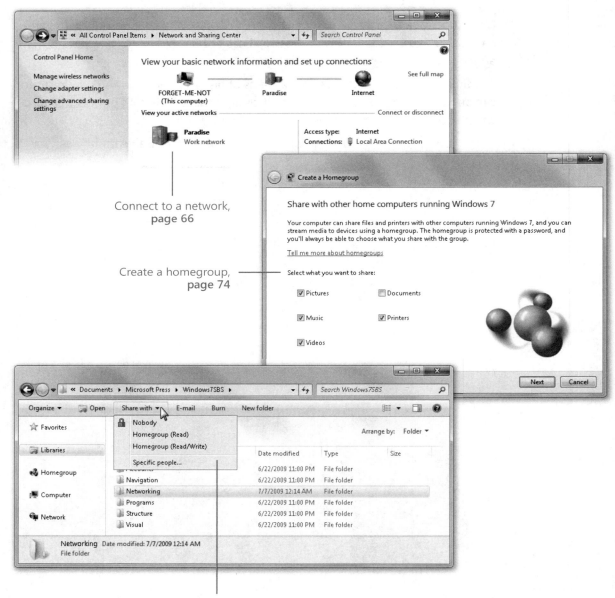

Connect to a network,
page 66

Create a homegroup,
page 74

Share files on your network,
page 85

# 3 Manage Your Network

---

**In this chapter, you will learn how to**

- ✔ Connect to a network.
- ✔ Create a homegroup.
- ✔ Work with a homegroup.
- ✔ Share files on your network.
- ✔ Manage a network connection.

---

In the early days of Microsoft, Bill Gates envisioned a future with "a computer on every desk and in every home." Today, the business world couldn't function without computers, and new terms such as "information worker" and "knowledge worker" have been coined to describe people who spend most of the day working with information on a computer screen. Computers make it possible for an increasing number of people to successfully run small businesses with large presences, or to maximize productivity by working from home. And on the home front, it's not uncommon for there to be two, three, four, or more computers in a home.

Whether you are an information worker or only a home computer user, your computer is probably connected to the Internet. But it's also becoming increasingly necessary to be connected to other computers in your work or home environment. When you establish a connection from a Windows 7 computer to a wired or wireless network, you designate the network as one of three types: Home, Work, or Public. The network type you choose governs the way your computer interacts with other computers and devices on the network. When you designate a network type as Home, you can choose to join the computer to a homegroup—a password-protected security group that enables you to easily and securely share information and devices with other homegroup member computers.

**Important** If your computer is connected to a domain, as is frequently the case in a large business environment, the network type is set by the network administrator to Domain and can't be changed. The information in this chapter pertains specifically to non-domain networks.

In this chapter, you'll first learn how to connect your computer to an existing network in a home, work, or public environment. You'll learn about the Windows 7 tools you can use to find information about a network and the computers and devices connected to it. You'll learn how to create a homegroup and work with an existing homegroup. You'll also learn how to find information about the connection from your network to the Internet, and learn some basic network connection troubleshooting skills. Finally, you'll explore ways to share information stored on your computer with other users on your network and how to access information that other users share with you.

**Important** This chapter assumes that you are connecting to an existing, functioning network. This chapter does not include instructions for setting up or configuring networking hardware. When setting up a network infrastructure, be sure to follow the instructions provided by the hardware manufacturer.

> **Practice Files** Before you can complete the exercises in this chapter, you need to install the practice file specified in "Using the Practice Files" at the beginning of this book to its default location. The practice file you will use to complete the exercises in this chapter is in the Networking practice file folder.

# Connecting to a Network

A network is a group of computers that communicate with each other through a wired or wireless connection. A network can be as small as two computers or as large as the Internet. In the context of this book, we primarily use the term *network* to mean the connection between computers in one physical location that are connected to each other, and to the Internet, through a network router.

If your computer has an enabled network adapter, whether or not it is actively connected to a network, a connection icon appears in the notification area at the right end of the Windows Taskbar. The connection icon indicates whether your network adapter is an Ethernet adapter or a wireless adapter (the wireless connection icon depicts signal strength bars). When the computer is not connected to a network, a red X appears on the connection icon. If a wireless connection is available, a yellow starburst appears on the wireless connection icon.

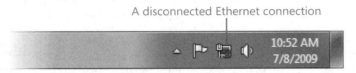
A disconnected Ethernet connection

*The connection icon indicates the adapter type and connection status.*

Pointing to or clicking the connection icon displays information about the current network connection status. When the computer is not connected to a network, pointing to the connection icon displays information about whether a network connection is currently available. Right-clicking the connection icon displays a shortcut menu with links to the Network And Sharing Center and troubleshooting tools.

If your computer is a desktop computer you'll probably connect it to only one network. If your computer is a portable computer, you might connect it to networks in many locations: at home, at work, at a friend's or relative's house, at the library, at a coffee shop...wherever you want to connect to the Internet you will first need to connect to a network. Each time you connect your computer to a network that you haven't previously connected to, Windows 7 creates a network profile with the network name specified by the network router, and prompts you to specify whether that network is a home network, a work network, or a public network.

When you physically connect your computer to a network by using an Ethernet cable, Windows 7 automatically creates the network connection. To connect to a wireless network for the first time, you need to make the connection.

To connect to an available wireless network:

1.  Click the available wireless connection icon in the notification area of the taskbar.

    A list of available connections appears.

*The connection icon adjacent to each available connection indicates its signal strength.*

2. In the Wireless Network Connection area, point to any network connection.

A ScreenTip displays information about the connection.

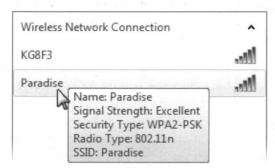

*To learn the security type of a network, point to the network in the connection list.*

3. Click the connection you want to connect to, and then click the Connect button that appears.

Windows 7 connects to the selected network. If additional information is required, such as a WEP key or WPA password, Windows prompts you to enter it.

**Tip** If you work in an organization that uses Active Directory Domain Services to authenticate (confirm the credentials of) users on a Windows Server domain and your computer is connected to the domain, the network connection type will automatically be Domain, and you will not be able to change it. Instead, you will log on to the domain by using your domain user name and password.

When you select the connection type, Windows creates a network profile for that connection and applies the settings specific to that connection type to your computer. Each network profile includes the following settings:

- **Network discovery** Determines whether the computer can see and be seen by other computers connected to the network.

- **File and printer sharing** Determines whether network users can access files and printers that you have shared.

- **Public folder sharing** Determines whether network users can access files stored in the public folders on your computer.

- **Media streaming** Determines whether network users can access music, videos, and pictures stored in your media library.

- **File sharing connections** Determines the security requirements for devices that connect to your computer's file sharing connections.

- **Password-protected sharing**  Determines whether shared files are available to any network user or only to those users with user accounts on your computer.

- **HomeGroup connections**  Determines whether user account credentials are necessary to connect to computers joined to your homegroup. Available only for network profiles associated with the Home Network and Work Network connection types.

**Tip**  Computers running Windows 7 can co-exist on a network with computers running earlier versions of Windows. Other computers and devices on the network do not affect the available network connection types or their settings. However, at the time of this writing, network connection types and homegroups weren't available on a computer running a version of Windows earlier than Windows 7.

## Home and Work Network Settings

Selecting the Home Network or Work Network connection type connects your computer to the network and configures the network profile to include network discovery, file and printer sharing, public folder sharing, media streaming, and password-protected sharing. Your computer is visible to other computers on the network. You don't necessarily have permission to access these computers or devices, but you can see that they are connected to the network and other network members can see that you are.

When your computer is connected to a home network, you can choose to join it to a homegroup. When your computer is connected to a work network, you can choose to join it to a custom workgroup or to a domain. (Ask your network administrator about these options.)

**See Also**  For more information about homegroups, see "Creating a Homegroup" and "Working with a Homegroup" later in this chapter.

## Public Network Settings

You'll probably connect to a public network only when you want to connect to the Internet from a portable computer. (Individual computers cannot connect directly to the Internet; they have to connect to an intermediary network that provides the Internet connection.) For example, you might connect to a free, pay-per-use, or subscription-based public network at an airport, restaurant, library, hotel, or other location. (I was at a highway rest stop last month that offered free Internet access from the picnic area!) If the network is provided free of charge, you might have immediate Internet access. Frequently, though, you will need to provide information, credentials, or payment in order to connect from the public network to the Internet.

When you connect to any network that you don't explicitly trust, choose the Public Network connection type to protect your privacy. Selecting the Public Network connection type connects your computer to the network without it being visible to other network users.

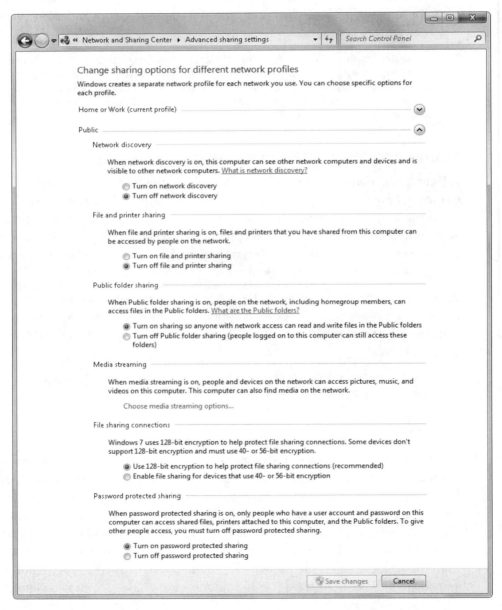

*Public Network settings.*

## Wireless Network Security

If you have a wireless network router, it is important that you secure the network properly to prevent unauthorized users from connecting to it via the Internet and gaining access to the computers on your network, as well as to your Internet connection.

When you set up your wireless router, be sure to follow the instructions that come with it. You'll usually be required to connect the router directly to a computer (by using an Ethernet cable) and run a setup program. During the setup process, you can do several things to increase the security of your wireless network, such as:

- Change the administrative password from the default password shared by all routers of that type to something unique. (Some manufacturers even use blank passwords.)

- Secure the network with an appropriate level of encryption. Establish a Wired Equivalent Privacy (WEP) key or Wi-Fi Protected Access (WPA) password to prevent unauthorized users from connecting to your wireless network.

  Your router configuration might offer multiple levels of WEP encryption, controlled by the length of the WEP key. A 10-character WEP key provides 64-bit encryption, and a 26-character key provides 128-bit encryption.

  WPA is a far more secure encryption standard than WEP. If you have a gigabit network router (which transmits data at 1,000 KB/sec, as opposed to the standard 100 KB/second), you should use WPA encryption. WPA encryption supports gigabit data transmission; WEP encryption does not.

  **Tip** The wireless protocol is expressed in the form 80211.x. Most routers support one or more of the following: 80211.b (10 KB/sec), 80211.g (100 KB/sec), and 80211.n (1,000 KB/sec).

- When creating a security key or password, use a combination of letters and numbers that you can remember—for example, a series of birthdays, or your street address. If the key is particularly long or difficult, you might want to keep a printed copy of it handy for when visitors want to connect their mobile computers to your wireless network.

## Network Information

Depending on the environment you're working in, you might not know the structure of the network your computer is connected to, or all the computers and devices that are connected to your network. Windows 7 provides several tools for viewing information about your network and Internet connections.

- **Network window** Displays a visual representation of the computers and devices on your network that are currently online and in compliance with the network profile for this connection, as well as the devices that support the network infra-structure, such as the network router. The Network window displays only those devices that are "visible" to your computer based on your current network settings.

  **Tip** The items shown in the Computer area of the Network window are almost always physical computers, but from time to time another device can sneak in there. For example, a network printer might identify itself in the Computer area by a name such as *NPI67BB3*, or something equally mysterious. For information about network printers, see "Sharing a Local Printer" and "Connecting to a Remote Printer" in Chapter 12, "Set Up Hardware Devices."

- **Network and Sharing Center** Displays information about the connection from your computer to the Internet and the type of active network connections you have, as well as links to tools you can use to manage network connections.

- **Network Map** Displays a comprehensive visual representation of all the computers on your network.

In this exercise, you'll display information about the network your computer is connected to.

**SET UP** You don't need any practice files to complete this exercise. Ensure that your computer is connected to a network of any type, and then follow the steps.

1. On the **Start** menu, click **Computer**.

   The Computer window opens in Windows Explorer.

2. In the **Navigation** pane, click the **Network** group.

   The Network window opens.

   **Troubleshooting** If an Information bar appears at the top of the window to inform you that file sharing is turned off, click the Information bar and then click Turn On Network Discovery And File Sharing.

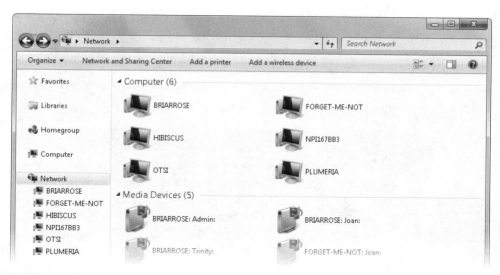

*Your Network window will show the devices on your network.*

**3.** On the toolbar of the **Network** window, click **Network and Sharing Center**.

The Network And Sharing Center opens.

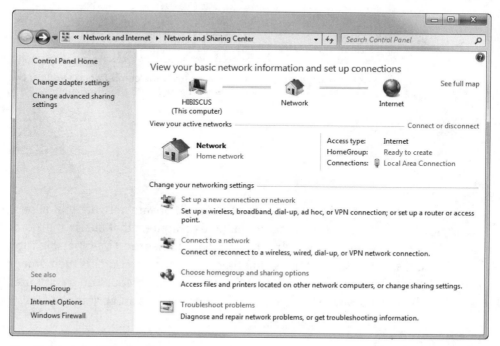

*The Network And Sharing Center.*

**Tip** You can also open the Network And Sharing Center by clicking the Network icon in the notification area of the taskbar and then clicking Network And Sharing Center, or by displaying Control Panel in Category view and then, under Network And Internet, clicking View Network Status And Tasks.

4. In the upper-right corner of the **Network and Sharing Center**, click **See full map**.

The Network Map window opens.

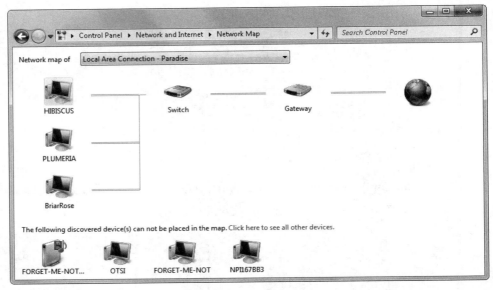

The Network Map displays connections from the computers on your network to the Internet. You can click a computer or device on the Network Map to open it.

 **CLEAN UP** Close the Network Map window.

# Creating a Homegroup

You can think of a homegroup as a type of private network that allows secure access to selected content stored on multiple computers that all use the Home Network connection type to connect to the network. Homegroup membership is on a per-computer basis, not a per-user basis. (In other words, the computer is the homegroup member, not the user.) However, each person who has a user account on a computer that is joined to the homegroup can make resources, such as files and printers, available to other homegroup members.

Only one homegroup can exist on any one home network; it exists as long as it has at least one member. (The member computer doesn't have to be online, or even on, for the homegroup to remain in existence.) The homegroup doesn't have a name, and it doesn't require any sort of administration. Access to the homegroup is protected by a password that is generated randomly when the homegroup is created. No information other than the password is associated with the homegroup or required to join it.

When you connect your computer to a network and stipulate that the connection is of the Home Network connection type, Windows 7 finds out whether a homegroup already exists on the network and a wizard presents you with the option of either creating a homegroup (if none exists) or joining your computer to an existing homegroup. You do not have to create or join a homegroup to establish the Home Network connection; you can decline the option by canceling or closing the wizard.

In this exercise, you'll create and join a homegroup.

 **SET UP** You don't need any practice files to complete this exercise. Before beginning this exercise, ensure that your computer is connected to a network that is designated as a home network and does not already have an active homegroup. Display Control Panel in Category view, and then follow the steps.

1. In **Control Panel**, under **Network and Internet**, click **Choose homegroup and sharing options**.

   The HomeGroup window of Control Panel opens.

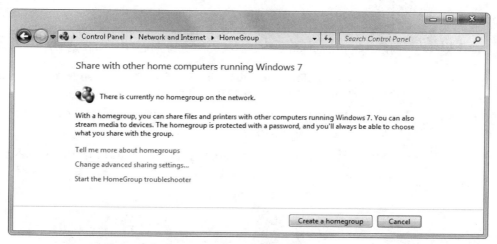

*The HomeGroup window on a computer with a Home Network connection to a network that doesn't already have a homegroup.*

**Tip** Homegroups are new in Windows 7 and are not accessible to computers running earlier versions of Windows or a non-Windows operating system.

2. In the **HomeGroup** window, click **Create a homegroup**.

The Create A Homegroup wizard starts.

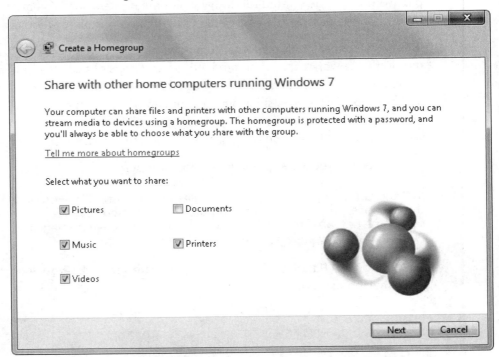

By default, all libraries other than the Documents library are selected for sharing.

**See Also** For information about libraries, see "Understanding Files, Folders, and Libraries" in Chapter 4, "Navigate Windows and Folders."

3. On the first page of the **Create a Homegroup** wizard, clear the **Pictures** check box, and then click **Next**.

Windows 7 creates the homegroup, and then the wizard displays the homegroup password.

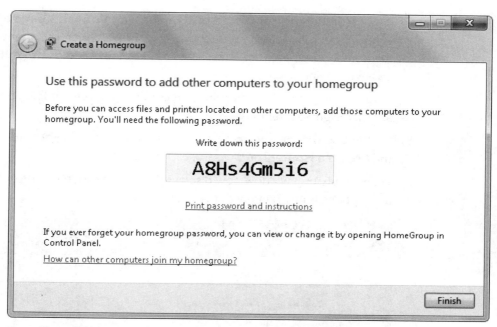

*You will need this password to join other computers to the homegroup.*

**4.** Click the **Print password and instructions** link.

The View And Print Your Homegroup Password window opens.

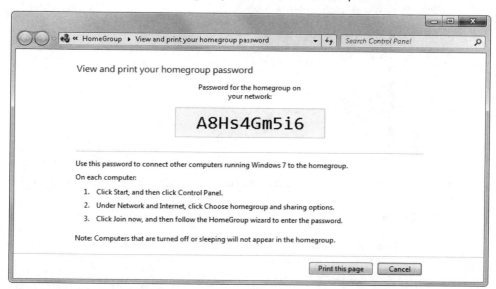

*You can provide the homegroup password and instructions to other home network computer users by printing the contents of this window.*

5. If your computer is connected to a printer, click **Print this page** and then, in the **Print** dialog box, select a printer and click **Print**. Otherwise, manually record the homegroup password, and then close the **View and print your homegroup password** window.

Save the password that you print or record in a convenient location; we'll use it in another exercise later in this chapter.

6. On the **Use this password to add other computers to your homegroup** page of the **Create a Homegroup** wizard, click **Finish**.

The HomeGroup window now displays your homegroup resource sharing settings and options for working with the homegroup.

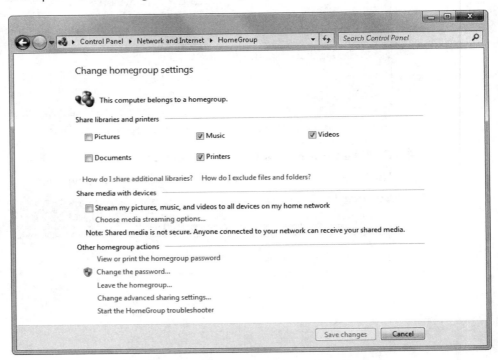

*The HomeGroup window on a computer that is joined to a homegroup.*

**CLEAN UP** Close the HomeGroup window.

**See Also** For information about changing the resources shared with your homegroup, see "Sharing Files on Your Network" later in this chapter.

# Working with a Homegroup

A homegroup doesn't have a management interface or require an administrator; it's simply an entity that exists on your network as long as it has at least one member. If all the computers leave the homegroup, it ceases to exist with no negative side effects. Any computer user can join the computer to a homegroup by using the homegroup password. On a multiple-user computer, the homegroup sharing settings of each user account are separate, so that if one user joins the computer to a homegroup and shares her Documents library, for example, other users' documents are still kept private.

## Joining an Existing Homegroup

After a homegroup is created on a home network, when you connect your computer to the network with a Home Network connection, the Join A Homegroup wizard offers you the option of joining the homegroup. If your computer already has a Home Network connection to the network but is not a member of the existing homegroup, you can start the wizard manually. The only information you need to join the homegroup is the homegroup password. The person who created the homegroup or a person who has since retrieved the password might have printed out and kept the password page, but if not, it's quite simple to locate.

To locate the password for an existing homegroup:

1. Log on to any computer that is joined to the homegroup.

   **Tip** You might have to ask another person to log on to his or her computer and retrieve the password for you.

2. In the HomeGroup window of Control Panel, click View Or Print The Homegroup Password.

## Homegroup Settings for Shared Computers

When any user of a computer that has multiple user accounts joins the computer to a homegroup, the computer is joined to the homegroup on behalf of all its users. However, each user has control over the resources that he or she shares with other homegroup members.

Windows 7 does not actively notify you that another user has joined your computer to a homegroup, but if you display the HomeGroup window of Control Panel, Windows 7 alerts you to this fact and prompts you to specify your homegroup resource sharing settings.

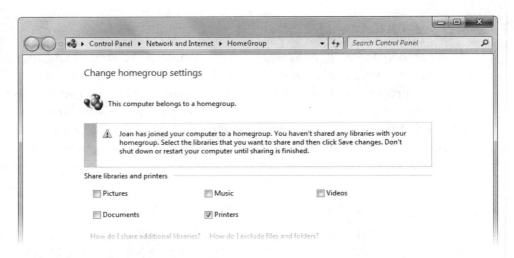

*Each user controls his or her own homegroup sharing settings.*

The only resource sharing setting that is common to all user accounts of a homegroup member computer is the Printers setting. When any user shares or excludes printers from the shared homegroup resources, the printers are shared or excluded on behalf of the computer rather than the user.

**See Also**  For information about changing the resources shared with other homegroup members, see "Sharing Files on Your Network" later in this chapter.

## Leaving a Homegroup

If at any time you decide that you no longer want to share resources with other home-group members, you can remove your computer from the homegroup with no adverse effects. It is not necessary to disconnect from the network.

To remove your computer from a homegroup:

1.  In the Network And Sharing Center, click Choose Homegroup And Sharing Options.

2.  In the HomeGroup window of Control Panel, click Leave The Homegroup.

3.  In the Leave The Homegroup wizard, click Leave The Homegroup. Then, when the wizard confirms that you have successfully left the homegroup, click Finish.

**Tip**  Changing the network connection type from Home Network to Work Network or Public Network also removes a computer from a homegroup. If you use this method and then later change the connection type back to Home Network, your computer will automatically rejoin the homegroup.

In this exercise, you'll connect your computer to an existing homegroup.

**Tip** You can complete this exercise only if you have multiple computers connected to a Home Network connection and a homegroup has been created from another Windows 7 computer on your network.

**SET UP** You don't need any practice files to complete this exercise. Before beginning this exercise, ensure that your computer is not connected to a homegroup. Obtain the homegroup password from the computer that created the homegroup, and then follow the steps.

1. On the **Start** menu, click **Control Panel**.

2. In **Control Panel**, click the **Network and Internet** category, and then click **Network and Sharing Center**. (If Control Panel is in Icons view, simply click **Network and Sharing Center**.)

   The Network And Sharing Center opens. Your network connection is shown in the basic network map and in the View Your Active Networks area.

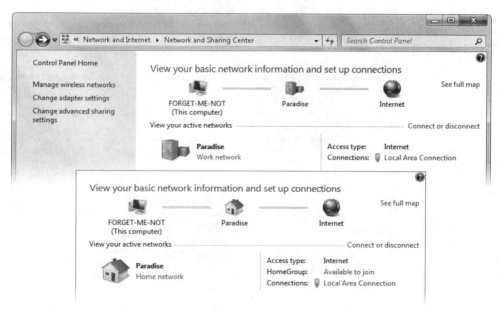

*The office building icon indicates a Work Network connection, and the house icon indicates a Home Network connection.*

3. If **Home network** is shown next to the current network connection in the **View your active networks** area, do the following:

   a. In the **View your active networks** area, to the right of **HomeGroup**, click **Available to join**.

   b. When the **HomeGroup** window opens, click **Join now**.

   c. Skip to step 6.

4. If **Work network** is shown next to the current network connection in the **View your active networks** area, click **Work network**.

   The Set Network Location dialog box opens.

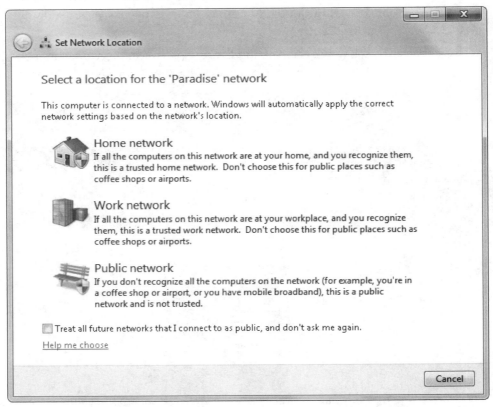

*You can join a homegroup only if your connection type is Home Network.*

**5.** In the **Set Network Location** dialog box, click **Home network** to apply the Home Network settings to your connection.

The Join A Homegroup wizard starts.

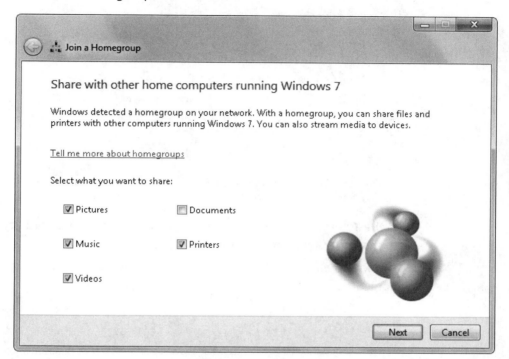

*Windows 7 automatically detects an existing homegroup and gives you the option of joining it.*

> **Tip** If you do not want to join the homegroup, you can click Cancel in the Join A Homegroup wizard. Your network connection type will still be Home Network; you simply won't be participating in the homegroup.

**6.** On the **Share with other home computers running Windows 7** page of the **Join a Homegroup** wizard, select or clear the check boxes to indicate the resources you want to share with other homegroup members. Then click **Next**.

The Type The Homegroup Password page opens.

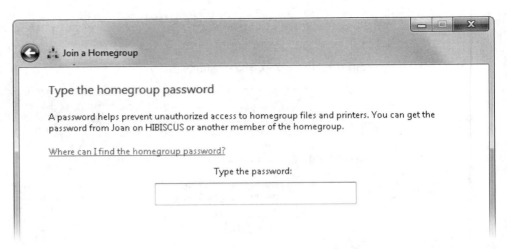

*The information on this page includes the name of the user who originally created the homegroup and the computer the homegroup was created from.*

7. In the **Type the password** box, enter the homegroup password you obtained for this exercise. Then click **Next**.

The wizard authenticates the homegroup password and joins your computer to the homegroup.

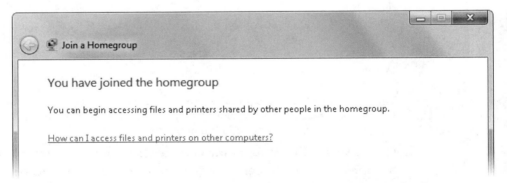

*After joining a homegroup, you can access files and printers shared by other homegroup members.*

**Troubleshooting** If the wizard can't connect the computer to the homegroup, the message "HomeGroup encountered an error" appears below the password box, with a link to the HomeGroup troubleshooter. For information about troubleshooters, see "Managing a Network Connection" later in this chapter.

8. On the final page of the **Join a Homegroup** wizard, click **Finish**.

 **CLEAN UP** Close the HomeGroup window of Control Panel.

# Sharing Files on Your Network

If you have more than one computer in your organization, you might find it convenient to share files and file storage locations with other people on your network. And if you have more than one computer in your household, you might want to share resources with family members, whether or not your computer is joined to a homegroup. For example, you might:

- Share project-related files with specific team members.
- From your portable computer, work on a file that is stored on your desktop computer.
- Share household management documents with your family members.
- Collect all your family photos in one place by having all your family members save their digital photos to a shared external hard drive.

There are several ways to share files with users (including yourself) who are logged on to other computers in your network. To share files by using any of these methods, you must first make sure network discovery and file and printer sharing are turned on so that your computer and any resources you choose to share are visible to other network computers and devices. Network discovery and file and printer sharing are turned on by default for Home Network and Work Network connection types.

**Tip** When network discovery is on, your computer is visible in Windows Explorer, in the Network group window on a Windows 7 computer or in the Network folder window on a Windows XP or Windows Vista computer. When file and printer sharing is turned on, any resources you choose to share from the computer are also visible in the Network group or Network folder windows.

All the file sharing options we discuss in this topic assume that network discovery and file and printer sharing are turned on.

To verify that your computer is set up to share files with other network computer users:

1. In the left pane of the Network And Sharing Center, click Change Advanced Sharing Settings.

2. In the Home Or Work area of the Advanced Sharing Settings window, do the following:

   ○ Under Network Discovery, verify that Turn On Network Discovery is selected.

   ○ Under File And Printer Sharing, verify that Turn On File And Printer Sharing is selected.

3. If you have changed any settings, at the bottom of the Advanced Sharing Settings window, click Save Changes. Otherwise, click Cancel.

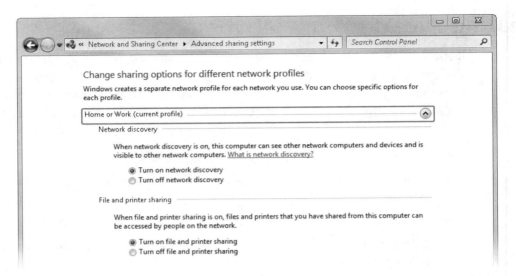

*To share files and printers with other network computer users, the Network Discovery and File And Printer Sharing settings must be on.*

When you share a folder, you can specify the people (in the form of user accounts or groups of users) you are sharing the folder with and what each person (or group) can do with the folder contents. The permission level options are:

- **Read**  The user can open a file from the shared folder but cannot save any changes to the file in the shared folder.

- **Read/Write**  The user can open and edit a file and save changes to the file in the shared folder.

The default permission level is Read. If you want to allow a network user or group of users to modify shared files, you must explicitly assign the Read/Write permission level.

Files and printers that you share are available only when your computer is on, and not when it is in Sleep mode.

## Public Folders

Files that you store in the public folders (Public Documents, Public Downloads, Public Music, Public Pictures, and Public Videos) are always accessible to any user logged on to your computer. Public folder sharing with other network computer users is turned on by default for Home Network, Work Network, and Public Network connections. This means that the contents of the public folders on your computer are visible to any user connected to the network, unless you turn off public folder sharing for a specific connection type.

If you frequently connect to public networks, consider carefully whether you want to share the contents of your computer's public folders with strangers. If not, you can easily turn off this feature to safeguard your privacy.

To prevent public network users from accessing your public folders:

1. In the left pane of the Network And Sharing Center, click Change Advanced Sharing Settings.

2. In the Public area of the Advanced Sharing Settings window, under Public Folder Sharing, click Turn Off Public Folder Sharing.

   With this setting off, the public folders on your computer can be accessed only from your computer, and not from the network.

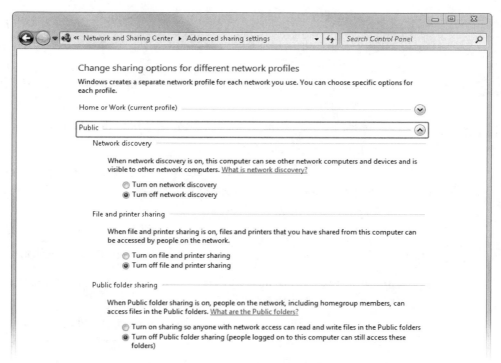

*If you don't want computer users on a public network to have access to files stored in your public folders, you must turn off public folder sharing for Public network profiles.*

3. At the bottom of the Advanced Sharing Settings window, click Save Changes.

**See Also** For more information about public folders, see "Understanding Files, Folders, and Libraries" in Chapter 4, "Navigate Windows and Folders." For information about the Network And Sharing Center, see "Connecting to a Network" earlier in this chapter.

## Homegroup Resources

When your computer is a member of a homegroup, you can share files with other home-group members while still keeping the files hidden from computers that aren't homegroup members. (Remember that computers, rather than users, are the homegroup members.) When you first create or join your computer to a homegroup, you have the option of sharing the built-in Documents, Pictures, Music, and/or Videos libraries. The choices you make at that time are not binding; you can change the library selections at any time. You can add or remove libraries from the shared homegroup resources at any time. Files that you store in a library that you share with your homegroup, whether in your personal folders or the public folders, are accessible to any user logged on to a computer that is a member of the homegroup.

To share built-in libraries with other homegroup computers for the first time:

1. Ensure that your network connection is designated as the Home type, and is joined to a homegroup.

2. In the Network And Sharing Center, under Change Your Networking.Settings, click Choose Homegroup And Sharing Options.

3. In the HomeGroup window, click Choose What You Want To Share.

    The HomeGroup wizard starts.

4. Select or clear check boxes to designate the libraries you want to share with the homegroup and to indicate whether to share printers that are connected to your computer, and then click Next.

5. On the last page of the HomeGroup wizard, click Finish.

To change the built-in libraries that you're sharing with the homegroup:

1. In the Network And Sharing Center, under Change Your Networking Settings, click Choose Homegroup And Sharing Options.

2. In the HomeGroup window, under Share Libraries And Printers, select or clear check boxes to designate the libraries you want to share with the homegroup and to indi-cate whether to share printers that are connected to your computer.

3. Under Share Media With Devices, select the Stream My Pictures, Music, And Videos To All Devices On My Home Network check box if you want to share the contents of your media library.

4. At the bottom of the HomeGroup window, click Save Changes.

**Tip** Although libraries that you create aren't listed with the built-in libraries, you can share a custom library by following the procedure for sharing individual files, folders, and libraries, which we discuss next.

## Individual Files, Folders, and Libraries

Regardless of whether your computer is a member of a homegroup, you can share a single file, a folder, or a built-in or custom library with users of other computers on your network. You can control access to the shared file, folder, or library by specifying the user accounts or groups of users who can access the shared resource and assigning a specific level of access for each user account or group.

**Tip** Certain folders that Windows creates, such as Program Files, Users, and Windows, are protected by the system and can be shared only through the advanced sharing settings.

To share a file, folder, or library:

1. Display the folder or library in Windows Explorer. To share a single file, display the folder or library the file is stored in.

2. To share a folder or library, click it, and click Share With on the toolbar. To share a single file, right-click it, and click Share With.

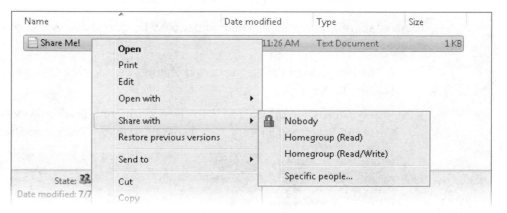

*You can share an entire folder or an individual file.*

3. On the Share With menu, either click a Homegroup permission-level option (and then you're done) or click Specific People and then follow the remaining steps.

4. In the File Sharing window, click the arrow at the right end of the empty box to display a list that includes all local user accounts, Everyone, and Homegroup.

5. Click the user account or group you want to share the file, folder, or library with, and then click Add.

6. In the Permission Level column, click the arrow corresponding to the user account or group you added, and then click the type of access you want to allow.

7. Click Share, and then, after the item is shared, click Done.

When you select a shared file in Windows Explorer, the State field appears in the Details pane of the Windows Explorer window with the designation *Shared*. When you select a shared folder in Windows Explorer or display its contents, the Shared With field, which identifies who can access the folder, also appears in the Details pane or in a ScreenTip when you point to the Shared icon.

*In the Details pane, an icon depicting two people indicates that the selected item is shared.*

As with other network file-sharing methods, an additional layer of control is provided by the advanced sharing settings. By default, if you choose to share a resource with everyone on your network, only a person with a user account on your computer can access the shared resource from another computer. You can remove this restriction so that any network computer user has access.

To make shared resources available to people who don't have user accounts on your computer:

1. In the left pane of the Network And Sharing Center, click Change Advanced Sharing Settings.

2. In the Home Or Work area of the Advanced Sharing Settings window, under Password Protected Sharing, click Turn Off Password Protected Sharing.

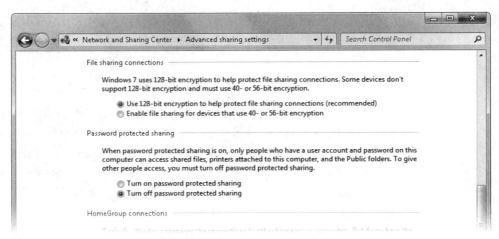

*Clicking Turn Off Password Protected Sharing doesn't turn off sharing; it removes the requirement for local user account credentials.*

3. At the bottom of the Advanced Sharing Settings window, click Save Changes.

**Tip** If you collaborate with a team of people on a document, working with the document in a shared folder entails the risk of one person overwriting another person's changes, even if you restrict access to the folder. To eliminate this risk, you need to use a system with version control. If your organization has a collaboration site built with Microsoft SharePoint products and technologies, such as Microsoft Office SharePoint Server 2007, you can store the document in a document library so that only one person at a time can check out and work on the document.

## Storage Drives

You can share an entire storage drive—either a disk drive that is built in to your computer, or an internal or external storage device such as a freestanding storage disk or a USB flash drive. For example, you might:

- Share an internal hard disk drive, on which you store only project-related resources, with all the computers on your work network, so that your co-workers have access to them.
- Share an external hard disk drive with all the computers on your home network, so that all your family members can save digital photos in one place for safekeeping.

To share a drive:

1. On the Start menu, click Computer.

   The Computer window opens. In the Navigation pane of the Computer window, the Computer group is expanded to display the disk drives and storage devices connected to your computer.

2. In the Computer group in the Navigation pane of the Computer window, click the drive you want to share to display its contents in the right pane. Don't select any file or folder in the Content pane.

   **See Also** For information about navigating in Windows Explorer, see "Finding Your Way Around Your Computer" in Chapter 4, "Navigate Windows and Folders."

3. On the toolbar, click Share With, and then click Advanced Sharing.

4. On the Sharing tab of the drive's Properties dialog box, click Advanced Sharing.

5. In the Advanced Sharing dialog box, select the Share This Folder check box.

   The Share Name box displays the drive letter of the drive you're sharing. You can replace the drive letter with a more user-friendly name.

*You can identify a shared drive by its drive letter or, to more clearly distinguish it from other network drives, you can assign it a name.*

6. Click Permissions. Then in the Permissions dialog box, click Add.

7. In the Select Users Or Groups dialog box, type the name of the user account, group, or computer you want to share the drive with, and then click Check Names.

   Windows 7 indicates a valid name by underlining it.

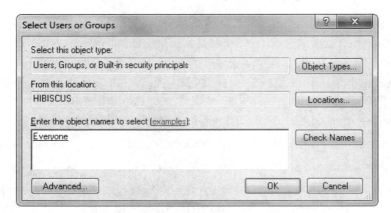

*You can enter multiple names, separated by semicolons.*

**Tip** To display a list of valid users and groups, click Advanced and then, in the second Select Users Or Groups dialog box that opens, click Find Now.

8. Click OK to return to the Permissions dialog box.

   The specified user account or group appears in the Group Or User Names list.

9. In the Permissions For list, select the check boxes of the permission levels you want to grant to the specified user account or group, and then click Apply.

   Windows applies the selected permissions.

*You can set the permission level for each user account or group.*

10. Click OK in the Permissions dialog box and in the Advanced Sharing dialog box. Then close the drive's Properties dialog box.

**See Also** For information about connecting to shared folders, see "Connecting to Network Resources" in Chapter 4, "Navigate Windows and Folders." For information about connecting to shared printers, see "Sharing a Local Printer" and "Connecting to a Remote Printer" in Chapter 12, "Set Up Hardware Devices."

In this exercise, you'll share a folder on your computer with everyone on your network.

**SET UP** You need the Networking folder located in your Documents\Microsoft Press\ Windows7SBS folder to complete this exercise.

1. On the **Windows Taskbar**, click the pinned **Windows Explorer** button.

   Windows Explorer starts and displays the Libraries window.

2. In the right pane of the **Libraries** window, double-click **Documents**, double-click **Microsoft Press**, double-click **Windows7SBS**, and then click (don't double-click) the **Networking** folder.

   **See Also** For information about navigating in Windows Explorer, see "Finding Your Way Around Your Computer" in Chapter 4, "Navigate Windows and Folders."

3. On the toolbar, click **Share with**.

   The Share With list displays the basic sharing options.

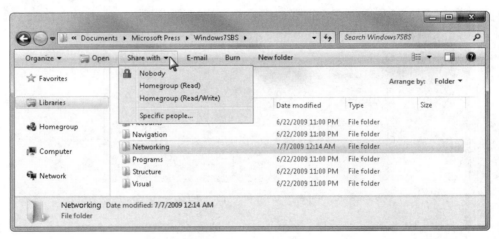

*It takes only two clicks to share a folder with other people on your network or with other homegroup members.*

**Tip** The Homegroup options appear on the Share With list regardless of whether the computer is part of a homegroup. If the computer is not a homegroup member, clicking either Homegroup option displays the HomeGroup page of Control Panel, from which you can create or join a homegroup.

4. In the **Share with** list, click **Specific people**.

   The File Sharing wizard starts.

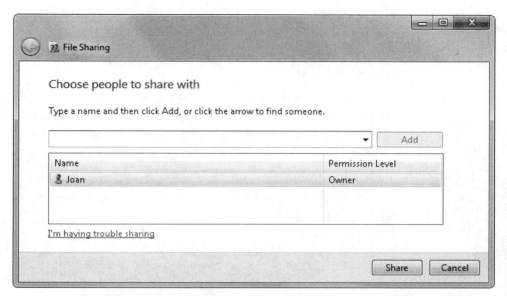

*The File Sharing wizard displays a list of the user accounts and groups the folder is shared with.*

**Tip** If your computer is a member of a homegroup and you have shared the Documents library with the homegroup, the homegroup appears in this list.

**5.** In the **File Sharing** wizard, click the arrow at the right end of the empty box.

A list of local user accounts appears.

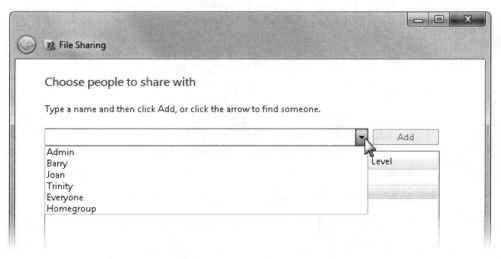

*Choose from a list of local user accounts or more general groups.*

**Tip** If your computer is not a member of a homegroup, the list includes a Create A New User option instead of the Homegroup option.

6. In the list of user accounts and groups, click **Everyone**. Then in the **File Sharing** wizard, click **Add**.

   *Everyone* appears in the Name column, with *Read* in the corresponding Permission Level column. These file-sharing settings give read-only access to the Networking folder to any network computer user who meets the requirements set by the Password Protected Sharing settings.

7. In the **File Sharing** wizard, click **Share**.

   Windows 7 confirms the location of the shared folder, which is now visible to other network computer users.

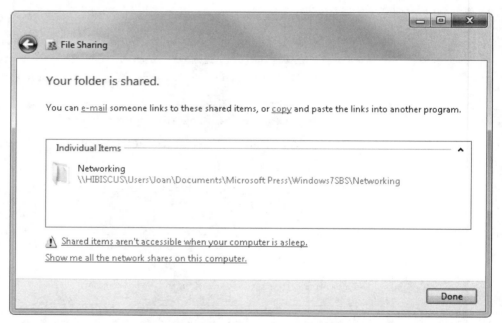

*The File Sharing wizard gives sharing details and instructions for notifying users about the shared folder.*

8. In the **File Sharing** wizard, click **Done**.

   In Windows Explorer, the Details pane now includes sharing information about the selected folder.

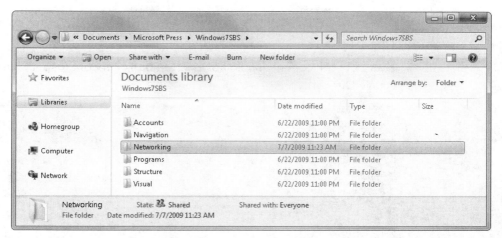

*In the Details pane, the State field indicates that the folder is shared with the users shown in the Shared With field.*

 **CLEAN UP** If you don't want to continue sharing the Networking folder, click the folder in the Content pane, click Share With on the toolbar, and then click Nobody. Then close the Windows7SBS folder window.

# Managing a Network Connection

A large organization usually has one or more network technicians (if not an entire IT department) who maintain the organization's hardware and keep the internal and external network connections running smoothly. In a small to medium organization, or in a household, it helps if you know enough about your network to be able to function as your own network technician.

For example, it's a good idea to be able to find information about your computer network, including information about the connection from your computer to the network and from the network to the Internet. If you work on a portable computer and connect it to networks other than your own, you'll want to know how to change the network connection type. That way, if you connect to a wireless network (for example, at a friend's house), choose the Home Network connection type, and then realize that the network is unsecured, you can easily change the network connection type from Home Network to Public Network to safeguard your system.

To change the network connection type:

1. Open the Network And Sharing Center.

   Your network connection is shown in the basic network map and in the View Your Active Networks area.

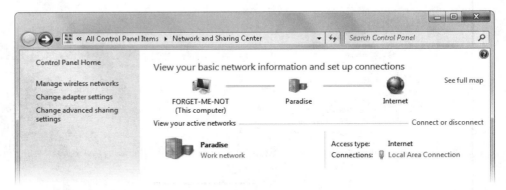

*The icon indicates the network connection type.*

2. In the View Your Active Networks area, click the current network connection type (for example, Work Network) that appears to the right of the network icon.

   The Set Network Location dialog box opens.

3. In the Set Network Location dialog box, click the new network connection type.

   Windows 7 applies the settings for the selected network connection to your computer. If the new connection type is Home Network, the Create A Homegroup wizard or the Join A Homegroup wizard starts. You can work through the wizard to create or join a homegroup, or click Cancel to close the wizard and remain disconnected from the homegroup.

If you experience problems that you think may be related to the network adapter installed in your computer, you can view information about it from the Network Connections window of Control Panel. This window displays connectivity information for each adapter and for each dial-up or virtual private network (VPN) connection on your computer. You can work with a connection by right-clicking the connection and then clicking a command on the shortcut menu that appears, or by clicking buttons on the Network Connections window toolbar.

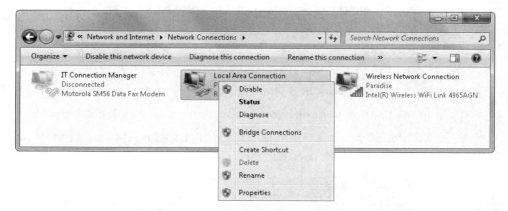

*You can enable, disable, and check the status of each network adapter. The status information includes the connection speed .*

A network of any size includes several components that affect the network connection. Your network might include one or more wired routers, wireless routers, or switches. These hardware devices, as well as the cables that connect them, and the external connection to your Internet service provider, can sometimes go haywire. When you do experience a connection problem, either when connecting to the Internet or when connecting to another computer on your network, you can use one of the handy troubleshooting programs included with Windows 7. These troubleshooting programs (also called *troubleshooters*) can help you identify and resolve the problem.

**Tip** Many computer problems can be resolved by restarting the computer, so this would be a good first step in any troubleshooting effort. When you experience a network or Internet connection problem, first determine whether the problem occurs only on your computer, or also on other computers on your network. You can frequently resolve Internet connection problems that affect the entire network by restarting the router that connects your network to your Internet service provider.

You can locate all the available troubleshooters from the Troubleshooting window of Control Panel. Links to specific categories of troubleshooters are found in related windows, and links to specific troubleshooters appear when needed—for example, if one of the Homegroup wizards encounters a problem creating or joining a homegroup, a link to the HomeGroup troubleshooter appears in the wizard.

In this exercise, you'll investigate the network-related troubleshooting programs.

 **SET UP** You don't need any practice files to complete this exercise; just follow the steps.

1. Open the **Network and Sharing Center**.

2. In the **Change your networking settings** area, click **Troubleshoot problems**.

   Windows 7 scans your computer and then displays the troubleshooting programs related to network connectivity.

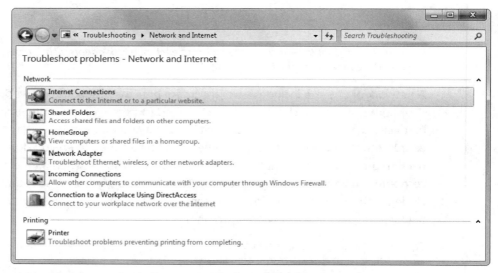

*Six troubleshooters are available to help you resolve network problems.*

3. Click any one of the troubleshooters that interests you.

   The troubleshooter starts, scans your system, and then leads you through a diagnostic process.

4. On each page of the selected troubleshooter, click the option that best describes your situation.

   Don't be afraid to test it out with incorrect answers—the troubleshooter won't make changes to your system without your approval.

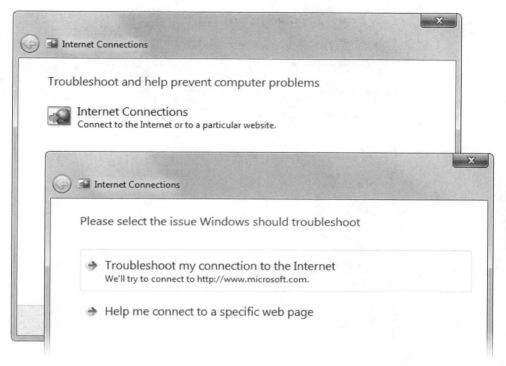

*Each troubleshooter is designed to address very specific issues.*

Assuming that you're not currently experiencing any issues, it's unlikely that the troubleshooter will identify any problems.

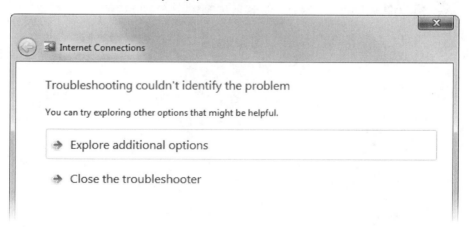

*The Internet Connections troubleshooter found nothing wrong with the settings it is designed to evaluate.*

5. Click **Explore additional options**.

The troubleshooter displays links to online resources.

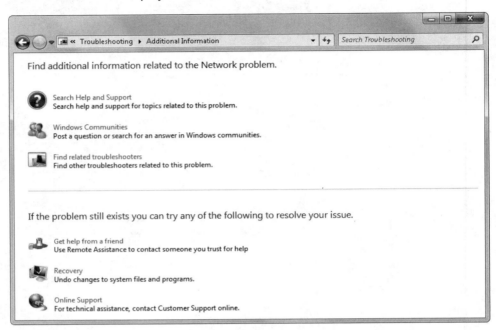

*The troubleshooter locates additional avenues that might enable you to resolve the connection problem.*

 **CLEAN UP** Close the Additional Information window.

# Key Points

- When your computer's wireless network adapter is active, Windows 7 detects any available wireless networks so you can easily connect your computer to one.

- You control the security settings for a network connection by designating the connection type as Home Network, Work Network, or Public Network. You can tailor the sharing and security settings for each connection type to suit your preferences.

- You can securely share resources among computers connected to a home network by joining them to a homegroup.

- You can change the network connection type for your current connection. If your computer is a member of a homegroup, changing the connection type from Home Network to another removes the computer from the homegroup, but changing back automatically rejoins the homegroup.

- You can share files, folders, libraries, and drives so that other network computer users can access them.

- Windows 7 includes many built-in troubleshooting tools to help you identify and resolve problems with network and Internet connections as well as in other areas.

# Chapter at a Glance

Work with windows, **page 106**

Understand files, folders,
and libraries, **page 115**

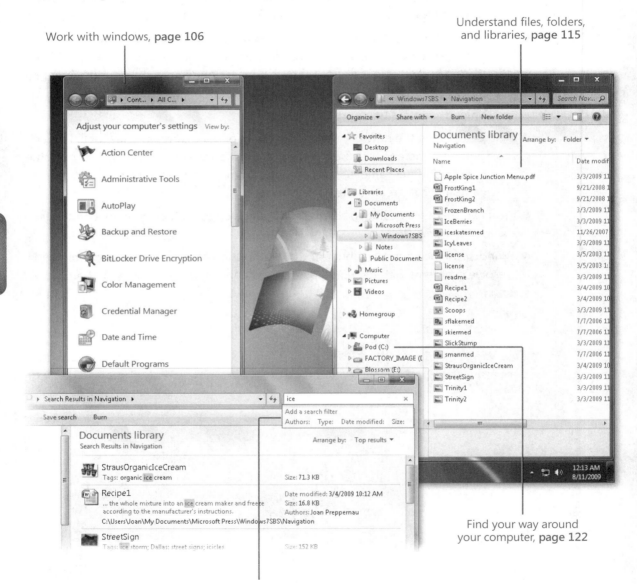

Find your way around
your computer, **page 122**

Find specific information,
**page 134**

# 4 Navigate Windows and Folders

---

**In this chapter, you will learn how to:**

- ✔ Work with windows.
- ✔ Understand files, folders, and libraries.
- ✔ Find your way around your computer.
- ✔ Connect to network resources.
- ✔ Find specific information.

---

To simplify the way you work with files on your computer, Windows uses a hierarchical storage system to organize information on your computer in a way similar to the way you would organize information in an office. Instead of organizing pieces of paper in cardboard folders in filing cabinets, you organize electronic files in electronic folders on the storage disks accessible to your computer.

You use Windows Explorer to look at the folders and files stored on your computer. With earlier versions of Windows, the Windows Explorer window could display the contents of only one folder at a time. With Windows 7, you can look at the contents of multiple folders in one window, by adding the folders to a library. This new feature allows you to easily access files while still maintaining an organizational system.

No matter how organized you are and how skillful you become at working with libraries, sometimes you might not remember where you stored a particular file. No problem! Windows 7 includes powerful search features that can help you almost instantly locate files and other information on your computer.

In this chapter, you'll first learn how to size, arrange, hide, and otherwise manage windows on your desktop. You'll learn about the standard file storage structure Windows 7 uses, and about the types of files you'll find on your Windows 7 computer. Then you'll explore the Windows 7 file storage structure. You'll also experiment with searching for files by using the different search methods that are available.

> **Practice Files**  Before you can complete the exercises in this chapter, you need to install the practice files specified in "Using the Practice Files" at the beginning of this book to their default location. The practice files you will use to complete the exercises in this chapter are in the Navigation practice file folder.

# Working with Windows

As the name of the Windows operating system indicates, most of the information you view on your computer is displayed in a window. Files open in program windows (windows that host the program controls), and folders open in Windows Explorer windows (windows that display the folder contents). Regardless of the content they display, all windows share certain common characteristics and can be manipulated in the same ways. You can change the appearance of windows by using controls built into their frames, as well as controls available from the desktop and from the Windows Taskbar. Windows 7 provides many new window-management controls that are very cool as well as useful.

**See Also**  For more information about the features of folder windows, see "Understanding Files, Folders, and Libraries" later in this chapter.

## Sizing, Moving, and Arranging Windows

You can minimize, maximize, restore, or close a window by clicking the buttons at the right end of the title bar. Additionally, you can use the following techniques to change the size or position of an individual window:

- To change the location of a window, but not its size, drag it.

  **Tip**  To drag a window, point to its title bar, press and hold the mouse button, and then move the mouse.

- To change only the height of a window, drag the top or bottom border of its frame.

- To maximize the height of a window without changing its width, drag the top border of its frame to the top edge of the screen or the bottom border of its frame to the bottom edge of the screen.

- To change the width of a window, drag the left or right border of its frame.

- To simultaneously change the height and width of a window, drag any corner of its frame.

  **Tip**  You cannot resize a maximized window by dragging an edge of its frame; you must first restore the window to its non-maximized state.

- To maximize the height and width of a window so that the window fills the screen, drag it until the mouse pointer touches the top edge of the screen, or click the Maximize button.

- To resize a window to the maximum height and half the screen width, drag it until the mouse pointer touches the left or right edge of the screen. When you release the mouse button, the window expands to fill half the available horizontal space.

  **Tip** You can use this technique to compare the contents of two windows; simply drag one to the left and one to the right.

- To restore a maximized or half-width window to its original size, drag its title bar away from the edge of the screen, or click the Restore Down button.

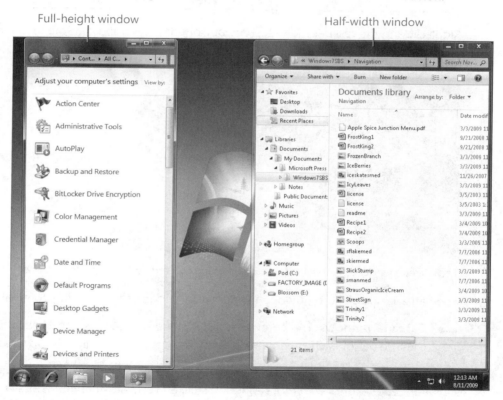

*You can automatically resize windows by dragging them to an edge of the screen.*

**Tip** When you resize a window by using a dragging technique, the change isn't permanent until you release the mouse button. When you drag a window to the top, left, or right edge of the screen to resize it, an outline representing the resized window appears. If you don't want to resize the window to match the outline, simply drag away from that location before releasing the mouse button.

You can use the keyboard shortcuts shown in the following table to work with the open window.

| Press this | To do this |
| --- | --- |
| Windows logo key+Up Arrow | Maximize the window |
| Windows logo key+Down Arrow | Resize the window from maximized to its original size or from its original size to minimized |
| Windows logo key+Home | Minimize or restore all other windows |
| Windows logo key+Left Arrow or Windows logo key+Right Arrow | Snap the window to the left or right edge of the screen |
| Alt+Tab | Switch between open windows |

Right-clicking the taskbar (not a taskbar button) displays a shortcut menu of commands you can use to manage all the open windows as a group.

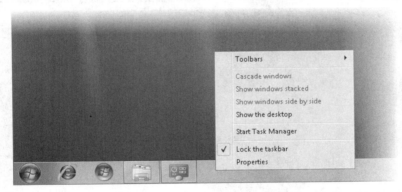

*The taskbar shortcut menu includes four commands for manipulating open windows.*

You can arrange all currently open windows by clicking the following commands:

- **Cascade windows** This command displays the windows on top of each other, with the title bar of each window visible and the contents of only the top window visible.

- **Show windows stacked** This command displays the content of all the windows arranged in a grid, with more windows stacked vertically than horizontally. For example, eight windows are arranged in two columns of four.

- **Show windows side by side** This command displays the content of all the windows arranged in a grid, with more windows stacked horizontally than vertically. For example, eight windows are arranged in four columns of two.

- **Show the desktop** This command minimizes all the windows.

In every arrangement, the open windows are sized similarly, regardless of their size before you arranged them.

**See Also**  When windows are arranged,an Undo command appears on the taskbar shortcut menu. For information about other the taskbar shortcut menu commands, see "Modifying the Taskbar" in Chapter 10, "Change System Settings."

## Hiding and Displaying Windows

In addition to the Show The Desktop command on the taskbar shortcut menu, you can use the following techniques to control the display of multiple open windows:

- Pointing to the Show Desktop button at the right end of the Windows Taskbar makes all the open windows temporarily translucent so that you can see through them to the desktop. The taskbar, desktop shortcuts, and gadgets remain visible. This new feature is called Aero Peek, and is one of the features that works only on hardware that supports Aero functionality.

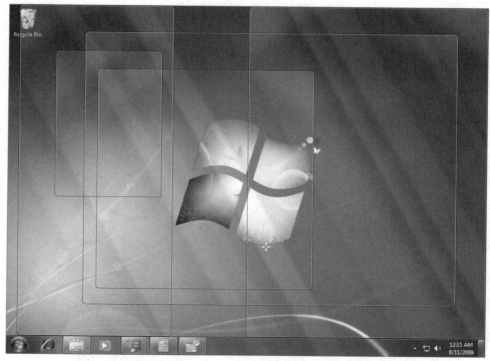

*The effect of pointing to the Show Desktop button, located at the right end of the taskbar.*

**Keyboard Shortcut**  You can peek at the desktop by pressing the Windows logo key+Spacebar.

● Clicking the Show Desktop button minimizes all the open windows. Clicking it again returns the windows to their previous sizes and locations.

● Shaking the active window minimizes all other open windows. To shake a window, point to its title bar, press the mouse button, and wiggle the mouse. To shake a window when you're working on a portable computer that has a touch pad, point to its title bar, and then wiggle your finger on the touch pad.

In this exercise, you'll experiment with the Windows 7 window-management techniques.

**SET UP** You don't need any practice files to complete this exercise. Log on to Windows 7, and then follow the steps.

1. Click the **Start** button. At the top of the right pane of the **Start** menu, point to **Pictures**.

The icon at the top of the Start menu changes from your user account picture to a representation of a stack of pictures, and a ScreenTip displays a description of what will happen when you click the button.

*You can open common windows from the right pane of the Start menu.*

2. On the **Start** menu, click **Pictures**.

The Pictures library opens in Windows Explorer.

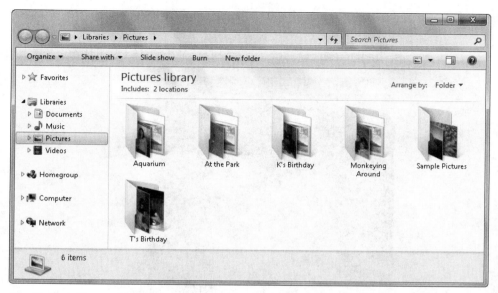

*The Pictures library displays the contents of your personal Pictures folder and the Public Pictures folder.*

**See Also** We'll discuss libraries in "Understanding Files, Folders, and Libraries," and work with Windows Explorer in "Finding Your Way Around Your Computer," both later in this chapter.

3. If the **Pictures** window is maximized when it opens, click the **Restore Down** button, near the right end of the window title bar, so that the window fills only part of the screen.

**Tip** The second button from the right end of a window title bar is the Restore Down button when the window fills the entire screen, and the Maximize button when it does not.

4. Drag the **Pictures** window by its title bar until the mouse pointer touches the top edge of the screen, but do not release the mouse button.

An outline of a maximized window appears, indicating the effect of releasing the mouse button in that location.

5. Release the mouse button.

The window size maximizes to fill all but the taskbar area of the screen.

6. Drag the window away from the top edge of the screen.

   The window returns to its previous size.

7. Drag the window by its title bar until the mouse pointer touches the right side of the screen.

   When you release the mouse button, the window fills the right half of the screen.

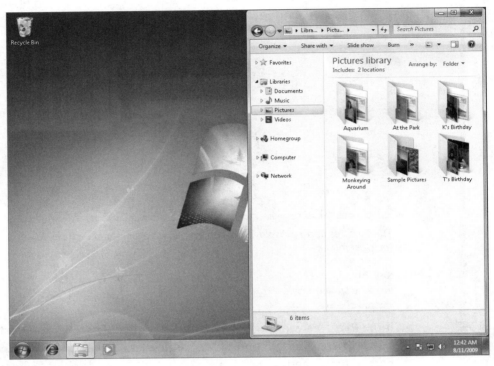

*The effect of dragging a window to the right side of the screen.*

8. On the taskbar, right-click the **Windows Explorer** button.

   The Windows Explorer shortcut menu appears. From the shortcut menu, you can open a new Windows Explorer window, or you can open a folder that you frequently access.

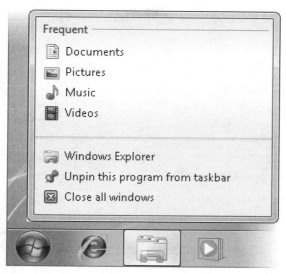

*The Windows Explorer shortcut menu.*

**9.** On the shortcut menu, click **Windows Explorer**.

Windows Explorer opens a new window.

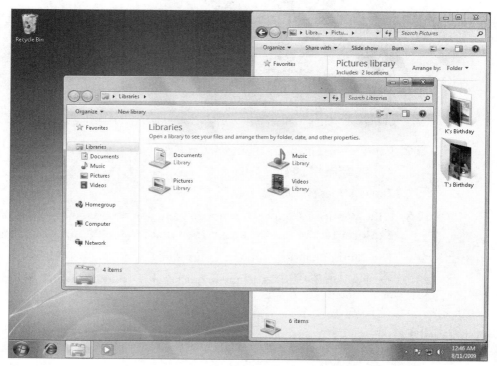

*If you don't specify a folder, Windows Explorer displays the Libraries folder when it starts.*

10. At the right end of the taskbar, point to the **Show desktop** button.

    The open windows become transparent.

11. Click the **Show desktop** button.

    The open windows disappear.

12. Click the **Show desktop** button again.

    The windows reappear.

13. Point to the **Libraries** window title bar, hold down the mouse button, and then wiggle the mouse to shake the window.

    The Pictures window is minimized under the Windows Explorer taskbar button.

14. On the taskbar, point to the **Windows Explorer** button.

    Thumbnails of the available Windows Explorer windows appear in a thumbnail pane above the taskbar button.

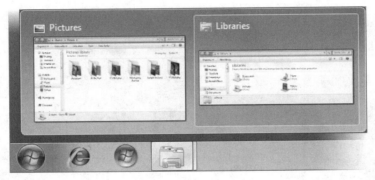

*In the thumbnail pane, a blue background indicates the active window.*

15. Point to the **Libraries** thumbnail, and then click the **Close** button that appears in its upper-right corner.

    The Libraries window closes.

16. If the Windows Explorer thumbnail pane has closed, point to the **Windows Explorer** taskbar button again. Then point to the **Pictures** thumbnail.

    The Pictures window appears temporarily when you point to its thumbnail.

    **Tip** You can use this technique to quickly check the content of a window without activating it.

17. In the **Windows Explorer** thumbnail pane, click the **Pictures** thumbnail.

    The Pictures window opens on the right half of the screen.

18. At the right end of the **Pictures** window title bar, click the **Close** button.

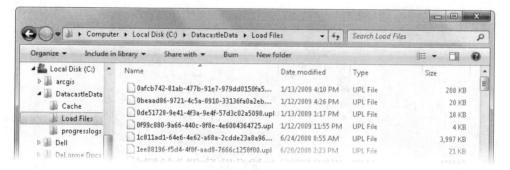

**CLEAN UP** Close any open windows before continuing to the next exercise.

# Understanding Files, Folders, and Libraries

Files associated with programs and tools, as well as the files you create to contain your information, are stored in a hierarchical structure of folders on hard disk drives and other storage devices (such as CDs, DVDs, or USB flash drives). You can look at a representation of this storage structure by displaying the contents of the available drives in Windows Explorer.

*Files are stored on each disk drive in a series of hierarchical folders.*

**Tip** This graphic displays the contents of a folder in Details view. You change the way folders and files are depicted in the Content pane by selecting a view from the Views list. For more information, see "Viewing Folders and Files in Different Ways" in Chapter 5, "Manage Folders and Files."

Each drive is identified by a letter, and in some cases by a description. Your computer's primary hard drive (the one where the operating system is installed) is almost always identified by the letter C. (By tradition, the letters A and B are reserved for floppy disk drives, which have been superseded by higher-capacity storage media and seem to be becoming quite rare.) If your computer has additional hard drives, they are assigned the next sequential letters, followed by any removable media drives.

**Tip** You can't assign a specific drive letter to a local drive in Windows Explorer, but you can name each drive. For information, see "Changing the Computer Name" in Chapter 10, "Change System Settings." You can assign a letter to a local drive in the Disk Management console, and you can assign a drive letter to a shared network folder or drive when you connect to it. For information, see "Connecting to Network Resources" later in this chapter.

In Windows Explorer, you can display a collection of related files and folders in a library. Libraries are virtual folders that aren't physically present on the hard disk but that display the contents of multiple folders as though the files were stored together in one location. The top-level view of a library displays the files and folders stored at the top level, called the *root*, of all the folders included in the library.

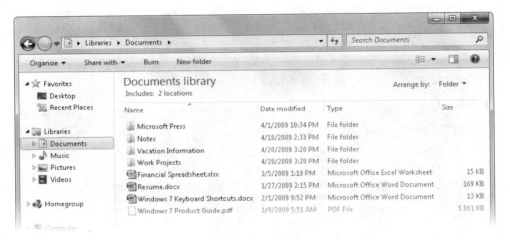

*The Documents library displays all the folders that are included in your personal Documents folder and the public Documents folder, as well as the files and folders stored in the root of those folders.*

The default Windows 7 installation includes four standard libraries—Documents, Music, Pictures, and Videos. Each of these libraries includes your corresponding personal folder and the corresponding public folder. In addition to the standard libraries, you can create your own libraries, and a folder can belong to more than one library. For example, suppose you are working on a Fall Promotion project for a client, Contoso Pharmaceuticals. If you create one library that displays all the folders of your current projects and another library that displays all the folders associated with Contoso, you can include the Fall Promotion folder in both libraries.

**See Also** For more information about how to make any default or custom library available to other users or computers on your network, see "Working with a Homegroup" and "Sharing Files on Your Network," both in Chapter 3, "Manage Your Network."

# File Types

There are many different types of files, but they all fall into these two basic categories:

- **Files used or created by programs** These include executable files and dynamic-link libraries (DLLs). Some of these files may be hidden (not shown in a standard folder window view) to protect them from being inadvertently changed or deleted.

  **Tip** When files are hidden you can't select or delete them, or delete the folder structure they're stored in; a folder might appear empty, but if it contains one or more hidden files, you cannot delete it. You can choose to display and work with hidden files, folders, and drives by clicking that option in the Folder Options dialog box, which is discussed in "Viewing Folders and Files in Different Ways" in Chapter 5, "Manage Folders and Files."

- **Files created by you** These include documents, worksheets, graphics, text files, presentations, audio clips, video clips, and other things that you can open, look at, and change by using one or more programs.

The files installed with a program and those it creates for its own use are organized the way the program expects to find them, and you shouldn't move or remove them. However, you have complete control of the organization of the files you create (such as documents and worksheets), and knowing how to manage these files is essential if you want to be able to use your computer efficiently.

# Windows System Folders

When Windows 7 was installed on your computer, it created three system folders:

- **Program Files folder** Most programs (including the programs and tools that come with Windows 7) install the files they need in subfolders of the Program Files folder. You may have the option to choose a different folder, but there's rarely a reason to do so. After you install a program you shouldn't move, copy, rename, or delete its folders and files; if you do, you might not be able to run or uninstall the program.

- **User account folder** The first time you log on to the computer with a new user account, Windows 7 creates a folder for that user account in the Users folder. The user account folder contains 12 subfolders, which we refer to in this book as your personal folders. Eleven of your personal folders are visible in your user account folder: Contacts, Desktop, Documents, Downloads, Favorites, Links, Music, Pictures, Saved Games, Searches, and Videos. One folder is hidden—the AppData folder that contains information about your user account settings for Windows and for programs that you use. As you work on your computer and personalize Windows, it saves information and settings specific to your user profile in these folders.

**Tip** You can display your personal folders by clicking your user account name that appears at the top of the right pane of the Start menu.

In addition to the user account–specific folder for each user account that is active on the computer, the Users folder also contains a Public folder, the contents of which are accessible to anyone logged on to the computer. The Public folder contains nine subfolders. Six of these are visible: Documents, Downloads, Music, Pictures, Recorded TV, and Videos. Three hidden subfolders—Desktop, Favorites, and Library—contain information about settings that are common to all user accounts on the computer. If you want to make files available to anyone who logs on to the computer, you can store them in the public folders rather than your personal folders.

**Tip** To clearly differentiate your personal folders from the public folders, Windows 7 refers to your personal folders as My Documents, My Music, My Pictures, and My Videos, and to the public folders as Public Documents, Public Music, Public Pictures, and Public Videos. The default Documents, Music, Pictures, and Videos libraries include the corresponding personal and public folders.

● **Windows folder** Most of the critical operating system files are stored in this folder. You can look, but unless you really know what you are doing, don't touch! Most Windows 7 users will never need to access the files in the Windows folder.

**Troubleshooting** If you upgraded your computer from an earlier version of Windows, the Windows folder from the earlier version might still remain on your computer. However, it will have been renamed to Windows.old during the upgrade process to avoid confusion.

## Folder Window Features

In Windows Explorer, every folder window displays two consistent elements: the title bar and the toolbar; you can't hide either of these elements.

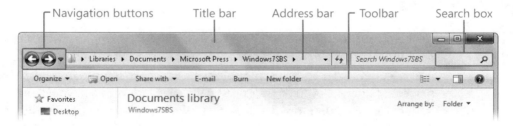

*All folder windows include the title bar and toolbar.*

The title bar always contains the following tools for moving around and for locating information:

- **Navigation buttons** The Back and Forward buttons move between previously visited window content, rather than up and down in the storage folder hierarchy. The Recent Pages button (the arrow to the right of the Forward button) displays a list of folders you have viewed; you can return to any folder by clicking it in the list.

- **Address bar** Beginning on the left with the icon representing the item type, the Address bar displays the path from one of the primary navigation groups (Computer, Control Panel, Homegroup, Libraries, Network, Recycle Bin, or your user account folder) to the folder whose contents are currently displayed in the folder window.

  - If the entire path doesn't fit in the Address bar, a left-pointing chevron appears next to the folder icon.

  - Clicking the arrow or chevron next to the folder icon displays a menu of common storage locations and any path locations that don't fit in the Address bar.

  - Clicking the folder icon displays the path to the folder from the root of the storage drive (sometimes referred to as the absolute path) or, for system folders, to the primary navigation group.

  - Clicking the arrow that appears after a folder name displays a list of its subfolders and certain high-level folders; you can switch to another location by clicking it in the list.

- **Search box** From the Search box of any folder window, you can quickly search for letters, words, or phrases occurring in the name or content of any file in that folder.

  - Type a search term in the Search box to immediately filter the folder contents. The Search Results list displays the names of files containing the search term and, for most file types, a content snippet and the absolute path to the file. Within the file name and the visible content snippet, the search term is highlighted.

  - Click the Clear button (the X) at the right end of the Search box to clear the search results and return to the folder window contents.

  **See Also** For more information about locating files and folders, see "Finding Specific Information" later in this chapter.

Unlike the title bar, the toolbar can vary based on the contents of the folder displayed in the folder window. The buttons on the toolbar represent context-specific commands for working with the folder and its content. For example, the buttons change for compressed folders (.zip files) or if you select one or more files. When more buttons are available than can be shown, chevrons (>>) appear at the right end of the toolbar; clicking the chevrons displays a list of other commands.

**See Also** For information about compressed folders, see the sidebar "Compressing Folders and Files" in Chapter 5, "Manage Folders and Files." For information about selecting files, see "Moving and Copying Folders and Files" in the same chapter.

In addition to the title bar and the toolbar, the layout of a folder window includes other standard and optional components. You can display and hide many folder window components.

*Typical folder window components.*

In addition to the title bar and toolbar, these components are available for every folder window:

- **Menu bar** If you prefer to manage the display of content by clicking commands on menus rather than using the toolbar buttons and column headers, you can display a traditional menu bar at the top of the window, between the title bar and the toolbar. (The menu bar is not open by default.)

- **Navigation pane** This vertical pane is open by default on the left side of the window. It displays a hierarchical view of the computer's storage structure, as well as the storage structure of any available network, organized in five groups: Favorites, Libraries, Homegroup, Computer, and Network. You can browse to folders on your computer or network by clicking locations in this pane.

  - To display the contents of a folder, click the folder name.
  - To expand a folder in the Navigation pane, point to the pane, and then click the white arrow that appears to the left of the folder.
  - To collapse an expanded folder, click the black arrow that appears to its left.

  You can resize or close the Navigation pane to provide additional working space in the folder window.

- **Content pane** This primary pane displays the contents of the selected folder as a textual or iconic list. You can't close the Content pane.

- **Details pane** This pane is open by default at the bottom of the window. It displays information about the selected folder or file. You can resize or close it.

- **Preview pane** This vertical pane is closed by default, but when open, it appears on the right side of the window. It displays a preview of the file selected in the Content pane. The Preview pane can display the contents of image files, Microsoft Word documents, Microsoft Excel workbooks, Microsoft PowerPoint presentations, PDF files, and other common file types. When the Preview pane is open, it is resizable.

**Tip** When you display the contents of a library, the folder window also includes a horizontal Library pane above the Content pane. The Library pane details the arrangement of the contents and the number of folders included in the library.

## Displaying and Hiding Panes

Each pane of a window displays a specific type of information. You can display and hide window panes to show or hide information, or to change the amount of space available in the Content pane. For example, if your folders typically contain many files and you are adept at navigating in the Address bar, you might want to turn off the Navigation, Detail, and Preview panes so that the Content pane occupies the entire folder window. To display or hide any window pane, click Organize on the toolbar, point to Layout, and then click the pane you want to change.

**Keyboard Shortcut** You can display or hide the Preview pane by clicking Alt+P.

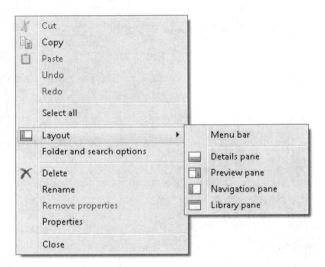

*You control which window panes are visible.*

**Tip** You can change the size of a pane by pointing to its border and dragging in the direction you want to increase or decrease its size. This technique is useful if you want to display more information in one pane without closing the other panes.

# Finding Your Way Around Your Computer

You view all the drives, folders, and files that are part of your computer's storage system, as well as those on any computers you are connected to through a network, in Windows Explorer.

You can start Windows Explorer in several ways; for example, you can:

- Click the Windows Explorer taskbar button to start Windows Explorer and display the Libraries folder.

  **Keyboard Shortcut** Press the Windows Logo key+E to start Windows Explorer and display the Computer folder.

- Click any of the folder links in the right pane of the Start menu.

  - Click your user account name to display your personal folders.

  - Click Documents, Pictures, or Music to display the corresponding library.

  - Click Computer to display the hard disk drives and storage devices available to your computer.

- Right-click a folder in the left pane of the Start menu, and then click Open or Explore to display the folder contents in the Content pane and the path to the folder expanded in the Navigation pane.

- Double-click a folder on the desktop or in any window to display the folder contents in the Content pane.

**See Also** Windows Explorer also displays the hardware devices (such as monitors, printers, and cameras) connected to your computer—both directly and over a network. For information about working with hardware, see Chapter 12, "Set Up Hardware Devices."

You can navigate through the folder hierarchy on each drive, displaying the contents of folders within folders until you find the file you want. This navigation process is called *browsing*. However, you don't have to browse to find the programs, tools, and information you need in your daily work. You don't even have to know precisely where things are stored, because Windows 7 provides a system of links that you can use to navigate directly to its settings and tools, to programs, and to certain classes of information. You have already seen evidence of this link system with the icons on the desktop and the links on the Start menu, but links are also used in other key components of Windows 7, which we will explore here and in other topics of this book.

**See Also** For more information about browsing drives and networks, see "Sharing Files on Your Network" in Chapter 3, "Manage Your Network."

To explore your computer's storage system, you can use the Computer window as a convenient entry point. The devices represented in the Computer window are divided into groups. Internal hard disk drives (those physically installed in your computer) and external hard disk drives (those connected to your computer by a cable) are shown first, followed by internal removable storage drives (floppy disk, CD, and DVD drives) and external removable storage devices (such as USB flash drives), and then storage locations you access through a network connection. For each drive or device, the total storage space and available storage space are given, both as actual measurements and visually as a colored progress bar. The length of the progress bar indicates the portion of the total storage space that is in use. The default bar color is aqua; when less than 10 percent of the storage space on a disk or device remains available, the bar color changes to red.

**Tip** The Computer window displays only groups that contain storage devices; if a group isn't active it isn't listed in the window.

In this exercise, you'll explore the storage structure of your computer and learn different ways of getting to the information stored on your computer.

 **SET UP** You don't need any practice files to complete this exercise; just follow the steps.

1. In the right pane of the **Start** menu, point to **Computer**.

   The Start menu icon changes from your user account picture to a representation of a computer system, and a ScreenTip displays a description of what you can do from the Computer window.

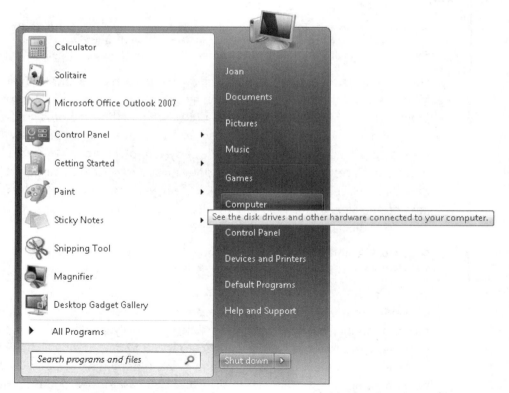

*You can open the Computer window to display information about your computer's storage devices.*

2.  On the **Start** menu, click **Computer**.

The Computer window opens in Windows Explorer.

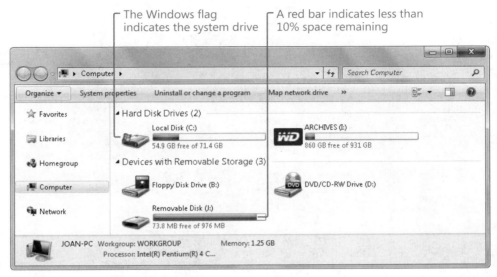

*In the Content pane of the Computer window, icons identify each drive or device type.*

**Troubleshooting**  The Content pane of your Computer window will display the number and types of drives your computer can access and will probably not be identical to the pane shown here.

From this window, you can navigate through the storage structure of your computer in four ways: by double-clicking locations in the Content pane, by expanding locations in the Navigation pane, by clicking locations in the Address bar, or by searching for files and folders from the Search box.

3.  If any groups in the **Navigation** pane are expanded to display their contents, collapse them by pointing to the pane and then clicking the black arrow that appears to the left of the group's name.

4.  If the drives and devices shown in the **Content** pane of your **Computer** window are represented by words or icons in a different way than shown in our graphic, click the **Views** arrow on the toolbar and then, in the **Views** list, click **Tiles**.

5.  In the **Navigation** pane, expand the **Computer** group.

The group includes the storage disks and devices currently available to your computer, as well as any media drives that contain media.

**Important**  Clicking any drive, whether internal or external, in the expanded Computer group displays the contents of the top level of the drive's storage structure, called the *root*, in the Content pane. The root of a drive often contains system files and folders that should not be modified or moved in any way.

6. In the **Navigation** pane, expand **Local Disk (C:)**, and then in the list of folders that appears, click **Users**.

The Users folder window opens.

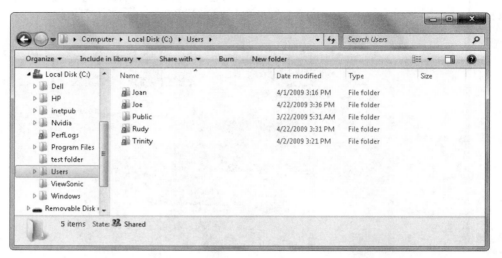

*The Users window displays folders for each active user account on the computer.*

7. In the **Content** pane, double-click the folder corresponding to your user account name.

The Content pane displays your personal folders, other than the hidden AppData folder.

8. In the **Address** bar, click the arrow to the right of **Users**.

A list of user account folders appears.

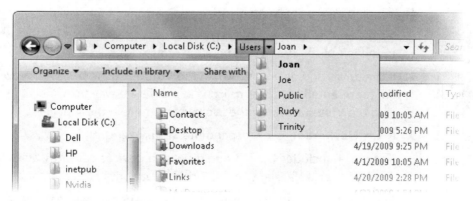

*In the list of user account folders, bold text indicates the folder in the path to the current location.*

9. In the list of user account folders, click **Public**.

    The Content pane displays the folders available to all users of your computer, and to network users with permission to connect to your computer.

    **See Also** For information about connecting to other computers on your network, see "Connecting to Network Resources" later in this chapter.

10. Point to the **Navigation** pane, and click the black arrow to the left of **Computer** to collapse the group. Then click the white arrow to the left of **Libraries** to display the available libraries.

11. In the **Navigation** pane, click the white arrow to the left of **Documents**.

    The Documents library expands.

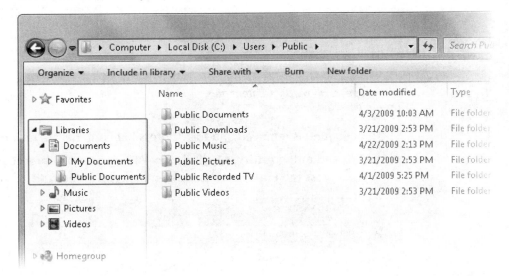

*You can reach the Public Documents folder from the Libraries group in the Navigation pane, as well as by browsing to it through the computer's folder structure.*

12. In the **Navigation** pane, under the **Documents** library, click **My Documents**.

    The Content pane displays the contents of the My Documents folder.

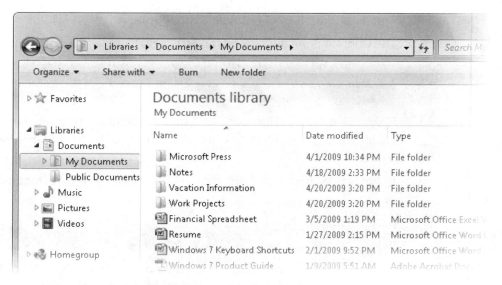

*Because you accessed your personal documents folder from the Libraries group, the Library pane appears above the Content pane, and the Address bar displays a library icon and a path beginning with Libraries.*

The highlighting is removed and the Address bar contents are now more visible.

**13.** At the left end of the **Address** bar, click the library icon that precedes the folder path. Then press the **End** key or click an empty area of the **Address** bar.

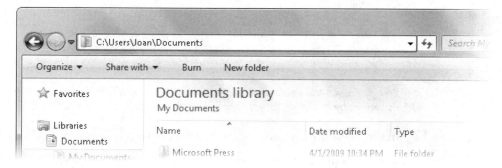

*Clicking the folder icon displays the absolute path of the current location.*

Notice that the actual name of your personal documents folder is Documents, not My Documents. The name *My Documents* is used in the library to distinguish your Documents folder from the Public Documents folder.

**14.** In the **Navigation** pane, click the **Documents** library.

The contents of all the folders included in the Documents library, both personal and public, appear in the Content pane.

**Tip** If there are no folders or files in your Public Documents folder, the content shown in the Content pane won't change.

**15.** In the **Library** pane, click the button to the right of **Arrange by**.

The Arrange By menu appears.

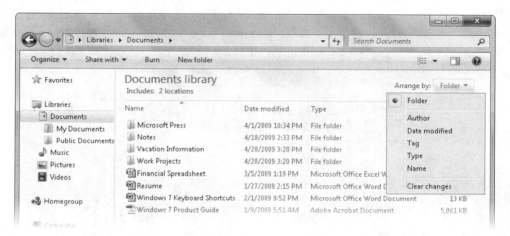

*You can view library contents arranged in folders; grouped by author, date modified, tag, or type; or listed in alphanumeric order by file name.*

**16.** Try the different arrangements to see how each displays files and folders.

 **CLEAN UP** Close the Documents window.

# Connecting to Network Resources

If your computer is connected to a work network or to a home network, you might want to access folders that are located on other computers on the network.

**See Also** For information about sharing folders and drives, see "Sharing Files on Your Network" in Chapter 3, "Manage Your Network."

## Navigating to a Shared Folder

In Chapter 3, "Manage Your Network," you learned how to share files, folders, and drives with other people on your network, either by sharing them with homegroup members (computers), if your computer is part of a homegroup, or by sharing them with all or selected network users (people). You also learned about sharing files by placing them in public folders, and how to control whether public folders are visible to other network computers.

If your computer is connected to a network, you can use Windows Explorer to navigate not only to drives and resources on your own computer, but also to drives and resources across your entire network.

You can view files, folders, and drives that other network users have shared with you in the same way that you view information on your own computer. Open the Computer window and then, in the Navigation pane, click the Network group. The Network window shows all the computers that are currently available through the network that your computer is connected to.

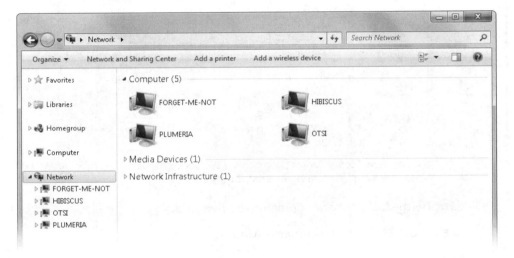

*The Network window.*

Navigate to shared resources on the computers by expanding the Network group computers and their folders in the Navigation pane, or by double-clicking computers and folders in the Content pane.

## Mapping a Network Drive

If you want to access a specific network drive or folder on a regular basis—for example, if you frequently connect to a shared external hard drive—you can map the drive in Windows Explorer to make it more easily available. When you map a drive, you assign it a local drive letter so that it appears along with other available storage devices and locations when you view the contents of your computer. You can map a drive for the duration of the current computing session, or instruct Windows to reconnect to that drive every time you log on.

To map a drive:

1. On the Start menu, click Computer.
2. On the Computer window toolbar, click Map A Network Drive.

   The Map Network Drive wizard starts.

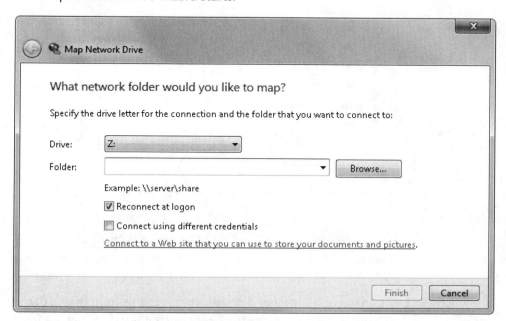

*If you haven't previously mapped a drive, the wizard suggests "Z" as the drive letter for the drive you're mapping.*

3. If you want to change the letter that represents the mapped drive when viewing your computer contents, click the Drive list, and then click the letter you want.
4. If you know the UNC path to the drive or folder you want to map, type it in the Folder box, and then skip to step 8.
5. To browse to the drive or folder you want to map, click the Browse button.

   The Browse For Folder dialog box opens, displaying a list of the computers that are available on your network.

6. Click the white arrow to the left of a computer name to display a list of shared folders on that computer.

   If a computer doesn't have any shared resources, the arrow disappears; otherwise, the arrow color changes to black to indicate that the computer folder is expanded. You can hide the content list for any folder by clicking its black arrow.

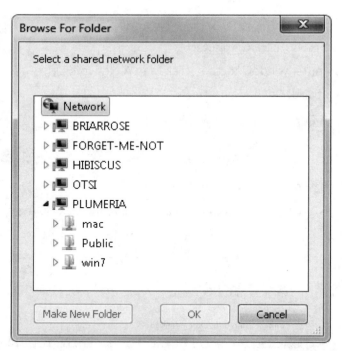

*If public folder sharing is turned on for a computer, its Public folder appears in the shared folder list.*

7. Click the computer that hosts the folder you want to map a drive to. If necessary, expand the shared folder to display its subfolders. When the folder you want to map to is selected, click OK.

The UNC path to the folder appears in the Folder box.

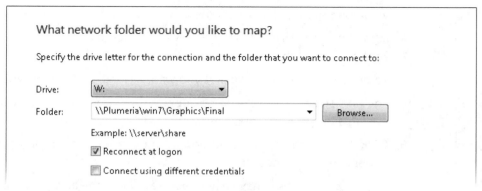

*You select the drive letter that will represent the shared folder's connection to your computer.*

8. If you want to connect to the mapped drive only until the end of the current Windows session, clear the Reconnect At Logon check box.

9. If the user account you log on to your computer with doesn't match the user account you need to log on to the computer hosting the shared folder, select the Connect Using Different Credentials check box.

10. In the Map Network Drive window, click Finish.

    Windows connects to the shared folder and opens it in a folder window.

11. In the Navigation pane of the folder window, click Computer.

    The mapped drive appears in the Network Location area of the Computer folder window.

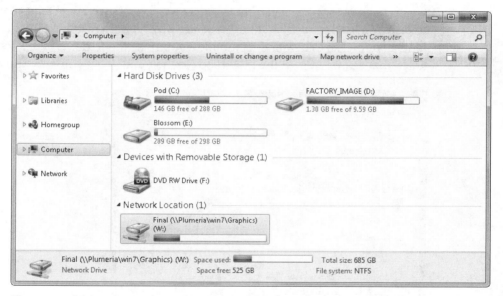

*The mapped drive also appears when you expand the Computer group in the Navigation pane.*

To remove a mapped drive, right-click the drive in the Computer window, and then click Disconnect.

**Tip** If you connect to a specific network drive from time to time but don't want or need to map a folder to it, you might find it useful to create a desktop shortcut to the folder or to add it to the pinned items area at the top of your Start menu. For more information, see "Creating Shortcuts" in Chapter 5, "Manage Folders and Files."

# Finding Specific Information

Recent advancements in online and computer search technology have made the instant location of information and files so simple that it's easy to forget how tedious tracking down the same items would have been in the past. The Windows Search technology that is built in to Windows 7 is quite simply excellent. We touted the search capabilities in Windows Vista as one of its top three features, but the Windows 7 search engine is better.

## Windows Search

Using Windows Search, you can find programs, files, messages, and message attachments on your computer almost instantly. You don't need to know the name or location of the file or item you want to find; simply type a word or phrase in the Start menu Search box to display a list of matching items, organized by type. To restrict your search to the contents of a specific folder (and its subfolders), display the folder in Windows Explorer and enter your search term in the Search box in the upper-right corner of the window.

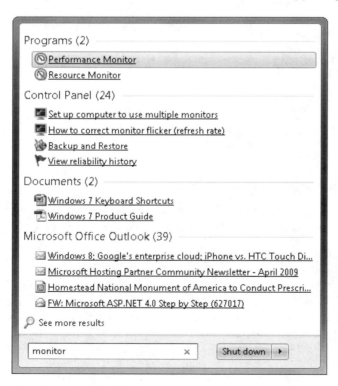

*Search results are divided into categories. Click any category heading to display a list of all the search results in that category.*

How does Windows Search find items so quickly? Behind the scenes, Windows Search maintains an index of all the key words in, and associated with, the files stored on your computer—program names, common tasks, and the file names and content (when possible) of documents, audio and video recordings, images, e-mail messages, Web pages, and other data files. Windows Search automatically indexes the most common file types (such as Word documents, text files, and e-mail messages) and doesn't index file types you are less likely to search (such as operating system files). For certain types of files (such as PowerPoint presentations), Windows Search indexes the file properties and the file content, but for others (such as PowerPoint slide templates) it indexes only the file properties. (It does not include the system files; such an index would be huge and would slow down the search process.) When you enter a search term, Windows looks for the term in the index instead of searching the actual files on your hard disk.

**Tip**  By default, Windows doesn't index encrypted files because a search by another computer user could reveal the encrypted data. You can add encrypted files to the search index if you first put in place a full-volume data-encryption solution, such as Windows BitLocker Drive Encryption. For information about BitLocker, see *Windows 7 Step by Step Deluxe Edition*, by Joan Preppernau and Joyce Cox (Microsoft Press, 2010).

If a simple search from the Start menu Search box or the Search box in a Windows Explorer window doesn't locate the item you are looking for, you can perform more advanced searches in the Search Results folder. Your search criteria can include the date a file was created, its size, part of its name or title, its author, and any tags you might have listed as properties of the file.

**See Also**  For information about file properties, see "Working with Folder and File Properties" in Chapter 5, "Manage Folders and Files."

You can save a set of search parameters so that you can display updated results at any time. Saved searches are added to the Favorites group in Windows Explorer and are also available from your personal Searches folder.

## Windows Search Parameters

You can change which file types and locations are included in the Windows Search index at any time. You can change the search settings in the following places:

- **On the Search tab of the Folder Options dialog box**  You can open the Folder Options dialog box by clicking Organize on the toolbar of any Windows Explorer window and then clicking Folder And Search Options on the Organize menu.

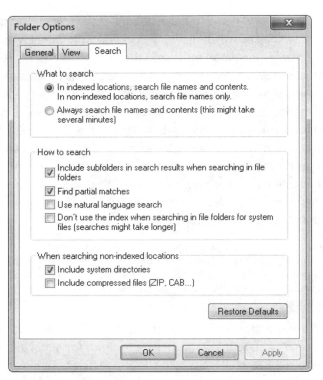

*On the Search tab of the Folder Options dialog box, you can make simple changes to search settings.*

You can specify whether Windows Search returns results from file contents as well as from file names; whether results of folder-specific searches include files located in subfolders; whether a search returns results that don't exactly match the search term (for example, returning results containing rocker as well as rocking); and other options related to the standard Windows Search scope.

● **From the Indexed Locations dialog box**  You can open the Indexed Locations dialog box by displaying Control Panel in Large Icons view or Small Icons view, clicking Indexing Options, and then clicking Modify in the Indexing Options dialog box.

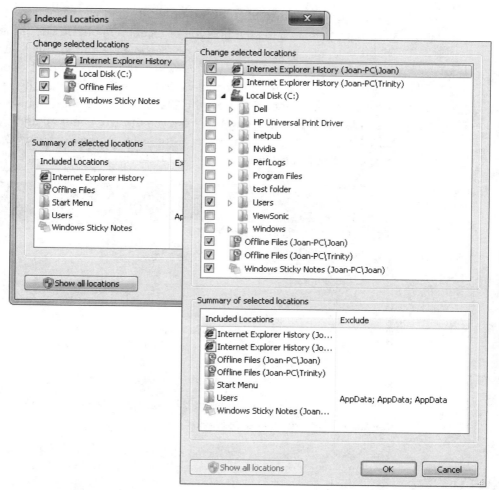

*In the Indexed Locations dialog box, you can view simple or expanded versions of the locations included in the search index.*

In the Change Selected Locations list, you can select or clear the check boxes of specific folders to indicate which ones should be included in the search index.

- **The Search and Indexing troubleshooter** If Windows Search isn't finding specific files that you search for, the file type or location might be out of the current index scope, or in rare cases, there could be a problem with the index file. The Search And Indexing troubleshooter will guide you through a simple troubleshooting process to determine what changes need to be made so that the search results meet your expectations. To start the Search And Indexing troubleshooter, open the Indexing Options dialog box from the Control Panel All Items window and click Advanced. Then, on the Index Settings tab of the Advanced Options dialog box, click the Troubleshoot Search And Indexing link.

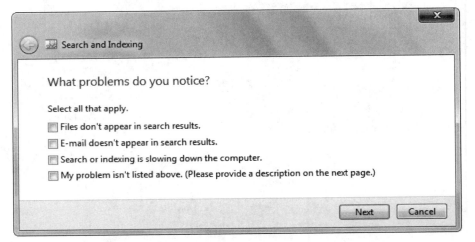

*The Search and Indexing troubleshooter.*

**Tip** Windows 7 has about two dozen built-in utilities, referred to as *troubleshooters*, that guide you through the processes of resolving various problems. For information about the available troubleshooters, see *Windows 7 Step by Step Deluxe Edition* by Joan Preppernau and Joyce Cox (Microsoft Press, 2010).

You can identify the type of problem you're having or simply have the troubleshooter check your computer against a list of common issues. After running the troubleshooter, click the See Detailed Results link to display a list of everything the troubleshooter checked.

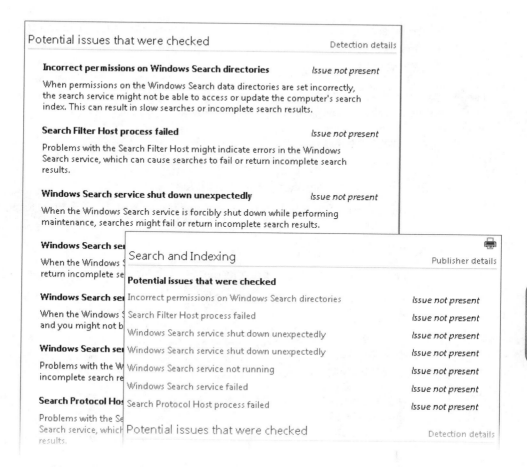

Potential issues that were checked                    Detection details

**Incorrect permissions on Windows Search directories**        *Issue not present*

When permissions on the Windows Search data directories are set incorrectly,
the search service might not be able to access or update the computer's search
index. This can result in slow searches or incomplete search results.

**Search Filter Host process failed**                          *Issue not present*

Problems with the Search Filter Host might indicate errors in the Windows
Search service, which can cause searches to fail or return incomplete search
results.

**Windows Search service shut down unexpectedly**             *Issue not present*

When the Windows Search service is forcibly shut down while performing
maintenance, searches might fail or return incomplete search results.

Search and Indexing                                    Publisher details

**Potential issues that were checked**

Incorrect permissions on Windows Search directories        *Issue not present*

Search Filter Host process failed                          *Issue not present*

Windows Search service shut down unexpectedly             *Issue not present*

Windows Search service shut down unexpectedly             *Issue not present*

Windows Search service not running                         *Issue not present*

Windows Search service failed                              *Issue not present*

Search Protocol Host process failed                        *Issue not present*

Potential issues that were checked                    Detection details

*The Search and Indexing troubleshooter details.*

From the Advanced Options dialog box, you can also do the following things that
require administrator permission:

- Include encrypted files in the index.
- Add a type of file to the index.
- Change the indexing level for a type of file.
- Change the location of the index file.
- Restore the default settings.
- Rebuild the index file from scratch.

**Tip** If you have a lot of data on your computer, rebuilding the index file can be a very
lengthy process, and is not one you would want to undertake without good reason.

In this exercise, you'll quickly locate items on your computer. You will then use advanced criteria in the Search Results folder to look for other files and will open the Preview pane to help identify the correct file.

**SET UP** You need the practice files located in your Documents\Microsoft Press\ Windows7SBS\Navigation folder to complete this exercise.

1. Click the **Start** button.

   The Start menu opens with the cursor blinking in the Start menu Search box.

2. In the **Start** menu **Search** box, type **ice**.

   As you type the search term, Windows filters the program files, folders, and e-mail messages stored on your computer.

3. Point to each file in the search results in turn.

   A ScreenTip displays the properties of each file you point to.

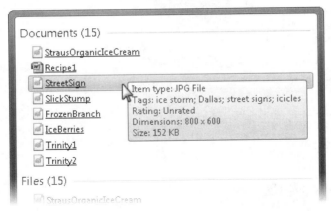

*The properties shown in a ScreenTip vary based on the file type.*

If you get in the habit of entering properties for your files, this handy trick can help you quickly identify the file you want.

**See Also** For information about file properties, see "Working with Folder and File Properties" in Chapter 5, "Manage Folders and Files."

4. At the bottom of the search results list, click **See more results**.

   The Search Results In Indexed Locations window opens, displaying the full list of results. You can change the view and sort the files the same way you would with any folder.

**See Also** For information about sorting and filtering folder contents, see "Viewing Folders and Files in Different Ways" in Chapter 5, "Manage Folders and Files."

5. Scroll the center pane to view all the search results.

In the center pane, file properties and content matching the search term are high-lighted. If no highlighting is visible in the search results shown, the matching content is further into the file than the snippet shown. Your search term appears in the Search box located in the upper-right corner of the window.

6. Click in the **Search** box to the right of the word *ice*.

The Add A Search Filter list appears.

*From the Add A Search Filter list in the Search Results window, you can quickly filter search results by common properties.*

7. At the right end of the **Search** box, click the **Clear Search** button.

The Search Results In Indexed Locations window displays the cumulative results of recent searches.

8. Close the **Search Results in Indexed Locations** window.

9. On the **Start** menu, click **Documents**.

The Documents library opens.

10. Navigate to your **Documents\Microsoft Press\Windows7SBS** folder and display its contents in the Content pane.

11. In the upper-right corner of the folder window, click in the Search box displaying **Search Windows7SBS**.

    A list of previous search terms appears.

12. In the list of previous search terms, click **ice**.

    The Search Results In Windows7SBS window displays the files in the Windows7SBS folder that match the search term.

13. Click in the **Search** box, after the word *ice*.

    The Add A Search Filter list appears below the search term, with options appropriate for searching in a library.

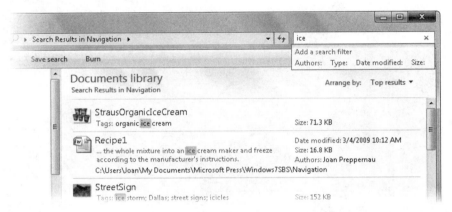

*You can enter search filters directly in the Add A Search Filter box or select properties from the list.*

14. In the **Add a search filter** list, click **Type**. Then scroll the list to see the results.

    The word *type* appears to the right of the term in the Search box to indicate which filter will be applied to the search results.

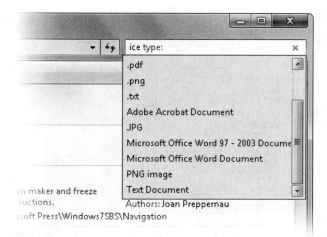

*When filtering a list by file type, you can choose from the file extensions or the corresponding file type descriptions represented by the search results.*

**15.** In the **type** list, click **.JPG**.

The search results change to reflect the filters you've applied.

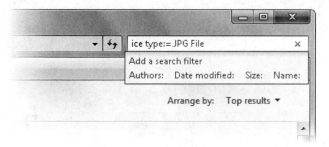

*The current filters are shown in the Search box, and the filter list changes to include additional options.*

**16.** In the **Search** box, after *.JPG*, type **cream**.

The results list displays one file that matches all the search criteria.

**Tip**  You can use wildcard characters to locate files that include your search term in the middle of another word.

*You can change the scope of a search by clicking any of the locations in the Search Again In list at the bottom of the search results.*

**17.** In the **Search** box, select and delete **type:=.JPG cream**. Then type **storm**.

The search results display photographic images taken after an ice storm.

**18.** On the toolbar, click **Save search**.

The Save As dialog box opens.

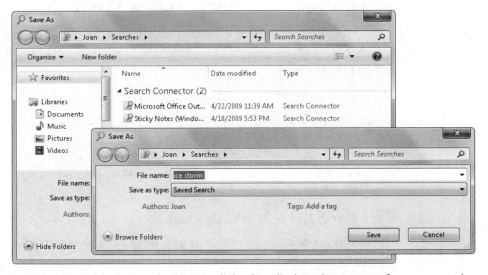

*In its Browse Folders state, the Save As dialog box displays the content of your personal Searches folder.*

**Tip** You can display or hide the Navigation and Content panes in the Save As dialog box either by clicking Browse Folders or Hide Folders, or by dragging the bottom border of the dialog box to resize it.

19. In the **Save As** dialog box, click **Save** to accept the default name and save the search in the Searches folder.

   The folder window now displays the contents of the new Searches\ice storm folder.

20. At the top of the **Navigation** pane, expand the **Favorites** group.

   The Navigation pane and Content pane display the contents of the Favorites group.

*The saved search is available in your Favorites group.*

You can display up-to-date search results for the term *storm* at any time by opening the saved search from the Favorites group.

 **CLEAN UP** Close the Favorites window.

# Key Points

- All windows share common characteristics. You can work with them in standard ways, such as by sizing, moving, arranging, and hiding them.
- Files are organized on your computer in a hierarchical storage structure.
- Windows Explorer provides several ways to move around your computer's storage system. Becoming familiar with them will increase your ability to quickly navigate to specific files.
- You can quickly locate information on your computer by entering a search term in either the Search box on the Start menu or the Search box in the upper-right corner of a folder window.
- You can refine a search by filtering the search results, for example, to show only files of a specific type.

# Chapter at a Glance

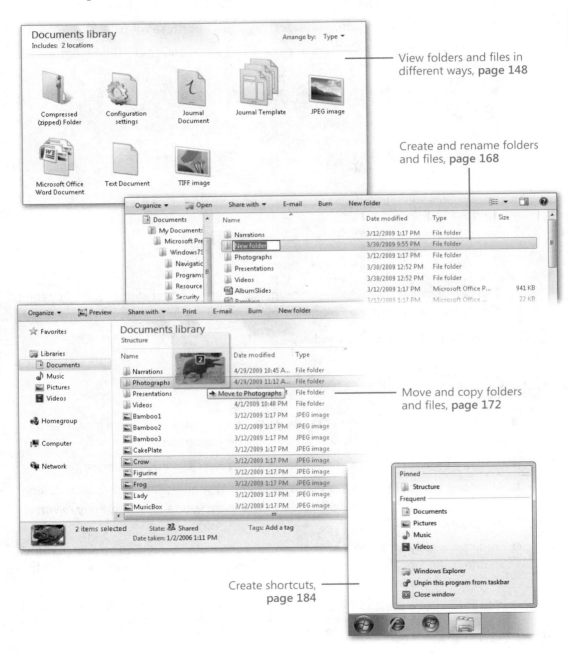

View folders and files in different ways, **page 148**

Create and rename folders and files, **page 168**

Move and copy folders and files, **page 172**

Create shortcuts, **page 184**

# 5 Manage Folders and Files

In this chapter, you will learn how to

- ✔ View folders and files in different ways.
- ✔ Work with folder and file properties.
- ✔ Create and rename folders and files.
- ✔ Move and copy folders and files.
- ✔ Delete and recover folders and files.
- ✔ Create shortcuts.

Whether you store your files in your personal folders or in the public folders, they are displayed in the corresponding library. For example, the picture files in both your personal and public Pictures folders appear in the Pictures library. If you work with a lot of files that are stored directly in the folders rather than in subfolders, the libraries will quickly come to display too many files for you to efficiently view them. In that case, you'll probably find it helpful to create a logical folder structure so that you can easily display sets of related files. It is important to design a simple structure and to use it consistently.

**Tip** We strongly recommend that you store all your private documents, spreadsheets, databases, and similar files in subfolders of your My Documents folder, and any files you want to share with other users in subfolders of the Public Documents folder. Similarly, store all your private pictures in My Pictures and those you want to share in Public Pictures; and so on for music and video files. When you follow this process, backing up your work is a simple matter of backing up only the libraries.

Before you can create your storage structure, you need to know the folder window navigation techniques discussed in Chapter 4, "Navigate Windows and Folders," and you need to know how to view and select files. Setting up the structure is a matter of creating the necessary folders and organizing folders and files appropriately. If folders and files you frequently use end up buried several levels down in your storage-structure hierarchy, you can provide easy access by creating shortcuts to them on the desktop or in the Windows Explorer Navigation pane.

In this chapter, you'll explore different ways to view folders and files in a folder window. You'll also see how to associate properties with folders and files to make it easier to organize and find information. Then you'll create, rename, move, copy, delete, and recover folders and files. Finally, you'll create and arrange shortcuts, both in various locations on the desktop and in Windows Explorer.

> **Practice Files**  Before you can complete the exercises in this chapter, you need to install the practice files specified in "Using the Practice Files" at the beginning of this book to their default location. The practice files you will use to complete the exercises in this chapter are in the Structure practice file folder.

# Viewing Folders and Files in Different Ways

While working through the exercises in Chapter 4, "Navigate Windows and Folders," you might have noticed that the contents of different folders are displayed in different ways in the Content pane of the folder window. Sometimes folders and files are listed with information such as the date and size, and sometimes they appear as icons representing the type of each file. You can change the appearance of folders and files in the Content pane by changing the view and by grouping the contents.

**See Also**  For information about changing the panes displayed in a window, see "Understanding Files, Folders, and Libraries" in Chapter 4, "Navigate Windows and Folders."

## Changing the Folder View

Different views are best suited to different tasks. For example, when you are looking for a specific graphic among those stored in a folder, you might find it useful to be able to see the graphic thumbnails in the Content pane. Whatever the default view of a folder is, you have complete control over the view, and often the one you choose will be a matter of personal preference.

The available views include the following:

- **Icons**  The four Icon views (Extra Large, Large, Medium, and Small) display an icon and file name for each folder or file in the current folder. In all but Small Icons view, the icons display either the file type, or in the case of graphic files (including Microsoft PowerPoint presentations), the actual file content.

- **List**  This view is similar to Small Icons view in that it shows the names of the files and folders accompanied by a small icon representing the file type. The only difference is that the items are arranged in columns instead of in rows.

- **Details**  This view displays a list of files and folders, each accompanied by a small icon representing the item type and its properties, arranged in a tabular format, with column headings. The properties shown by default for each file or folder are Name, Date Modified, Type, and Size. You can hide any of these properties, and you can display a variety of other properties that might be pertinent to specific types of files, including Author and Title.

  **Tip**  You can size a property's column to fit its contents by pointing to the right border of its heading and double-clicking when the two-headed pointer appears.

- **Tiles**  For folders, this view displays a medium-size icon and the folder name and type. For files, the icon displays the content of the file and is accompanied by the file name, type, and file size.

- **Content**  For folders, this view displays an icon, the folder name, and the date. For files, the icon displays the content of the file and is accompanied by the file name, type, file size, and date. Also shown are any tags.

  **See Also**  For information about tags, see "Working with Folder and File Properties" later in this chapter.

**Tip**  In the Extra Large Icons, Large Icons, Medium Icons, Tiles, and Content views, folder icons display the actual contents of the folder, depicted as pages and pictures.

There are three ways to change the folder view:

- On the folder window toolbar, click the Views button repeatedly to cycle through the views.

- Click the Views arrow, and in the Views list, click the view you want.

- Right-click the Content pane, click View, and then in the View list, click the view you want.

**Tip**  You can optimize a folder for a specific type of content by applying the Documents, Pictures, Music, or Videos template from the Customize tab of the folder's Properties dialog box. One characteristic of the folder template is the default folder view. You can override the default view at any time by making a selection from the Views list.

**See Also**  For information about folder types, see "Working with Folder and File Properties" later in this chapter.

## Grouping Folder Content

By default, the folders and files in a folder window are visible as individual items. In a library window, you can group items by author, modification date, tag, file type, or file name.

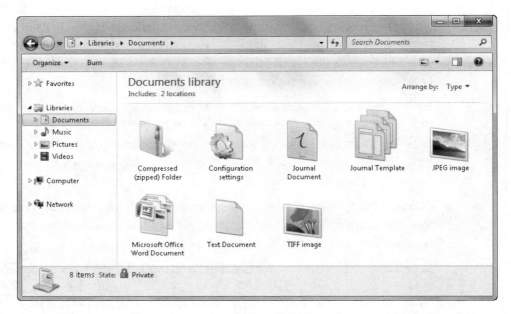

*Grouped items appear in stacks; you can display all the items in a group by double-clicking the stack.*

**Tip** When displaying a folder that is shared with other users on your network, the State indicator appears in the Details pane of Windows Explorer. For information about sharing folders, see "Sharing Files on Your Network" in Chapter 3, "Manage Your Network."

To group items in a library window:

1. Display the Library pane.

2. On the Arrange By menu at the right end of the Library pane, click Author, Date Modified, Tag, Type, or Name.

You can group items in any view, and you can change the folder view of a folder displaying grouped items.

## Sorting and Filtering Folder Content

By default, the folders and files in a folder window are shown in alphanumeric order by name. All subfolders are shown first, followed by all files. You can change the order of the items in the Content pane by sorting them by any of the properties displayed in Details view.

To display or hide a property in Details view:

1. Right-click any column heading, and then click More.

2. In the Choose Details dialog box, select the check box of a property you want to display, or clear the check box of a property you want to hide, and then click OK.

To sort items in a folder window:

● In Details view, click a column heading to sort the folder contents in ascending or descending order by that property. Click the heading a second time to sort the contents in the opposite order.

● In any view, right-click the Content pane, click Sort By, and then click the property by which you want to sort the items. Click Ascending or Descending on the shortcut menu to change the sort order of the selected property.

In Details view, you can display only items that match specific criteria by filtering them. For example, you can display only the items you worked with on a particular day.

To filter items in a folder window:

1. Point to the column heading of the property by which you want to filter the folder contents, and then click the arrow that appears.

   A list of values that exist for that property appears. This list can consist of a range of alpha values (for the Name column), a specific date or range of dates (for the Date Modified column), specific values (for the Type column), or a range of numeric values (for the Size column).

2. In the list, select the check boxes of the values you want to match. Then click away from the list to close it.

   Windows Explorer instantly filters the folder content to display only the items that match the values you specified. A check mark at the right end of a column heading indicates a property used to filter the folder content.

3. To remove a filter, click the check mark in the column heading to display the filter list, clear the check box or boxes, and then click away from the list.

## Changing Folder Options

In the Folder Options dialog box, which you display by clicking Organize on the toolbar and then clicking Folder And Search Options, you can customize folder windows by changing settings on these two tabs:

- **General** On this tab, you can change how you browse folders, whether you click or double-click to open items, and how the Navigation pane behaves.

- **View** On this tab, you can change the default view for all folders and change specific display/hide settings.

For example, on the View tab you can specify whether Windows Explorer and all Windows programs should display file name extensions, which are hidden by default. Every file name has an extension, separated from the name itself by a period, that designates the file's type or the program in which it was created. If you often need to know the type of a file, it might be easier to turn on the display of file name extensions so that they are visible in all views than to have to constantly switch to Details, Tiles, or Content view to see the file type.

In this exercise, you'll customize a folder window, and then switch views. You'll also explore the Folder Options dialog box.

 **SET UP** You need the practice files and folders located in your Documents\ Microsoft Press\Windows7SBS\Structure folder to complete this exercise.

1. On the **Start** menu, click **Computer**.

   The Computer window opens.

2. If the **Details** pane is open at the bottom of the window, click **Organize** on the toolbar, click **Layout**, on the Organize menu, and then in the list, click **Details Pane** to hide the pane.

3. If the **Navigation** pane is open on the left side of the window, or the **Preview** pane is open on the right side of the window, repeat step 2 to close it.

Now the only open pane is the Content pane, which you cannot hide.

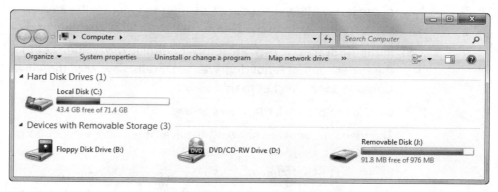

*When you hide the Details and Navigation panes, the Content pane occupies the entire area below the toolbar.*

**Tip** Your Computer window will display the disk drives and devices connected to your computer, rather than those shown in our graphic. If the current folder view in the Computer window is not Tiles, which is the default for this window, the window contents will be represented by icons or words instead of by tiles.

**4.** In the **Address** bar, click the arrow to the left of **Computer**, and then click your user account name to display your personal folders.

**5.** In the **Content** pane, double-click **My Documents**, double-click **Microsoft Press**, double-click **Windows7SBS**, double-click **Structure**, and then double-click **Presentations**.

The Presentations folder contains two files. If your computer is set to the default settings, they are currently displayed in Details view.

**6.** At the right end of the toolbar, click the **Views** button (not its arrow) five times to cycle through the most common views: **Tiles**, **Content**, **Large Icons**, **List**, and **Details**. End with Details view.

Each time you change the view by clicking the Views button, the icon on the button changes to represent the new view.

7. Point to the **Name** column heading, and then point to its right border, to the right of the arrow. When the pointer changes to a double-headed arrow, double-click to decrease the width of the **Name** column to fit its contents.

8. In the **Address** bar, click **Structure** to display the contents of that folder. Then, if the folder content is not displayed in **Details** view, click the **Views** button until the **Content** pane switches to that view.

9. On the toolbar, click the **Views** arrow.

The Views list appears, showing the available folder view options.

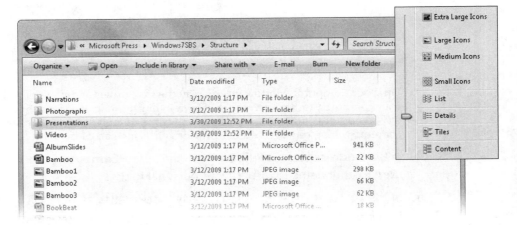

*The slider on the left side of the Views list indicates the current view.*

10. Slowly drag the slider to the top of the **Views** list and then to the bottom of the list without releasing the mouse button, noticing the effect on the display in the **Content** pane.

11. In the **Views** list, click **Medium Icons**.

The view changes so that each folder and file is represented by an icon.

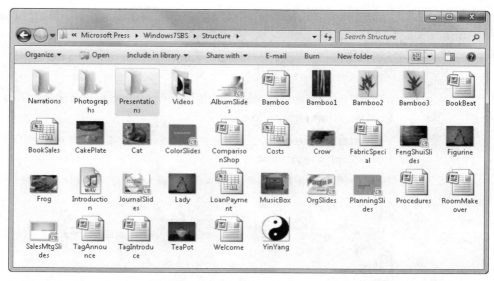

*In Medium Icons view, graphic files are represented by thumbnails showing their images, and folders and other files are represented by icons representing their type.*

**12.** In the **Views** list, click **Details**.

**13.** Point to the **Name**, **Date Modified**, **Type**, and **Size** column headings in turn.

As the pointer passes over each heading, the heading background changes color to indicate that it is active, and an arrow appears at the heading's right end. You can click the arrow to filter the contents on that property in various ways.

**14.** Click the **Size** column heading (not the arrow that appears at its right end) to sort the files in order of file size.

The arrow at the top of the Size column heading indicates the sort order: downward-pointing for largest to smallest and upward-pointing for smallest to largest.

**15.** Click **Size** again to reverse the sort order.

The arrow at the top of the Size column heading now points the other way.

**16.** Point to the **Type** column heading, and then click the arrow that appears at its right end.

A list of all the file types in the folder appears. You can filter the folder contents by any of these file types.

**17.** In the **Type** filter list, select the **JPEG image** and **Microsoft Office PowerPoint Presentation** check boxes.

Windows Explorer hides all the files and folders that are not JPEG images or PowerPoint presentations.

**Troubleshooting** If your list shows JPG File or PPTX File, click those instead.

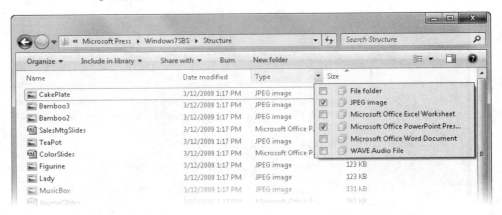

*The Content pane displays only the files and folders that match the selected filters.*

**18.** Click away from the filter list (for example, click the window title bar).

The filter list closes.

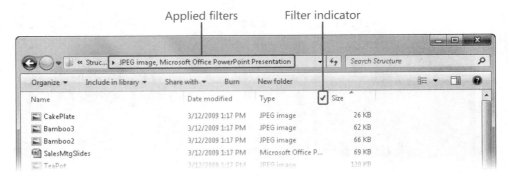

*The filters named in the Address bar have been applied to the property that has a check mark at the right end of its column heading.*

**19.** In the **Address** bar, click the arrow to the left of the currently applied filters.

A list of all the filters that can be applied to the indicated property is displayed.

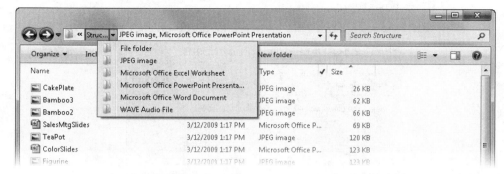

*From this list, you can change the filter applied to the indicated property, but you can select only one value.*

 **20.** In the upper-left corner of the window, click the **Back** button to remove the current filter.

**21.** Right-click any column heading.

A properties list appears.

*In the properties list, check marks indicate the properties currently displayed in Details view.*

**Tip** The Name property is unavailable (gray) because the file name is always displayed.

**22.** In the properties list, click **Authors**.

A new column appears, displaying Authors property values for the files that have them.

**23.** Right-click any column heading, and then click **More**.

The Choose Details dialog box opens.

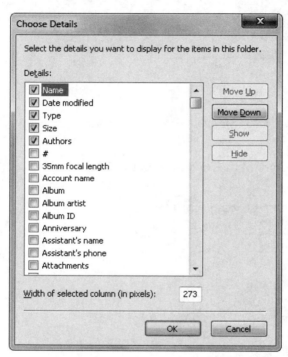

*The Choose Details dialog box includes more than 270 file properties that you can display in Details view. The currently displayed properties appear at the top of the Details list. Other properties are in alphabetical order.*

**24.** Scroll through the **Details** list to see all the file properties you can display in **Details** view. Then clear the **Authors** check box, and click **OK**.

The Authors column disappears from the folder window.

**25.** Click the **Name** column heading to sort the files alphanumerically by name. Then in the **Views** list, click **Tiles**.

The sort order is retained when you switch to a different view.

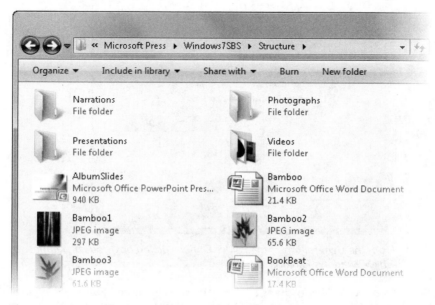

*Tiles view displays an icon or thumbnail for each item, along with its name, file type, and file size.*

**26.** On the **Organize** menu, click **Folder and search options**.

The Folder Options dialog box opens.

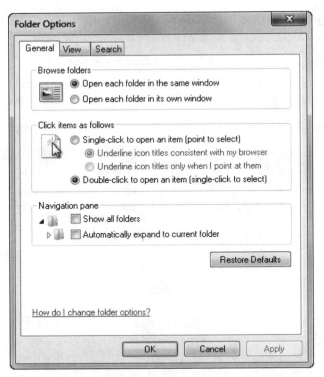

*From the General tab of the Folder Options dialog box, you can change the basic ways in which Windows Explorer works.*

**Important** If you change any of the settings in the Folder Options dialog box, the instructions in this book might not work for your computer. We recommend that only experienced users of Windows Explorer change these options.

**27.** In the **Folder Options** dialog box, click the **View** tab.

The options on this tab control many aspects of folder and file display.

**Tip** When you first start working in Windows 7, the default view for each folder is determined by its type. If you apply the current folder view to all folders of a particular type and then change your mind, you can click Reset Folders on the View tab of the Folder Options dialog box to restore the type-based default views. For information about folder types, see "Working with Folder and File Properties" later in this chapter.

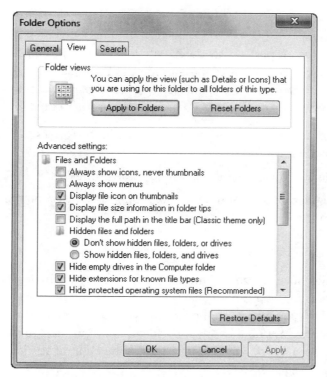

*From the View tab of the Folder Options dialog box, you can set the default view for all folders of the current type, and you can change specific view settings.*

**28.** Scroll the **Advanced settings** list, and notice the ways you can change the folder window display.

By default, Windows 7 system folders and files that have been assigned a hidden attribute are not shown, and extensions for known file types are hidden. If you want to be able to determine the type of a file in all views, you can display file names with their extensions (for example, cat.jpg) for all types of files by clearing the Hide Extensions For Known File Types check box.

**29.** Click **Cancel** to close the **Folder Options** dialog box without changing any settings.

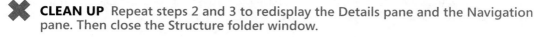 **CLEAN UP** Repeat steps 2 and 3 to redisplay the Details pane and the Navigation pane. Then close the Structure folder window.

# Working with Folder and File Properties

Every file or folder has properties associated with it, including its name, modification date, and type. You can view some of these properties by displaying the folder window in Details view. Some properties, such as the file type, are displayed in other views as well. Regardless of the view, you can display file or folder properties in the following ways:

- Select a file or folder to display some properties in the Details pane at the bottom of the folder window.
- Point to a file to display a ScreenTip listing some properties.
- Right-click a file or folder, and then click Properties to view all the available properties in the Properties dialog box.

## File Properties

Some file properties, such as size and modification date, are maintained by Windows 7 and, for obvious reasons, you cannot change them. Other properties are maintained by the program in which you work with the file, and you can assign or change them in that program or in Windows Explorer at any time. Because properties can make it easier to search for a particular file, you might want to get in the habit of assigning the following properties, if they are available:

- Title (helpful if the file name is not an intuitive indicator of the contents of the file)
- Authors
- Subject (helpful for graphics files)
- Tags (also known as *keywords*; helpful for identifying potential terms that people might use to search for the file)
- Comments
- Rating (for graphics files; from zero to five stars)

**Tip** Some types of files, including .rtf files, .txt files, and .png files, do not have associated file properties other than those maintained by Windows. Other types of files, such as those created in Microsoft Office programs, have properties that are accessible only if the associated program is installed on your computer.

You can add a title, author information, or tags to some types of files directly in the Details pane of the folder window, and you can add and change all the editable properties in a file's Properties dialog box. This dialog box has four tabs:

- **General**  This tab displays overview information about the file. You can change the default program used to open the file, and you can set attributes that control archiving and encryption.

- **Security**  You cannot set a password for a file or folder in Windows, but you can assign access permissions to specific users or groups of users on this tab.

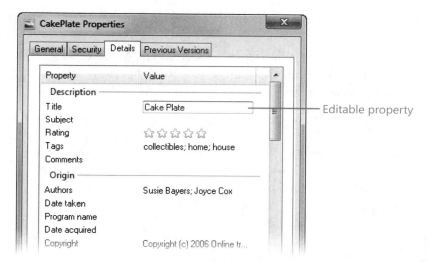

On the Details tab of the Properties dialog box, you can assign and change a file's editable properties.

**Tip**  You can assign a rating to an image file that supports ratings on either the Details tab of the Properties dialog box or in the Details pane of the folder window. Pointing to a star on the Rating scale changes the color of the star and its predecessors to gold. Clicking a star records the change. For example, to assign a four-star rating, click the fourth star. The color of the first four stars changes to gold to indicate the rating.

- **Details**  This tab lists all the properties assigned to the file, which vary depending on the file type. If a property can be added or changed, pointing to the right of the property in the Value column displays a box containing the existing property or instructions about the type of information to add.

- **Previous Versions**  This tab lists other versions of the file, saved with Windows Backup restore points, that you can revert to.

**See Also**  For information about folder and file security, restore points, and restoring previous versions of files, see *Windows 7 Step by Step Deluxe Edition*, by Joan Preppernau and Joyce Cox (Microsoft Press, 2010).

## Folder Properties

The Properties dialog box for folders has the same General, Security, and Previous Versions tabs providing the same information as the corresponding tabs in a file's Properties dialog box. It also includes a Sharing tab on which you can set options for sharing the folder with colleagues on a network.

**See Also** For information about sharing folders, see "Sharing Files on Your Network" in Chapter 3, "Manage Your Network."

When you view some folders from the Computers group of the Navigation pane (not from the Libraries group) and then display the Properties dialog box, the dialog box also has a Customize tab.

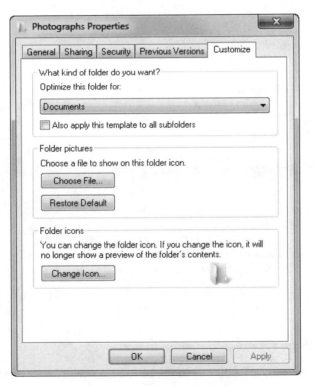

*On the Customize tab of the Properties dialog box for a folder, you can assign a template and change the appearance of the folder icon.*

On the Customize tab, you an specify the following.

- The template that controls the tools available on the toolbar in the folder window and the default view in which the folder's contents are displayed in the Content pane.

You can optimize folders for the type of content you store in them by assigning one of four templates: Documents, Pictures, Music, and Videos. If it makes more sense to store all related files, no matter what their type, in a single folder, you can assign the catch-all General Items template to the folder.

● The picture that appears on the folder icon (available only for those folder icons that display an image).

● The icon that represents the folder.

**Tip** The Properties dialog box of a system-created folder, such as the Program Files folder, does not include a Customize tab. Some folders have a Customize tab but don't include the options to change the folder icon or the picture on the icon.

In this exercise, you'll view the properties of a selected file in the Details pane, add file properties from the Details pane and from the Properties dialog box, and apply a template to a folder.

**SET UP** You need the practice files and folders located in your Documents\Microsoft Press\ Windows7SBS\Structure folder to complete this exercise. Start Windows Explorer, and ensure that the Navigation and Details panes are open and the Preview and Library panes are closed. From the Libraries group in the Navigation pane, display the Structure folder contents in Details view, and then follow the steps.

1. In the **Content** pane, click the **CakePlate** image file.

   The Details pane at the bottom of the folder window displays some of the selected file's properties.

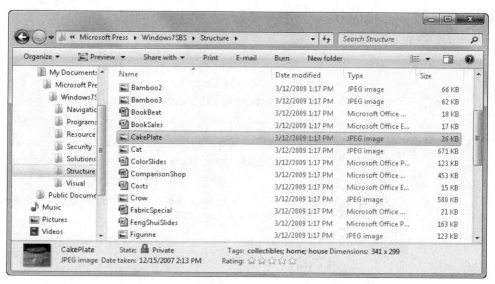

*The properties of an image file include its size in pixels and its rating.*

**2.** In the **Content** pane, click the **Cat** file. Then in the **Details** pane, click **Add a tag**.

The Tags property changes to a text box in which you can enter keywords.

**3.** In the **Tags** box, type **animals**, and then click **Save**.

**Tip** Windows Explorer automatically inserts a semicolon after your entry. Multiple tags must be separated by semicolons.

Windows 7 updates the file properties, and the tag appears in the Details pane.

**4.** In the **Content** pane, point to **Cat**.

A ScreenTip displays several of the file's properties.

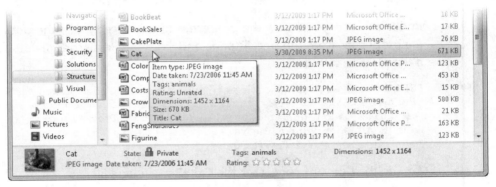

*The properties of the selected file include the tag you just created.*

**5.** Right-click **Cat**, click **Properties**, and then in the **Cat Properties** dialog box, click the **Details** tab.

**6.** Point to **animals** to the right of **Tags**, click an empty area of the box that appears, type **critters**, and then click **OK**.

**7.** In the **Content** pane, click the **Crow** image file, and then on the **Organize** menu, click **Properties**. On the **Details** tab of the **Crow Properties** dialog box, point to the right of **Tags**, click the box to activate it for editing, type **c**, and then wait a few seconds.

A list of tags appears. The tag list includes all tags currently in use that contain the letter you typed in the Tags box. When you search your computer for files, search results include files with names or tags that match the search term.

**See Also** For information about searching for files, see "Finding Specific Information" in Chapter 4, "Navigate Windows and Folders."

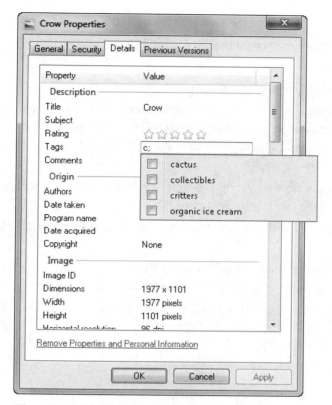

*File properties include "tags" you assign to the file.*

**8.** Select the **critters** check box to assign that tag to the **Crow** file.

Now when you search for all files associated with *critters*, this file will be part of the search results.

**9.** Click **OK** to close the dialog box.

**10.** At the top of the **Content** pane, double-click the **Videos** folder.

The folder contents appear in Details view. The Type column indicates that the item in this folder is a Windows Media Audio/Video file.

**Troubleshooting** The default view for a folder can be overridden by selections you make from the Views list. If the Videos folder is not displayed in Details view, switch to that view before continuing with the exercise.

**11.** Right-click a blank area of the **Content** pane, and then click **Properties**.

Because you are accessing this folder from a library, the Properties dialog box has no Customize tab.

**12.** Close the **Videos Properties** dialog box.

**13.** In the **Navigation** pane, expand the **Computer** group, and navigate to the **C:\Users\ <user account name>\My Documents\Microsoft Press\Windows7SBS\ Structure\Videos** folder. Right-click a blank area of the **Content** pane, and then click **Properties**.

Because you are now accessing the Videos folder from the Computer group, the Properties dialog box has a Customize tab.

**14.** Click the **Customize** tab, and in the **Optimize this folder for** list, click **Videos**. Then click **OK**.

The folder contents now appear in Large Icons view, because the Videos template designates that view as the one most suited to quickly identifying videos.

**Tip** Changing the folder type doesn't affect the display of the folder contents when you view it from inside a library. Libraries independently control the display of folder contents.

 **CLEAN UP** Close the Videos folder window.

**Tip** You can quickly remove the properties from a file you have created (but not from a folder) by selecting the file and then clicking Remove Properties on the Organize menu. In the Remove Properties dialog box, you can select the properties you want to remove. (You can also open the Remove Properties dialog box by clicking the Remove Properties And Personal Information link at the bottom of the Details tab of the file's Properties dialog box.)

# Creating and Renaming Folders and Files

With each program you use on your computer, you create files of a specific type. The files you create with most programs are only temporary until you save them on your hard disk or in another location, such as on a USB flash drive. (Certain programs that create more complex files must save a file or file structure to a specific location when creating a file.) Each program may have a default location for saving new files—for example, in your Documents folder or in a program-specific folder.

**See Also** For more information about file types, see "Specifying Default Programs" in Chapter 11, "Work with Programs."

As you create files, you'll find it easier to keep them organized logically if you also create folders in which to store the files. If you work with only a few files, your folder structure can be fairly simple. However, as you accumulate more and more files, you might need to refine the structure by creating new folders and renaming existing folders and files to accurately reflect their content.

In this exercise, you'll create a folder and two files: a text document and a picture. You'll then rename a file and a folder.

**SET UP** You need the practice files and folders located in your Documents\Microsoft Press\ Windows7SBS\Structure folder to complete this exercise. Start Windows Explorer, and ensure that the Navigation and Details panes are open and the Preview and Library panes are closed. From the Libraries group in the Navigation pane, display the Structure folder contents in Details view, and then follow the steps.

1. On the toolbar, click **New folder**.

   **Troubleshooting** The New Folder button appears on the toolbar only when no specific file is selected.

   A new folder appears in the Navigation pane (if the Structure folder is expanded) and in the Content pane.

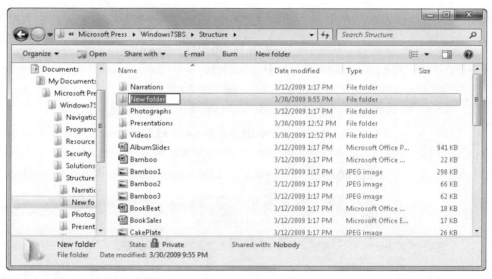

*In the Content pane, the new folder's temporary name is selected so that you can easily change it.*

   **Troubleshooting** If the folder name is not selected for editing, press F2.

2. With the folder name selected for editing, type **My New Folder**, and then press **Enter**.

   The renamed folder moves into alphanumeric order.

3. Press **Enter** again to open the empty folder.

4. Right-click anywhere in the **Content** pane, and then click **New**.

   The New menu appears. You can create a variety of items from this menu.

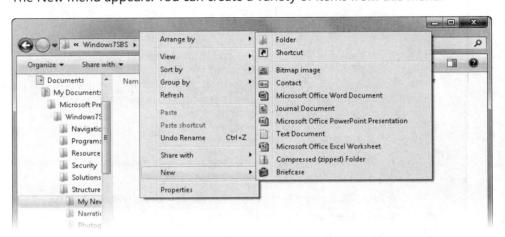

*The contents of the New menu vary depending on the programs that are installed.*

5. On the **New** menu, click **Text Document**.

   A new text document is created, with its temporary name *New Text Document* selected so that you can change it.

6. Double-click **New**, type **My** followed by a space, and then press **Enter**.

7. If the **Name**, **Date modified**, **Type**, and **Size** property columns are not visible in the window, adjust the column widths so that they are.

   The properties of the My Text Document file are displayed in the Content pane.

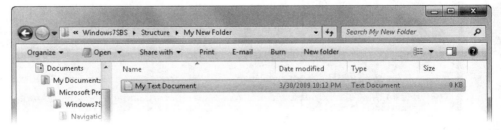

*In Details view, you see the new file's name, creation date, type, and size (0 KB, because the file is empty).*

**See Also** For information about sizing columns in Details view, see "Viewing Folders and Files in Different Ways" earlier in this chapter.

8. Press **Enter** again to open the file.

The text document opens in Microsoft Notepad, the text-editing program that comes with Windows 7.

**Troubleshooting** If the text document opens in a different program, that program has been designated as your default text editor. The next two steps in this exercise will be the same regardless of the program you use.

9. Type **This is a text file.**

10. Click the **Close** button to close the file, and click **Save** when prompted to save your changes.

After you save the file, its size in the Content pane is 1 KB, because the size is rounded up to the nearest whole kilobyte. The actual size of the file is about 20 bytes, as reported in the Details pane. (You might have to click the file in the Content pane to update the Details pane.)

11. Right-click a blank area of the **Content** pane, click **New**, and then click **Bitmap Image**.

A new image file is created, with the name *New Bitmap Image* selected so that you can change it.

**Tip** A bitmap image is made up of dots, called *pixels*, and is saved in the bitmap (.bmp) format.

12. Change the name of the file to **My Bitmap Image**.

When you rename the file, it moves to the top of the file list to maintain the alphanumeric sort order.

13. Right-click the image file, and then click **Edit**.

The blank image file opens in Microsoft Paint, the simple graphics program that comes with Windows 7.

**Troubleshooting** If the image opens in a different program, that program has been designated as your default graphics editor. The next step in this exercise will be the same regardless of the program you use.

14. Experiment with the Paint tools while creating a picture of any kind. (Click a tool, move the pointer over the blank canvas, and drag the pointer to use the tool.) When you're done, close the file, saving your changes.

In the Content pane, the Size column reflects the size of the graphic. The Details pane displays a thumbnail depicting the graphic you created, and reports the file's dimensions as well as its size. If you want, you can switch to one of the icon views to see an image of the graphic.

**15.** Right-click **My Bitmap Image**, click **Rename** to activate the file name for editing, and click to the right of *Image*. Press the **Backspace** key to delete *Image*, type **Graphic**, and then press **Enter**.

> **Tip**  By default, file name extensions are hidden. On the rare occasion when you need to change an extension, you will need to first display extensions for all files by clearing the Hide Extensions For Known File Types check box on the View tab of the Folder Options dialog box. For more information, see "Viewing Folders and Files in Different Ways" earlier in this chapter.

**16.** On the **Organize** menu, click **Undo** to change the name back to the original *My Bitmap Image*.

**17.** Click the **Back** button to redisplay the contents of the **Structure** folder.

**18.** With **My New Folder** selected in the **Content** pane, click the folder again to select its name for editing.

> **Troubleshooting**  If clicking the folder once doesn't activate the name for editing, click it once again. Be careful not to double-click, which will display the contents of the folder. If that happens, click the Back button, and try again.

**19.** Type **My Work** as the new name of the folder, and then press **Enter**.

 **CLEAN UP**  Close the Structure folder window. You will reuse the folder and files you created in this exercise for another exercise later in this chapter.

# Moving and Copying Folders and Files

You can easily move and copy folders and files from one location to another. The methods of moving and copying are the same for both folders and files.

Before you can move or copy files and folders, you need to select them. For efficiency, it helps to be familiar with various ways to select multiple items in the Content pane of a folder window. Briefly, these techniques are as follows:

- Select all the items in a folder by clicking Select All on the Organize menu.

  > **Keyboard Shortcut**  You can select all the files and folders in a folder by clicking any one item and then pressing Ctrl+A.

- Select contiguous folders and/or files by clicking the first item, holding down the Shift key, and clicking the last item.

- Select noncontiguous items by clicking the first item, holding down the Ctrl key, and clicking each other item you want to add to the selection.

- If a check box appears to the left of the Name column heading in Details view, you can select all the items in the displayed folder by selecting the check box. You can select an individual item by pointing to it and selecting its check box.

  **Tip** Depending on your installation of Windows 7, check boxes might be turned on or off by default. To turn them on, click Folder And Search Options on the Organize menu, display the View tab of the Folder Options dialog box, select the Use Check Boxes To Select Items check box in the Advanced Settings list, and then click OK.

When multiple files are selected, the Details pane indicates the number of items and the total size of the selection. (Because the file sizes in the Content pane are rounded up, the total in the Details pane will be more accurate.) If folders and files are included in the selection, the Details pane indicates the number of items but not the cumulative size.

You can use a variety of methods to move or copy one or more selected files or folders.

To move a selected item from one folder to another:

- Click Cut on the Organize menu, or right-click the selection and click Cut. Display the folder where you want to move the item and then click Paste on the Organize menu, or right-click a blank area of the folder and click Paste. Or select the folder where you want to move the item, right-click the selected folder, and then click Paste.

  **Tip** When you cut or copy a folder or file, the item is stored in a storage area called the *Clipboard* so that you can then paste one or more copies of it elsewhere.

- Use the left mouse button to drag the selection to the desired location.

- Use the right mouse button to drag the selection to the desired location, and then click Move Here on the shortcut menu that appears when you release the mouse button.

  **Tip** When you drag a folder or file, the item is not stored on the Clipboard.

  **Keyboard Shortcut** You can cut an item to the Clipboard by pressing Ctrl+X, and paste the Clipboard contents by pressing Ctrl+V.

To create a copy of a selected item:

- Click Copy on the Organize menu, or right-click the selection and click Copy. Display the folder where you want to copy the item, and then click Paste on the Organize menu, or right-click a blank area of the folder and click Paste. Or select the folder where you want to move the item, right-click the selected folder, and then click Paste.

  **Tip** You can use these methods to create a copy of a file in its original folder. Windows Explorer will append – *Copy* to the original filename.

- Hold down the Ctrl key, use the left mouse button to drag the selection to the desired location, release the mouse button, and then release the Ctrl key.

● Use the right mouse button to drag the selection to the desired location, and then click Copy Here on the shortcut menu that appears when you release the mouse button.

**Keyboard Shortcut** You can copy an item to the Clipboard by pressing Ctrl+C, and paste the Clipboard contents by pressing Ctrl+V.

In this exercise, you'll make copies of files and folders and then move files between folders.

**SET UP** You need the practice files and folders located in your Documents\Microsoft Press\ Windows7SBS\Structure folder to complete this exercise. Start Windows Explorer, and from the Libraries group in the Navigation pane, display the Structure folder contents in Details view. Ensure that the Navigation, Library, and Details panes are open and the Preview pane is closed, and then follow the steps.

1. In the **Content** pane, click the **Introduction** audio file to select it. Then on the **Organize** menu, click **Copy**.

    No visible change occurs, but the file has been stored on the Clipboard.

2. At the top of the **Content** pane, right-click the **Narrations** folder, and then click **Paste**.

    **Troubleshooting** Be sure to right-click the folder name rather than the blank space to the right of the name. If the folder doesn't appear to be selected when you right-click it, step 2 will paste a copy of the file into the original Structure folder rather than the intended Narrations folder.

    The folder's modification date changes to reflect that you have modified its contents.

3. Double-click the **Narrations** folder.

    The folder's contents are displayed in the Content pane.

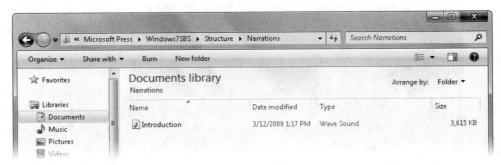

*The Narrations folder now contains a copy of the Introduction file. The original file remains in the Structure folder.*

**Tip** The Narrations folder is designated as a Music folder. The special properties of the folder template aren't available when you access it from the Libraries group, but if you access this folder from the Computer group, a Play All button appears on the toolbar so that you can play the audio file if you want. For more information, see the sidebar "Folder Templates in Libraries" later in this topic.

4. Click the **Back** button to return to the Structure folder. In the **Content** pane, right-click the **Cat** image, and then click **Cut**.

The Cat image file remains in place.

| Name | Date modified | Type | Size |
|------|---------------|------|------|
| CakePlate | 3/12/2009 1:17 PM | JPEG image | 26 KB |
| Cat | 3/12/2009 1:17 PM | JPEG image | 671 KB |
| ColorSlides | 3/12/2009 1:17 PM | Microsoft Office PowerPoint Pre... | 123 KB |
| ComparisonShop | 3/12/2009 1:17 PM | Microsoft Office Word Document | 453 KB |
| Costs | 3/12/2009 1:17 PM | Microsoft Office Excel Worksheet | 15 KB |
| Crow | 3/12/2009 1:17 PM | JPEG image | 580 KB |

*The Cat file's icon is dimmed to indicate that you have cut it from the folder.*

5. At the top of the **Content** pane, right-click the **Photographs** folder, and then click **Paste**.

The Cat image moves to the Photographs folder.

**Tip** If you move or copy a selection to the incorrect location, you can reverse the action by clicking Undo on the Organize menu before you take any other action.

**Keyboard Shortcut** You can undo the most recent action by pressing Ctrl+Z, and restore an undone action, or repeat the most recent action, by pressing Ctrl+Y.

6. Click the **Type** column heading to sort the files by type.

7. If necessary, scroll the **Content** pane until you can see the **Photographs** folder and the **Crow** and **Frog** files.

8. Click **Crow**, hold down the **Ctrl** key, click **Frog**, and then release the **Ctrl** key. Drag the selected files upward to the **Photographs** folder, and pause before releasing the mouse button.

The destination folder is highlighted, and a ScreenTip appears.

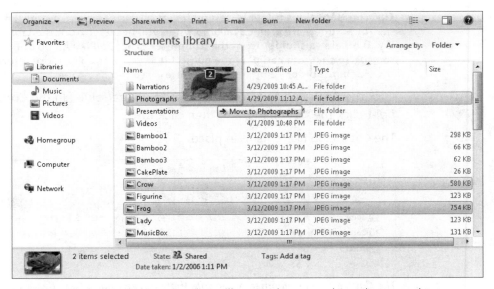

*The ScreenTip indicates the action that will occur when you release the mouse button.*

9. Release the mouse button to move the files.

10. In the **Navigation** pane, expand the practice file folders until the **Structure** folder is expanded (if it isn't already expanded).

11. From the **Content** pane, right-drag the **MusicBox** file to the **Photographs** folder in the **Navigation** pane.

    A shortcut menu appears.

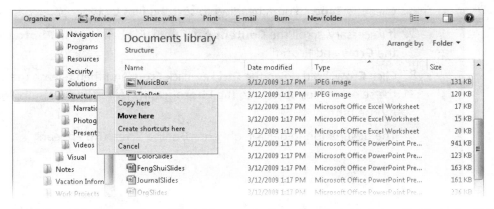

*Dragging while holding down the right mouse button allows you to choose the desired action from a shortcut menu.*

**12.** Click **Move here**.

The selected file moves to the folder.

**13.** In the **Navigation** pane, click the **Photographs** folder to display its contents in the **Content** pane. Then in the **Views** list, click **Extra Large Icons**.

**14.** Click the first image in the **Content** pane (**Cat**).

The toolbar changes to display context-specific commands.

*Commands you might want to carry out with the selected image are represented by buttons on the toolbar.*

✖ **CLEAN UP**  Close the Photographs folder window.

## Compressing Folders and Files

When you buy a computer these days, it likely comes with a hard disk that will store several gigabytes (GB) of information. A gigabyte is 1 billion bytes, and a byte is a unit of information that is the equivalent of one character. Some of your files will be very small—1 to 2 kilobytes (KB), or 1000 to 2000 characters—and others might be quite large—several megabytes (MB), or several million characters. The small ones are easy to copy and move around, but large files or large groups of files are easier to copy and move from one place to another, or to send by e-mail, if you compress them.

**Tip** Compressing is frequently referred to as *zipping*.

You can compress the files you create, program files, or even entire folders. The result is a compressed folder that is identified by a zipper on its folder icon.

To compress a file or folder:

1.  In the Content pane, select the file, files, or folder you want to compress.

2.  Right-click the selection, click Send To, and then click Compressed (Zipped) Folder.

    A compressed folder named for one of the selected files is created. The folder name is selected so that you can change it.

3.  Edit the name as necessary, and then press Enter.

To view the contents of a compressed folder, you can click it in the Navigation pane or double-click it in the Contents pane, just like any other folder. The Content pane then displays the files that have been compressed into the zipped folder. The Extract All Files button on the toolbar and the zipped folder icon in the Details pane indicate that you are viewing a compressed folder rather than a standard folder.

To extract the files from a compressed folder:

1. Display the contents of the compressed folder in the Content pane. Then, on the toolbar, click Extract All Files.

   The Extract Compressed (Zipped) Folders dialog box opens.

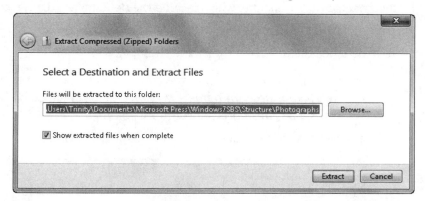

   *You can specify the location to which you want to extract the contents of the folder.*

   **Tip** You can also display this dialog box by right-clicking the compressed folder in either the Navigation pane or the Content pane and then clicking Extract All.

   The default extraction location is a new folder with the same name as the compressed folder, created in the folder that contains the compressed folder.

2. If you want to extract the files to a folder other than the one indicated in the Files Will Be Extracted To This Folder box, click Browse and then, in the Select A Destination dialog box, navigate to the desired folder.

3. Click Extract.

## Folder Templates in Libraries

The Pictures folder template has been applied to the Photographs folder. However, the template functionality isn't available when you access the folder through the Libraries group. If you browse to the folder from the Computer group, you can see the effects of the template, which include the default view (Large Icons) and a Slide Show button on the toolbar.

To experience the effects of the Pictures template:

1. From the Computer group in the Navigation pane, browse to the C:\Users\<*your account name*>\My Documents\Microsoft Press\ Windows7SBS\Structure\Photographs folder.

   The folder's contents are displayed in Large Icons view.

   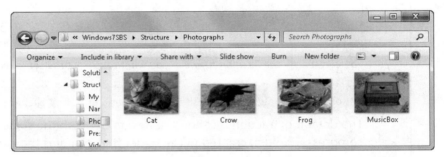

   *When the contents of a Picture folder are displayed, the toolbar includes a Slide Show button.*

2. Click the first image in the Content pane (Cat), and then, on the toolbar, click Slide Show.

   The Cat image is displayed full-screen. After three seconds, the Crow image appears, followed by the Frog and MusicBox images.

3. After the slide show cycles through all four images, press Esc to end the slide show.

**Tip** If pressing Esc doesn't end the slide show, right-click the active image, and then click Exit.

# Deleting and Recovering Folders and Files

Periodically, you'll want to delete folders and files you no longer need. Removing a file from your computer is a two-step process: You first delete the file, which moves it to the Recycle Bin—a holding area on your hard disk from which it's possible to restore an item if you realize you need it. Then you empty the Recycle Bin, which permanently erases its contents.

By default, Windows prompts you to confirm the deletion of files and folders. If you prefer, you can turn off this setting by clearing the Display Delete Confirmation Dialog check box in the Recycle Bin Properties dialog box.

You can recover a deleted file from the Recycle Bin at any time until you empty the Recycle Bin. When you recover a file, Windows restores the file to its original location. You can't open and work with files directly from the Recycle Bin.

In this exercise, you'll delete one of the files you created in an earlier exercise in this chapter, and then you'll delete the entire folder. You'll also recover both the folder and the file from the Recycle Bin.

**SET UP** You need the My Work folder and the My Text Document and My Bitmap Image files that you created earlier, as well as the practice files in your Documents\ Microsoft Press\Windows7SBS\Structure folder, to complete this exercise. (If you did not create the folder and files, you can use a folder and files of your own.) Display the contents of the My Work folder from the Libraries group, and then follow the steps.

1. In the **Content** pane, click **My Bitmap Image** to select it. Then press the **Delete** key.

   **Tip** You cannot delete a file by pressing the Backspace key.

   The Delete File dialog box opens.

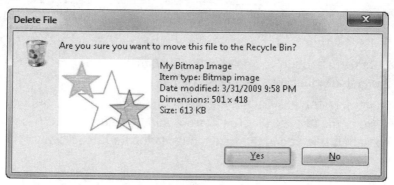

*Windows prompts you to confirm the deletion.*

2. Click **Yes** to confirm the deletion and send the file to the Recycle Bin.

   The My Bitmap Image file disappears from the folder.

3. On the **Organize** menu, click **Undo**.

   The My Bitmap Image file reappears in the My Work folder.

4. Repeat steps 1 and 2 to delete the My Bitmap Image file again.

5. In the **Address** bar, click **Structure** to display the contents of the **Structure** folder.

6. In the **Content** pane, right-click the **Introduction** file, click **Delete**, and then click **Yes** when prompted to confirm the deletion.

7. In the **Content** pane, click the **My Work** folder. On the **Organize** menu, click **Delete**, and then confirm the deletion.

8. On the desktop, double-click the **Recycle Bin** icon.

   The Recycle Bin window opens.

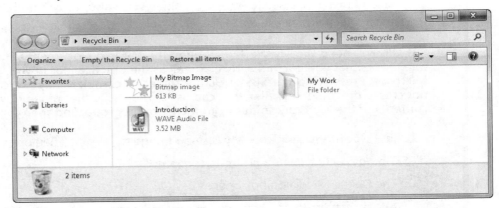

*The Content pane of the Recycle Bin window displays all the files and folders you have deleted.*

Note that although you deleted the My Bitmap Image file from the My Work folder, it is an individual item in the Recycle Bin.

The Empty The Recycle Bin button on the toolbar permanently deletes all the items in the Recycle Bin. The Restore All Items button, which is visible only when no item is selected in the folder, puts all the items back where they came from.

9. In the **Content** pane, click the **Introduction** file and then, on the toolbar, click **Restore this item**.

10. Restore first the **My Work** folder and then the **My Bitmap Image** file.

   **Tip** You can't choose specific files to be restored from a deleted folder; you can restore only the entire folder. If you restore the My Bitmap Image file before you restore the My Work folder from which it was deleted, Windows 7 re-creates the folder. (However, this version of the folder will not contain the My Text Document file.) If you then restore the deleted My Work folder, Windows 7 asks whether you want to merge the two folders into one.

11. Close the **Recycle Bin** window.

   **Important** Your Recycle Bin may contain additional files that you deleted before working through this exercise. Complete step 12 of this exercise only if you are certain that you no longer need any of the files.

12. On the desktop, right-click the **Recycle Bin** icon, and click **Empty Recycle Bin**. Then click **Yes** to confirm that you want to delete the remaining files in the bin.

13. Display the contents of the restored **My Work** folder to verify that both its files have been restored.

 **CLEAN UP** Close the My Work folder window.

---

### Recycle Bin Size

The contents of the Recycle Bin take up space on your hard disk. By default, 10 percent of a disk up to 40 GB in size is allocated to the Recycle Bin, plus 5 percent of any space over 40 GB. If your hard disk is divided into partitions, the Recycle Bin might quickly become full. For example, if the Recycle Bin is on a 10 GB partition, only 1 GB is available for deleted files.

When deleting a very large file, Windows might inform you that the file is too large to store in the Recycle Bin and that it will delete it permanently. If you're sure you won't need to recover the file, you can give the go-ahead; if not, you can cancel the deletion. On a small hard disk or drive partition, you might see this "too large" message quite often.

You might need to restrict the amount of space used by the Recycle Bin, or you might want to instruct Windows to bypass the Recycle Bin entirely. Both of these options are available from the Recycle Bin Properties dialog box.

# Creating Shortcuts

You can make folders and files that you use often more easily accessible by creating shortcuts to them—on the desktop, on the Start menu, on the taskbar, or in the Windows Explorer Favorites group.

## Desktop Shortcuts

Desktop shortcuts are links on your desktop to programs, folders, and files in other locations. These shortcuts can come from several sources:

- Windows 7 creates desktop shortcuts to five locations: the Recycle Bin, the Computer window, your personal files, your Network, and Control Panel. However, by default it displays only the Recycle Bin icon. You can display the others by selecting them in the Desktop Icon Settings window, which you open by clicking Change Desktop Icons in the Personalization window of Control Panel.

- Many programs give you the option of creating one or more desktop shortcuts during installation; some less-polite programs create shortcuts without asking.

- You can create your own desktop shortcuts to files, folders, programs, and Web pages.

The five system-created desktop shortcuts are represented by their own labeled icons. A desktop shortcut created by you or by a program is represented by a program-specific icon with a small arrow in its lower-left corner.

To create a desktop shortcut:

- Right-click an empty area of the desktop, click New, click Shortcut, and provide the path to the shortcut target.

When you no longer need a desktop shortcut that you have created, or that was created for you by an installation program, you can delete it without affecting the shortcut target (the program, folder, file, or page that the shortcut is linked to).

To keep your desktop tidy, you can arrange shortcuts in various ways. Some people like to line up their icons and shortcuts in regimented rows, some like to arrange them as a sort of frame around the perimeter of their screen, and others like to group them by type in various locations. You can organize your icons and shortcuts manually, or if you are happy with simple arrangements, you can have Windows 7 arrange them for you.

**Tip** To quickly create a desktop shortcut to another computer on your network, display the Network window, right-click the computer, and then click Create Shortcut.

## Start Menu Pinned Items

You can gain quick access to folders, files, and programs by adding links to them to the pinned items area at the top of the left pane of the Start menu.

**Tip** If the pinned items list becomes longer than the space available, causing the Start menu to exceed the height of the desktop, the list first encroaches on the Recently Used Programs list and then runs off the bottom of the page, without any indication that part of the list is not visible. Removing items from the list reveals the hidden items.

To pin an item to the Start menu, display the folder containing the item in Windows Explorer, drag the item to the Start button, and release the mouse button when the Pin To Start Menu ScreenTip appears. If you want to pin the item in a specific location, pause until the Start menu expands, and then drop the item anywhere in the pinned items area that you want. A horizontal line indicates the insertion location for the new pinned item. Similarly, you can rearrange pinned items by dragging them into whatever order you want.

You can pin an item from the desktop or from the Recently Used Programs list or All Programs list of the Start menu by right-clicking the item and then clicking Pin To Start Menu.

If you no longer need a folder, file, or program to be pinned to the Start menu, you can delete it from the Start menu by right-clicking it and then clicking Remove From This List or Unpin From Start Menu.

## Taskbar Pinned Items

You can pin programs to the Windows Taskbar for quick access, and you can pin files and folders to the programs that open them. If the pinned program buttons exceed the width of the taskbar, the taskbar expands to multiple rows that you can scroll.

**Tip** The ability to pin programs directly to the taskbar replaces the Quick Launch toolbar used for the same purpose in previous editions of Windows. Although the Quick Launch toolbar is no longer necessary, it is still available as part of the Windows code and you can display it if you really want to, by following instructions that you can find on the Internet.

To pin a program to the taskbar, display the folder or menu containing the program, and locate and select the program's executable file. (This file is usually identified as an Application in the Type column in Details view.) Drag the file to the place you want it on the taskbar, and release the mouse button when the Pin To Taskbar ScreenTip appears. Other taskbar buttons move to indicate the insertion location for the new pinned program.

To pin a file or folder to the taskbar, display the folder that contains it, and then drag the file or folder to the taskbar. A ScreenTip appears, specifying the default program for opening the file or folder. (For example, Pin To Notepad appears for a text document and Pin To Windows Explorer appears for a folder). When you release the mouse button, the file or folder is pinned to the corresponding program. (If the program isn't already pinned to the taskbar, Windows pins it there for you.) You can quickly access the pinned file or folder by right-clicking the pinned program and then clicking the file or folder on the shortcut menu that appears.

**See Also**   For information about changing where and how pinned items appear on the taskbar, see "Modifying the Taskbar" in Chapter 10, "Change System Settings."

You can change the order of pinned programs on the taskbar by dragging them. To remove a pinned program from the taskbar, right-click it and then click Unpin This Program From Taskbar.

## Favorites Group

If you frequently need access to a folder to either open or save files in it, you can add it to the Favorites group that appears at the top of the Windows Explorer Navigation pane. The Favorites group is available not only in Windows Explorer, but also in program dialog boxes that interact with Windows, such as the Open dialog box in a Microsoft Office program. You can add a folder that is on your computer or on another computer on your network to this group.

**See Also**   For information about accessing folders on other computers, see "Connecting to Network Resources" in Chapter 4, "Navigate Windows and Folders."

To add a folder to the Favorites group, display the folder (not its contents) in the Windows Explorer Content pane, drag the folder to the Favorites group in the Navigation pane, and release the mouse button when the Create Link In Favorites ScreenTip appears.

**Tip**   Dropping a folder on top of another folder in the Favorites group moves the dragged folder into the target folder, instead of creating a link in the group. Be sure to drop the dragged folder directly on the Favorites group heading or when a horizontal line indicates a location between other folders in the group.

You can change the order of folders in the Favorites group by dragging them. To remove a folder from the group, right-click the folder, and then click Remove.

In this exercise, you'll create desktop shortcuts, work with desktop icons, and pin items to the Start menu and taskbar.

 **SET UP** You need your Documents\Microsoft Press\Windows7SBS folder and the Structure subfolder to complete this exercise. Minimize or close any open windows, and then follow the steps.

1. Right-click an open area of the desktop, and then click **Personalize**.

2. In the left pane of the **Personalization** window, click **Change desktop icons**.

   The Desktop Icon Settings dialog box opens.

*In the Desktop Icon Settings dialog box, you can specify which of the five standard system areas are represented by desktop icons.*

The standard icons might be replaced when you select a theme that includes one or more personalized icons. You also have the option of changing the visual representation of each system area to an icon of your choice.

**See Also** For information about other personalization options, including themes, see Chapter 9, "Change Visual Elements."

3. Select the **User's Files** check box, and click **OK**. Then close the **Personalization** window.

The icon representing your personal folders, labeled with your user account name, appears on the desktop. Double-clicking the icon will open your user account folder in Windows Explorer.

**4.** Right-click an open area of the desktop, click **New**, and then click **Shortcut**.

A generic desktop shortcut, displaying a blank page icon and the label *New Shortcut*, appears on the desktop in the area where you clicked, and the Create Shortcut wizard starts. This wizard will prompt you for the information necessary to create a desktop shortcut.

**5.** In the **Create Shortcut** wizard, click **Browse**. In the **Browse for Files or Folders** dialog box, click the arrow to the left of **Libraries** to expand the folder. Then expand **Documents**, **My Documents**, and **Microsoft Press**. In the **Microsoft Press** folder, click **Windows7SBS**.

The Windows7SBS folder is highlighted to show that it is selected.

*You can browse to and select the folder or file for which you want to create a shortcut.*

**Troubleshooting** The specified path exists only if you installed the practice files for this book to the default installation location.

6. In the **Browse for Files or Folders** dialog box, click **OK**.

   The absolute path to the selected folder is displayed in the Type The Location Of The Item box.

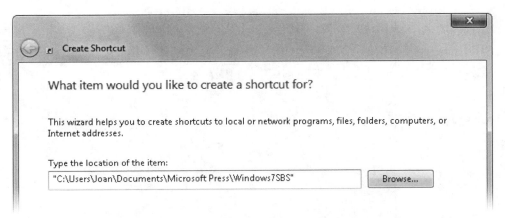

*The Type The Location Of The Item box displays the absolute path to the Windows7SBS folder contained in your Documents library.*

**See Also** For more information about libraries, see "Understanding Files, Folders, and Libraries" in Chapter 4, "Navigate Windows and Folders."

7. Click **Next**. Then on the wizard's final page, click **Finish** to change the icon and label of the generic shortcut to make them specific to the selected folder.

   **Tip** In the wizard, you can change the name that appears below the shortcut by replacing the text in the Type A Name For This Shortcut box with the name you want. After you create the shortcut, you can change its name by clicking its icon, clicking its name to select it for editing, and then typing the new name.

   Now you can open the folder containing the practice files for this book simply by double-clicking the shortcut.

   **Tip** You can change the size of your desktop icons and desktop shortcuts by right-clicking the desktop, pointing to View, and then clicking Large Icons or Small Icons. (The default selection is Medium Icons.)

8. Right-click an open area of the desktop, click **New**, and then click **Shortcut**.

9. In the **Create Shortcut** wizard, in the **Type the location of the item** box, type **www.msn.com**. Then click **Next**.

   **Tip** When you are creating a shortcut to a Web site or page that follows a standard naming convention, it is not necessary to include *http://* in the location; the shortcut works with or without it.

10. In the **Type a name for this shortcut** box, replace *New Internet Shortcut* with **MSN Web Site**. Then click **Finish**.

The wizard creates a shortcut to the specified site.

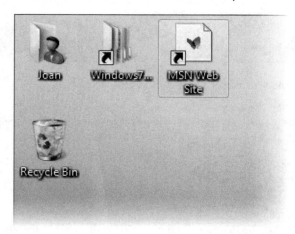

*The Web site shortcut is represented by the Internet Explorer icon, or by a custom icon specified by the site code.*

11. Drag your desktop shortcuts to random positions on the desktop.

Notice that as you drop the shortcuts, they align to an invisible grid.

12. Right-click an open area of the desktop, and click **View**.

The View shortcut menu appears.

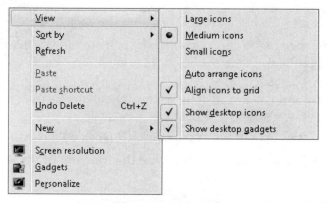

*By default, desktop icons are aligned to an invisible grid, so they appear in neat rows and columns.*

**13.** On the **View** shortcut menu, click **Auto arrange icons**.

Windows 7 neatly arranges the icons on the left side of the desktop.

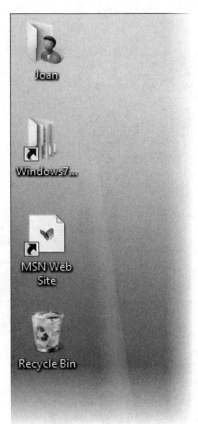

*Icons are arranged automatically in columns on the desktop.*

**14.** Drag the bottom icon to the upper-right corner of the desktop.

When you release the mouse button, the icon moves to the upper-left corner of the desktop, instead. Because the Auto Arrange feature is turned on, you cannot move the icons away from the group at the left edge of the screen, but you can rearrange them vertically.

**Tip** When the first column is full, subsequent icons form additional columns. You can move icons vertically and horizontally within the columns. When you move or delete an icon, Windows rearranges the remaining icons.

**15.** Drag the **Windows7SBS** desktop shortcut to the **Start** button, pause until the **Start** menu expands, drag the icon to the pinned items section, and pause again.

A horizontal line shows where the new pinned item will be inserted.

*The horizontal line and ScreenTip indicate that the pointer is in the pinned items section of the Start menu.*

**16.** Release the mouse button.

The desktop shortcut appears in the pinned items section.

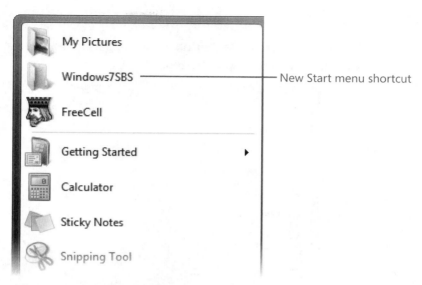

The Windows7SBS folder is pinned to the Start menu.

Notice that although you dragged a desktop shortcut (as indicated by the arrow in its lower-left corner) to the Start menu, the pinned item is a link directly to the folder.

**Tip** To pin a program to the Start menu, drag it from the All Programs list to the Start button, pause until the Start menu opens, and then continue dragging up to the pinned programs section.

**17.** In the pinned items section of the **Start** menu, click the **Windows7SBS** folder.

The folder opens in Windows Explorer.

**18.** In the **Windows7SBS** folder window, click the **Structure** folder to select it. Then drag it to the taskbar.

A ScreenTip tells you where the selected item will be pinned.

When the pointer reaches the taskbar, the ScreenTip changes to Pin To Windows Explorer.

**Troubleshooting** As you drag the folder across the desktop, the ScreenTip reads *Move To Desktop*. Dropping the folder on the desktop while this ScreenTip is displayed moves the folder from its current location to the desktop.

**19.** Release the mouse button.

The Windows Explorer taskbar button menu appears. (This menu also appears when you right-click the taskbar button.)

*The folder has been added to the Pinned section of the Windows Explorer taskbar button menu.*

**20.** On the **Windows Explorer** taskbar button menu, click the **Structure** folder.

The folder opens in a new Windows Explorer window.

**21.** Drag the **Bamboo1** image file to the taskbar, releasing the mouse button when the ScreenTip displays *Pin to Paint*.

**Troubleshooting** If a slashed circle (⊘) appears when you drag the file to the taskbar, then the file type is not associated with a program that is supported by the taskbar. If this occurs, right-click the Bamboo1 file, click Open With, and then click Choose Default Program. In the Open With dialog box, click Paint, and then click OK. Then close the Paint window that opens, and repeat step 21.

A Paint button appears on the taskbar, with its menu expanded and the Bamboo1 file in the Pinned section.

**22.** Drag the **Paint** taskbar button to the left end of the taskbar, to the right of the **Start** button.

The other taskbar buttons move aside.

**23.** Right-click the **Paint** taskbar button, point to **Bamboo1**, and then click the **Unpin from this list** button that appears on the right.

The file disappears from the Pinned section, but the program remains pinned to the taskbar.

**24.** On the **Paint** taskbar button menu, click **Unpin this program from taskbar**.

The Paint taskbar button disappears.

**25.** Close the **Structure** folder window. In the **Windows7SBS** folder window, drag the **Structure** folder from the **Content** pane to the **Favorites** group heading in the **Navigation** pane.

**Troubleshooting** Be sure to drop the folder on the Favorites heading and not in the group content.

The folder appears at the bottom of the list.

**26.** In the **Navigation** pane, drag the folder upward, and drop it below the **Desktop** folder.

A horizontal line shows where the new favorite will be inserted.

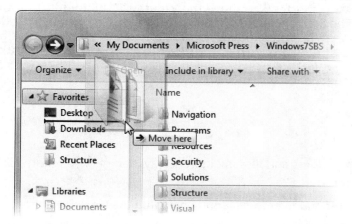

*The horizontal line and ScreenTip indicate where the item will appear in the Favorites group.*

**27.** In the **Favorites** group, click the **Desktop** folder.

The Desktop folder contents appear in the Content pane.

*In the Desktop folder window, all the available desktop icons are visible, along with the desktop shortcuts you created at the beginning of this exercise.*

 **CLEAN UP** Close all open windows. If you want, delete the Windows7SBS and MSN Web Site desktop shortcuts, remove the Windows7SBS folder from the pinned items area of the Start menu, unpin the Structure folder from the Windows Explorer taskbar button menu, and remove the same folder from the Favorites group. Then repeat steps 1 through 3 to display the desktop icons you want. If you don't like the Auto Arrange feature, right-click an open area of the desktop, click View, and then click Auto Arrange Icons to turn it off.

# Key Points

- Displaying folders and files in different ways can help you more easily identify their contents.

- You can sort and filter folder contents to find the file you want.

- The properties stored with a file can be viewed, and some properties can be changed, in the file's Properties dialog box.

- To organize folders and files in a logical structure, you can create folders, and you can rename, move, copy, and delete both folders and files.

- Desktop shortcuts provide a quick way to open the folders, files, programs, and Web sites you access most frequently. You can also add objects to the Start menu or taskbar, or add them to your Favorites group.

# Part 2

# Experiencing the World Wide Web

# Chapter at a Glance

Connect to the Internet, **page 201**

Display Web sites, **page 208**

Work with tabs and pages, **page 214**

# 6 Connect to the Web

**In this chapter, you will learn how to**

✔ Connect to the Internet.

✔ Set up Internet Explorer 8.

✔ Display Web sites.

✔ Work with tabs and pages.

The Internet is a worldwide computer network consisting of millions of smaller networks that exchange information. Originally constructed and used by governments and large organizations for the exchange of text-based data, the Internet evolved almost overnight with the implementation by English computer scientist Sir Timothy Berners-Lee in 1990 of a prototype for the World Wide Web, now referred to simply as *the Web*. While combining the existing concept of hypertext with the communication structure of the Internet, Berners-Lee developed the system of hyperlinks (links from content to other content in the same or a different document) and Uniform Resource Locators (URLs), that paved the way for the global exchange of information we take for granted today.

**Tip** The prefix *hyper* comes from the Ancient Greek language; it means *over*, *above*, *beyond*, or *excessive*, and is commonly used in Web terminology. *Hypertext* refers to text that you can link from or to. *Hypermedia* refers to audio, video, and graphic elements you can link from or to. *Hyperlinks* connect hypertext and hypermedia elements. Together these terms bring to mind an image of bits of information frenetically zinging all over the world, and that seems like a reasonably appropriate representation of the Web.

Browsing the Web (commonly referred to as *surfing the Web*) has become a form of entertainment in itself, as well as a simple and powerful research tool that literally puts a world of information at your fingertips. Students, teachers, business people, shoppers, gamers, and others can now find almost any information or entertainment they want on the Web. With a high-speed Internet connection, you can stream live radio programs, recorded television programs, and movies from the Internet to your computer, for display on a computer monitor or television screen, in far less time than it takes to go to a video rental store.

**Tip** The Internet is the physical network over which information travels. The Web is the information space you access through a Web browser such as Internet Explorer or Firefox. The Internet transports Web traffic and other traffic including e-mail and file-transfer operations. Different protocols are used for each of these types of Internet-based communication. For information about protocols, see the sidebar "Anatomy of a Web Address" later in this chapter.

Moreover, the Web is no longer a one-way information highway for individual computer users. The advent of personal Web spaces, called *Web logs* or *blogs*, means that anyone can post anything on the Web for family, friends, and complete strangers to view and respond to. Blogs range from personal diaries and ways for communities to keep in touch to sources of information on a specific topic that are replacing traditional media in importance. They can provide on-the-spot news about current events, and because they are not constrained by printing and production processes, they can "scoop" other media with late-breaking news. Blogs are also uncensored and largely unregulated, meaning that viewers need to bear in mind that the information presented on a blog is not necessarily unbiased or correct.

Windows Internet Explorer 8, which is installed with most editions of Windows 7, is a Web browser with which you can easily find, view, search, print, and save Web pages while shielding your computer and the people who use it from exposure to malicious or objectionable content. Internet Explorer provides a framework in which you can view Web pages, and an engine with which you can perform basic tasks.

**See Also** For information about configuring security zones and restricting the viewing and downloading of objectionable content over the Internet, see Chapter 8, "Manage Internet Explorer."

In this chapter, you'll learn how to configure Internet Explorer 8 to best fit your needs and how to use some of the great features not available in previous versions of Internet Explorer. You'll also personalize the Internet Explorer browser window and content display.

---

**Practice Files** You won't need any practice files to complete the exercises in this chapter. See "Using the Practice Files" at the beginning of this book for more information.

# Connecting to the Internet

Internet access has become prevalent in workplaces and homes around the world. Many companies have an Internet presence (a Web site) and use Internet-based services to streamline operations. In the past, many employers were concerned that allowing Internet access from company-owned computers would mean a loss of productivity, because people could receive and send personal e-mail messages, divulge privileged information, indulge in surreptitious Web surfing, or download objectionable content. These days, more and more employers are coming to the conclusion that Internet access can actually enhance the productivity of people in some jobs, and many companies now provide organization-wide access.

In addition, Internet access is fast becoming one of the primary reasons for buying a home computer. Setting up a connection from your computer to the Internet is easier than ever with Windows 7. The most difficult part of the process will likely be finding out what types of connections are available from Internet service providers (ISPs) in your area and deciding which one you want to use.

To use the Internet, you must connect your computer to the ISP by using one of the following types of connections:

- **Wired connection** If your computer PC has an Ethernet adapter, you can physically connect the computer to a router by using an Ethernet cable. You can connect the computer directly to the router, to a network switch that is connected to the router, or to a network socket that is connected to the router (usually via cables hidden in the walls). The router handles the connection to the ISP.

- **Wireless connection** If your computer has a wireless network adapter, you can establish a cable-free connection to a wireless router. The wireless router may be connected by an Ethernet cable to another router that handles the connection to the ISP, or directly to the incoming connection (for example, to a cable service outlet).

- **Dial-up** If your computer has a telephone modem and your ISP offers dial-up access, you can physically connect the computer to a telephone socket by using a standard telephone cord. The modem establishes a connection to the ISP through your telephone line by placing a phone call. The connection is active only for the duration of the phone call.

Whichever type of connection you use, you can set it up from the Network And Sharing Center.

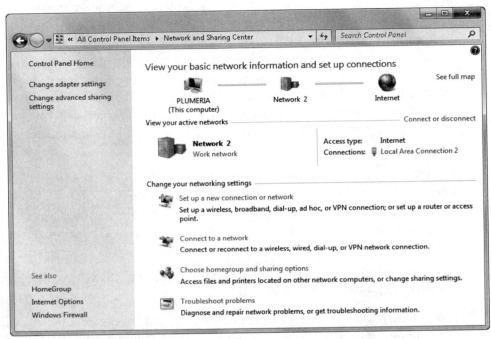

*The Network And Sharing Center, showing typical network and Internet connections.*

You can open the Network And Sharing Center in the following ways:

- In Control Panel, click Network And Internet, and then click Network And Sharing Center.
- On the Start menu, enter *network* in the Start menu Search box, and then click Network And Sharing Center in the search results list.

To create an Internet connection through an ISP, you need to first set up an account directly with the ISP, who will provide the information you need to complete the connection process in the Network And Sharing Center, such as:

- The specific IP address or the address of the DHCP server
- DNS addresses and domain names
- POP3 or IMAP settings for incoming e-mail
- SMTP settings for outgoing e-mail

**Tip** Depending on the area in which you live, you may have access to several ISPs. If you're looking for an ISP, your telephone service provider and your cable television provider are good places to start. You might also have options through a satellite television service provider, a satellite broadband service provider, or a wireless broadband service provider. If you live in a rural community, contact your local town hall for a recommendation. The town administrator will also be able to provide information about companies that have applied for permits to expand their services into your area.

# Setting Up Internet Explorer 8

The first time you start Internet Explorer, the Set Up Windows Internet Explorer 8 wizard starts. With this wizard, you can indicate whether you want to turn on the Suggested Sites feature and then either choose a package of default settings (the "express settings") for the remaining features or choose a specific setting for each feature (the "custom settings").

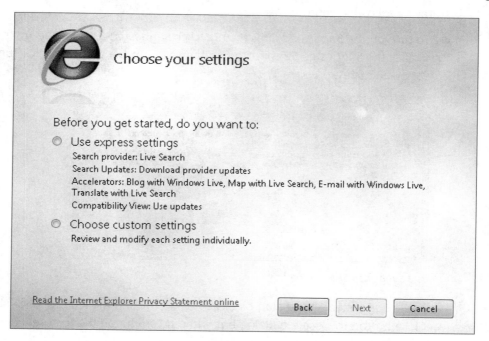

*Express settings may vary depending on your previous Internet Explorer use.*

When choosing custom settings, you can accept the default search provider and Accelerators, or you can choose to display all the available options so that you can select the ones you want.

**Troubleshooting** If you select the Choose Custom Settings option, after you complete the wizard Internet Explorer displays the custom setting options on new tabs of the current browser window. You have to click the tabs to display the options, and then select the settings you want. For information about tabs, see "Working with Tabs and Pages" later in this chapter.

If you don't want to complete the selection process, you can click Cancel on any page of the wizard to run Internet Explorer with the default settings. The wizard will start automatically and prompt you to make your selections the first time you start Internet Explorer each day, or you can set your Suggested Site, Compatibility View, and search engine preferences manually.

**See Also** For information about setting search engine preferences, see "Finding, Saving, and Returning to Web Sites" in Chapter 7, "Work with Web Pages and Sites."

You can turn on and set preferences for the Suggested Sites and Compatibility View features by following these steps:

- To turn on the Suggested Sites feature, click Suggested Sites on the Tools menu, or click the Suggested Sites button on the Favorites bar and then click Turn On Suggested Sites.

*The Suggested Sites dialog box.*

In the Suggested Sites dialog box, click Yes to turn on the feature. Click No or the Close button to close the dialog box without turning on the feature.

- To turn off the Suggested Sites feature, click Suggested Sites on the Tools menu.
- To manage the display of sites in Compatibility View, click Compatibility View Settings on the Tools menu.

*In the Compatibility View Settings dialog box, you can specify sites that you want to view in Compatibility View.*

**Tip** Some Web sites designed for older browsers may not display properly, or may cause Internet Explorer 8 to stop working properly. If you have trouble opening a site in Internet Explorer 8, add it to the Compatibility View site list, and then open it.

- If you don't want to display the Compatibility View button at the right end of the Address bar, right-click a blank part of the toolbar area and then click Compatibility View Button.

## Anatomy of a Web Address

The words, letters, numbers, and symbols that appear in the Address bar of your Internet Explorer browser window when you connect to a Web site or page might look like a logical address or like a bunch of gobbledygook. Even when you connect to a simple Web site address such as http://www.microsoft.com, the Address box contents change to include additional information about the specific page displayed. Every character has a specific purpose. Here's a breakdown of a typical Web page address and a description of what each part does.

http://movies.msn.com/showtimes/today.aspx?zip='76226'

| Protocol | Subdomain | Domain name | Folder | Page | Query |
|----------|-----------|-------------|--------|------|-------|
| http | movies | msn.com | showtimes | today.aspx | ?zip='76226' |

The *protocol* tells your Web browser what type of connection to make to the destination site. The most common protocol is *http* (Hypertext Transfer Protocol, the protocol that delivers information over the World Wide Web). Another common Web protocol is *https* (HTTP over a secure connection). In a URL, the protocol is followed by a colon and two forward slashes (://).

**Tip** There are dozens of protocols for many different types of communication, including Internet connections, e-mail delivery, file sharing, local and remote network connections, and a plethora of others. Some of the more familiar protocols include ADSL, DHCP, DNS, FTP, HTTPS, IMAP, IP, ISDN, POP3, SMTP, SOAP, TCP, and Telnet.

The *domain name* is the base address of the site. The top-level domain (TLD), such as *.com*, is part of the domain name. Each domain name is purchased and registered by an organization or individual and is assigned to an IP address representing the location of the site content on a server. Domain names and IP addresses are managed by ICANN (the Internet Corporation for Assigned Names and Numbers), a non-profit corporation based in California. Although ICANN is an American corporation, it manages Internet-related tasks worldwide in cooperation with international agencies.

When you enter the domain, your computer connects to the Internet to find out the IP address currently assigned to that domain. Then it connects to the server located at that IP address and displays the content located on that server. Because the alphabetic domain name leads you to the less-obvious IP address, the domain name is sometimes referred to as a *friendly name*.

If an address includes a *subdomain*, it points to a specific site, usually one of a group of sites presented under the umbrella of one domain name. The sites represented by the subdomains don't need to be of the same type and don't need to reside in the same location. For example, Contoso Corporation might have the registered domain name contoso.com. The company's public Web site might be located at http://www.contoso.com. The company might also have the following subdomains:

- *sharepoint* that connects to its collaboration site (http://sharepoint.contoso.com)
- *mail* that connects to its Web e-mail server (http://mail.contoso.com)
- *shopping* that connects to a secure online shopping cart application (https://shopping.contoso.com)

A *folder name* indicates the location in the Web site structure of the page on screen. In the same way that you store files within a logical folder structure on your hard disk drive, a Web site administrator might arrange files in a logical structure within the site. Single forward slashes (/) separate folders from other address elements, in the same way that single backward slashes (\) separate folders in the Windows Explorer Address bar.

The *page name* represents the specific file containing the content and/or code that generates the information displayed on the screen. The page name includes a file name extension indicating the file type. Common page name extensions include .htm for HTML files containing static content, and .aspx for Active Server Pages (ASP pages) displaying dynamic content gathered from a database or other source within a framework governed by code in the file.

An HTML page name might include a bookmark, preceded by a pound sign (#), indicating a specific location in a file. An ASP page name might include a query, preceded by a question mark (?), indicating the search term that generated the page content. In the example given at the beginning of this topic, the query *?zip='76226'* is intended to return showtimes for movies playing in the geographical area identified by the ZIP Code 76226.

When you connect to a simple Web site address, Internet Explorer uses the protocol to establish the communication method, connects to the server hosting the domain or subdomain, and then displays the page designated by the Web site administrator as the home page for the site. The typical home page is named *default* or *index*, but the Web site administrator can designate any page at the top level of the site as the home page.

> **Tip** TLDs are governed by an international organization. Each TLD has a specific meaning: There are generic TLDs (such as .com and .net) that are available to anyone, sponsored TLDs (such as .edu, .gov, and .travel) that belong to private agencies or organizations, and two-letter country code TLDs that are intended to represent the country of origin or use of a site's content. Country code TLDs are frequently used for other purposes, however; for example, the TLD .am is assigned to Armenia, and .fm is assigned to the Federated States of Micronesia, but many radio stations have Web site addresses ending in these TLDs.
>
> A recent "unrestricted generic TLD" program that was approved in 2008 will allow organizations and individuals to reserve their own TLDs that don't fit the existing rules. For example, Microsoft could apply for the TLD .msft. The initial fee to have your application evaluated has been set at $185,000, so it's unlikely a lot of individuals will be applying for the honor in the near future.

# Displaying Web Sites

Whether or not Internet Explorer 8 is your default browser, you can start it by clicking the pinned Internet Explorer button on the Windows Taskbar, and then use it to explore the Web. With all browsers, you navigate to a specific Web site by typing its address, or Uniform Resource Locator (URL), in an address box and then clicking hyperlinks to move to specific Web pages.

**Tip** Your computer keyboard may include a button that you can press to open an Internet browser window. For information about special keyboard keys, see "Your Keyboard" in "Information for New Computer Users" at the beginning of this book.

Internet Explorer 8 has several new features, including the following:

- **Suggested Sites** When this feature is turned on, Internet Explorer tracks your Internet site visits and recommends other sites that fit your personal browsing history. Links to these sites are available from the Suggested Sites Web Slice on the Favorites bar. If the menu isn't there, Suggested Sites is turned off. The Suggested Sites feature does not work when InPrivate Browsing is active.

  **See Also** For information about the InPrivate Browsing feature, see the sidebar "Keeping Your Browsing Information Private" in Chapter 8, "Manage Internet Explorer."

- **Compatibility View** This feature displays Web sites as though you are using Windows Internet Explorer 7, thus negating any incompatibilities between Web sites designed for older browsers and the new Internet Explorer 8 technologies. You can turn on this feature for the current Web site by clicking the Compatibility View button that appears to the right of the Address bar. After you choose Compatibility View for a site, Internet Explorer remembers the site and automatically displays it in Compatibility View on future visits.

**Tip** The Compatibility View button appears to the right of the Address box only when you are displaying a Web site that does not include Internet Explorer 8 among its browser options. The button background is blue when Internet Explorer is displaying the site in Compatibility View.

● **Accelerators** With these convenient tools, you can interact with Web page content directly from the page. Accelerators enable you to do things such as add Web page content to your blog, send information in an e-mail message, display a location on a map, locate related information, or translate content, with just one click.

● **Web Slices** With these automatically updating information feeds, you can display up-to-date information from certain sites without leaving the current Web page.

● **Visual Search** This add-on displays thumbnails of the pages found as a result of a search from the Internet Explorer Search box.

**See Also** For more information about Accelerators, Web Slices, and Visual Search, see "Working with Web Page Content" in Chapter 7, "Work with Web Pages and Sites."

## Specifying Sites and Pages

When you want to display a Web site or page, you can either start Internet Explorer as part of the process of displaying the site or page or start Internet Explorer first and then specify the site or page.

To display a site or page and start Internet Explorer:

● Type the URL in the Start menu Search box, and then press Enter.

● Click an active link in a Microsoft Office Word document, Microsoft Office Excel worksheet, or other document that supports hyperlinks.

● Click a desktop shortcut icon that points to the site or page.

To display a site or page on the current tab of an Internet Explorer window:

● Type the URL in the Address bar, and then either click the Go button or press Enter.

● Type a partial URL or site name of a previously visited site and then, in the list that appears below the Address bar, click the URL or site.

● If the URL begins with *www.* and ends with *.com*, type the domain root name (the part between *www.* and *.com*) in the Address bar, and then press Ctrl+Enter.

To display a site or page on a new tab of an Internet Explorer window:

- Click the New Tab button, type the URL in the Address bar, and then either click the Go button or press Enter.
- Type the URL in the Address bar, and then press Alt+Enter.
- Type the URL in the Start menu Search box, and then either press Enter or click the URL in the Internet section of the search results list.
- In Internet Explorer, right-click a link, and then click Open In New Tab.
- Right-click the Internet Explorer taskbar button, and then click the site URL or page title in the Frequent list.

## Internet Explorer 8 Interface Elements

Internet Explorer displays Web content in a standard window that you manage as you would any other window. In the default Internet Explorer configuration, additional controls for working in and managing Internet Explorer are available on toolbars at the top and bottom of the window.

The Favorites bar and the Command bar appear above the Internet Explorer Content pane, below the navigation buttons, Address bar, and Search box.

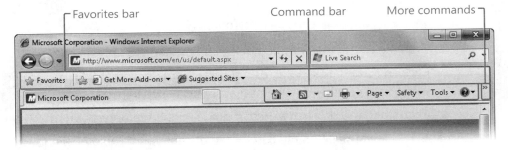

*By default, commands for working with and managing Internet Explorer are available from the Favorites bar and the Command bar.*

**Tip**  By default, buttons on the Favorites bar are labeled with Web page titles pulled from the page code. You can change the labeling convention, and thus the width of the buttons. To do so, right-click any Favorites bar button, point to Customize Title Widths, and then click Long Titles, Short Titles, or Icons Only.

You can change the title on a specific button. To do so, right-click the button, and click Rename. In the Rename dialog box, type the label you want, and then click OK.

If the contents of the Favorites bar or the Command bar exceed its width, a button (labeled with a chevron) appears at the bar's right end. Click the button to display a menu of the other available items.

The Favorites bar includes the following tools:

- **Favorites button** Click this button to open the Favorites Center. In this pane, you can save and organize links to Web sites and Web pages on the Favorites tab, and save and organize RSS feeds on the Feeds tab. You can also view your browsing history on the History tab.

- **Add to Favorites Bar button** Click this button to create a link to the current page on the Favorites bar.

- **Get More Add-ons menu** From this menu, you can obtain recommended add-ons and access the Internet Explorer Add-ons Gallery.

- **Suggested Sites menu** From this menu, you can open sites that match your browsing history and turn the Suggested Sites feature on or off.

You can personalize the Favorites bar by adding Web Slices, RSS feeds, and links to it.

The Command bar includes the following tools:

- **Home button and menu** Click this button to display your home page(s). Click the arrow to display a menu of commands for adding or changing home pages.

- **Feeds button and list** When this button is active, click it to subscribe to the first Web Slice or RSS feed on the page. Click the arrow to display a list of all the Web feeds on the page.

  **See Also** For information about Web Slices and RSS feeds, see "Working with Web Page Content" in Chapter 7, "Work with Web Pages and Sites."

- **Read Mail button** Click this button to open your default e-mail program Inbox.

- **Print button and menu** Click the button to print the current page using the default print settings. Click the arrow to display a menu of commands for printing and previewing Web pages.

- **Page menu** This menu includes commands for working with and managing the appearance of Web page content.

- **Safety menu** This menu includes commands for managing your history, privacy, and security when browsing the Internet.

- **Tools menu** This menu includes commands for managing your browsing session and most Internet Explorer features.

If you prefer to select commands from traditional text-based menus, you can choose to display the Menu bar, from which all the commands on the Favorites bar and Command bar, as well as a few others, are available. (To display the Menu bar, click Toolbars on the Tools menu and then click Menu Bar.)

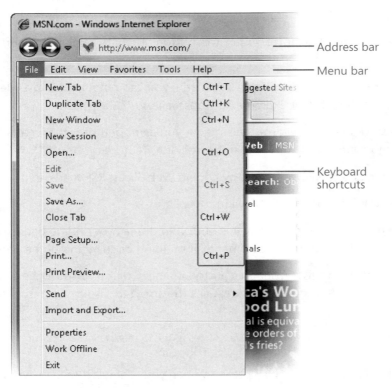

*The menus display keyboard shortcuts for all commands that have them.*

At the bottom of the window, the status bar displays information about your current browsing session, including the target URL of any link you point to or click, a progress bar when Internet Explorer loads a new page, the security level of the browsing session, an alert for any page elements that are blocked from loading, and the zoom level.

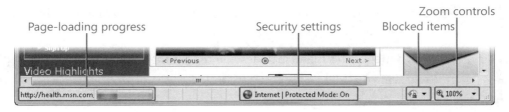

*The Internet Explorer status bar.*

To hide or display an Internet Explorer toolbar:

1.  Point to Toolbars on the Tools menu, or right-click a blank part of the toolbar area.

2.  On the Toolbars menu or the shortcut menu, click the toolbar you want to display or hide.

    A check mark on the menu indicates an active toolbar.

When you display a page in Internet Explorer 8, the page's URL is shown in the Address bar. Internet Explorer 8 emphasizes the site's domain name by displaying it in black letters and the other elements of the page address in gray letters.

*The Internet Explorer Address bar.*

You can use the buttons at the right end of the Address bar to work with pages as follows:

- To display the page as though you were using Internet Explorer 7, click the Compatibility View button.

- To reload a page, click the Refresh button or press F5.

    Refreshing a page displays the most current page content.

- To stop loading a page, click the Stop button.

    You might want to stop loading a page if you mistakenly click a link to a Web page that you don't want to display, if a page is downloading content that you don't want, or if a page is loading unusually slowly.

**See Also** For information about other interface elements, such as the navigation buttons, tab controls, and Search box, see "Finding, Saving, and Returning to Web Sites" in Chapter 7, "Work with Web Pages and Sites."

# Working with Tabs and Pages

In the past, if you wanted to view multiple Web pages at the same time it was necessary to open multiple Web browser windows. Versions of Internet Explorer starting with Internet Explorer 7 offer tabbed browsing, which enables you to display multiple Web sites or pages on separate tabs of one Internet Explorer program window. Tabbed browsing is convenient because it takes far less time to open a new tab than it does to open a new browser window, and it's much easier to move between open sites by clicking the tabs at the top of one window than by switching between windows.

*You can switch between pages by clicking the page tabs, and open a new tab by clicking the New Tab button.*

You can manage page tabs in an Internet Explorer window in the following ways:

- To open a new tab, click the New Tab button to the right of the active tabs.

  **Tip** The inactive New Tab button is blank. Pointing to the button causes the New Tab icon to appear.

- To close the current tab if more than one tab is open, click the Close button at the right end of the tab.

- To close a tab other than the current one if more than one tab is open, right-click the tab and then click Close Tab.

- To close all tabs but one if more than one tab is open, right-click the tab you want to keep, and then click Close Other Tabs.

Tabbed browsing is turned on by default. You can turn it off so that each browser window displays only one page of content, or change the way Internet Explorer works with tabs, by selecting check boxes in the Tabbed Browsing Settings dialog box.

To open the Tabbed Browsing Settings dialog box, first click Internet Options on the Tools menu and then, on the General tab of the Internet Options dialog box, under Tabs, click Settings. You can also set options for pop-ups and links in this dialog box.

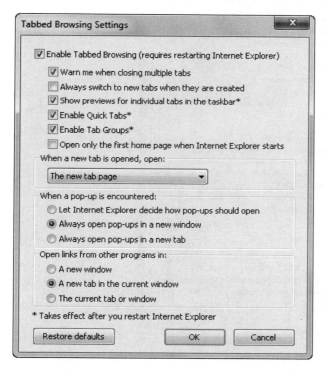

*In the Tabbed Browsing Settings dialog box, you can turn the Tabbed Browsing feature on or off and control the way Internet Explorer handles tabs, pop-up windows, and links.*

**See Also**  For information about pop-up windows, see "Blocking Pop-Up Windows" in Chapter 8, "Manage Internet Explorer."

Additional options for tabbed and non-tabbed browsing are available from the Advanced tab of the Internet Options dialog box.

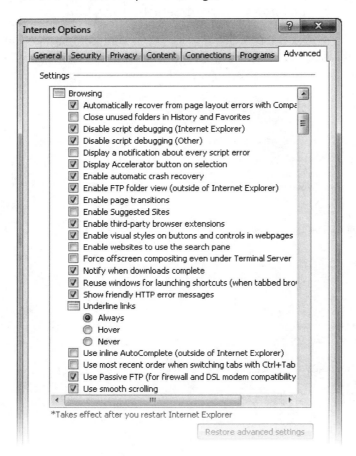

*On the Advanced tab of the Internet Options dialog box, you can further customize your browsing experience.*

**Tip** From time to time, Microsoft releases a new version of Internet Explorer. You can always find the latest version of Internet Explorer at www.microsoft.com/windows/ie/.

There are several ways to switch between Web pages that are open on multiple tabs in one window or in multiple windows. When several tabs are open, it can be difficult to know which tab represents the page you want to switch to. You can view and switch between open pages in the following ways:

- If you know the tab you want to switch to, you can simply click the tab.
- You can cycle through the tabs in a window by pressing Ctrl+Tab.

- When the tabs exceed the available space, you can click the scroll buttons that appear to the left and right of the visible tabs.

- On each tab, you can move between the pages you have previously visited by clicking the Back and Forward buttons.
- You can display a specific page by clicking the Recent Pages button to the right of the Forward button and then, in the Recent Pages list, clicking the title of the page you want to display.

*In the Recent Pages list, a check mark indicates the current page, and an arrow indicates the page you will move to if you click the mouse button.*

● You can display the page title and thumbnail of each tab of the current browser window by clicking the Quick Tabs button to the left of the first tab. Then click any thumbnail to display that tab, or click its Close button to close the tab and remove the thumbnail from the Quick Tabs window.

*The Quick Tabs window displays thumbnails of each tab of the current Internet Explorer window.*

● You can display thumbnails of the tabs open in all browser windows by pointing to the pinned Internet Explorer button on the Windows Taskbar. Then point to any thumbnail to preview the tab content, and click a thumbnail to switch to that tab.

*Pointing to the Internet Explorer button displays thumbnails of all tabs open in all browser windows.*

**Tip**  Do you want to have Web site for your business? You can build and host a site for free through Office Live. For more information, visit www.officelive.com/free-website/.

In this exercise, you'll start Internet Explorer, specify basic settings, and use various methods to open pages. You'll navigate between sites and pages, close some sites, and then close them all.

**SET UP** You don't need any practice files to complete this exercise; all you need is an active Internet connection.

1. On the **Windows Taskbar**, click the **Internet Explorer** button.

   If you haven't previously set up Internet Explorer, a wizard starts.

*The Set Up Windows Internet Explorer 8 wizard leads you through the process of setting your preferences.*

2. If the **Set Up Windows Internet Explorer 8** wizard starts, click **Next** to walk through the wizard or click **Ask me later** to close the wizard without making selections.

   Internet Explorer displays your current home page.

   **See Also** For information about personalizing the Internet Explorer settings, see "Setting Up Internet Explorer 8" earlier in this chapter. For information about changing the site that opens when you start Internet Explorer, see "Personalizing Internet Explorer 8" in Chapter 8, "Manage Internet Explorer."

3. Click once in the **Address** box to select the URL of the currently displayed page. Type **www.microsoft.com** to replace the current URL, and then either click the **Go** button or press **Enter**.

Internet Explorer adds http:// to the beginning of the URL before submitting it.

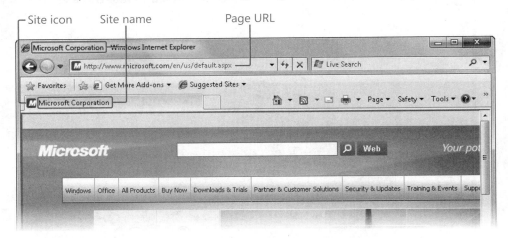

*The Microsoft Web site replaces your home page on the current tab.*

**Tip** The Go button appears at the right end of the Address bar when you are editing the Address bar content. Otherwise, the Refresh button appears in its place.

Because the home page of the Microsoft Web site is something other than simply default.htm, the URL in the Address bar changes to reflect the path to the file of the displayed page. The tab displays the icon and site name specified by the site, as does the Internet Explorer title bar. (If the site does not specify a name, the tab and the title bar display the URL.)

4. In the **Address** box, select the current URL, type **otsi**, and then press **Ctrl+Enter** to expand the URL to http://www.otsi.com.

Our company's Web site opens on the current tab. Because the file for the home page of this site is default.htm, the Address bar displays only the simple URL.

Because this page includes content that isn't designed specifically for Internet Explorer 8, the Compatibility View button appears near the right end of the Address bar.

**Tip** Incompatible content might be part of the fixed content of a page, or it might be part of linked content displayed on the page, such as an advertisement provided by a different company.

5. In the **Address** box, replace *www.otsi* with **movies.msn**. Then press **Alt+Enter** to open the specified Web site on a new tab.

Internet Explorer opens a new tab and submits the URL.

Optional Compatibility View button ⌐    ⌐ Refresh button

*Internet Explorer displays the MSN Movies site on the new tab.*

6. Click the **Start** button (or press the **Windows logo** key).

When the Start menu opens, the cursor is already in the Start menu Search box in the lower-left corner of the menu.

7. In the **Start** menu **Search** box, type **http:// money.msn.com**. Then press **Enter**.

The home page of the MSN Money site opens on a new tab of the existing Internet Explorer window.

**Tip** Internet Explorer records the Web sites you visit on the History tab of your Favorites Center so that you can easily locate a site you have previously viewed. You can save sites and locations on the Favorites tab of your Favorites Center so that you can return to them whenever you want.

8. On the MSN Money home page, below the title, click a link to a specific section of the MSN Money site (News, Investing, and so on).

The home page of that section replaces the site home page you were viewing.

9. Right-click another link.

A menu of options for working with that linked page appears.

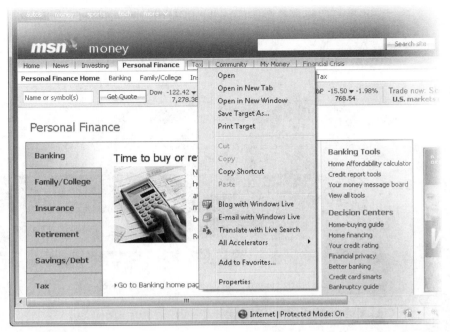

*Right-clicking a link displays a shortcut menu of options pertaining to the link target.*

**10.** On the shortcut menu, click **Open in New Tab**.

**Tip** Clicking Open In New Window opens a separate Internet Explorer window. Clicking Save Target As saves a copy of the HTML page in the location you specify.

Internet Explorer opens a new tab to the right of the current tab and displays the selected page on that tab, but does not switch to it; the tab displaying the page you linked from is still on top of the others. The color of the two tabs displaying MSN Money pages changes to indicate that the tabs are related.

**11.** In the tab area, click the newly opened tab to bring it to the top. (If you followed the instructions exactly so far, it is the fourth of four tabs.)

The selected page tab comes to the top of the stack.

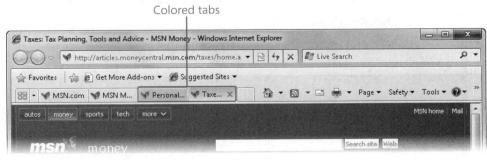

*Internet Explorer 8 indicates related pages by changing the color of their tabs.*

**12.** Click the original **MSN Money** tab (the third tab) and then, to the left of the **Address** bar, click the **Back** button to return to the MSN Money home page.

If you visited only two pages on this tab, only the Back button or Forward button is active at any time. If you explored more than two pages, both buttons are active.

**13.** To the right of the **Back** and **Forward** buttons, click the **Recent Pages** button, and then click a page that doesn't have a check mark next to it to return to that page.

**14.** On the current **MSN Money** tab, click the **Close Tab** button.

The tab closes. The tab to its right slides to the left and, because its related tab is no longer open, its color changes to the standard tab color.

**15.** On the **Internet Explorer** window title bar, click the **Close** button.

Internet Explorer prompts you to confirm that you want to close all the tabs.

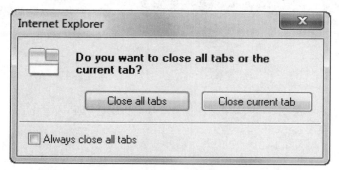

*When multiple tabs are open, Internet Explorer notifies you before closing.*

**Tip** This is one of the settings you can change in the Tabbed Browsing Settings dialog box. But before you do, bear in mind that this warning can sometimes come in handy.

**16.** In the dialog box, click **Close all tabs** to close all the tabs and exit Internet Explorer.

# Key Points

- You can connect your computer to the Internet through a wired, wireless, or dial-up connection. You need to have an account with an ISP that provides a connection from your location to the Internet.

- Internet Explorer displays Web content in a standard window that you manage as you would any other window.

- You can open multiple Web sites in one Internet Explorer window, so it's faster and easier to open and switch between sites and pages.

- You can open and move between pages on the same tab or in new tabs. Related tabs are color-coded so you can easily distinguish them.

# Chapter at a Glance

Work with Web page content, **page 226**

Send Web pages
and links, **page 256**

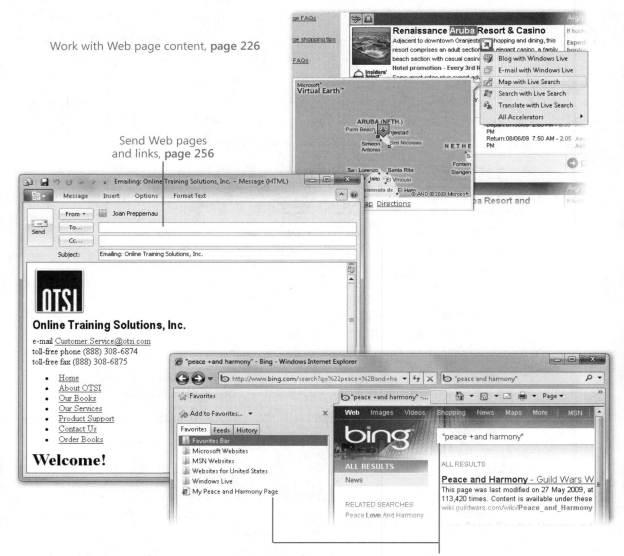

Find, save, and return
to Web sites, **page 240**

# 7 Work with Web Pages and Sites

In this chapter, you will learn how to

✔ Work with Web page content.
✔ Subscribe to Web feeds.
✔ Find, save, and return to Web sites.
✔ Send Web pages and links.

The Internet is an amazing place, full of all types of information. Windows Internet Explorer 8 opens up a world of Web surfing possibilities beyond the basic viewing of words and pictures on Web pages. You can take action on content that interests you, and ensure that you're always up to date on the latest information available on the Web sites and blogs that matter most to you. It's easier than ever to locate information about the topics you're interested in—you can choose from a tremendous number of search providers offering specialized search and decision-making tools. You can use precise search terminology to narrow the results down to those most likely to contain the information you want. Basic information is displayed within the search results so that, in some cases, you might locate the information you're looking for without having to actually display the site. Some search engines now include images as well as words in their search results.

When you locate a Web site that provides information you want, you can save the site so you can easily return to it later. If you want to share information from a Web site, you can send Web page content, or a link to the Web page, to other people by using e-mail.

In this chapter, you'll learn how to work with Accelerators, RSS feeds, and Web Slices. You'll learn techniques for conducting effective Web searches, and you'll learn how to use Internet Explorer to save and share information.

> **Practice Files** You won't need any practice files to complete the exercises in this chapter. See "Using the Practice Files" at the beginning of this book for more information.

# Working with Web Page Content

Internet Explorer 8 includes several nifty new tools that you can use to work with content on a Web page. Chief among these are add-ons, called Accelerators, that let you quickly perform Web page content–related tasks directly from a Web page.

When you select page content that triggers one or more Accelerators, the Accelerator icon appears. Clicking the icon displays the Accelerator menu. The default Accelerator menu includes tools for blogging about, e-mailing, mapping, and translating content, and for searching the Web for additional, related content.

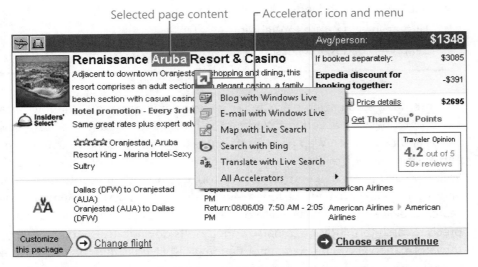

*The Accelerator menu displays the default Accelerators in each category.*

Accelerators are classified into specific categories, including Blogging, Bookmarks, Dictionaries and Reference, E-mail, Finance, Mapping, Music , News, Photos and Videos, Search, Sharing, Shopping, Social Networking, Toolbars, Translation, Travel, and Weather. Each Accelerator is assigned to only one category. The Accelerator you choose as the default for that category appears on the default Accelerator menu. Other Accelerators you install on your computer are only one more click away, on the All Accelerators submenu.

The action required to start an Accelerator, and the results of the Accelerator, vary depending on the individual tool. Some Accelerators display information when you point to them; others open an associated Web site (on a separate tab of the same Internet Explorer window) when you click them.

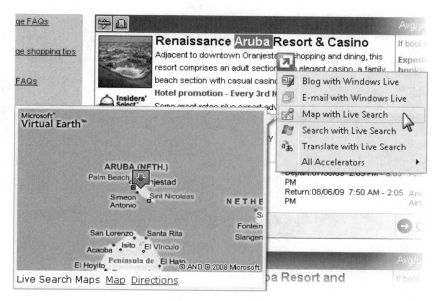

*Some Accelerators display their results when you point to them on the menu.*

Accelerators are available to help you shop (at specific stores or to locate bargains), perform research, convert currency, and get stock quotes; to share (on your favorite social networking site), bookmark, define, and evaluate information you select on a Web page; to locate movies, videos, music auctions, events, jobs, and missing packages. Among all the available Accelerators (well over 100 before the release of Windows 7), there are bound to be at least a few you didn't know you couldn't live without.

You can install Accelerators from the Internet Explorer Add-ons Gallery. To locate Accelerators that you can add to your installation of Internet Explorer:

1.  On the Internet Explorer Command bar, click Page.

2.  On the Page menu, click All Accelerators, and then click Find More Accelerators.

The Add-ons Gallery opens, displaying the Accelerators page. All available Accelerators appear in the Add-ons Gallery, including those that are already installed on your computer.

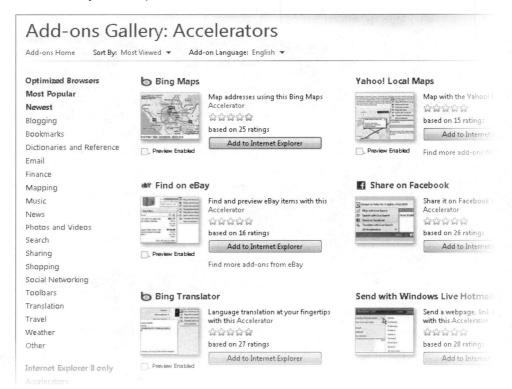

*In the Add-ons Gallery, Accelerators that display a content preview when you point to them on the menu are indicated by Preview Enabled under the Accelerator image.*

3. Click the name or thumbnail representation of any Accelerator to display more information about it, including user reviews.

**Tip** In the Add-ons Gallery, click Accelerators (under the Internet Explorer 8 only heading) to display all the available Accelerators, or click any category under that to filter the Accelerators. Click any category at the top of the page to display the Accelerators, plug-ins, search providers, Web Slices, and other add-ons in that category.

You can change the sort order of the gallery items (to Alphabetical, Most Recent, Most Viewed, or Rating) by clicking the current sort order at the top of the page.

4. Click the Add To Internet Explorer button next to an Accelerator you want to install.

The Add Accelerator dialog box opens.

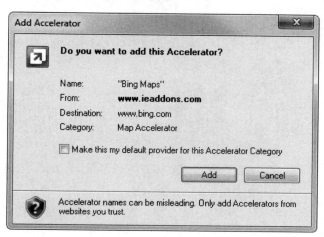

*The Accelerator you select as the default provider for each category appears on the default Accelerator menu.*

**Tip** If the selected Accelerator is already installed on your computer, the Add Accelerator dialog box presents the option to replace the existing installation.

5. In the Add Accelerator dialog box, select the Make This My Default Provider... check box if you want this Accelerator to appear on the Accelerator menu in place of any other in its category. Then click Add.

To manage your current Accelerators and locate others:

1. On the Internet Explorer Page menu, click All Accelerators, and then click Manage Accelerators.

The Manage Add-ons window opens, displaying the Accelerators page.

Accelerators with *Default* in the Status column appear on the Accelerator menu. Accelerators with *Enabled* in the Status column appear on the All Accelerators submenu. Accelerators with *Disabled* in the Status column aren't on either menu, but can be quickly available if you choose to enable them.

2. Click any Accelerator to display information about it in the pane at the bottom of the page.

*The Accelerators page of the Manage Add-ons window displays a list of the Accelerators currently available on your computer.*

3. Click Remove As Default to move the selected Accelerator from the main menu to the submenu, Disable to remove it from either menu, or Remove to uninstall it.

4. In the lower-left corner of the Manage Add-ons window, click Find More Accelerators to display the Accelerators page of the Internet Explorer Add-ons Gallery.

# Subscribing to Web Feeds

You can save time by having Web content delivered to you from your favorite sites and blogs. Internet Explorer 8 supports two methods of automatic content delivery: RSS feeds and Web Slices.

## RSS Feeds

Really Simple Syndication (RSS) is a technology with which Web sites and blogs can send information to you so that you don't have to visit the site. When you subscribe to an RSS feed, the RSS provider automatically sends (feeds) content updates to you. You can view the current content in many programs, including Internet Explorer, Windows Live Mail, Microsoft Outlook, and dedicated newsreader programs. You can subscribe to an RSS feed from any site that offers one. Although RSS is a recent technology, RSS feeds are available for thousands of Web sites. If you regularly visit certain Web sites or blogs, you can save time by scanning synopses of all the new articles from that site or blog within one advertisement-free interface. When you locate an article that you want to read the full text of, simply click the article's link to display it.

You can subscribe to RSS feeds directly from Internet Explorer 8. When you display a site or page that has one or more RSS feeds, the Feeds button on the Internet Explorer Command bar changes to an orange RSS Feeds button. If the page also contains Web Slices, the Feeds button changes to a green Web Slice button. Clicking the arrow to the right of the button displays the Feeds list, which includes all Web Slices and RSS feeds on the page.

*The RSS Feeds button appears on the Command bar when the page includes one or more RSS feeds, but no Web Slices.*

Clicking the RSS Feeds button displays the default feed on the page in Internet Explorer. To display a feed other than the default, click the RSS Feeds arrow and then click any feed in the list. In either case, the feed content replaces the current page content.

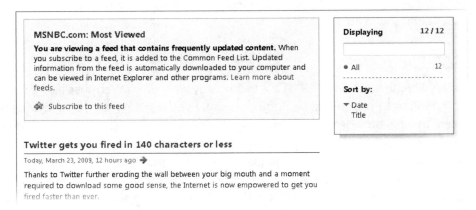

*If you haven't subscribed to the feed, subscription information appears at the top of the page.*

To subscribe to an RSS feed in Internet Explorer:

1. Display the feed content, and then click the Subscribe To This Feed link.

   The Subscribe To This Feed dialog box opens.

   *From the Subscribe To This Feed dialog box, you can add the feed to your Favorites Center and to your Favorites bar.*

2. If you want to add a button for this RSS feed to the Favorites bar, select the Add To Favorites Bar check box.

3. If you want to save the feed in a folder on the Favorites Center Feeds tab rather than directly on the tab, click the Create In arrow and then click the folder you want.

4. Click the Subscribe button to complete the process and return to the feed content.

Subscribing to an RSS feed adds it to the Feeds tab of your Favorites Center. You can open the feed at any time to view up-to-date article synopses, and click any headline that interests you to display the article. You can display any one of the feeds in your Favorites Center in the Feed Headlines gadget, if you've added that to your desktop.

**See Also** For more information about the Favorites Center, see "Finding, Saving, and Returning to Web Sites" later in this chapter. For information about gadgets, see "Using and Modifying Desktop Gadgets" in Chapter 11, "Work with Programs."

RSS feed subscriptions can include the publisher's recommendation for how often subscribers will receive updates. You can stipulate the minimum update frequency for the feeds you subscribe to from Internet Explorer 8.

● To change the update frequency and other settings of a specific RSS feed, right-click its button, or right-click its name on the Feeds tab of your Favorites Center, and then click Properties.

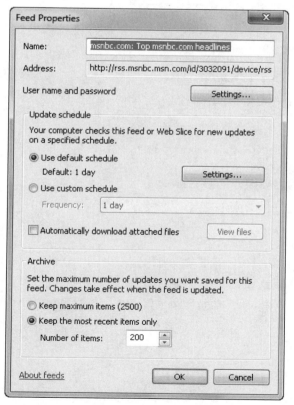

*The Feed Properties dialog box for the selected RSS feed.*

From the Feed Properties dialog box, you can provide your credentials for password-protected sites, specify a custom update schedule for the selected feed, and specify the number of feed items you want to keep on your computer.

● To change the way Internet Explorer manages all RSS feeds, click Settings in the Update Schedule area of any Feed Properties dialog box, or click Internet Options on the Tools menu and then on the Content tab of the Internet Options dialog box, click Settings in the Feeds And Web Slices area.

Either method opens the Feed And Web Slice Settings dialog box, from which you can change the update frequency for all RSS feeds. You can also control whether Internet Explorer marks feeds that you have read, whether feed reading view is on, whether Internet Explorer plays a sound when an RSS feed is found or updated, and whether Internet Explorer detects Web Slices in Web pages.

*From the Feed And Web Slice Settings dialog box, you can change the way Internet Explorer manages all feeds and Web Slices.*

## Newsreaders and Feed Directories

Your Favorites Center is available to you only on the computer it is stored on. If you want to access your news feeds from any computer, you can set up an account with an online newsreader that you can connect to over the Internet, such as one of the following:

● My MSN is a home page you can personalize with the elements you want to see when you start your Web browser, including RSS feeds. To use this site, you need to register an e-mail address as a Windows Live ID. For more information, visit my.msn.com.

● Google Reader displays all your RSS feeds without the extra information that might be on your My MSN page. To use this reader, you need a Google account. For more information, visit reader.google.com.

● My Yahoo! also supports RSS feeds. To use this reader, you need a Yahoo! account. For more information, visit my.yahoo.com.

These Web-based newsreaders, and sites such as the MSN RSS Directory at rss.msn.com, provide directories of RSS feeds. You can display or subscribe to a feed from the directory.

*To add an RSS feed to your online newsreader, click the corresponding button.*

## Web Slices

A Web Slice is a content feed that allows you to view up-to-date information from your Internet Explorer browser window without navigating away from the page you're currently viewing. When you subscribe to a Web Slice, a corresponding button appears on the Favorites bar. Internet Explorer periodically checks for updates to your Web Slices; when it finds one, the button on the Favorites bar flashes and its title becomes bold. You can then display a preview of the updated content by clicking the button.

*You can preview updated Web Slice content without leaving the current Web page.*

When you finish viewing the information in the Web Slice preview window, you can do any of the following:

- Click outside the preview window to close it.

- Click any hyperlink in the preview window to display that page on a new tab of the current Internet Explorer window.

- Interact with any tool in the preview window, such as a Search box, that links to content on the Web Slice source page.

- Click the Open button at the bottom of the preview window to display the Web Slice source page on the current tab.

  **Tip** The URL of the Web Slice source page appears at the bottom of the Web Slice preview window, to the right of the Open and Refresh buttons.

- Click the Refresh button at the bottom of the preview window to update the content preview.

**Tip** Until you explicitly allow Internet Explorer to subscribe to Web Slices, the Suggested Sites and Web Slices buttons appear on the Favorites bar, and no content is visible in their preview panes. You can allow subscription either by clicking Turn On Subscribing To Web Slices in the Suggested Sites or Web Slices preview pane, or by adding a Web Slice from the Add-ons Gallery. When subscription is enabled, the Get More Add-ons button replaces the Web Slices button on the Favorites bar. You can display the Add-ons Gallery by clicking Get More Add-ons and then clicking Find More In The Internet Explorer Add-ons Gallery.

Many Web Slices are available from the Add-ons Gallery, including Web Slices that help you stay up to date with e-mail, finances, music, news, weather, sports, traffic, television schedules, shopping, social networking, and more. You can quickly locate available Web Slices and add them to the Favorites bar by following these steps:

1.  On the Internet Explorer Favorites bar, click Get More Add-ons, and then click Find More In The Internet Explorer Add-ons Gallery.

2.  In the Add-ons Gallery, click Web Slices to display all the available Web Slices, or click a category to display the Accelerators, plug-ins, search providers, Web Slices, and other add-ons in that category.

    **Tip** All available Web Slices appear in the Add-ons Gallery, even those that are already installed on your computer.

3.  Click the Add To Internet Explorer button next to a Web Slice you want to download.

    The Add A Web Slice dialog box opens.

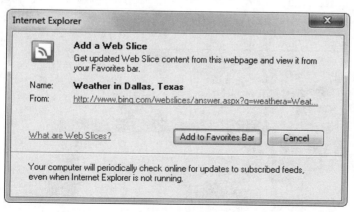

*When adding a Web Slice to the Favorites bar, you can view its source by clicking the From link in the dialog box.*

**Troubleshooting** If a Web page displaying the Web Slice opens rather than the Add A Web Slice dialog box, point to the Web Slice on the page, and then click the Web Slice button that appears. The Add A Web Slice dialog box will open, and you can proceed.

4.  In the Add A Web Slice dialog box, click Add To Favorites Bar.

When you display a page that contains one or more Web Slices, the Feeds button on the Internet Explorer Command bar changes to a green Add Web Slices button. Clicking the arrow to the right of the button displays the Feeds list.

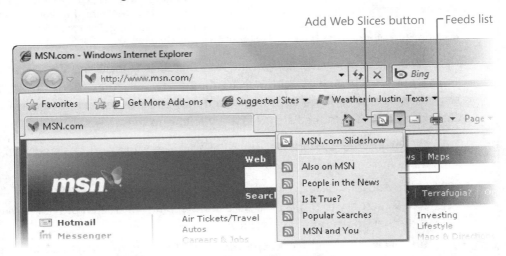

The Feeds list includes all Web Slices and RSS feeds on the page.

**Keyboard Shortcut** You can expand the Feeds list by pressing Alt+J.

A Web Slice button might also appear next to Web Slice–enabled content on the page. (The button might not appear until you point to the Web Slice–enabled content.)

*Web Slice buttons accompany all Web Slice–enabled content on the page.*

You can add a Web Slice from a page to the Favorites bar in the following ways. (Each method displays the Add A Web Slice dialog box; in the dialog box, click the Add To Favorites Bar button to complete the process.)

● To add the first (or only) Web Slice on the page, click the Add Web Slices button on the Command bar.

● To add a Web Slice other than the first or only Web Slice, click the Add Web Slices arrow and then, in the Feeds list, click the Web Slice you want to add.

● To add a Web Slice directly from the page, click the green Web Slice button located next to the Web Slice–enabled content, or point to the Web Slice–enabled content and click the Web Slice button that appears.

You can change the way Internet Explorer handles all Web Slices, and you can change the properties of any individual Web Slice.

● To prevent a specific Web Slice button title from becoming bold when the Web Slice is updated, right-click the button, and then click Bold On Update to remove the check mark preceding the command.

● To change the update frequency and other settings of a specific Web Slice, right-click its button, and then click Properties.

*In the Web Slice Properties dialog box for a selected Web Slice, you can provide your credentials and specify an update schedule for the Web Slice.*

- To change the way Internet Explorer manages all Web Slices, click Settings in any Web Slice Properties dialog box; or click Internet Options on the Tools menu and then, on the Content tab of the Internet Options dialog box, click Settings.

  Either method opens the Feed And Web Slice Settings dialog box (shown in the "RSS Feeds" section of this topic), from which you can change the update frequency for all Web Slices, play a sound when an update is available, and control whether the Web Slice icon appears at the top of a page when Web Slice–enabled content is available.

# Finding, Saving, and Returning to Web Sites

An amazing amount of information is available on the Internet. There is probably no topic that isn't discussed somewhere on a Web site or blog. Many sites, such as Wikipedia, exist solely for the purpose of providing information. Most companies today have some sort of Internet presence, even if it's only a listing in the online telephone directory. Even the smallest owner-operated company can have a Web site that presents a professional image and provides information to potential clients.

## Finding Sites

You can search for a Web site that provides information about a general topic by entering search terms into the Search box located in the upper-right corner of the Internet Explorer program window. Pressing Enter or clicking the Search button returns search results from your default search engine.

If you know the exact name of a company, you can locate its Web site by entering its name into the Search box. If you don't know the full name, you can enter as much of it as you do know, or enter a description of its products or services. For example, a search for *garbage collection Bartonville Texas* returns the name of the company that provides waste management services for that city.

Search terms can include the following:

- **One or more words separated by spaces** This search returns a list of sites containing some or all of the words but not necessarily together or in the order you enter.

  **Tip** Use a plus sign (+) to indicate a word that must be included in the search results, and a minus sign (−) to indicate a word that must not. For example, you can use the + operator to force the inclusion of a minor word (such as *and*) that a search engine might otherwise ignore.

● **Multiple words enclosed in quotation marks** This search returns a list of sites containing the entire search term exactly as you enter it (results may also include the search term with additional text appended, such as plural, gerund, or past-tense forms of the last word). For example, to search for a company's Web site, enter the entire company name in quotation marks, like this:

"Blue Yonder Airlines"

**Tip** If you know the e-mail address of a company employee, chances are the company's Web site is on the same domain as the e-mail address. For example, if Ben Smith works at Wingtip Toys and has the e-mail address ben@wingtiptoys.com, it is likely that the Wingtip Toys Web site address is www.wingtiptoys.com.

● **Boolean search operators** Boolean operators return more precise search results. For example, you can separate two words by using the following Boolean operators to get different results.

○ **AND or ()** Returns a list of sites that contain the words that precede and follow the operator. For example, a search for

chocolate AND "ice cream"

or

(chocolate "ice cream")

returns results containing *chocolate ice cream*, *chocolate macadamia nut ice cream* and *ice cream with chocolate sauce*.

○ **NOT** Returns a list of sites that contain the word(s) that precede the operator and don't contain the word(s) that follow it. For example, a search for

chocolate NOT "ice cream"

returns results containing *chocolate chip cookie* and *death by chocolate*, but not *chocolate ice cream*.

○ **OR** Returns a list of sites that contain either the word(s) that precede the operator or the words that follow it, but not both. For example, a search for

chocolate OR "ice cream"

returns results containing *chocolate* or *ice cream* but not *chocolate ice cream* or *ice cream with nuts and chocolate sprinkles*.

**Troubleshooting** You must enter AND, NOT, and OR in capital letters for the search engine to recognize them as Boolean operators.

Internet Explorer 8 offers you a choice of search engines (also called *search providers*). You don't need to commit to only one; it's easy to choose a search provider each time you perform a search. However, if you find that a particular provider gives you better results for specific types of information, you can set that provider as the default. Bing is the default search provider until you specify another.

As you enter a term in the Search box, the Suggestions list displays suggestions from the active search provider, and the History list displays sites you've visited that contain the search term. This feature can be very helpful when you're uncertain of either the exact term you want to enter or its spelling.

*Search filters a list of suggestions as you type.*

## Visual Search

Visual Search is an add-on to the Internet Explorer Search feature that finds and displays thumbnail images and additional information in the search results; so much information that you might not need to follow the link. Visual Search is not available from all search providers.

You can display a site from the search results on the current tab by clicking the link, or you can display it on a new tab by right-clicking the link and then clicking Open In New Tab. You also have the option of displaying the site in a new window.

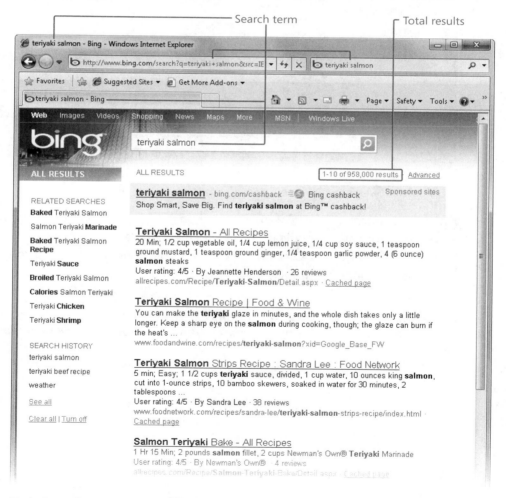

*Typical search results. Words and terms matching the search term are bold.*

Each search provider returns results in its own format, which usually includes a list of links, descriptions, and URLs.

If you locate a site that provides the type of information you're looking for and you'd like to see similar information from other resources, you can find related sites in the Suggested Sites list.

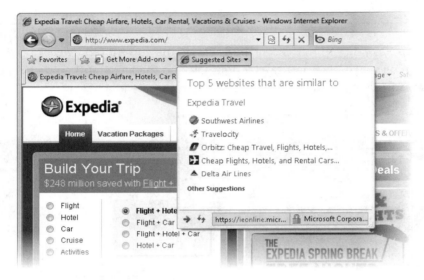

*The Suggested Sites feature presents a list of sites related to the current site content.*

When the Suggested Sites feature is turned on, Internet Explorer monitors your browsing history and periodically compares the metadata of the sites you've visited with a central list of sites. Clicking the Other Suggestions link at the bottom of the list opens a separate tab displaying a list of sites related to those you've visited in the past.

**Tip** You can turn the Suggested Sites feature on and off by clicking Suggested Sites on the Internet Explorer Tools menu. A check mark next to the feature name indicates that it is turned on.

## Choosing a Search Provider

During the process of setting up Internet Explorer, you can specify a default search provider by choosing the custom setting option in the Set Up Windows Internet Explorer wizard and then selecting your preferred providers on the Add Search Providers To Internet Explorer page that opens after you finish the wizard.

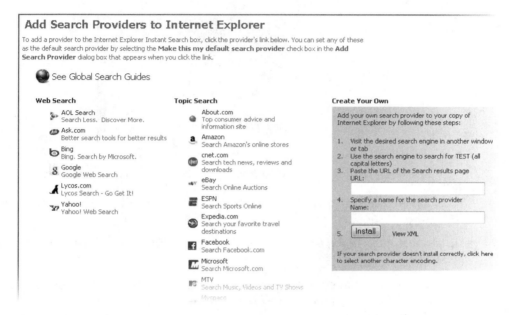

*You can add any search provider to the list by following the simple instructions on the Add Search Providers To Internet Explorer page.*

To add more search providers from any Internet Explorer window:

1. Click the Search arrow, and then click Find More Providers.

   The Add-ons Gallery opens, displaying the Search Providers page.

   **Tip** Search providers that support Visual Search are indicated by a conversation balloon icon and the words *Visual Search* below the provider's thumbnail image.

2. Click the Add To Internet Explorer button next to any search provider you want to have available to you.

3. In the Add Search Provider dialog box, select or clear the check boxes to indicate whether this is the default search provider, and whether to display search suggestions from this provider. Then click Add.

To search by using a search provider other than the default:

1. Click the Search arrow and then, in the list, click the search provider you want.

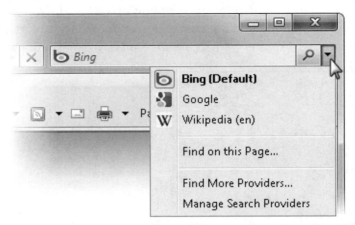

*You can choose a search provider from the list before entering the search term.*

2. Type the search term in the Search box, and then either click the Search button or press Enter.

**Tip** When not displaying a search term, the Search box displays the name of the active search provider.

Alternatively, you can enter the search term and then, on the bar below the list of search suggestions, click the icon of the search provider you want to use.

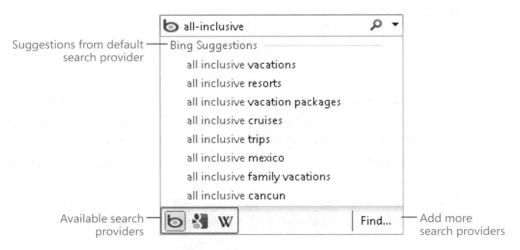

*You can also choose a search provider after entering the search term.*

## Saving Sites

If you want to save a link to a site so that you can quickly return to it later, you can add it to the Favorites tab of your Favorites Center or to the Favorites bar.

The Favorites tab is one of three tabs in your Favorites Center containing links to Web content. The other tabs are the Feeds tab, which we discussed earlier in this chapter, and the History tab, which keeps track of each site you visit so that you can find it even if you have not saved a link to it.

You can display the Favorites Center as a tabbed menu over the page content or as a tabbed pane on the left side of the Internet Explorer window.

Favorites Center as a tabbed menu    Site added to Favorites bar

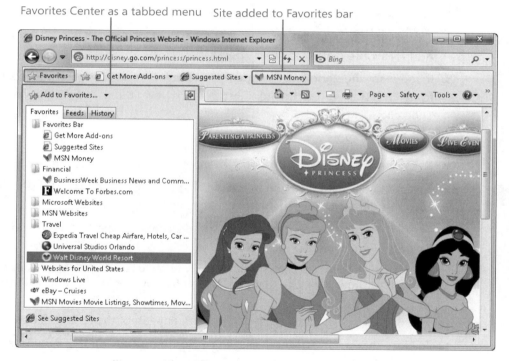

*Click the Favorites button to display the Favorites Center as a tabbed menu.*

**Tip** The Favorites button is located at the left end of the Favorites bar when the Favorites bar is open, or to the left of the page tabs when the Favorites bar is closed.

To add the current page to the Favorites bar:

● If the Favorites bar is open, click the Add To Favorites Bar button.

Adding a page to the Favorites bar also adds it to the Favorites Bar folder on the Favorites tab of your Favorites Center.

**Tip** You can move change the order of buttons on the Favorites bar by dragging them.

● If the Favorites bar is closed, click the Favorites button and then, in the Add To Favorites list at the top of the Favorites Center, click Add To Favorites Bar.

Using this method opens the Favorites bar and adds the page link.

To add the current page to the Favorites tab but not to the Favorites bar:

1. Click the Favorites button, and then click Add To Favorites.

2. If you want the page link to appear directly on the Favorites tab, click Add in the Add A Favorite dialog box that opens.

3. If you want the page link to appear within a folder on the Favorites tab, click the folder you want in the Create In list, or click New Folder and create the folder. Then click Add.

To work with the Favorites Center:

● To temporarily display the Favorites Center, click the Favorites button.

● To open the Favorites Center in a pane, first display it, and then click the Pin The Favorites Center button that appears in its upper-right corner.

The width of the page Content pane on the right changes to accommodate the Favorites Center pane on the left.

**Tip** When the Favorites Center is not open, you can open it as a pinned pane with a specific tab displayed by pointing to Explorer Bars on the Tools menu, and then clicking the tab you want.

● To expand or collapse a folder or group on any tab of the Favorites Center, click it.

● To close the Favorites Center, click the Favorites button. Or if the Favorites Center is pinned, click the Close button in its upper-right corner.

To display a page from any tab of your Favorites Center:

- To display a page on the current tab of the Internet Explorer window, click the page link.

- To display a page on a new tab of the Internet Explorer window, right-click the page link, and then click Open In New Tab.

- To display all the pages stored in a folder, right-click the folder, and then click Open In Tab Group.

To organize pages on the Favorites tab:

- To organize folders and pages alphabetically, right-click any folder or page title, and then click Sort By Name.

- To create a folder, right-click any folder or page title at the level you want the new folder, and then click Create New Folder. Type a folder name to replace the temporary name, and then press Enter.

- To move a page link to a folder, drag the page link to the folder. To move the page link to a specific position within the folder, pause over the folder until it expands, and then drag the page link to the position you want.

*A thick horizontal line indicates where the page link will appear. A blue arrow indicates a valid location; a red slashed circle indicates an invalid location.*

- To create a copy of a page link or a shortcut to a page link in a folder, hold down the right mouse button and drag the page link to the folder. After releasing the button, click Copy Here or Create Shortcuts Here.

- To carry out a more extensive organization of folders and pages, click the Add To Favorites arrow and then, in the list, click Organize Favorites.

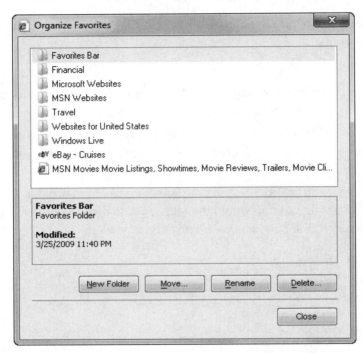

*In the Organize Favorites dialog box, you can create folders and delete, move, and rename folders and pages.*

In this exercise, you'll conduct a simple search, expand the available search resources, save a page as a favorite, and return to a previously visited page from the History tab of your Favorites Center.

**SET UP** You don't need any practice files to complete this exercise. Start Internet Explorer, and then follow the steps.

1. Click the **Search** arrow at the right end of the **Search** box, and then in the list, click **Bing**.

   Regardless of whether Bing is your default search provider, it is now the active search provider.

**2.** In the **Search** box, type **peace and harmony**

As you type, Bing displays suggested search terms matching your input.

**3.** Click the **Search** button, or press **Enter**.

The search results appear on the current tab of the Internet Explorer window.

**4.** Browse the search results, noting that some of the bold terms on the page aren't an exact match for the search term.

**5.** In the **Search** box, enclose the search term in quotes and insert a plus sign (+) in front of the word *and* so that the search term is

"peace +and harmony"

Then click the **Search** button or press **Enter**.

The bold terms in the new search results exactly match the search term. The Related Searches list on the left suggests other, similar terms.

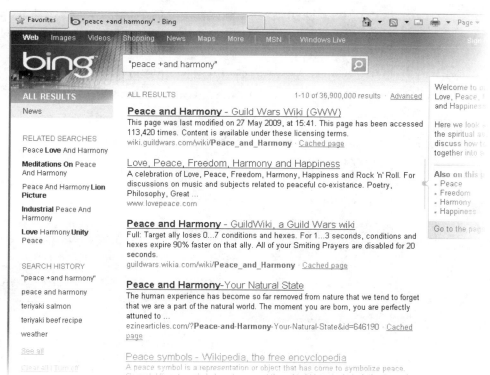

*Refining your search returns a more exact list of results.*

6. Browse the results and click any link to open that page.

7. On the **Favorites** bar, click the **Favorites** button, and then click **Add to Favorites**. The Add A Favorite dialog box opens.

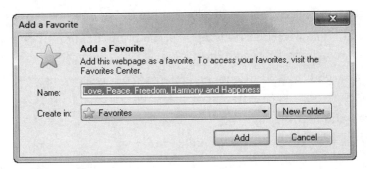

*The Add A Favorite dialog box.*

8. In the **Add a Favorite** dialog box, with the site name selected, type **My Peace and Harmony Page**. Then click **Add** to make the current page available from your **Favorites Center**.

9. In the browser window, click the **Back** button to return to the search results.

10. On the **Favorites** bar, click the **Favorites** button.

The Favorites pane expands, displaying the tab you most recently viewed.

11. In the upper-right corner of the **Favorites Center**, click the **Pin the Favorites Center** button.

Internet Explorer displays the Favorites Center in a new left pane of the browser window, and the content moves to the right.

*The pinned Favorites Center.*

12. If the **Favorites** tab is not displayed, click it, and verify that the *My Peace and Harmony Page* link is there. Then click the **History** tab and, with **View By Date** selected in the sort list, click **Today**.

The History tab displays an alphabetical list of the sites you have visited today.

*The History tab of the Favorites Center.*

**Tip** By default, Internet Explorer saves your browsing history for 20 days. To change the number of days, open the Internet Options dialog box. In the Browsing History area on the General tab, click Settings, and then enter the number of days (from 0 to 999) you want Internet Explorer to retain your browsing history.

13. In the list, click **search.live (search.live.com)**.

The list expands to display all the searches you performed today using the Live Search engine.

14. Experiment with other aspects of the **Favorites Center**. When you finish, click the **Close** button in the upper-right corner of the **Favorites Center**.

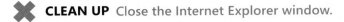 **CLEAN UP** Close the Internet Explorer window.

## Deleting Saved Information

Internet Explorer saves many types of information so that you don't need to remember or re-enter it. If you want to ensure that the saved information is not available to other computer users (particularly if you're loaning or selling your computer to another person), you can delete the saved information.

To clear some or all of your Internet Explorer history:

1.  On the Safety menu, click Delete Browsing History.

*The Delete Browsing History dialog box.*

2.  Select the check boxes of the types of information you want to remove.

3.  If you want to retain files associated with sites on your Favorites bar and on the Favorites tab of your Favorites Center, select the Preserve Favorites Website Data check box.

4.  Click Delete.

## Printing Web Pages

While you're browsing the Web, Internet Explorer makes it easy to print the Web page you're viewing, either on paper or to a file. Before printing the page, you can preview it and adjust settings such as the paper size, the orientation, and the margins.

● To print a Web page by using your default settings, click the Print button on the Command bar.

● To display a page as it will appear when printed, click Print Preview in the Print list.

From the Print Preview window, you can change the page orientation and adjust the print settings.

● To change the print settings without first previewing the page, click Page Setup in the Print list.

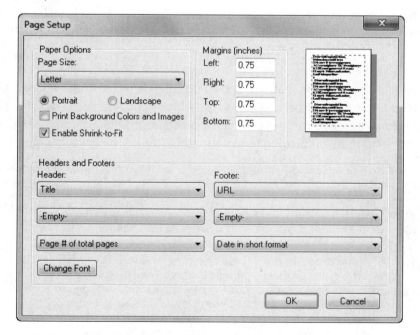

*In the Page Setup dialog box, you can specify the page header and footer as well as print settings such as page size, orientation, and margins.*

**Tip** If you have Microsoft OneNote 2007 or later installed on your computer, you can print Web pages to a OneNote notebook. You can quickly send the contents of a Web page and a link to that page to your default OneNote notebook by clicking Send To OneNote on the Internet Explorer Tools menu. You must have previously started OneNote at least one time before you can send information to it from Internet Explorer.

# Sending Web Pages and Links

Sharing information from Web pages can be very useful—for example, when you are researching information (such as travel plans) on behalf of a group, or if you come across an article that you know would be of interest to a co-worker, friend, or family member. If you have an e-mail program installed on your computer, you can share the information directly from Internet Explorer in two ways:

- You can send a copy of the page embedded in an e-mail message. (If you want to keep a copy of the page handy in an easily accessible electronic format, you can send it to yourself.) Links from the page you send remain active in the e-mail message.

- You can send the page URL in a plain-text message. Message recipients using e-mail programs that support active content can click the URL to display the Web page in a browser window. Recipients using e-mail programs that don't support active content can copy the URL and paste it into a browser to display the page.

**Troubleshooting** These options are available only when working in an e-mail program that is installed on your computer; not when working in a Web mail program that runs inside an Internet Explorer window.

If you have a Windows Live Hotmail account, you also have the option of sending the Web page or link through that account. To do so, click E-mail With Windows Live on the Page menu. This option opens Windows Live Hotmail on a separate tab of the same Internet Explorer window. Internet Explorer protects your account from use by other people by requiring that you first log in to your account.

**See Also** For information about setting the default e-mail program for Internet services, see the sidebar "Setting the Default E-Mail Program" in Chapter 8, "Manage Internet Explorer."

In this exercise, you'll first send an e-mail message with an embedded Web page, and then send another message with a link to a Web page.

**SET UP** You don't need any practice files to complete this exercise, but you do need to have an e-mail program installed on your computer, and an account configured in that program. Start your default e-mail program and log on to your e-mail account if necessary. Then start Internet Explorer and follow the steps.

1. Display any Web site in the Internet Explorer window.

2. On the **Command** bar, click the **Page** button.

The Page menu displays a list of actions you can perform with the current Web page.

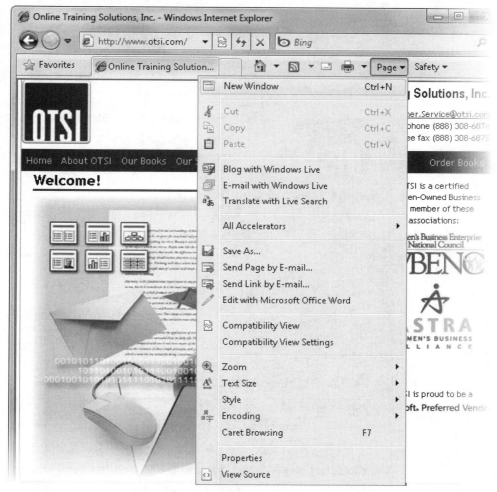

*Some commands on the Page menu are active only when content is selected.*

**3.** On the **Page** menu, click **Send Page by E-mail**.

An Internet Explorer Security dialog box opens, requesting permission to display the page content in an e-mail message.

**4.** In the **Internet Explorer Security** message box, click **Allow**.

A new HTML e-mail message opens in your default e-mail program.

*The contents of the currently displayed page are embedded in the message as individual HTML and graphic elements.*

You can select any text or graphic in the embedded page and work with it as you would work with other e-mail message content.

5. Address the e-mail message to yourself, and then send it. (Or if you prefer, close the message window without sending the message.)

You can work with the message you receive as you would with any other—you can view it, delete it, save it for later reference, or forward it to someone else.

6.  On the **Page** menu, click **Send Link by E-mail**.

    A new plain-text e-mail message opens. Notice the variation in the message subject.

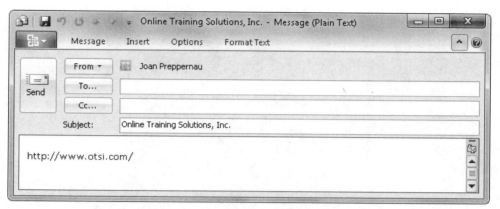

*The name of the current Web page is the message subject, and the page URL appears in the Content pane.*

7.  Address the e-mail message to yourself, and then send it. (Or, if you prefer, close the message window without sending the message.)

**CLEAN UP** Close the Internet Explorer window.

# Key Points

- Accelerators are add-ons to Internet Explorer that let you quickly perform content-related tasks directly from a Web page.

- You can receive information from Web sites and blogs that interest you by subscribing to their RSS feeds. Web Slices are a type of feed that alert you to updated information.

- You can search the Web for information by entering general or specific search terms in the Search box. You may choose whatever search provider you want.

- The Favorites Center keeps track of sites you save, feeds you subscribe to, and your Internet browsing history.

# Chapter at a Glance

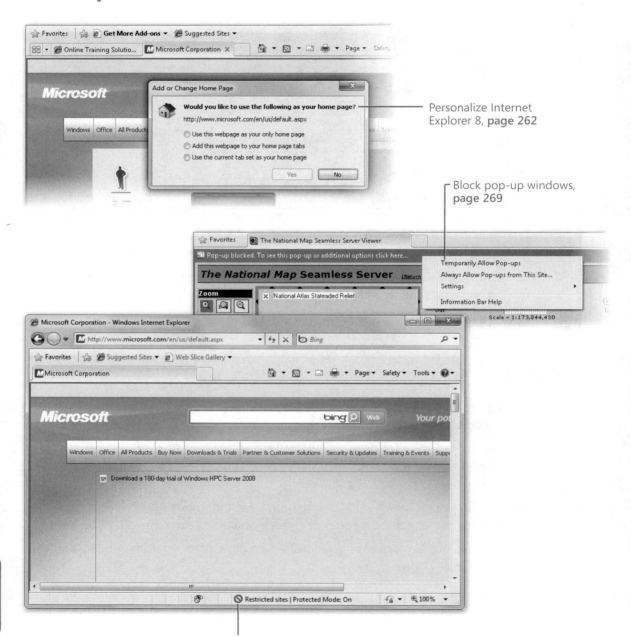

Personalize Internet Explorer 8, **page 262**

Block pop-up windows, **page 269**

Configure Internet security zones, **page 273**

# 8 Manage Internet Explorer

---

**In this chapter, you will learn how to**

✔ Personalize Internet Explorer 8.

✔ Block pop-up windows.

✔ Configure Internet security zones.

✔ Restrict objectionable content.

---

If you frequently visit specific Web sites, you might find it a convenient time-saver to have Windows Internet Explorer 8 automatically display those pages for you when you start the program. If you have trouble viewing information on Web pages, you can control the appearance of the information, including the default font, font size, and color used on Web pages that don't specify those settings.

In addition to these cosmetic changes, you can control many security-related settings, to reassure yourself that you (or your family members) will not have unpleasant experiences when browsing the Internet. You can specify whether programs may open secondary Internet Explorer program windows, as well as explicitly prevent the display of content you consider offensive.

In this chapter, you'll learn how to specify one or more Web pages to open automatically when you start Internet Explorer and how to change the appearance of the Web content that appears within the Internet Explorer program window. Then you'll learn several techniques and settings for protecting your computer from malicious content distributed over the Internet. Finally, you'll learn how to prevent the display of specific types of content during Web browsing sessions.

> **Practice Files** You won't need any practice files to complete the exercises in this chapter. See "Using the Practice Files" at the beginning of this book for more information.

# Personalizing Internet Explorer 8

As with so many Windows 7 elements, you can personalize Internet Explorer to display the content you want in the way you want.

**See Also**  For information about displaying and hiding Internet Explorer toolbars, see "Displaying Web Sites" in Chapter 6, "Connect to the Web."

## Changing Your Home Page

Each time you open a new Internet Explorer window by clicking the Internet Explorer button or command rather than a link to a specific Web site or page, the browser window opens and displays your home page. This is usually the main page of a site you visit often, such as MSN for general information, your company's home page for internal news, or a financial Web site for tracking your investments. You can display more than one home page—for example, if you look at three news sites each morning, you can set all three as home pages so that they open automatically on three tabs of the browser window when you start Internet Explorer. Or if you prefer to avoid the distraction of a commercial site, you can select a blank page as your home page and display a specific Web site only when you choose to visit one.

## Changing the Appearance of Web Content

Some Web sites set the formatting, such as fonts, font sizes, and text and background colors, used in their pages in order to control the way the site looks on your screen. Others don't. In the latter case, you can change the appearance of content displayed in the Internet Explorer window by changing the formatting. You might make these changes for personal preference or for readability if, for example, you have trouble distinguishing certain colors or find it difficult to read small text on a computer monitor.

To change the size of the text on Web pages that don't specifically set the text size:

- On the Internet Explorer Page menu, click Text Size, and then click the size you want: Smallest, Smaller, Medium (the default), Larger, or Largest.

**Tip**  To magnify everything in the Internet Explorer window, click the Change Zoom Level button in the lower-right corner of the window, and then click the zoom level you want.

**Keyboard Shortcut**  You can increase the zoom level of the Internet Explorer window in 25%, increments up to a maximum of 1000%, by pressing Ctrl+Plus Sign (+). You can decrease the zoom level in 25% increments, to a minimum of 10%, by pressing Ctrl+Minus Sign (–).

To change the font of the text on Web pages that don't specifically set the text font:

1. On the Internet Explorer Tools menu, click Internet Options.

2. On the General tab of the Internet Options dialog box, in the Appearance area, click Fonts.

   The Fonts dialog box opens.

*In the Fonts dialog box, you can specify the fonts for text on Web pages and in plain-text documents.*

3. In the Webpage Font list, click the font you want to use, and then click OK.

To change the text and background colors used on Web pages that don't specifically set the color:

1. On the Internet Explorer Tools menu, click Internet Options.

2. On the General tab of the Internet Options dialog box, in the Appearance area, click Colors.

3. In the Colors dialog box, clear the Use Windows Colors check box.

   Clearing this check box activates the Text, Background, Visited, and Unvisited settings. (The Visited and Unvisited settings control the appearance of hyperlinks you have explored and those you haven't, respectively.)

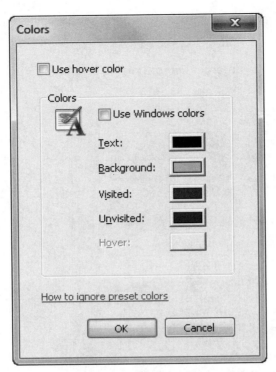

*In the Colors dialog box, you can specify non-standard colors for various Web page elements.*

4. Click the Text, Background, Visited, or Unvisited color button, select the color you want to use for that element, and then click OK.

5. If you want to highlight links that you point to with a color rather than having only the standard underlining, select the Use Hover Color check box at the top of the Colors dialog box, click the Hover color button, and select the color you want. (The default is red.)

6. In the Colors dialog box, click OK to save and apply your changes.

To change the font, font size, text colors, and background color of all Web pages (even Web pages that specify those elements):

1. Complete the previous steps to change the text size and font, and to set the text, background, hyperlink, and hover colors.

2. On the General tab of the Internet Options dialog box, in the Appearance area, click Accessibility.

The Accessibility dialog box opens.

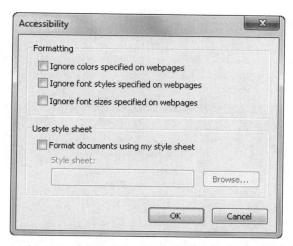

*In the Accessibility dialog box, you can apply non-standard settings to all Web pages.*

3.  In the Formatting area of the Accessibility dialog box, select the Ignore Colors Specified On Webpages check box, the Ignore Font Styles Specified On Webpages check box, and the Ignore Font Sizes Specified On Webpages check box.

    **Tip**  If you don't select these check boxes, Internet Explorer will use the colors and fonts specified in the Web page code.

4.  Click OK to close the dialog box and apply your changes.

In this exercise, you'll change your home page, add a second home page, and then set a blank home page.

**SET UP**  You don't need any practice files to complete this exercise. Start Internet Explorer, and then follow the steps.

1.  On the **Command** bar, click the **Home** button.

    Internet Explorer displays your home page on the current tab.

    **Tip**  Your home page may have been set by your computer manufacturer.

2.  Replace the URL in the **Address** bar with **microsoft.com**, and then press **Alt+Enter**.

    The home page of the Microsoft Web site opens on a new tab.

3.  On the **Command** bar, click the **Home** arrow, and then in the list, click **Add or Change Home Page**.

    The Add Or Change Home Page dialog box opens.

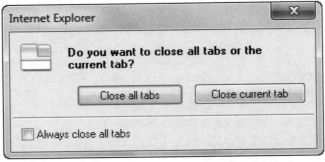

*The Add Or Change Home Page dialog box displays options for adding the current page as a home page.*

4. In the **Add or Change Home Page** dialog box, click **Use this webpage as your only home page**, and then click **Yes**.

5. At the right end of the Internet Explorer window title bar, click the **Close** button.

   A message box appears.

*When you try to close the browser window while multiple tabs are open, Internet Explorer prompts you to confirm that you want to close all the tabs.*

6. In the message box, click **Close all tabs** to close the program window.

7. On the taskbar, click the pinned **Internet Explorer** taskbar button.

   Internet Explorer restarts and displays only the home page of the Microsoft Web site.

8. Replace the URL in the **Address** bar with **msn**, and then press **Ctrl+Enter**.

   The home page of the MSN site opens on the current tab.

9. In the **Home** list, click **Add or Change Home Page**.

The Add Or Change Home Page dialog box displays a different set of options.

*When only one tab is open, the Add Or Change Home Page dialog box does not include the option to use the current set of tabs as your home page.*

10. In the **Add or Change Home Page** dialog box, click **Add this webpage to your home page tabs**, and then click **Yes**.

11. On the **Command** bar, click the **Home** button.

   The two home pages you have set are now open on separate tabs.

12. In the **Home** list, click **Remove**, and then click **Remove All**.

   The Delete Home Page dialog box opens.

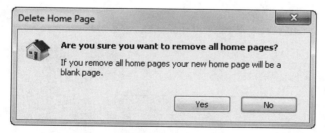

*You don't have to use a Web site as your home page; you can use a blank page instead.*

13. In the **Delete Home Page** dialog box, click **Yes**.

14. On the **Command** bar, click the **Home** button.

   Internet Explorer displays a blank page on the current tab, but does not close the second tab.

15. Close and then restart Internet Explorer.

   Internet Explorer displays only the blank page.

✖ **CLEAN UP** If you want to set a specific home page or pages before continuing, display the page(s), click the Home arrow, click Add Or Change Home Pages, and then set your home page(s).

## Setting the Default E-Mail Program

Often you will find information on the Internet that you want to share with others. One way to do this is to send a Web page or link directly from Internet Explorer, by clicking Send Page By E-mail or Send Link By E-mail on the Internet Explorer Page menu.

To send a Web page or link from Internet Explorer, you must first have installed and configured an e-mail program. You might use more than one e-mail program on your computer—for example, you might use Microsoft Outlook to connect to your work e-mail account and Windows Live Mail to connect to your personal e-mail account. Internet Explorer will automatically open a message in the e-mail program that is set as your default. You can change the e-mail program that Internet Explorer uses, from the Internet Options dialog box.

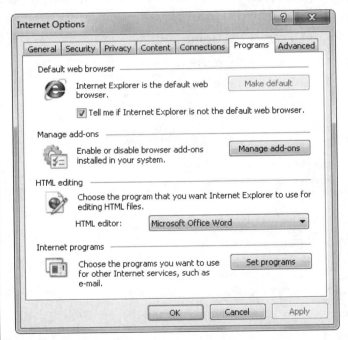

On the Programs tab of the Internet Options dialog box, you can specify which HTML editing and Internet programs you want to work with.

**See Also** For more information about choosing a default Web browser, e-mail client, media player, and other programs, see "Specifying Default Programs" in Chapter 11, "Work with Programs."

# Blocking Pop-Up Windows

Pop-up windows (or just *pop-ups*) are secondary Web browser windows that open in front of (or sometimes behind) the window you're working in when you display a Web site or click an advertising link. The content of these windows might be informational—for example, a new window might open when you click a link for more information or when you log on to a secure site—or in some cases might be irritating or malicious—for example, when browsing the Web for information you might come across display a page that causes several advertisements to pop up behind it. However, pop-ups frequently display annoying advertisements, adware (fake warning messages containing links to product sites), spyware (malicious software that can collect personal information from your computer), or other types of content you did not invite and probably don't want.

You can use the Internet Explorer Pop-up Blocker to prevent the display of unwanted pop-ups. The Pop-up Blocker is turned on by default. When a pop-up tries to open, an audio alert sounds, and the Information bar appears at the top of the Internet Explorer Content pane, notifying you that a pop-up has been blocked.

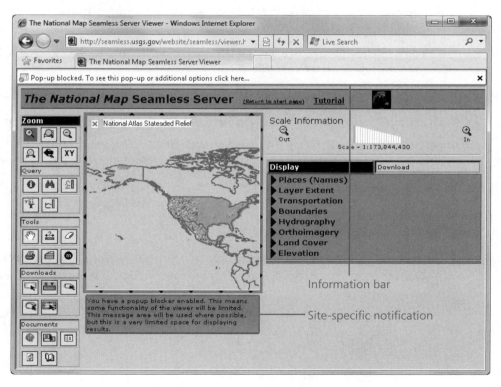

*Some sites display a notification when the Information bar appears.*

You can configure pop-up settings for the currently displayed site by clicking the Information bar and then clicking the option you want.

*Click the Information bar to display the site-specific Pop-up Blocker settings.*

When a pop-up is blocked, you have the following options:

- You can ignore the Information bar and not display the pop-up.
- You can allow pop-ups from the site you're displaying, for the duration of the current browsing session.
- You can allow pop-ups from the site you're displaying, for this and all future browsing sessions.

To turn off the Pop-up Blocker and allow all pop-ups from all sites:

- On the Tools menu, click Pop-up Blocker, and then click Turn Off Pop-up Blocker.

**Important** Unless you visit only Web sites you know to be safe, turning off the Pop-up Blocker entirely is not a good idea, because it exposes your computer to the risk of infection by malware.

You can allow all pop-ups from a specific site to open by adding the site to either the Pop-up Blocker list of allowed Web sites or your Trusted Sites list.

To modify Pop-up Blocker settings:

1. On the Internet Explorer Tools menu, click Pop-up Blocker, and then click Pop-up Blocker Settings; or click Settings on the Information bar menu and then click More Settings.

   The Pop-up Blocker Settings dialog box opens.

*From the Pop-up Blocker Settings dialog box, you can turn off the audio alert and/or Information bar notifying you when a pop-up is blocked, and configure the blocking level.*

2. Do any of the following:

   ○ To allow all pop-ups from a specific site and its subsites, enter the URL (for example, www.microsoft.com) in the Address Of Website To Allow box, and then click Add.

   ○ To allow all pop-ups from any site or subsite in a specific domain, enter the domain (for example, microsoft.com) in the Address Of Website To Allow box, and then click Add.

   ○ To disallow pop-ups from a site or group of sites, click the site or domain in the Allowed Sites list, and then click Remove.

3. Select the notification and blocking level options you want.

   You can set the blocking level to High (block all pop-ups), Medium (block most pop-ups), or Low (allow pop-ups from secure sites). The default is Medium.

4. Click Close to close the dialog box and apply your changes.

## Protecting Yourself from Phishing Sites

Some Web sites are set up to collect information about users who visit them and use that data for fraudulent purposes. These "phishing sites" (so named because they "fish" for information) aren't Web sites that you would visit on purpose; links to them are distributed in e-mail messages, usually purporting to be from a bank or other financial institution. The phishing site link in the message is usually disguised as a valid link, but has code behind it that sends you to a site that is not the one you think you are visiting.

Many phishing messages are immediately obvious due to the poor spelling and grammar they contain. Others claim to come from companies you don't actually have a financial relationship with. Even if you do business with the company, don't click the link! Instead, call the company to verify the validity of the request. Most reputable companies would never communicate with you about your personal or financial information in this way.

Internet Explorer 8 comes with the SmartScreen Filter—a new feature that helps protect you by blocking access to known phishing sites and to sites that distribute malicious software (malware). The filter is updated several times per hour using the latest security information from Microsoft and several industry partners. When you try to connect to a reported phishing or malware site, Internet Explorer highlights the page URL in red, and displays a page informing you that the site has been blocked. You have the option of continuing to the page at your own risk.

You can control the SmartScreen Filter from the Safety menu on the Internet Explorer Command bar. From this menu, you can use the SmartScreen Filter to manually check a Web site against the current database of reported sites, and you can report suspicious sites for investigation.

You can turn off the SmartScreen Filter, but we would advise you to do this only if you feel confident that you, or another user of your computer, will not inadvertently display any malicious sites.

# Configuring Internet Security Zones

With Windows Internet Explorer, you can set different levels of security for different types of Web sites. For example, you might feel perfectly comfortable running programs that originate from your organization's intranet site or from specific Web sites that you trust (such as your own), but not want to allow certain types of programs to run on your computer from the Internet.

Internet Explorer divides the types of Web sites you visit into these four security zones:

- **Internet** All external Web sites that are not on either the Trusted Sites list or the Restricted Sites list.

- **Local intranet** All Web sites that are part of your organization's local network.

- **Trusted** Specific Web sites that you have designated as trustworthy because you believe that content from these sites will not damage your computer or data.

- **Restricted** Specific Web sites that you have designated as untrustworthy because you believe that content from these sites might damage your computer or data.

You must specifically add Web sites to the Trusted Sites list and the Restricted Sites list; otherwise these zones are empty.

You can set the security level for each zone to one of five predefined levels, or you can customize the security level for your own or your organization's needs. The predefined security levels are:

- **High** This level is appropriate for any Web sites you don't trust, or if you want to have full control over the content that is downloaded to and run on your computer. This is the default security level for the Restricted Sites zone. Internet Explorer prevents potentially harmful content from running on your computer, which might mean that the functionality or display of some Web sites is impaired.

- **Medium-high** This level is appropriate for most Internet sites, and it is the default security level for the Internet zone. Internet Explorer prompts you before downloading any potentially unsafe content, and it does not download unsigned ActiveX controls (software components).

- **Medium**  This is the default security level for the Trusted Sites zone. Internet Explorer does not download unsigned ActiveX controls and prompts you for permission before downloading potentially unsafe content. Specific settings vary from the Medium-high security level.

- **Medium-low**  This is the default security level for the Local Intranet zone. Internet Explorer does not download unsigned ActiveX controls, but most other content runs without prompts.

- **Low**  This level is appropriate only for sites that you absolutely trust. Internet Explorer provides only minimal safeguards and warnings, and it downloads and runs most content without prompting you for permission.

Most people will find that the default settings are adequate for their needs, but from time to time you might want or need to customize a setting. Even if you never do, it's good to know what your options are so that you are confident that your Web browsing is done in a secure and sensible manner.

In this exercise, you'll examine your current Internet Explorer security zone settings, experiment with changing your security options, and add and remove a Web site from the Restricted Sites list.

**Important**  If you have personalized your Internet security settings for a specific purpose and do not want to reset them to the default settings, do not complete this exercise.

 **SET UP**  You don't need any practice files to complete this exercise. Start Internet Explorer, display a site of your choosing, and then follow the steps.

1. On the **Tools** menu, click **Internet Options**. Then in the **Internet Options** dialog box, click the **Security** tab.

   The Security tab displays the four security zones and the security level for the current zone.

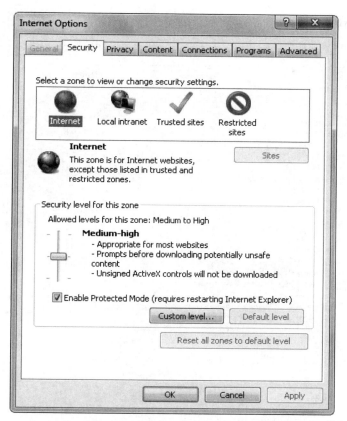

*Depending on your current security settings, the Security Level For This Zone area displays either a slide control or a custom setting.*

**Tip** You can also display this tab from Internet Explorer by double-clicking the zone name on the status bar.

2. If your screen shows a custom setting, click **Default level** to return the Internet zone to the default **Medium-high** security level.

Next you'll try customizing the security options.

**3.** Click **Custom level**.

The Security Settings dialog box for the currently selected Internet zone opens.

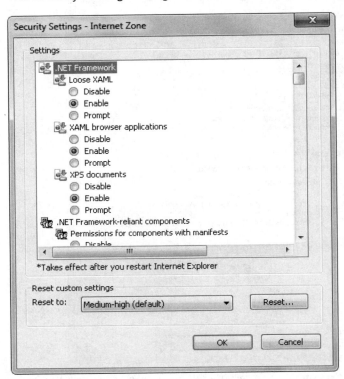

*The dialog box title bar displays the current zone. The default security level for the current zone is selected in the Reset To list.*

**See Also** The settings in the Security Settings dialog box are controlled by option buttons. For each setting, you can select only one option. For more information about option buttons and other dialog box controls, see "Dialog Boxes and Message Boxes" in "Information for New Computer Users" at the beginning of this book.

**4.** Scroll the **Settings** list to get an idea of the scope of settings controlled by the Internet Explorer security level.

Some of the setting names are self-explanatory; for others, it is not quite as easy to determine the effect they have on your browsing experience. All the settings are security-related and are there for your protection, so it's best not to make changes to settings you aren't familiar with.

5. About two-thirds of the way down the **Settings** list, in the **Miscellaneous** section, locate **Drag and drop or copy and paste files**.

   The default for this setting in the Medium-high security level is Enable.

6. Under **Drag and drop or copy and paste files**, click **Prompt**.

   This is a harmless setting to change, but one that will allow us to safely demonstrate the process of changing security settings.

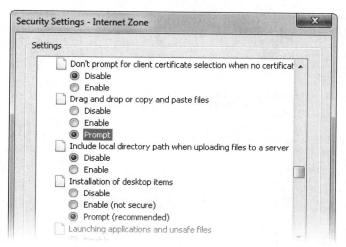

*Changing the Drag And Drop Or Copy And Paste Files setting to Prompt causes Internet Explorer to confirm that you want to perform these actions.*

7. In the **Security Settings** dialog box, click **OK**.

   Internet Explorer prompts you to confirm that you want to make changes to this security setting.

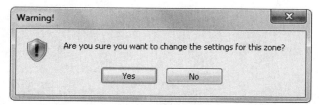

*A Warning icon emphasizes the potential risk of changing a security setting.*

**8.** In the **Warning** message box, click **Yes**.

In the Internet Options dialog box, the security level for the Internet zone is now set to Custom.

*When you customize the security level, the specific customizations are not indicated on the Security tab or in the Security Settings dialog box.*

**9.** In the **Select a zone to view or change security settings** pane, click **Restricted sites**.

The Security tab displays the settings for the Restricted Sites zone.

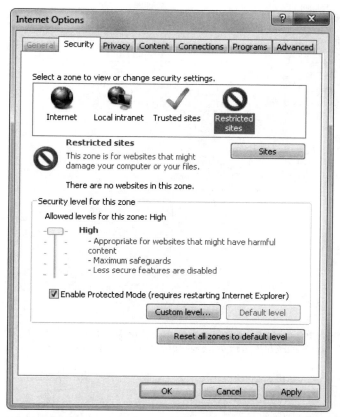

*The slide control is set to High, and it is dimmed to indicate that it cannot be moved.*

The security level for the Restricted Sites zone cannot be changed from High to another preset level, but you can customize specific settings in the Security Settings dialog box.

**10.** Click **Sites**.

The Restricted Sites dialog box opens.

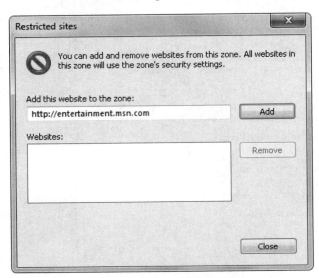

Restricted sites

You can add and remove websites from this zone. All websites in this zone will use the zone's security settings.

Add this website to the zone:

http://entertainment.msn.com

Add

Websites:

Remove

Close

*The address of the currently displayed site is in the Add This Website To The Zone box, so adding it to the Restricted Sites list is as simple as clicking the Add button.*

Depending on your previous Internet Explorer use, the Websites list might already contain one or more site addresses.

**11.** Replace the URL that appears in the **Add this website to the zone** box with **www.microsoft.com**, and then click **Add**.

**12.** In the **Restricted sites** dialog box, click **Close**. Then in the **Internet Properties** dialog box, click **OK**.

**13.** Replace the address that appears in the **Address** box in the Internet Explorer window with **microsoft**, and then press **Ctrl+Enter**.

Internet Explorer displays the Microsoft Corporation Web site. Content that is restricted by the security zone, such as scripts and active content, will not run or display.

Placeholder for restricted content      Current security zone

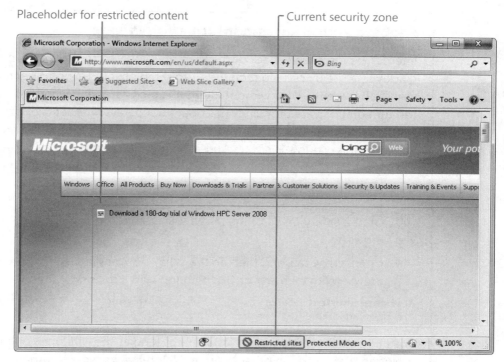

*The status bar at the bottom of the Internet Explorer window indicates that this site is in the Restricted Sites zone.*

**14.** Repeat step 1 to display the **Security** tab of the **Internet Options** dialog box. In the dialog box, click **Restricted sites**, and then click **Sites**.

**15.** In the **Websites** list, click **www.microsoft.com**. Click **Remove**, and then click **Close**.

**16.** In the **Select a zone** area, click **Internet**, and then click **Default level** to return the Internet zone to the default security settings.

 **CLEAN UP** Ensure that the Internet Explorer security settings are set the way you want them, and then close the Internet Options dialog box, before you proceed.

## Keeping Your Browsing Information Private

Internet Explorer keeps track of the Web sites you visit so that you can return quickly to a site by clicking it on the History tab of your Favorites Center. If you want to browse the Web without Internet Explorer tracking where you go, you can turn on InPrivate Browsing. This opens a separate Internet Explorer window in which an InPrivate label is shown to the left of the Address box. The browsing that you do in this window is not tracked—the pages and sites do not appear on the History tab, and temporary files and cookies are not saved on your computer.

To start an InPrivate Browsing session:

- On the Safety menu of the Internet Explorer Command bar, click InPrivate Browsing.

- Open a new tab, and then on the What Do You Want To Do Next page, click Browse With InPrivate or Open An InPrivate Browsing Window.

**Keyboard Shortcut** You can open an InPrivate Browsing window from the keyboard by pressing Ctrl+Shift+P.

The InPrivate Browsing session lasts only as long as the window is open. Any browsing that you do in other Internet Explorer windows is recorded as usual.

Another InPrivate tool, InPrivate Filtering, analyzes the Web pages you visit and gives you the option to block visible or hidden content that is not part of the Web page code and that it determines is distributed to multiple sites. Some companies collect information about you through this type of third-party content.

By default, InPrivate Filtering works in the background of your Internet Explorer session but does not notify you of or block third-party content. You can use InPrivate Filtering to either block all content that meets its criteria or to display a dialog box when it encounters this type of content.

To change the InPrivate Filtering settings:

1. Turn on InPrivate Filtering.

2. On the Safety menu of the Internet Explorer Command bar, click InPrivate Filtering Settings.

The InPrivate Filtering Settings dialog box opens.

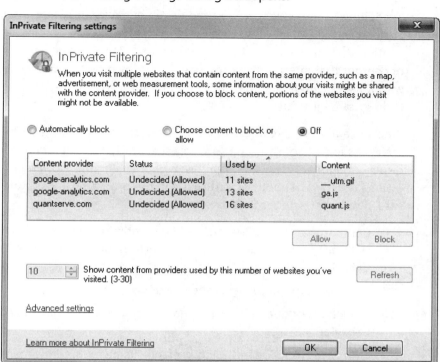

*The InPrivate Filtering Settings dialog box displays a list of the third-party content providers present on sites that you've visited.*

3. In the dialog box, click Automatically Block or Choose Content To Block Or Allow.

4. If you click Choose Content To Block Or Allow, you can click individual content providers in the list and then click Allow or Block.

5. In the InPrivate Filtering Settings dialog box, click OK.

By using tools such as InPrivate Browsing and InPrivate Filtering, you can avoid any concern that you might have about information that you don't specifically release being collected.

# Restricting Objectionable Content

In addition to the basic ways you can tailor your Web-browsing experience, Internet Explorer includes the Content Advisor, which offers peace of mind regarding the types of content that can be viewed on your computer. The Content Advisor controls the types of content that Internet Explorer may display by monitoring Web sites in accordance with ICRA (formerly the Internet Content Rating Association, now a part of the Family Online Safety Institute).

Web site authors and owners who are aware of Internet rating systems voluntarily submit their sites for rating. You can allow only sites with a certain rating, and you can block the display of unrated sites (although this might result in the blocking of a lot of sites whose owners don't know about or participate in the program). ICRA catalogs submitted Web sites in rating categories that cover:

- Content that creates feelings of fear or intimidation, sets a bad example for young children, or encourages children to perform or imitate dangerous or harmful behavior.

- Depictions of gambling or the use of weapons, alcohol, tobacco, or other drugs.

- Depictions of discrimination or encouragement to engage in discriminatory behavior.

- Offensive language including profanity, expletives, terms for bodily functions, anatomical references, obscene gestures, explicit sexual references, and otherwise vulgar, discriminatory, or crude language.

- Partial, frontal, or full nudity, revealing attire, and provocative displays.

- Mild or explicit sexual activity, passionate kissing, and clothed or non-explicit sexual touching.

- Violence, including aggressive, natural, or accidental violence; fighting in which creatures are injured or killed or damage is inflicted on realistic objects; injuring or killing of humans or non-threatening creatures; injuring or killing of humans with blood and gore; or wanton and gratuitous violence.

- User-generated content, such as conversations in chat rooms, that is not controlled by a site owner and might or might not be moderated.

For each of the content categories, you can specify the level of that type of content Internet Explorer may display: None, Limited, Some, or Unrestricted. (The Some option is available for only some of the categories.)

In this exercise, you'll configure the Content Advisor settings and then see Content Advisor in action.

 **SET UP** You don't need any practice files to complete this exercise. Start Internet Explorer, and then follow the steps.

1. On the Internet Explorer **Tools** menu, click **Internet Options**. Then in the **Internet Options** dialog box, click the **Content** tab.

   From the Content tab, you can access commands and controls related to Internet content that appears on your computer.

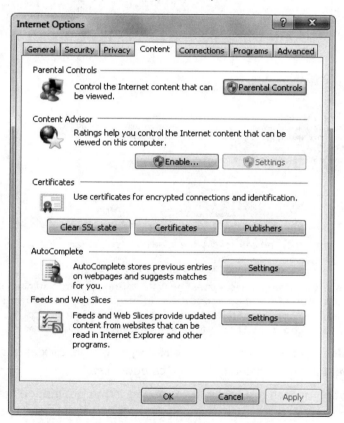

*Internet Explorer offers several content protection options.*

2. In the **Content Advisor** area, click **Enable**.

The Content Advisor dialog box opens, displaying the Ratings tab.

*From the Ratings tab, you can specify the allowable level of specific types of content that might be offensive or inappropriate.*

**Tip** By default, Content Advisor uses the ICRA rating system. You can add the SafeSurf rating system. For information about ICRA ratings and tips for ensuring safe Web browsing for kids, or to apply for an ICRA label for a Web site you control, visit www.fosi.org. For information about the SafeSurf ratings, visit www.safesurf.com.

3. In the **Select a category to view the rating levels** list, click each category in turn and move the slider located below the category list.

A description of each restriction level appears in the Description area below the slider.

4. Set the restriction level for each category as you want it, and then click the **Approved Sites** tab.

You can allow or block the display of specific sites, regardless of their content, by entering the site's URL in the Allow This Website box and then clicking the Always button (to allow the site) or the Never button (to block the site).

*A white check mark on a green icon indicates an approved site; a white bar on a red icon indicates a blocked site.*

**Tip** Don't be misled by the names of the tab and text box—you can block sites as well as allow them by adding them to the Approved Sites tab.

5. Add any sites you want to this list, and then click the **General** tab.

    If you activate Content Advisor without selecting Users Can See Websites That Have No Rating, Internet Explorer blocks the display of any site that doesn't include a rating information from the selected organization(s) in its site code.

*On the General tab, you can specify supervisor settings and add rating systems.*

6. For the purposes of this exercise, leave the **Users can see websites that have no rating** check box cleared, and the **Supervisor can type a password...** check box selected. Then in the **Supervisor password** area, click **Create password**.

   If you don't create a Content Advisor password ahead of time, Content Advisor prompts you to do so the first time you activate it.

7. In the **Create Supervisor Password** dialog box, type **P@ssw0rd** in the **Password** and **Confirm password** boxes, and click **OK**. Then click **OK** in the message box confirming that the password was successfully created.

   **Tip** You can display an Internet Explorer Web page that includes links to the available rating systems (currently only ICRA and SafeSurf) by clicking Find Rating Systems in the Rating Systems area.

8. In the **Content Advisor** dialog box, click **OK**. Then click **OK** in the message box confirming that Content Advisor has been enabled.

   In the Internet Options dialog box, the buttons in the Content Advisor area change to Disable and Settings.

9. Close the **Internet Options** dialog box, and then close the **Internet Explorer** window.

   The Content Advisor settings are applied to all Internet Explorer windows opened after this point. If you try to open a site that does not meet your criteria, Internet Explorer displays a dialog box restricting access to the site. You can browse the Web to see if you come across a site restricted by Content Advisor. (Keep in mind that Content Advisor evaluates only those sites that include their ratings within the site code.) You must enter the supervisor password to access any site that doesn't meet the criteria you specified.

10. Click the **Start** button, type **http://www.otsi.com** in the **Start** menu **Search** box, and then press **Enter**.

    Internet Explorer starts and attempts to display our company's Web site. Because the site code does not contain rating information, the Content Advisor dialog box opens.

*The Content Advisor dialog box opens when you attempt to display a site that hasn't been rated, or that has been rated by a rating system you didn't select.*

11. Click **Always allow this website to be viewed**, type **P@ssw0rd** in the **Password** box, and then click **OK**.

    **Tip**  The Always Allow This Website... option allows the display of any page within the structure of the currently displayed Web site. The Always Allow This Webpage... option allows only the specific page that is currently displayed (the page shown in the title bar).

    The home page of our Web site appears. (We promise there's no inappropriate content on the site!)

12. Click any of the site navigation links.

    Content Advisor again restricts you from displaying the page. Obviously, this type of constant restriction can be quite irritating. After you view a few other Web sites with your criteria in place, you might want to make adjustments to the Content Advisor settings to fine-tune the way it works.

13. In the **Content Advisor** dialog box, click **Cancel**.

14. On the **Tools** menu, click **Internet Options**. Then on the **Content** tab of the **Internet Options** dialog box, in the **Content Advisor** area, click **Disable**.

    The Supervisor Password Required dialog box opens.

*Only people who know the Content Advisor supervisor password can change its settings or disable it.*

15. In the **Supervisor Password Required** message box, type **P@ssw0rd** in the **Password** box, and then click **OK**.

    A message box appears, informing you that Content Advisor has been turned off.

16. In the **Content Advisor** message box, click **OK**.

**✖ CLEAN UP** Close the Internet Options dialog box and the Internet Explorer window.

**Tip** On the Advanced tab of the Internet Options dialog box are many settings that affect various aspects of Internet Explorer, such as accessibility, browsing, printing, and searching. For the most part, you are unlikely to need to change these options. However, if you find yourself wishing that some aspect of Internet Explorer worked a different way, you might want to display the Advanced tab to see if one of its options will do the trick.

**Protecting Children's Privacy**

In November 1998, the U.S. Congress passed the Children's Online Privacy Protection Act (COPPA), which requires that operators of U.S.-based online services or Web sites obtain parental consent before collecting, using, disclosing, or displaying the personal information of children under the age of 13. COPPA went into effect on April 21, 2000 and is governed by regulations established by the Federal Trade Commission.

More information about COPPA, including guides for parents, teachers, and Web site operators, is available at www.ftc.gov/bcp/menus/consumer/data/child.shtm.

# Key Points

- Not only can you change the home page that opens when you start Internet Explorer, but you can set multiple home pages to open.

- You can personalize the look of the browser window as well as the way content appears and performs within the window.

- Internet Explorer applies pre-set groups of security settings to sites that you visit. You can change the settings for a security zone. You can increase or decrease the safeguards applied to a specific site by adding it to the Restricted Sites list or to the Trusted Sites list.

- Windows 7 incorporates safeguards that help to shield computer users from objectionable Internet content. You can specify the level of protection you want.

Part 3

# Managing Your Computer

# Chapter at a Glance

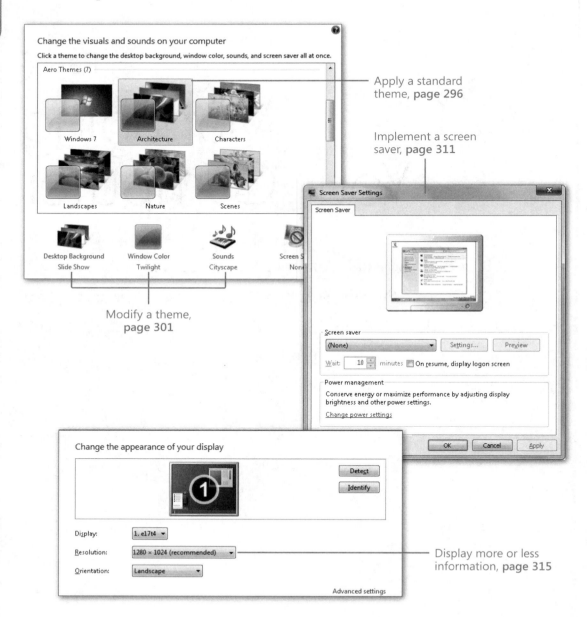

Apply a standard theme, **page 296**

Implement a screen saver, **page 311**

Modify a theme, **page 301**

Display more or less information, **page 315**

# 9 Change Visual Elements

**In this chapter, you will learn how to**

✔ Apply a standard theme.

✔ Modify a theme.

✔ Implement a screen saver.

✔ Display more or less information.

The appearance of the Start menu, Windows Taskbar, programs, windows, dialog boxes, and other items on your screen (collectively referred to as the *user interface*) is determined by the current visual theme and theme elements. The default Windows 7 theme elements include a desktop background graphic named Harmony, a sky-blue color scheme, transparent window frames, and a set of traditional sounds associated with computer events or actions. You can choose another built-in theme, download a theme, or create your own.

The elements of each theme are controlled by a variety of settings that you can change to suit your needs and preferences. You can also change other aspects of the user interface, such as what happens when you don't use the computer for a period of time and the amount of space taken up by the items displayed on your screen. Although such changes might seem merely cosmetic, proper management of the desktop work environment can greatly contribute to your efficiency. It's worth taking the time to explore the options so that you can personalize any aspect of your computer's appearance and functionality that distracts you or otherwise slows you down.

In this chapter, you'll change the appearance of Windows 7 by working with themes, backgrounds, and color schemes. You'll also select a screen saver and change the screen resolution of your computer display.

> **Practice Files** Before you can complete the exercises in this chapter, you need to install the practice files specified in "Using the Practice Files" at the beginning of this book to their default location. The practice files you will use to complete the exercises in this chapter are in the Visual practice file folder.

# Applying a Standard Theme

You can easily change the look of the Windows 7 user interface elements by applying a different theme. Each theme can include the following four elements:

- A desktop background image or color
- A color scheme that affects window frames, the Start menu, and the taskbar
- Sounds that are associated with specific actions
- A screen saver that starts after a period of inactivity

Windows 7 comes with a standard set of Aero themes that includes the following:

- Windows 7 (the default)
- Themes that include graphic backgrounds, such as Architecture, Characters, Landscapes, Nature, and Scenes
- Themes relevant to different regions of the world

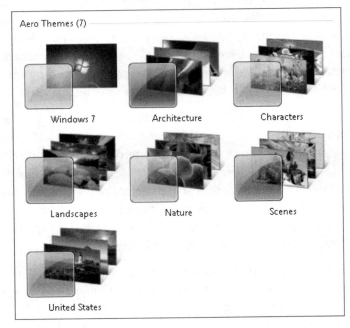

*The right pane of the Personalization window in Control Panel lists the available Aero themes.*

In addition, Windows 7 includes two basic themes designed for computer systems that don't support Aero graphics, and four high-contrast themes designed for people who need additional help viewing information on the screen.

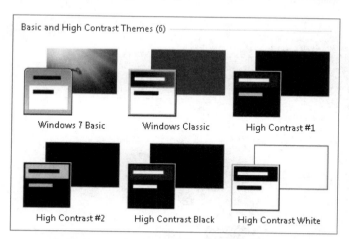

*Below the Aero themes in the Personalization window are six special-purpose themes.*

You can supplement the standard theme set by downloading additional themes or theme elements from the Internet.

**Tip** Computer manufacturers frequently provide additional themes featuring the computer brand information. When you purchase a new computer, the theme might be set to one of these themes.

In earlier versions of Windows, each theme included only one desktop background option. In Windows 7, a theme can include multiple desktop backgrounds that are displayed sequentially, like a slide show.

**See Also** For information about customizing a desktop background slide show, see "Modifying a Theme" later in this chapter.

In this exercise, you'll switch among various standard themes.

**SET UP** You don't need any practice files to complete this exercise; just follow the steps.

1. Open **Control Panel** in Category view, and size the window so that you can see the desktop background behind it.

2. In **Control Panel**, under **Appearance and Personalization**, click **Change the theme**.

The Personalization window opens.

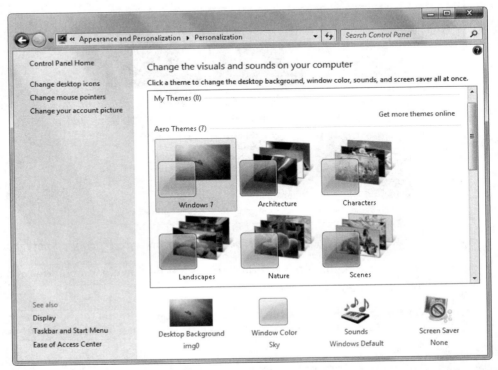

*In the Personalization window, standard and custom themes are available from the right pane.*

3. In the right pane, under **Aero Themes**, click each of the standard themes in turn, pausing to notice the effect behind the **Personalization** window.

At the bottom of the right pane, the Desktop Background and Window Color previews change to reflect the corresponding elements of your selection. As you select each scheme, Windows plays a sound from the corresponding sound scheme, and the name below the Sounds icon changes.

4. Click the **Landscapes** theme, and then, in the upper-right corner of the **Personalization** window, click the **Minimize** button.

One of the six corresponding desktop backgrounds fills the screen.

*The Landscapes theme includes six desktop backgrounds and a transparent gray color scheme.*

5. On the taskbar, click the **Control Panel** taskbar button to restore the **Personalization** window.

6. Scroll the right pane, and under **Basic and High Contrast Themes**, click each of the themes in turn.

   The first two themes are basic representations of traditional Windows themes. The last four themes feature solid window colors with no fancy graphics or transparency effects.

7. In the right pane, under **Aero Themes**, click the **Nature** theme.

 **CLEAN UP**  Close Control Panel, leaving the Nature theme selected for use in the next exercise.

## Downloading a Theme

Clicking Get More Themes Online in the My Themes section of the Personalization window takes you to the Personalize Your PC page of the Windows Web site. When you select a theme on this page, the File Download dialog box opens. You can apply the theme to Windows immediately by clicking Open, or save it to your computer by clicking Save.

When you apply a theme, Windows saves a folder containing the theme files in your personal Themes folder, and the theme appears under My Themes in the right pane of the Personalization window, with other non-standard themes. The downloaded theme remains in the My Themes list even if you apply a different theme.

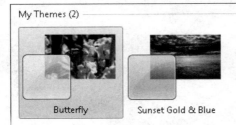

*Downloaded and custom themes appear in the My Themes section of the Personalization window and can be applied just like any other theme.*

**Tip** By default, your personal Themes folder is the AppData\Local\Microsoft\Windows\ Themes folder under your user account folder. The AppData folder is hidden by default.

When you download a theme, Windows saves a .themepack file containing the theme settings in your Downloads folder (unless you choose another location). Double-clicking the .themepack file adds the theme's files to your personal Themes folder and to the My Themes area of the Personalization window.

# Modifying a Theme

You can customize a theme by changing any of its four elements. If you save the customized theme, you can switch to it at any time. In this section, we discuss three theme elements you can change: the desktop background, the window color, and the sound scheme.

**See Also** For information about screen savers, see "Implementing a Screen Saver" later in this chapter.

## Desktop Background

You can easily change the background image displayed on the Windows desktop. To display the desktop background options, open the Personalization window of Control Panel, and then click Desktop Background.

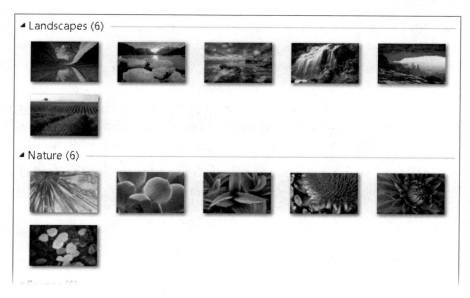

*In the Desktop Background window, you can select from a variety of backgrounds.*

Your choice of desktop background usually reflects your personal taste—what you like to see when your program windows are minimized or closed. Some people prefer simple backgrounds that don't obscure their desktop icons, and others prefer photos of family members, pets, or favorite places.

Windows 7 comes with many desktop background images to choose from, including photographs and abstract art. You can use any of the photos that come with Windows, or a digital image of your own. Or, if you want to keep things simple, you can opt for a plain, colored background. You can preview each background on your desktop before actually applying it.

Within any particular theme, you can use some or all of the associated desktop background images as a slide show, or you can select only one image.

When displaying an image as your desktop background, you can specify the position of the image as follows:

- **Fill**  One copy of the image is centered on the screen. The image fills the screen horizontally *and* vertically, and maintains its original aspect ratio. Parts of the image may overrun the left and right sides or the top and bottom edges (but not both).

- **Fit**  One copy of the image is centered on the screen. The image fills the screen horizontally *or* vertically, and maintains its original aspect ratio. Parts of the image may not fill the left and right sides or the top and bottom edges.

- **Stretch**  One copy of the image is centered on the screen. The image fills the screen horizontally *and* vertically, but does not maintain its original aspect ratio. No part of the image overruns the screen.

- **Tile** The image appears on the screen at its original size. One copy of the image is anchored in the upper-left corner of the screen, followed by as many copies as are necessary to fill the screen. Parts of the image may run past the right side or bottom edge of the screen.

- **Center** One copy of the image is centered on the screen at its original size.

Because Fit and Centered images can expose the desktop background, you also specify a desktop background color to appear behind the image.

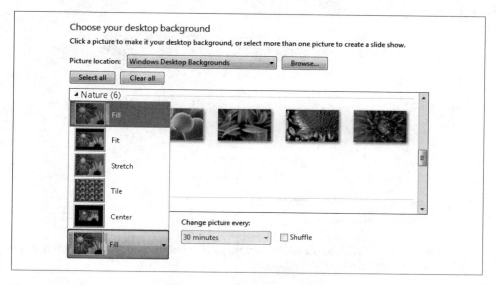

*You can change the way a picture is positioned on the desktop.*

For themes that include multiple desktop background images, you can specify whether Windows displays the pictures in a random or specific order, and how often the image changes—from once every 10 seconds to once each day.

## Window Color

From the Window Color And Appearance window of Control Panel, you can change the color used for window frames, the Start menu, and the taskbar. You can also change or turn off the transparent glass effect.

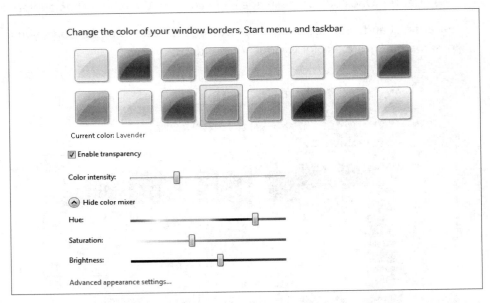

*The options in the Window Color And Appearance window control the appearance of window frames, the Start menu, and the taskbar.*

**Troubleshooting** The transparency effects are available only on hardware that supports Windows Aero technology, and only when an Aero theme is selected. Under other circumstances, the Windows Color and Appearance dialog box opens. From this dialog box, you can set properties for basic desktop elements..

Windows 7 offers 16 standard colors, but you can pick any color by displaying the color mixer and adjusting the Hue, Saturation, and Brightness settings. You can even vary the color's intensity until you get exactly the effect you want.

**Tip** If you have selected one of the Basic or High Contrast themes (or if your computer's hardware does not support advanced graphics) and you want to change the color assigned to a particular screen element, click Advanced Appearance Settings at the bottom of the Window Color And Appearance window. You can then change the color assignments in the Window Color And Appearance dialog box.

## Sounds

The themes that come with Windows 7 all include a sound scheme that assigns specific sounds to some, but not all, program events. Some use the default Windows sound scheme and others have sound schemes specifically chosen to reflect the theme. You can change the sound options from the Sound dialog box, which you open by clicking Sounds in the Personalization window of Control Panel.

*The theme's sound scheme controls the sounds assigned to program events.*

You can switch to a different scheme by clicking it in the Sound Scheme list. You can turn off sounds altogether by clicking No Sounds in this list. You can modify any scheme by clicking an event in the Program Events list and then clicking a sound in the Sounds list. When you finish assigning new sounds, you can save the customized scheme by clicking Save As and assigning the scheme a name. The scheme is then applied to the theme and is also available in the Sound Scheme list for use with any other theme.

## Custom Themes

When you make an adjustment to a theme, the new combination appears in the My Themes section of the Personalization window with the name *Unsaved Theme*. The Unsaved Theme remains available if you switch to a different theme, and it remains available from computing session to session.

However, you can have only one Unsaved Theme. If you want to create a variety of themes—for example, to suit your moods or to celebrate different holidays—you must explicitly save them with different names. When you first create a custom theme, you can click Save Theme in the My Themes section to save the file. You can then apply the theme at any time.

**Tip** If you close the Personalization window before saving the custom theme, the Save Theme option does not appear the next time you open the window. To save the theme, first apply it, and then right-click it in the My Themes list and click Save Theme.

If you no longer need a custom theme, you can delete it from the My Themes section of the Personalization window regardless of whether you have saved it or not. You cannot delete a built-in theme.

To delete a custom theme:

1. Make sure that the theme you want to delete is not applied.
2. In the My Themes section of the Personalization window, right-click the theme, and then click Delete Theme.
3. In the Delete File message box, confirm the deletion by clicking Yes.

In this exercise, you'll preview the built-in desktop background options. After switching to a plain, solid-color background, you will specify a non-transparent color for borders, the Start menu, and the taskbar. Then you'll save the combination as a custom theme.

**SET UP** You don't need any practice files to complete this exercise. Follow the steps Apply the Nature theme (see the previous exercise), open Control Panel, and then follow the steps.

1. In the **Appearance and Personalization** category of **Control Panel**, click **Change desktop background**.

   The Desktop Background window opens.

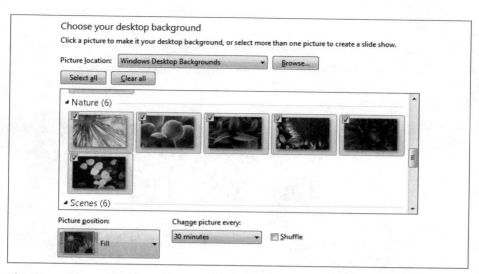

*The check marks in the upper-left corners of six Nature images indicate that those images will be displayed, rotating according to the Change Picture Every setting.*

The Desktop Background window displays thumbnails of the images available when Windows Desktop Backgrounds is selected in the Picture Location list. The thumbnails of the available images are grouped in themes, with the theme containing your current desktop background displayed. Any images in the theme that will be displayed as the desktop background are identified by a check mark in their upper-left corner. In this case, all of the Nature images have check marks.

2. With **Windows Desktop Backgrounds** selected in the **Picture Location** list, clear the check boxes of all but two of the **Nature** images. Then select the check boxes of two **Landscapes** images.

3. In the **Change picture every** list, click **10 seconds**, and then watch as a slide show of the two Nature images and the two Landscapes images is displayed on the desktop behind the window.

**Tip** To display the pictures in random order instead of sequentially, select the Shuffle check box.

4. In the **Picture Location** list, click **Pictures Library**.

The Desktop Background window changes to display the pictures in the Pictures library.

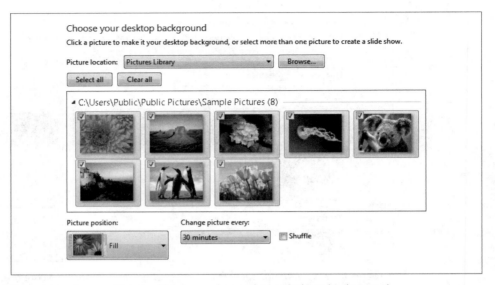

*Any picture in your Pictures library can be used as a desktop background.*

These photographs come with Windows 7 and are stored in the Public Pictures\
Sample Pictures folder. You can find a link to that folder in your personal Pictures
library. If you have stored any of your own pictures in this library, their thumbnails
are also available for display as your desktop background.

**Tip** To use pictures that are stored in a folder other than your Pictures library, click
Browse to the right of the Picture Location list, and then in the Browse For Folder
dialog box, navigate to that folder, and click OK. In the Desktop Background window,
the Picture Location box now shows the path of the selected folder, and thumbnails
of all the pictures stored in that folder are displayed so that you can click the pictures
you want to use as your desktop background.

5. In the **Picture Location** list, click **Top Rated Photos**.

The list now displays a subset of photographs that have a rating of four or five stars.

**Tip** You can rate the pictures in your Pictures library to limit the desktop display to
your favorites. For information about rating files, see "Working with Folder and File
Properties" in Chapter 5, "Manage Folders and Files."

6. Point to each picture in turn to display information about it, including its rating.
Then clear the check boxes of all the images except **Koala**, **Penguins**, and **Tulips**.

7. Below the thumbnails, in the **Picture position** list, click **Center**.

On your desktop, the picture changes to its actual dimensions. Depending on your screen resolution, this might result in blank space above and below the picture or on all four sides.

**Troubleshooting**  Results can vary depending on your hardware.

8. Below **Picture position**, click **Change background color**.

The Color dialog box opens.

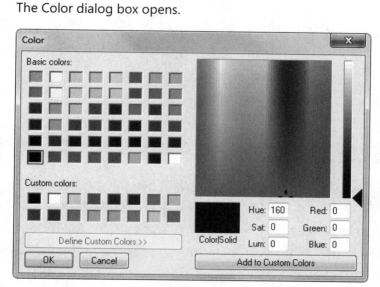

*You can select which color will surround the centered graphic.*

9. In the **Color** dialog box, click any color you like, and then click **OK**.

The blank space around the picture changes to the selected color.

10. After waiting a few seconds to see the picture behind the window change, in the **Picture Location** list, click **Solid Colors**.

The Desktop Background window changes to display a set of more than 30 basic colors.

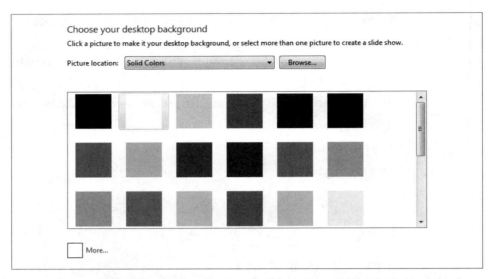

*If none of these colors suits your needs, you can click More to display the Color dialog box, from which you can select any color.*

**11.** Click the second color in the first row (white), and then click **Save changes** to apply your background selection and return to the **Personalization** window.

A thumbnail of the customized theme appears in the My Themes section.

**12.** At the bottom of the **Personalization** window, click **Window Color**.

**13.** In the **Window Color and Appearance** window, click the first color in the first row (**Sky**), and then drag the window by its title bar to the lower-left corner of the screen.

You can see the transparent glass effect through the taskbar.

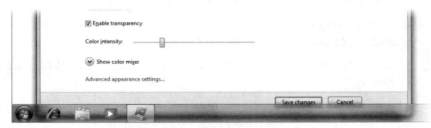

*When Enable Transparency is turned on, you can see through the taskbar, the frames of windows, and the Start menu.*

14. Clear the **Enable transparency** check box to see the effect of a solid window frame, and then reselect the check box.

15. At the bottom of the **Window Color and Appearance** window, click **Save changes**.

   The Unsaved Theme thumbnail in the My Themes section shows that the theme now has a light blue window color.

16. To the right of the **Unsaved Theme** thumbnail in the **My Themes** section, click **Save theme**.

   The Save Theme As dialog box opens.

*You can assign a name to a customized theme.*

17. In the **Save Theme As** dialog box, type **Theme1** as the name of the custom theme, and then click **Save**.

**✕ CLEAN UP** Change the desktop background to suit your preferences, and then close all open windows before moving on.

# Implementing a Screen Saver

Screen savers are blank screens or moving images that are displayed on your monitor after some period of inactivity. Originally, screen savers were used to prevent monitors from being permanently "imprinted" with a static image that remained on the screen for too long. Modern monitors are not susceptible to this kind of damage, but you might still want to use a screen saver for the following reasons:

● It hides the information on your screen when you are away from your desk.

● It personalizes your work area.

By default, the themes that come with Windows 7 do not include screen savers. However, you can customize any theme by adding one of the built-in screen savers, and you can download other animated screen savers from the Internet. For all screen savers, you can preview the effect, set the interval of inactivity before it will be displayed, and specify whether your password must be entered to unlock the screen saver after it is set in motion. For some screen savers, you can set options such as size, motion pattern, and style.

In this exercise, you'll preview the screen savers that come with Windows 7 and then select a screen saver that consists of a slide show of photographs.

 **SET UP** You need the images located in your Documents\Microsoft Press\Windows7SBS\ Visual folder to complete this exercise. Display the Appearance And Personalization window of Control Panel in Category view, and then follow the steps.

1. In the **Appearance and Personalization** window of **Control Panel**, under **Personalization**, click **Change screen saver**.

   The Screen Saver Settings dialog box opens.

*You can activate a screen saver and control when and how it appears.*

2. In the **Screen saver** list, click **Mystify**, and then click **Preview**. Move the mouse to redisplay the dialog box.

3. In the **Screen saver** list, click **3D Text**, and then click **Settings**.

   The 3D Text Settings dialog box opens.

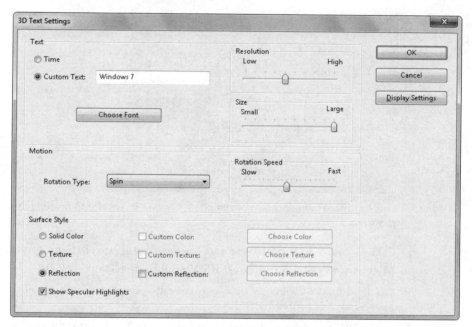

*You can specify your own text and control its appearance.*

**Troubleshooting**  If your hardware does not support Aero, the 3D Text screen saver might not be available. In that case, skip to step 6.

4. In the **Custom Text** box, drag across **Windows 7** to select it, and replace it with **My Screen Saver**. Change any other settings you want, and click **OK**. Then click **Preview**.

5. Move the mouse to redisplay the dialog box. Then in the **Screen saver** list, click other screen savers, and preview their effects.

6. In the **Screen saver** list, click **Photos**.

   The preview screen displays a slide show of the pictures in the Public Pictures\ Sample Pictures folder.

**Troubleshooting**  If you have saved pictures in your personal Pictures folder, they will also be part of the slide show.

7. Click **Settings**.

The Photos Screen Saver Settings dialog box opens.

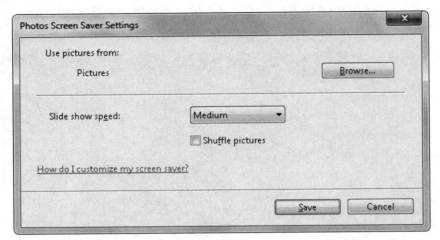

*You can specify the location of the photos to be used in the slide show and set the speed of the show.*

8. Click **Browse**. In the **Browse For Folder** dialog box, browse to your **Documents\ Microsoft Press\Windows7SBS\Visual** folder. Then click **OK**.

**Tip** If you have a folder of your own favorite photos on your computer, feel free to browse to that folder instead.

9. In the **Photos Screen Saver Settings** dialog box, in the **Slide show speed** list, click **Fast**. Then select the **Shuffle pictures** check box, and click **Save**.

In the Screen Saver Settings dialog box, the slide show preview cycles through the pictures in the selected folder. You can click Preview to see the full-screen slide show as it will appear when in action; move the mouse or press the Esc key to return to the dialog box.

**Tip** To require that a password be entered to unlock the screen saver and display the information currently open on your desktop, select the On Resume, Display Logon Screen check box.

10. Change the **Wait** setting to **1** minute, either by repeatedly clicking the down arrow or by selecting **10** and typing **1**. Then click **OK**.

**CLEAN UP** Change the screen saver to suit your preferences, and then close Control Panel.

# Displaying More or Less Information

When you purchase a computer monitor, one of the things you consider is its size, or display area, which is measured like a television screen: diagonally in inches. As important as the physical size, though, is the screen resolution the monitor supports, which is measured in pixels and is expressed as the number of pixels wide by the number of pixels high. Pixels are the individual dots that make up the picture displayed on your screen. Each pixel displays one color; depending on your screen resolution, the images you see on screen might consist of 500,000 to several million individual dots of color.

When personal computers first became popular, most computer monitors were capable of displaying only 640 pixels horizontally and 480 pixels vertically (a screen resolution of 640 × 480). Now most display at 1024 × 768 pixels, and some can display at 2560 × 1600 pixels (or perhaps by the time this book is published, even higher). In effect, as the screen resolution increases, the size of each pixel decreases, and more information can be shown in the same display area. In other words, as the screen resolution increases, so does the amount of information you can see on the screen...but it all appears smaller.

**Tip**  The maximum resolution is the highest resolution supported by your monitor or the highest resolution supported by the graphics card installed in your computer, whichever is lower.

**Keyboard Shortcut**  To take a closer look at on-screen content you can use the Magnifier. Press Windows logo key++ (the plus sign) to start Magnifier and zoom in on an area of the screen. Press Windows logo key+- (the minus sign) to zoom out.

Most computer systems provide a choice of at least two screen resolutions, but you might have many more choices. Some people prefer to work at a screen resolution of 1024 × 768 so that everything on the screen appears larger; others prefer to fit as much information on the screen as they possibly can. Recent statistics indicate that more than 90 percent of Internet users have their screen resolution set to 1024 × 768 or greater— up from 80 percent in 2007, 65 percent in 2005, and 46 percent in 2003.

Many monitors and portable computers have widescreen displays with resolutions such as 1280 × 720, intended to improve the experience of viewing movies on the computer by displaying them at the correct aspect ratio. These resolutions may be available on your computer regardless of the aspect ratio of your actual monitor.

In this exercise, you'll change your screen resolution to the minimum and maximum sizes supported by your computer.

**Troubleshooting**  Screen resolution capabilities are hardware specific. The settings available on your computer may be different from those shown or specified in this exercise.

**SET UP**  You don't need any practice files to complete this exercise. Open Control Panel, and then follow the steps.

1. In the **Appearance and Personalization** category, click **Adjust screen resolution**.

   The Screen Resolution window opens. You can also open this window directly by right-clicking the Windows 7 desktop and then clicking Screen Resolution.

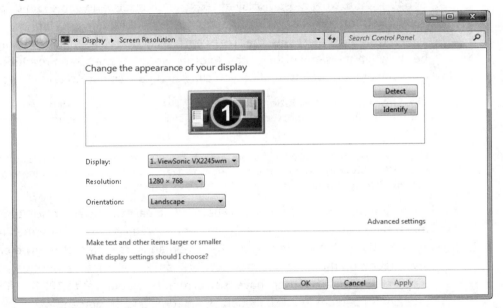

*In the Screen Resolution window, you can change the appearance of your display.*

**Tip**  If you have more than one monitor installed, select the monitor you want to change before proceeding with the next step. You can easily determine which monitor is which by clicking the Identify button. A large number, corresponding to one of the numbers displayed on the icons in the preview pane, flashes on each monitor.

**See Also**  For information about setting up multiple monitors, see "Displaying Your Desktop on Multiple Screens" in Chapter 12, "Set Up Hardware Devices."

2. Click the **Resolution** arrow to display its slider. Then drag the slider all the way down to choose the minimum resolution.

   The change is reflected in the thumbnail image of your monitor at the top of the window, but not on your screen.

3. Click away from the slider, and then click **Apply**.

4. In the **Display Settings** message box, click **Keep changes**.

   **Tip**  You have 15 seconds to decide whether to retain the changed resolution. If you click Keep Changes, the resolution is retained; if you click Revert or don't click either button, the resolution returns to its previous setting.

   Unless your monitor was already set to the minimum resolution, your display changes to the lowest resolution supported by your monitor and graphics card.

   **Tip**  When your display is set to the lowest resolution, Control Panel windows span the width of the screen.

5. In the **Resolution** list, drag the slider all the way to the top to choose the maximum resolution.

   You can either drag the slider to a marker or click above the marker you want.

6. Click away from the slider, and click **Apply**. Then in the **Display Settings** message box, click **Keep changes**.

   Your screen resolution changes to the maximum supported by your monitor and graphics card.

7. Experiment with the available screen resolutions. Apply the one you like best, and then in the **Screen Resolution** window, click **OK**.

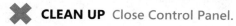 **CLEAN UP**  Close Control Panel.

# Key Points

- To personalize the Windows 7 user interface, you can easily apply a theme consisting of a desktop background, window colors, sounds, and a screen saver.

- You can customize a theme by changing any of its four elements, and save custom themes for later use.

- You can use a screen saver to hide information on your screen after a period of inactivity.

- To fit more or less information on your screen, you can change the resolution at which your monitor displays information.

# Chapter at a Glance

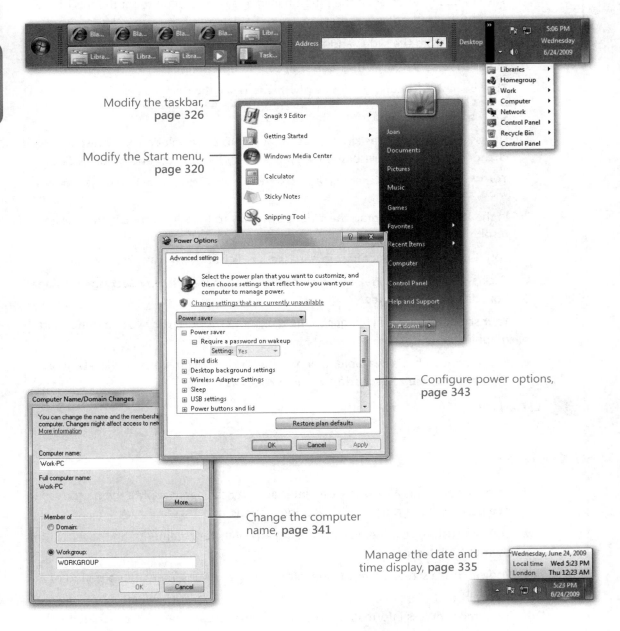

Modify the taskbar, **page 326**

Modify the Start menu, **page 320**

Configure power options, **page 343**

Change the computer name, **page 341**

Manage the date and time display, **page 335**

# 10 Change System Settings

---

**In this chapter, you will learn how to**

- ✔ Modify the Start menu and the taskbar.
- ✔ Manage the date and time display.
- ✔ Change the computer name.
- ✔ Configure power options.

---

When Windows 7 was installed on your computer, the computer manufacturer or the person performing the installation might have used the default system settings. Alternatively, they might have customized visible system elements, such as the computer name and drive names, which programs appear on the Start menu, and which icons appear on the taskbar. They might also have changed other settings that run more in the background, such as the available search providers and Accelerators, or the default programs for working with certain types of files.

Whether you're working with the default settings or with custom settings, you can easily change the appearance and functionality of many of the basic Windows 7 system elements. You might want to explore different configurations to see whether you can improve your efficiency, or some changes might be necessary rather than optional. For example, when you travel with a portable computer, you might need to change the computer's time-zone setting or power-management options.

In this chapter, you'll learn how to customize the Start menu and the taskbar to suit the way you work. You'll manually change the system time and restore the local time by synchronizing with an Internet time server, and then you'll add a different time zone to your clock's display. Finally, you'll see how to change your computer's name and its power settings.

**See Also** For information about changing the appearance and behavior of Windows Internet Explorer 8, see "Personalizing Internet Explorer 8" in Chapter 8, "Manage Internet Explorer." For information about changing your computer's security settings, see *Windows 7 Step by Step Deluxe Edition*, by Joan Preppernau and Joyce Cox (Microsoft Press, 2010).

> **Practice Files** You won't need any practice files to complete the exercises in this chapter. See "Using the Practice Files" at the beginning of this book for more information.

# Modifying the Start Menu

The Start menu is your primary interface for starting programs, locating files, and working with system utilities. You can customize the Start menu in many ways. For example, you can:

- Specify the maximum number of recently used programs shown in the left pane—up to 30, depending on your screen resolution.

- Specify the maximum number of files shown in program-specific jump lists and in the Recent Items list, and control whether the Recent Items link appears in the right pane of the Start menu.

  **See Also** The maximum number of files you specify controls not only the files that appear on Start menu jump lists, but also the number of items that appear on taskbar-button shortcut menus. For more information about taskbar buttons, see "Using the Windows Taskbar" in Chapter 1, "Explore Windows 7."

- Display or hide the Favorites menu, from which you can open the Web sites and pages you save from Internet Explorer.

- Display or hide links to the Computer, Control Panel, and Games windows, as well as links to folder windows for your Documents, Downloads, Music, Pictures, Recorded TV, and Videos folders and your personal Users subfolder. By default, clicking a link displays the associated contents in a window or folder window. For greater efficiency, you can display the contents as a menu from which you can make a choice.

- Display or hide links to the Connect To, Default Programs, Devices And Printers, Help, Homegroup, Network, and Search windows. These links aren't available as menus because they don't contain other groups or folders.

● Display or hide the System Administrative Tools, either in the All Programs menu or as a menu in the right pane.

**Tip** If you frequently work with command-line commands, you might find it convenient to add the Run command to the right pane of the Start menu. Clicking the Run link opens a dialog box in which you can enter system commands as you would in the Command Prompt window.

● Control the items and areas available for the Search function.

● Change the look and behavior of the Start menu in the following ways:

  ○ Change the size of the icons that appear on the Start menu.

  ○ Activate the display of shortcut menus when you right-click a Start menu item.

  ○ Allow the rearranging of Start menu items by dragging them.

  ○ Highlight newly installed programs.

  ○ Open submenus by pointing to them rather than clicking.

  ○ Arrange the All Programs list in alphabetical order.

**See Also** For information about pinning items to the Start menu, see "Creating Shortcuts" in Chapter 5, "Manage Folders and Files."

In this exercise, you'll hide and redisplay the recently opened programs list and change the number of programs it shows. You'll also hide the Default Programs and Devices And Printers links and display the Recent Items and Favorites menus.

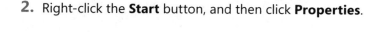

**SET UP** You don't need any practice files to complete this exercise; just follow the steps.

1. Display the **Start** menu, and notice the programs that appear in the recently opened programs list in the menu's left pane.

   **Keyboard Shortcut** Press the Windows logo key to open or close the Start menu.

   **Tip** If your recently opened programs list is empty, you can still follow along with the exercise.

2. Right-click the **Start** button, and then click **Properties**.

The Taskbar And Start Menu Properties dialog box opens, displaying the Start Menu tab.

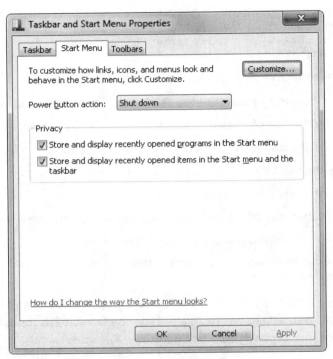

*On the Start Menu tab, you can change the default Power button action and remove lists of recent programs from the Start menu.*

**Tip** If you want to delete the recently used programs list from the left pane of the Start menu instead of simply hiding the list, clear the Store And Display Recently Opened Programs In The Start Menu check box, and then click Apply. Select the check box and click Apply to start accumulating recently used programs again.

**3.** Click **Customize**.

The Customize Start Menu dialog box opens.

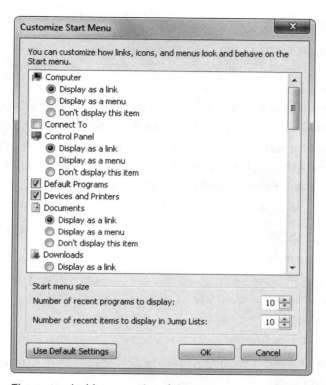

*The customizable properties of the Start menu are available from the Customize Start Menu dialog box.*

4. Click **Use Default Settings** in the lower-left corner of the dialog box to ensure that you are using the default settings, and then scroll through the list to view the ways in which you can customize the **Start** menu.

5. In the **Start menu size** area, change the **Number of recent programs to display** setting to **0**, and click **OK**. Then in the **Taskbar and Start Menu Properties** dialog box, click **Apply** to activate your change.

6. Display the **Start** menu.

   The recently opened programs list is hidden, and the horizontal line separating it from the pinned items area (if you've pinned items to the Start menu) is no longer visible.

7. Close the **Start** menu, and return to the **Start Menu** tab of the **Taskbar and Start Menu Properties** dialog box. Then click **Customize**.

8. In the **Start menu size** area of the **Customize Start Menu** dialog box, change the **Number of recent programs to display** setting to **6**, and click **OK**. Then in the **Taskbar and Start Menu Properties** dialog box, click **Apply**.

   **See Also** The other option in the Start Menu Size area controls the number of items to display in jump lists. For information about jump lists, and about pinning programs to the Start menu, see "Using the Start Menu" in Chapter 1, "Explore Windows 7."

9. Display the **Start** menu.

   Up to six programs appear in the recently used programs list. Notice that items were hidden, but not removed from the list, when you set the number of programs to 0 in step 5.

   Before continuing, notice the items that appear in the right pane of the Start menu.

10. Close the **Start** menu. Then in the **Taskbar and Start Menu Properties** dialog box, click **Customize**.

11. In the list of settings in the **Customize Start Menu** dialog box, clear the **Default Programs** and **Devices and Printers** check boxes.

12. Scroll the list, select the **Favorites menu** and **Recent Items** check boxes, and click **OK**. Then click **Apply**.

13. Display the **Start** menu.

    The right pane of the Start menu reflects the changes you just made.

*The Favorites and Recent Items menus have been added to the right pane of the Start menu.*

**14.** Close the **Start** menu, and then in the **Taskbar and Start Menu Properties** dialog box, click **OK**.

**CLEAN UP** Customize the Start menu the way you want it, or reset the Start menu to the default settings by clicking Use Default Settings in the Customize Start Menu dialog box.

# Modifying the Taskbar

Windows 7 gives you more ways to customize the taskbar than previous versions of Windows did. In addition to pinning items to the taskbar and determining where and how pinned items appear, you can change the position and size of the taskbar, hide it when it is not in use, display and customize taskbar toolbars, and customize taskbar buttons and the notification area.

**See Also** For information about pinning items to the taskbar, see "Creating Shortcuts" in Chapter 5, "Manage Folders and Files."

## Position and Size

By default, the taskbar is docked at the bottom of the desktop and displays one row of buttons. Right-clicking the taskbar (not a taskbar button) displays a shortcut menu of commands.

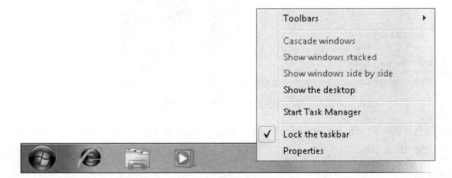

*A check mark indicates a selected option.*

**See Also** For information about using taskbar shortcut menu commands to arrange open windows, see "Working with Windows" in Chapter 4, "Navigate Windows and Folders."

To manually move the taskbar or change its size, you must first unlock it by clicking Lock The Taskbar to remove the check mark. When the taskbar is unlocked, you can control its position and size in the following ways:

- You can dock the taskbar at the top, bottom, or on either side of the desktop by dragging it to the edge of the screen against which you want to dock it.

  **Tip** If your computer system includes multiple screen displays, you can dock the taskbar against any edge of any screen.

● When the taskbar is docked at the top or bottom, you can expand it to be up to half the height of your screen by dragging its border down or up.

● When the taskbar is docked on the left or right, you can expand it to be up to half the width of your screen by dragging its border right or left.

**See Also** You can change the location of the taskbar without unlocking it. For information, see "Taskbar Properties" later in this topic.

## Taskbar Toolbars

Taskbar toolbars provide shortcuts to frequently used folders, files, and even some Internet Explorer functions. From the Toolbars submenu on the taskbar shortcut menu, you can display or hide four built-in toolbars, as well as create a custom toolbar.

**Tip** Your Toolbars submenu might include more than four toolbars. Additional toolbars might have been made available by your computer manufacturer or by the programs you have installed.

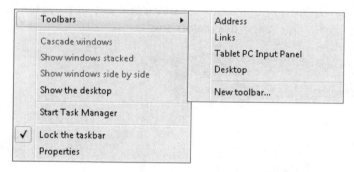

*You can add toolbars to the taskbar to streamline your workflow.*

The built-in toolbars include the following:

● **Address** You can start or switch to Internet Explorer and display a Web site by entering its URL in this toolbar.

● **Links** This toolbar displays a list of the sites and pages on your Internet Explorer Favorites bar.

**See Also** For information about Internet Explorer Favorites, see "Finding, Saving, and Returning to Web Sites" in Chapter 7, "Work with Web Pages and Sites."

● **Tablet PC Input Panel** This toolbar controls the display of the Tablet PC Input Panel, which is available on computers with and without touch input. From the Tablet PC Input Panel, you can enter information into the computer by "writing" with a tablet pen or mouse pointer, or by clicking keys on an on-screen keyboard.

> **Tip** When the Tablet PC Input Panel toolbar is displayed, clicking its only button displays the panel. Clicking the panel's Close button hides the panel under a tab at the side of the screen, and clicking either the tab or the toolbar button displays the panel again. You remove the panel completely from the screen by clicking Tools on the panel's toolbar and then clicking Exit.

● **Desktop** This toolbar displays links to libraries, homegroup and network resources, your personal folders, your computer drives, Control Panel, the Recycle Bin, and any shortcuts, files, and folders that appear on your desktop. (All of these items are actually stored in a Desktop folder on your hard drive.)

When a toolbar contains more links than can be shown in the space allocated to it, chevrons appear at its right end. Clicking the chevrons displays a list of the hidden links, in which you can click the one you want.

## Taskbar Properties

Clicking Properties at the bottom of the taskbar shortcut menu displays the Taskbar tab of the Taskbar And Start Menu Properties dialog box.

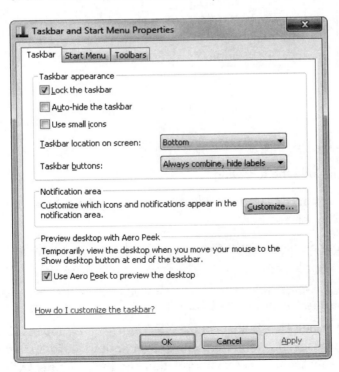

*On the Taskbar tab, you can change the location, appearance, and behavior of the taskbar.*

If you want to be able to use all your screen space for your current tasks, you can select the Auto-hide The Taskbar check box to stipulate that the taskbar should be hidden when you're not using it, instead of always appearing on top of other windows. When the taskbar is hidden, you can display it by pointing to the edge of the screen where it is docked.

On the Taskbar tab, you can also control the location of the taskbar and the appearance and behavior of taskbar buttons.

**Tip** The shortcut menu that appears when you right-click a taskbar button for a program includes a Frequent list of the pages or files you have most recently worked with in that program. Because this list resembles the lists available from the Start menu, it is controlled by the Store And Display Recently Opened Items In The Start Menu And The Taskbar setting on the Start Menu tab. If this check box is selected, the number of items accumulated in the Frequent list is controlled by the Number Of Recent Items To Display In Jump Lists setting in the Customize Start Menu dialog box.

## Notification Area

The notification area at the right end of the taskbar provides access to frequently used system functions and to any installed programs and devices that display icons in this area. Some common icons include the following:

- **Action Center** This icon appears if you need to install an update, or if an element of your security system (such as antivirus software) is missing or fails. A white X in a red circle indicates that some action is necessary. Pointing to the icon displays an action summary. Clicking the icon displays related commands.

- **Clock** This icon appears only when there is insufficient room for the time and date to be displayed, in short or long format, in the notification area. Clicking this icon displays date and time details. Right-clicking the icon displays a shortcut menu with options for configuring the date and time.

   **See Also** For information about configuring the date and time, see "Managing the Date and Time Display" later in this chapter.

- **Connection** This icon represents your network and Internet connections. The appearance of the icon depends on the type of network adapter your computer has. One version of the icon represents an Ethernet adapter; the other represents a wireless network adapter. Lack of an active connection is indicated by a red X on the icon. When the computer is not connected to a network, an available connection is indicated by a yellow starburst.

   **See Also** For information about networks, see "Connecting to a Network" in Chapter 3, "Manage Your Network."

- **Power** If you are using a portable computer, this icon displays the battery charge remaining and indicates whether the battery is currently charging (in other words, whether the computer is plugged in).

- **Printer** This icon appears temporarily when you send a document to the printer.

  **See Also** For information about printers, see "Installing Peripheral Devices" in Chapter 12, "Set Up Hardware Devices."

- **Show Hidden Icons** Clicking this button temporarily displays any icons that are hidden when inactive.

- **Volume** Clicking this icon displays a slider with which you can turn down or turn up the speaker volume. Right-clicking the icon displays a shortcut menu of volume-related actions.

- **Windows Update** This icon appears in the notification area when Windows Update is downloading or installing updates. Pointing to the icon displays Windows Update status information.

In addition, the programs installed on your computer might display program-specific icons in the notification area.

You can customize the appearance and behavior of notification area icons by clicking Customize in the Notification Area section of the Taskbar tab of the Taskbar And Start Menu Properties dialog box.

In this exercise, you'll dock the taskbar at the top of the screen, increase its size, and change the way it displays buttons. You'll then cause the taskbar to hide when not in use, and add toolbars to it. Finally, you'll explore ways to hide and display the icons in the notification area.

**SET UP** You don't need any practice files to complete this exercise. Exit any running programs, close any open windows, and then follow the steps.

1. On the **Windows Taskbar**, click the pinned **Internet Explorer** button. Then right-click the **Internet Explorer** button, and click **Internet Explorer**. Repeat the second part of the step until at least four Internet Explorer windows are open.

2. Repeat step 1 with the pinned **Windows Explorer** button to open at least four Windows Explorer windows.

3. Right-click a blank area of the taskbar, and then, if a check mark appears to the left of **Lock the Taskbar**, click that command to unlock the taskbar.

**4.** Point to a blank area of the taskbar, and drag it to the top of the screen.

**5.** Point to the bottom border of the taskbar. When the pointer changes to a double-headed arrow, drag the border down until the taskbar is two rows high.

Notice that although there is enough space for all the open windows to display their own buttons on the taskbar, they remain grouped under their respective program buttons.

*When the taskbar is two or more rows high, the day of the week appears with the date and time.*

**6.** Right-click a blank area of the taskbar, and then click **Properties**.

The Taskbar And Start Menu Properties dialog box opens, displaying the Taskbar tab.

*The Taskbar Location On Screen setting reflects the current taskbar position.*

7. In the **Taskbar appearance** area, click **Never combine** in the **Taskbar buttons** list. Then click **Apply**.

All the open windows are now represented by their own buttons on the taskbar.

*Instead of grouping similar windows under one button, you can display a button for each open window.*

**Tip** The size and position of the taskbar buttons depends on your screen resolution, which controls the width of the taskbar. At a lower resolution (narrower taskbar), the buttons will be narrower; at a higher resolution (wider taskbar), more buttons will fit on the top row. You can change the size and position of taskbar buttons and menus by dragging them around the taskbar.

8. In the **Taskbar and Start Menu Properties** dialog box, select the **Auto-hide the taskbar** check box, and then click **Apply**.

The taskbar disappears. It is now hidden at the top of the screen.

9. In the **Taskbar and Start Menu Properties** dialog box, click the **Toolbars** tab.

This tab displays the built-in toolbars available for display on the taskbar.

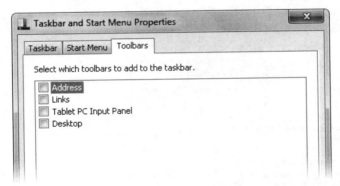

*You can display as many of the built-in toolbars on the taskbar as you want.*

**Tip** Another way to display a toolbar on the taskbar is to click Toolbars on the taskbar shortcut menu and then click the toolbar you want.

10. Select the **Address** and **Desktop** check boxes, and then click **Apply**.

The taskbar appears briefly, displaying the Address bar and the Desktop toolbar.

11. Point to the top of the screen, and when the taskbar appears, click the chevrons at the right end of the **Desktop** toolbar.

A menu displays links for all the items accessible from this toolbar.

*The Desktop toolbar provides one-click access to several frequently used windows.*

**Tip** You can type a URL or a folder path in the Address bar and then press Enter to open the target destination, either on a new tab of an open Internet Explorer window or in a new Windows Explorer window.

**12.** In the **Taskbar and Start Menu Properties** dialog box, click the **Taskbar** tab. Then in the **Notification Area** section, click **Customize**.

The Notification Area Icons window opens.

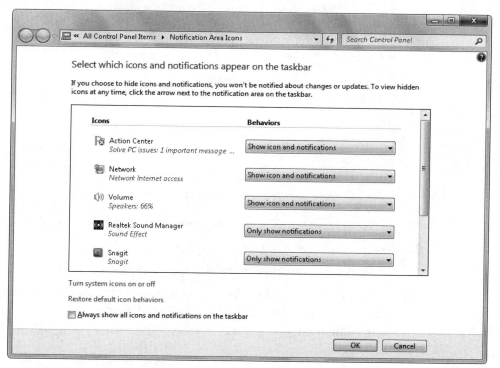

*In the Notification Area Icons window, you can control the behavior of each icon in the notification area.*

13. In the **Notification Area Icons** window, scroll the list of icons to review their behavior settings.

   From the list adjacent to each icon, you can select Show Icon And Notifications, Hide Icon And Notifications, or Only Show Notifications.

14. Below the icon list, click **Turn system icons on or off**.

   The System Icons window opens.

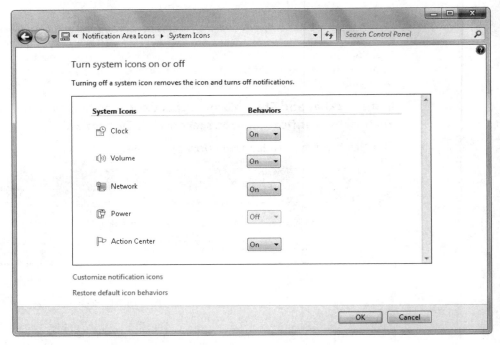

*You can display or hide the standard system icons.*

15. In the **System Icons** window, set the behavior for **Clock** to **Off**. Then click **OK**.

16. Point to the top of the screen to display the taskbar.

   The time, day, and date no longer appear in the notification area.

17. In the **Notification Area Icons** window, click **Turn system icons on or off** again. Then at the bottom of the **System Icons** window, click **Restore default icon behaviors**, and click **OK**.

18.  Point to the top of the screen to display the taskbar, where the time, day, and date are once again displayed.

 **CLEAN UP** Close all open windows. Then adjust the position, size, and behavior of the taskbar to suit your needs before continuing.

**Tip** If you choose to keep your taskbar hidden when not in use, you will need to display it whenever we instruct you to work with it in an exercise.

# Managing the Date and Time Display

Your computer system has an internal clock that keeps track of the date and time, even when the computer is turned off. By default, Windows 7 displays this system date and time in the notification area at the right end of the taskbar. The internal clock controls a number of behind-the-scenes settings and is also used by Windows and your programs to maintain an accurate record of happenings on your computer.

**See Also** For information about hiding the date and time, see "Modifying the Taskbar" earlier in this chapter.

You can set the system date and time manually or, if your computer is connected to the Internet, you can synchronize the system date and time with an Internet-based time server. If you have a continuous Internet connection, by default your computer synchronizes itself at 1:00 A.M. every Sunday of every week.

**Tip** If your computer is part of a domain network, the time is centrally controlled from the domain server and you can change it only temporarily (until the next time your computer is synchronized with the domain clock).

Internet-based time servers transmit the current Coordinated Universal Time to your computer. This time is known as UTC, an acronym based on a compromise between the English and French terms. UTC is a standard based on International Atomic Time that corresponds to the time at the Royal Observatory in Greenwich, England. UTC is within one second of Greenwich Mean Time (GMT). If your computer isn't located in the UTC/GMT time zone, you need to adjust the time zone so that your computer displays the correct time. If your computer is in a region that participates in Daylight Saving Time, you also need to indicate that fact, so that your computer adjusts from Standard Time to Daylight Saving Time and back again on the appropriate days.

If you move or travel, you can easily reset your computer to a different time zone, provided you have administrator credentials. If you want to keep track of the time in a different time zone, you can activate up to two additional clocks; for example, if you work in a regional office, you might want to keep track of the time at your company headquarters. Any additional clocks are displayed in the ScreenTip that appears when you point to the date and time in the notification area or in the window that opens when you click the date and time.

**Tip** You must be logged on as an administrator to change the time zone. You can add a time zone when you're logged on as a standard user.

In this exercise, you'll manually reset your system time and then connect to an Internet time server for an automatic update. You'll also add a clock to track the time in a different time zone.

 **SET UP** You don't need any practice files to complete this exercise. Be sure that your computer is connected to the Internet, close any open windows, and then follow the steps.

1. In the notification area of the taskbar, click the date and time.

   The date and time details appear.

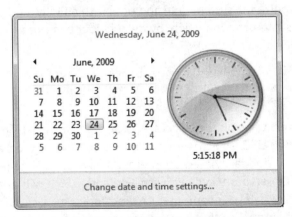

*Clicking the clock displays a calendar for the current month and the time in both analog and digital formats, with both clocks changing in one-second increments.*

2.  In the clock details window, click **Change date and time settings**.

The Date And Time dialog box opens.

From the Date And Time tab, you can change the current system date and time, and the time zone.

3.  Click **Change date and time**.

The Date And Time Settings dialog box opens.

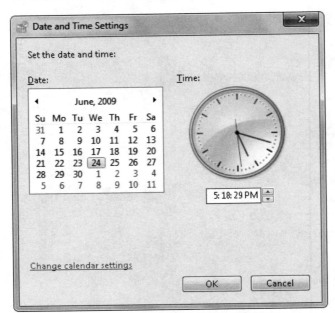

*You can set the local date and time in the Date And Time Settings dialog box.*

**Tip** Different regions of the world use different formats for dates and times. Clicking Change Calendar Settings displays the Date tab of the Customize Format dialog box, where you can specify the formats for your region. (This dialog box also opens when you click Change The Date, Time, Or Number Format in the Clock, Language, And Region window of Control Panel, and then click Additional Settings on the Formats tab of the Region and Language dialog box.)

4. At the left end of the digital clock, double-click the hour segment (anywhere before the first colon), and then click the up arrow to the right of the clock once to change the hour.

   The analog clock reflects your change, and both clocks stop advancing. You can also use this technique to change the minutes, seconds, and AM/PM setting.

5. Click **OK** to close the **Date and Time Settings** dialog box.

   The clock in the notification area changes to reflect the new time.

6. In the **Date and Time** dialog box, click the **Internet Time** tab.

The current synchronization behavior is displayed.

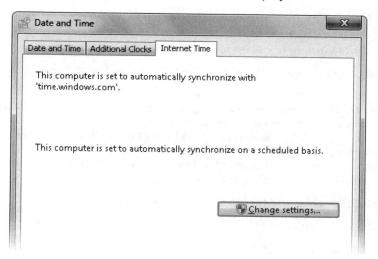

*By default, Windows synchronizes the computer's system clock with an Internet time server.*

**Troubleshooting** If your computer is on a domain, the contents of the Internet Time tab will appear dimmed and you will not be able to synchronize with an Internet time server. In that case, skip to step 10.

**7.** Click **Change settings**.

The Internet Time Settings dialog box opens.

*You can synchronize with an Internet time server whenever you want.*

8. With the **Synchronize with an Internet time server** check box selected, click **Update now**.

   **Troubleshooting** If you wait a while before clicking Update Now, Windows 7 might display an error message. Simply click Update Now a second time.

   Your computer connects to the selected time server and updates your system time.

   **Tip** You can select the Internet time server you want to use from the Server list. The default server is time.windows.com, which is maintained by Microsoft. The four servers with *nist* in their names are maintained by the National Institute of Standards and Technology (NIST) at various locations around the United States. The time.nist.gov server is at the National Center for Atmospheric Research in Boulder, Colorado; time-nw.nist.gov is at Microsoft in Redmond, Washington; and time-a.nist.gov and time-b.nist.gov are at NIST in Gaithersburg, Maryland.

9. Click **OK** to close the **Internet Time Settings** dialog box.

10. In the **Date and Time** dialog box, click the **Additional Clocks** tab.

    You can use the settings on this tab to display one or two additional clocks on the taskbar.

*You can display the time in two additional time zones.*

**11.** Select the first **Show this clock** check box. In the **Select time zone** list, click **UTC Coordinated Universal Time**. In the **Enter display name** box, replace *Clock 1* with **London**. Then click **OK**.

The date and time displayed on the taskbar remain the same.

**12.** In the notification area of the taskbar, point to the clock.

A ScreenTip displays your system time and the corresponding time in London.

*The additional time zones are displayed in a ScreenTip when you point to the clock.*

 **CLEAN UP** Delete the additional clock or set it to the time zone you want before continuing.

# Changing the Computer Name

Every computer is identified by a name. You can quickly view the computer name by clicking the Computer group in any Windows Explorer window. The name then appears in the Details pane at the bottom of the window.

The computer name was assigned either by the computer manufacturer or by the person who installed or upgraded Windows on the computer. Manufacturers tend to assign names associated with their companies, such as *Toshiba*. During the installation or upgrade process, people often accept the name suggested by Windows 7, which is based on the name assigned to the initial administrator account, such as *Joan-PC*. Neither of these naming conventions is specific enough to uniquely identify the computer—for example, you might have several Toshiba computers on your network, or you might be the primary administrator of several computers.

During the installation or upgrade process, or at any time thereafter, you can change the name of your computer to one that is meaningful or helpful to you.

To change the computer name:

1. On the Start menu, right-click Computer, and then click Properties.

   The System window opens.

2. In the Computer Name, Domain, And Workgroup Settings area, click Change Settings.

3. On the Computer Name tab of the System Properties dialog box, click Change.

   The Computer Name/Domain Changes dialog box opens.

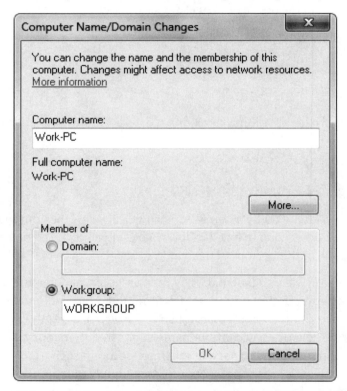

*At the top of the dialog box, a warning tells you that changing the settings in this dialog box might affect access to network resources.*

4. In the Computer Name/Domain Changes dialog box, replace the existing computer name with the name you want, and then click OK.

5. Click OK to acknowledge that the name change won't take effect until you restart your computer, and then close the System Properties dialog box.

6. In the Windows message box, click Restart Now or, if it isn't convenient to restart your computer at this time, click Restart Later.

7. Close the System window.

The folder representing your computer on the Start menu and in Windows Explorer is identified by the name *Computer*. If you want, you can change the name of the Computer folder.

To change the Computer folder name:

1. On the Start menu, right-click Computer, and then click Rename.

2. With Computer selected for editing, type the name you want to appear, and then press Enter.

   **Tip**  Like other folder and file names, the Computer folder name can't contain an asterisk (*), backslash (\), colon (:), greater than sign (>), less than sign (<), pipe (|), question mark (?), quotation marks ("), or slash (/). If you try to type one of these symbols, Windows refuses to accept it and displays a message that the symbol is not allowed. If the folder name includes a space, Windows displays up to two lines of characters on the Start menu.

# Configuring Power Options

Your computer's power-management options are organized into three built-in power plans: Balanced, Power Saver, and High Performance. Each power plan defines settings that control how your computer uses power. All three plans determine how long your computer is idle before the display is turned off and before activating Sleep mode, with the default settings as outlined in the following table.

| Power plan | Turn off display | Activate Sleep mode |
| --- | --- | --- |
| Balanced | 10 minutes | 30 minutes |
| Power Saver | 5 minutes | 15 minutes |
| High Performance | 15 minutes | Never |

If you are working on a portable computer that is running on battery power, the Power Saver plan will increase the length of time the battery charge lasts. If your work involves intense computer processes that are affected by your computer's performance, or if you want to keep the computer display from dimming when you don't use it for a short period of time, the High Performance plan might work best for you. The Balanced plan is designed to provide enough processing speed for daily work while minimizing power consumption.

If none of the built-in plans meets your needs, you can create your own power plan. For example, you might want to create a variation of one of the built-in plans for a specific purpose, such as a high-performance variation that never turns off the display for use during video conference calls. You could then switch to this power plan before a conference call and switch back when you resume your work.

In this exercise, you'll examine your computer's power settings and see how to change them. You'll then create a variation of the High Performance plan.

 **SET UP** You don't need any practice files to complete this exercise. Open the Performance And Information Tools window of Control Panel, and then follow the steps.

1. In the left pane of the **Performance and Information Tools** window, click **Adjust power settings**.

 2. In the **Power Options** window, click the arrow to the right of **Show additional plans**.

The Power Options window expands.

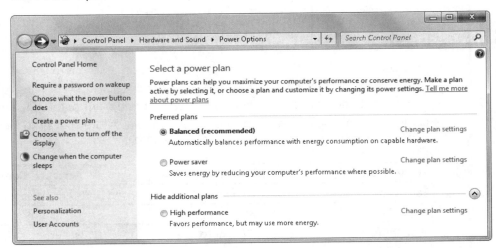

*Windows 7 includes three default power plans offering energy savings, performance, or a balance between the two.*

**Troubleshooting** The available power options may vary based on your computer hardware.

3. To the right of **Power saver**, click **Change plan settings**.

The Edit Plan Settings window opens.

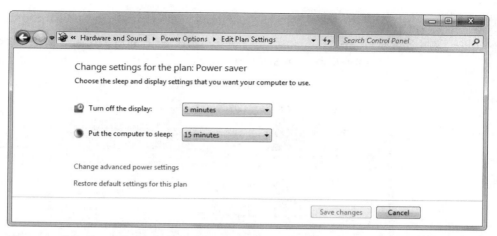

*You can adjust the periods of idle time before Windows 7 turns off the display and puts the computer into Sleep mode.*

4. Click **Change advanced power settings**.

   The Power Options dialog box opens, with the power saver options listed.

*You can change any of the power plan settings to suit the way you work.*

**Troubleshooting**  Your list of options might be different from the one shown. Windows 7 displays only the power settings that you can adjust for your computer.

5. Scroll the list of settings, expanding categories to view the options.

6. Click **Cancel** to close the **Power Options** dialog box, and click **Cancel** again to close the **Edit Plan Settings** window and return to the **Power Options** window.

7. In the left pane of the **Power Options** window, click **Create a power plan**.

   The Create A Power Plan wizard starts.

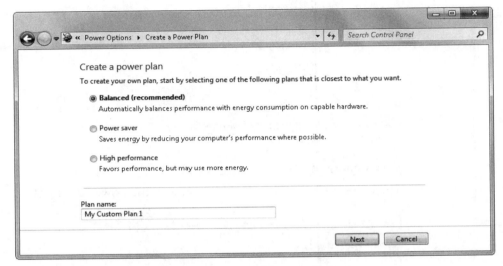

*You can create your own power plan by customizing a built-in plan.*

8. Click **High performance**, and in the **Plan name** box, type Always On. Then click **Next**.

9. In the **Edit Plan Settings** window, click **Never** in the **Turn off the display** list, and then click **Create**.

   In the Power Options window, Always On appears in the list of Preferred Plans and is selected as the current plan.

10. Click **Balanced** to switch to that built-in plan.

11. To the right of **Always On**, click **Change plan settings**.

12. In the **Edit Plan Settings** window, click **Delete this plan**. Then confirm the deletion by clicking **OK** in the **Power Options** message window.

**CLEAN UP** Choose the power plan you want, and close the Power Options window.

**Tip** If you make changes to a power plan and then want to restore the default settings, select the plan in the Power Options window, and click Change Plan Settings. Then in the Edit Plan Settings window, click Restore Default Settings For This Plan. Finally, click Yes in the confirmation message box, and click Cancel to close the Edit Plan Settings window.

# Key Points

- To help you work most efficiently, you can customize the Start menu, taskbar, and notification area.

- You can manually update the date and time shown on your computer, or your computer can automatically update the date and time by connecting to an Internet time server.

- If your computer's name does not readily identify it, you can change the name that appears on the Start menu and on your network.

- You can control your computer's use of power by switching power plans. You can also create custom power plans to suit the way you work.

# Chapter at a Glance

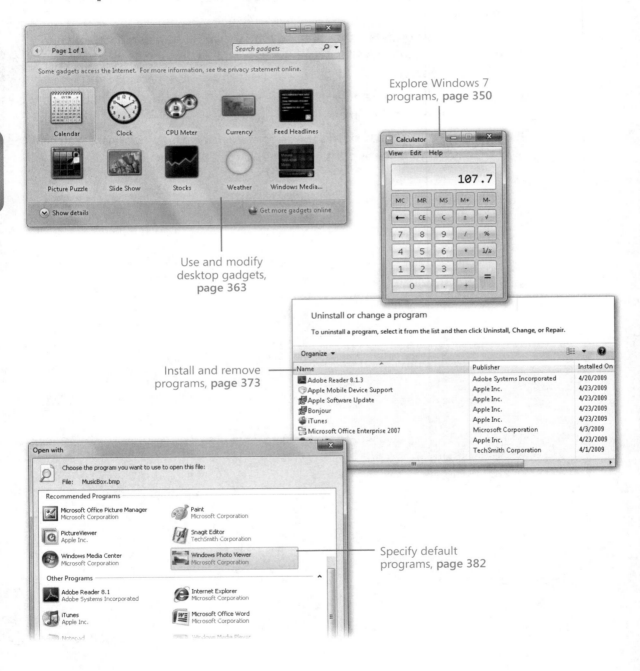

Explore Windows 7 programs, **page 350**

Use and modify desktop gadgets, **page 363**

Install and remove programs, **page 373**

Specify default programs, **page 382**

# 11 Work with Programs

---

**In this chapter, you will learn how to**

- ✔ Explore Windows 7 programs.
- ✔ Use and modify desktop gadgets.
- ✔ Explore Windows Live programs and services.
- ✔ Install and remove programs.
- ✔ Start programs automatically.
- ✔ Specify default programs.

---

Nowadays, you can purchase a computer, plug it in, and start working without installing any additional software. New name-brand computers usually come with the operating system already installed. A package of useful programs is often included with the operating system so that you can quickly accomplish simple tasks. And your computer might also come with commercial software packages for more complex tasks, such as word processing. Sooner or later, however, you will want to install additional programs.

Most of the programs installed on your computer have a link on the Start menu. You can start a program by clicking its link or by opening a file of a type that is associated with the program. For example, if Windows Photo Viewer is your default image viewer, double-clicking an image file in Windows Explorer starts Windows Photo Viewer and then displays the graphic. If you are more likely to want to work with digital photographs in an image-editing program, you can instruct Windows to open any file with a .jpg extension in that program when you double-click it. Another way to save clicks and keystrokes, and therefore save time, is to have Windows start programs for you when you log on to Windows 7. You can easily use techniques like these to make working with programs more efficient.

In this chapter, you'll start by exploring the programs that come with Windows 7 in the form of gadgets, the Windows 7 utility programs, and the programs that are made available through Windows Live. Then you'll learn about installing new programs on your computer and removing programs you no longer need. You'll set up a program to start automatically when you turn on your computer, and finally, you'll specify which program will open files of a particular type when you double-click them.

> **Practice Files** Before you can complete the exercises in this chapter, you need to install the practice files specified in "Using the Practice Files" at the beginning of this book to their default location. The practice files you will use to complete the exercises in this chapter are in the Programs practice file folder.

# Exploring Windows 7 Programs

Each release of Windows has brought with it new and improved features, tools, and programs. Windows 7 includes many programs, some familiar and some new.

> ## Absent Programs
>
> If you're an experienced Windows user, you might notice that several programs available in previous versions of Windows are missing. Microsoft has removed some of the programs that weren't directly associated with the operating system from Windows. Specific programs that were available in earlier versions of Windows and are not in Windows 7 include:
>
> - Windows Live Messenger (formerly Windows Messenger)
> - Windows Mail (formerly Microsoft Outlook Express)
> - Windows Contacts
> - Windows Calendar
> - Windows Meeting Space
>
> Some of the programs that are no longer included with Windows are among those you can download, free of charge, from the Windows Live Web site located at home.live.com.
>
> **See Also** For more information about the programs and services available through Windows Live, see "Exploring Windows Live Programs and Services" later in this chapter.

## Windows Essentials

A fresh installation of Windows 7 includes many programs that you can use to manage your Windows computing experience, create things, or communicate. The programs that you are most likely to use are:

- **Windows Internet Explorer 8**  The latest version of Internet Explorer introduces many new features, some of which were borrowed from other popular Web browsers. Internet Explorer still holds the lead in worldwide browser usage, but the popularity of Firefox seems to have encouraged Microsoft to reach higher. The winners in this competition are Internet Explorer users, who can now enjoy an expanded feature set as well as seamless interaction between their Web browser and common information-management programs, such as Microsoft Word, Microsoft OneNote, Windows Live Mail, and Windows Live Writer.

  **See Also**  For information about using and managing Internet Explorer 8, see Part 2 of this book, "Experiencing the World Wide Web."

- **Desktop Gadget Gallery**  This new feature replaces the Windows Sidebar introduced with Windows Vista. From the Desktop Gadget Gallery, you can place gadgets that display a variety of information directly onto your desktop. You can move the gadgets to any location on the desktop, and tailor the information each gadget displays to suit your needs—you can even have multiple instances of one gadget, each displaying different aspects of the same type of information.

*You can display the date and time, the current weather in your home town and your current location, as well as a slideshow of your favorite photos.*

**See Also**  For information about managing desktop gadgets, see "Using and Modifying Desktop Gadgets" later in this chapter.

- **Windows Update** This essential tool monitors the Microsoft Update site and alerts you to updates available for your operating system, for Microsoft programs installed on your computer, and for device drivers that interact with the devices connected to your computer.

  **See Also** For information about Windows Update, see "Updating Windows System Files" in Chapter 1, "Explore Windows 7."

## Media Management

Digital media is now available to the average consumer in somewhat overwhelming quantities. Many devices are available for streaming media from the Internet and for recording, playing, and processing still photos, video and audio clips.

- **Windows Media Center** Originally, Microsoft offered a separate Media Center edition of the Windows operating system for people who wanted to run a dedicated in-home media server, but now Media Center is built right into Windows 7 so that anyone with the interest and know-how can take advantage of it. Using Media Center, you can view movies, recorded television programs, and photo slideshows on your computer screen just as you would by hooking a playback device to your television. If your computer has an internal or external TV tuner, you can stream network television directly from your television service provider to your computer and record your favorite shows. And many televisions available now have built-in computer input ports, so you can play audio and video through that nice new 50-inch, flat-screen TV. You can listen to live radio programs, music from your personal music library, and music from online sources, all on one machine (and watch a slideshow of your vacation photos at the same time). This is not nearly as difficult as it might sound, and with the rapidly dropping price of computers featuring 500 gigabytes (GB) or more of storage space, you can take the opportunity to store all your music and digital media in one place and then enjoy it with ease.

- **Windows Media Player** An easy-to-use program for playing recorded music and videos from your personal library, including content that you access or purchase online.

- **Windows DVD Maker** A simple means by which you can create professional-looking DVDs of your photos, videos, and music, complete with chapters, titles, and special effects. This is a great way to preserve baby photos and videos and share them with family and friends.

## Communication Tools

Windows 7 comes with two free word-processing programs and a simple graphics program, as well as several other programs with which you can convey information.

- **Notepad** You can use this simple text editor to edit unformatted documents or HTML files.

- **WordPad** This more sophisticated word-processing program supports rich text formatting and character and paragraph styles.

- **Paint** You can use this simple graphics program to produce drawings in a variety of graphics formats (including .bmp, .gif, .jpg, .png, and .tif) and to save screen images captured by using the Print Screen utility.

  **Tip** WordPad and Paint have been updated with a Windows Ribbon command interface similar to the Microsoft Office Fluent Ribbon introduced with many of the Office 2007 programs.

- **Windows Fax and Scan** Using this program, you can send and receive faxes through an analog phone line and a modem, or through a fax server. Received faxes appear in your Inbox in the Windows Fax And Scan window and can be viewed in much the same way as an e-mail message in an e-mail program. If a scanner is connected to your computer, you can also use Windows Fax And Scan to scan text documents and graphics to your computer as digital files that you can then send as faxes or e-mail message attachments. Most modern scanners are plug-and-play devices that you can simply plug into an appropriate port on your computer.

---

### XPS Files

Like the Portable Document Format (PDF), the XML Paper Specification (XPS) format allows a file to be saved in such a way that it can be viewed but not changed without the use of special software.

Windows 7 comes with the XPS Viewer, in which you can view XPS files. Windows 7 also comes with the software required to create XPS files from any program from which you can print. Simply open the file in its originating program, display the Print dialog box, specify the Microsoft XPS Document Writer as the printer, and click Print. When prompted, save the file with the name and in the location you want.

## Utilities

Utilities are handy little tools that you might find yourself using quite frequently. These programs and many others are available from the Accessories folder of the All Programs menu.

- **Calculator** In Windows 7, the Calculator has been transformed into a multi-dimensional tool that can meet a variety of specialized calculating needs.

- **Math Input Panel** Designed for Tablet PC users, Math Input Panel converts simple and complex mathematic equations to text.

- **Sticky Notes** You can use this program to attach electronic notes to your computer desktop in the same way you'd stick the paper version of a sticky note to your physical desktop.

- **Snipping Tool** Using this tool, you can capture an image of a screen area and then annotate it with handwritten notes, save it as an .html, .png, .gif, or .jpg file, and send it by e-mail.

- **Windows Journal** Designed for use with a Tablet PC, Journal records your handwritten and typed notes and imports existing notes and pictures.

---

### Utilities for Geeks

Experienced computer users who want to be able to run programs and manage their computers in traditional ways might find the following utilities useful:

- **Command Prompt** A legacy from the early days of personal computing, this utility allows you to control the computer with MS-DOS commands. (MS-DOS was the first Microsoft operating system.)

- **Windows PowerShell** With a text-based interface similar to that of Command Prompt, Windows PowerShell provides command-line tools for automating administrative tasks that can be leveraged by users who are familiar with operating systems such as Windows, MS-DOS, UNIX, Linux, and Mac OS.

- **Windows XP Mode** A solution for users running programs that are not compatible with versions of Windows later than Windows XP (such as customized accounting packages), XP Mode creates a virtual machine running Windows XP (with Service Pack 3) within Windows 7. You can then install the programs you want on the virtual machine, and run them, within the virtual machine, directly from your Windows 7 computer.

## Games

Finally, we get to the fun stuff. For those who enjoy the distraction of simple computer games, Windows 7 comes with many preinstalled games: Chess Titans, FreeCell, Hearts, Mahjong Titans, Minesweeper, Purble Place, Solitaire, and Spider Solitaire. In addition to these single-player games there are versions of Backgammon, Checkers, and Spades that you can play over the Internet against random players from around the world. There's also a link for downloading more games from Microsoft.

In this exercise, you'll work with three utilities that you might find useful: the Calculator, Sticky Notes, and the Snipping Tool. You'll perform a couple of quick calculations, work with different Calculator modes, attach Sticky Notes to your screen to remind yourself about important tasks, and use the Snipping Tool to capture part of a document as a graphics file.

 **SET UP** You need the MakeOver document located in your Documents\Microsoft Press\Windows7SBS\Programs folder to complete this exercise.

1. On the **Start** menu, click **Calculator**.

   **Troubleshooting** If the Calculator does not appear in the left pane of the Start menu, click All Programs, click Accessories, and then click Calculator.

2. In sequence, click the following **Calculator** buttons: **17.95\*6=**.

   The Calculator displays the result of your calculation.

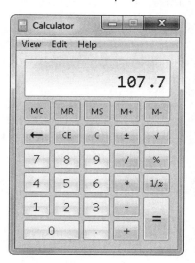

   *You enter formulas in the Calculator by clicking numbers and operators, just as you would on a physical calculator.*

3. On the **View** menu, click **Scientific**.

The Calculator switches to the selected mode.

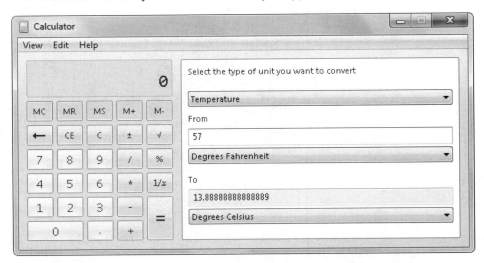

*Scientific mode is one of four Calculator modes.*

4. Repeat step 3 to display first **Programmer** mode, then **Statistics** mode, and then **Standard** mode.

5. On the **View** menu, click **Unit Conversion**. In the **Select the type of unit you want to convert** list, click **Temperature**, and in the **From** list (below the box displaying *Enter value*), click **Degrees Fahrenheit**. Finally, type **57** in the **From** box.

The Calculator instantly converts the value you type.

*With the Calculator, it's easy to convert temperatures from one scale to another.*

6. Explore the other options available on the menus, and then in the upper-right corner of the **Calculator** window, click the **Close** button.

7. On the **Start** menu, click **Sticky Notes**.

   **Troubleshooting** If Sticky Notes does not appear in the left pane of the Start menu, click All Programs, click Accessories, and then click Sticky Notes.

   A colored square resembling a paper sticky note, with a blinking cursor, appears on your desktop.

8. Without moving the cursor, type **Submit expense report**.

   The words you type appear at the cursor in a script font.

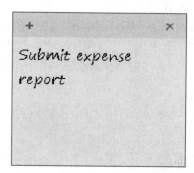

*You can use Sticky Notes to post reminders of important tasks on your desktop.*

9. Drag the sticky note by its top bar to the right side of the desktop, below any displayed gadgets.

   The sticky note remains wherever you drop it; it doesn't snap to a grid as the desktop gadgets do.

10. In the upper-left corner of the sticky note, click the **New Note** button.

   A second sticky note appears on the desktop, to the left of the original note.

   **Tip** The notes produced in Sticky Notes look similar to those produced in the Notes gadget on the Windows Vista Sidebar and to those produced in the Microsoft Outlook Notes feature. However, Sticky Notes does not offer as much functionality as either of those products. You can't change the sticky note color or font, and each sticky note is an individual entity rather than a multipage item like the Sidebar gadget. Sticky notes do show up in Windows search results, however, which makes them quite convenient when you want to save information for later.

11. In the new sticky note, type **Reserve conference room**.

12. In the upper-right corner of the first note, click the **Delete Note** button, and then in the **Sticky Notes** message box, click **Yes** to confirm the deletion.

**13.** In **Windows Explorer**, navigate to your **Documents\Microsoft Press\ Windows7SBS\Programs** folder, and double-click the **MakeOver** document.

The document opens in the program designated as the default for working with Word documents, which might be Microsoft Office Word 2007 (or a later version) if it is installed, or might be WordPad, which comes with Windows 7.

**Troubleshooting** If the document opens in WordPad, an Information bar below the WordPad Ribbon informs you that WordPad doesn't support all the formatting included in this document, which was created with Word 2007. The unsupported formatting won't have any effect on this exercise, but if you prefer, you can dismiss the Information bar by clicking the Close button at its right end.

**14.** On the **Start** menu, click **Snipping Tool**.

**Troubleshooting** If the Snipping Tool does not appear in the left pane of the Start menu, click All Programs, click Accessories, and then click Snipping Tool.

The Snipping Tool window appears on top of the open document, and the pointer changes to a hollow cross.

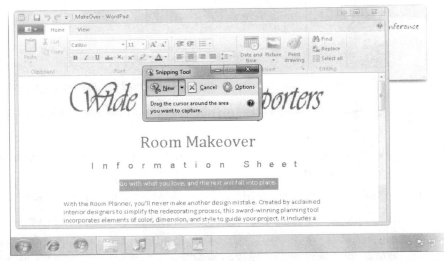

*When you start the Snipping Tool, the entire screen is dimmed to show that nothing is currently selected for snipping.*

**15.** In the document window, point to the upper-left corner of the company logo, and then drag diagonally down and to the right, until the selection rectangle contains the logo and the paragraph with the red background.

The selected area is no longer dimmed.

*You can select as much of the screen information as you want.*

16. Release the mouse button.

The Snipping Tool displays the snippet in a separate window.

*The snippet is centered within a background document that provides space for markup.*

17. With the **Pen** button selected on the toolbar, drag to draw a circle around the letter *W* in the word *World*, and then draw an arrow pointing to the red paragraph of text.

18. On the toolbar, click the **Highlighter** button, and then drag across the word *Makeover*.

The snippet reflects your markup.

*You can mark up a snippet with pens of various shapes and colors, as well as a highlighter.*

**Tip** You can remove any markup that you don't want by using the Eraser tool. (The Snipping Tool utility doesn't support the standard Undo command.) Other toolbar buttons allow you to copy the snippet so that you can paste it elsewhere and to use an associated e-mail program to send the snippet either embedded in or attached to a message.

19. On the toolbar, click the **Save Snip** button. Then in the **File name** box of the **Save As** dialog box, type **MakeOverHeader**, and click **Save** to save the snippet in your Pictures library.

**20.** On the **Snipping Tool** window title bar, click the **Close** button. Then close the document window.

**21.** In **Windows Explorer**, navigate to your **Pictures** library, and open the **MakeOverHeader** file.

If you saved the file in PNG format and haven't selected another program as the default for that file format, the file opens in Windows Photo Gallery.

*The image file has the same dimensions as the area you selected in the document, and your pen and highlighter markings have been incorporated into the image.*

**Tip** You can save a snippet as a .png file, a .gif file, a .jpg file, or an .htm file by selecting the format you want in the Save As Type list. Portable Network Graphic (.png) is the default format.

 **CLEAN UP** Close the image window and Windows Explorer. If you want, remove the sticky note from the desktop.

## Turning Windows Programs and Features On and Off

Some of the programs and features that are installed with Windows 7 are not immediately available for use because they are not turned on by default. Some are on by default only in specific editions of Windows 7, and some off by default in all editions. You can turn Windows programs and features on and off at any time. If your computer's performance seems unsatisfactory, you can turn off Windows programs and features that you don't use to conserve system resources. You can always turn them back on if you find you need them.

**See Also** For information about monitoring and managing computer performance, see *Windows 7 Step by Step Deluxe Edition*, by Joan Preppernau and Joyce Cox (Microsoft Press, 2010).

To turn Windows programs and features on or off:

1. In the left pane of the Programs And Features window of Control Panel, click Turn Windows Features On Or Off.

   The Windows Features window opens.

*In the Windows Features dialog box, you can specify the features you want to run.*

If all the components of a feature are installed, its check box is selected. If none are installed, its check box is cleared. If some but not all components are installed, its check box is shaded.

2. Select the check boxes of any features you want to turn on, or clear the check boxes of any you want to turn off, and then click OK.

**Tip** To view or manage features with multiple components, click the plus sign to the left of the feature name to expand the component list, and then select and clear the check boxes of individual components.

A message box tells you that configuring the change might take several minutes. When the process is complete, the message box and the Windows Features dialog box close.

# Using and Modifying Desktop Gadgets

Gadgets provide dynamic, up-to-date information or entertainment on your desktop. (In Windows 7, gadgets appear directly on the desktop instead of on the Windows Sidebar that was part of Windows Vista.) Windows 7 provides 10 gadgets in the Desktop Gadget Gallery, and you can find many more online, in the Windows Live Gallery. The following gadgets come with Windows 7:

- **Calendar** Displays today's date, this month's calendar, or both.

  **Tip** When the date is displayed, double-click it to switch to the calendar. When the calendar is displayed, double-click a date to display it. Click the Larger Size button on the gadget's control panel to display both, and click the Smaller Size button to return to the most recently active view.

- **Clock** Displays the current time in the current time zone. You can choose from eight faces, name the clock, change the time zone, and add a second hand.

- **CPU Meter** Displays the percentage of your computer's central processing unit (CPU) that is currently being used, as well as the percentage of its random access memory (RAM).

  **Tip** If your computer has two or more processors (for example, if it is a dual core or quad core system), you can download CPU meters from the Windows Live Gallery that display the status of each core.

- **Currency**  Displays the current equivalent of one currency in another currency. You can add currencies and data providers.

- **Feed Headlines**  Displays four of up to 100 headlines from a variety of RSS feeds. You can restrict the number of headlines and the type of feed.

  **Tip** Click any headline to display a synopsis of the article in a separate window, and click the Read Online link in the window to display the entire article in your Web browser.

- **Picture Puzzle**  Displays a 4-by-4 grid containing 15 jumbled picture pieces and one blank square. You move the pieces around to reassemble the picture. There are 11 pictures to choose from.

- **Slide Show**  Displays a rotating set of pictures from the folder you select. You can set the transition speed and effect, as well as the display order.

- **Weather**  Displays the temperature and an image representing the type of weather in a specified location. You can change the location and show temperature in Fahrenheit or Celsius.

  **Tip** Point to the city name to display a description of the current weather conditions, or click the city name to display the corresponding MSN Weather page, which provides weather maps, averages, and daily, hourly, and 10-day forecasts for the selected city. Click the Larger Size button on the gadget's control panel to display the day's forecasted high and low and a 3-day forecast.

- **Windows Media Center**  Provides quick access to the music and pictures in your Windows Media Center catalog.

If you purchased a new computer with Windows 7 already installed, the manufacturer might have made other gadgets available.

You can add a gadget from the Desktop Gadget Gallery to your desktop by double-clicking it, by right-clicking it and then clicking Add, or by dragging it onto the desktop. After you add a gadget to your desktop, you can move it, change its size, or turn it off at any time.

**See Also** Several of the gadgets access the Internet, so UAC should be set to alert you if a program attempts to make changes to your system. For information about UAC, see "Understanding User Accounts and Permissions" in Chapter 2, "Manage User Accounts."

In this exercise, you'll add the Clock gadget to your desktop and customize the gadget to show the time in a different time zone. You'll also display news headlines and the weather in two different cities.

 **SET UP** You don't need any practice files to complete this exercise; just follow the steps.

1. On the **Start** menu, click **All Programs**, and then click **Desktop Gadget Gallery**.

   The Desktop Gadget Gallery opens.

*These nine gadgets ship with Windows 7.*

   **Tip** You can also open the Desktop Gadget Gallery by right-clicking the desktop and then clicking Gadgets.

2. At the bottom of the gallery, click **Show details**, and then click each gadget in turn to see its description.

3. Double-click the **Clock** gadget to display an analog clock in the upper-right corner of your desktop (or near the corner, if that position is already occupied).

4. Point to the clock to display the gadget control panel, and then click the **Options** button, labeled with a wrench icon.

The Clock dialog box opens.

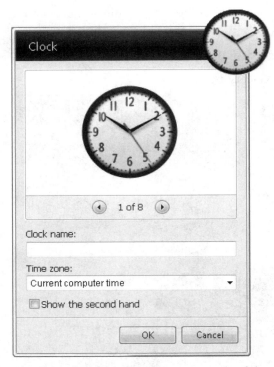

*The Clock dialog box displays an example of the current clock and provides options for changing it.*

5. Below the clock, click the **Next** button repeatedly to preview the other available clock faces.

6. Display clock face **6**, type your name in the **Clock name** box, change the **Time zone** setting to **(UTC) Coordinated Universal Time**, select the **Show the second hand** check box, and then click **OK**.

The Clock gadget changes to reflect the settings you chose.

*You can use the Clock gadget to display the time in the part of the world where a colleague, friend, or relative lives.*

7. From the **Desktop Gadget Gallery**, drag the **Feed Headlines** gadget to the desktop and drop it to the left of the clock. Then if the headlines are not immediately displayed, click **View Headlines**.

   The gadget loads current news headlines and then cycles through them four at a time. You can move backward or forward through the headlines by clicking the arrows at the bottom of the gadget.

8. Point to any headline that interests you to display the entire headline in a tooltip. Then click the headline.

   A window displays a synopsis of the associated article.

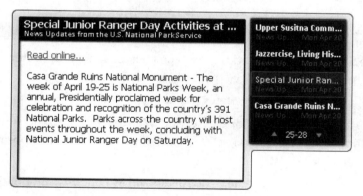

*You can view the entire article by clicking the headline at the top of the synopsis window.*

9. In the **Desktop Gadget Gallery**, double-click the **Weather** gadget twice to display two instances of the gadget on the right side of your desktop.

   The default settings display the current weather in New York, NY.

10. Point to the first **Weather** gadget, and then on its gadget control panel, click the **Options** button.

The Weather dialog box opens.

*In the Weather dialog box, you can specify a location and the temperature scale.*

11. In the **Select current location** box, type your location, press **Enter**, and if necessary, click the location in the list of those identified. Then click **OK**.

   **Tip** If you live in the United States, you can type your ZIP Code instead of your location.

12. Repeat steps 10 and 11 for the second **Weather** gadget, this time entering **London, UK** as the location, clicking **Celsius** in the **Show temperature in** section, and then clicking **OK**.

The weather location on the gadget is shown as London, GBR (for Great Britain).

13. Point to the **Feed Headlines** gadget, and then on its gadget control panel, click the **Close** button.

14. Point to the **Weather** gadget for London, point to the **Drag gadget** button at the bottom of its gadget control panel, and then drag the gadget to the top of the screen, somewhere to the left of the **Clock** gadget.

> **Tip** You can also drag the gadget itself by any part that isn't a hyperlink.

When you get close to the top edge of the screen, the gadget snaps into place. However, Windows 7 desktop gadgets aren't restricted to one area of the screen, as the Windows Vista Sidebar gadgets were; you can place them anywhere you like.

> **Tip** If you're feeling adventurous, you can click Get More Gadgets Online in the lower-right corner of the Desktop Gadgets Gallery, browse the gadget gallery on the Microsoft Web site, and download any gadgets you want.

 **CLEAN UP** Close the Desktop Gadget Gallery window. Then adjust the settings of the gadgets currently on your screen to suit your needs, or remove them entirely.

# Exploring Windows Live Programs and Services

If you've used earlier versions of Windows, you might have noticed that some familiar programs that came with those earlier versions do not come with Windows 7. You can download current versions of some of these programs, free of charge, from the Windows Live Web site located at home.live.com. All you need is a Windows Live ID, which is simply a registered e-mail address. Hotmail e-mail accounts, Messenger instant messaging accounts, and Xbox LIVE gaming accounts are automatically registered as Windows Live IDs.

> **Tip** If you don't have a Windows Live ID, you can easily sign up for one at home.live.com.

So what is Windows Live? It is two collections of programs and services—Windows Live Essentials and Windows Live Online Services—that are designed to extend the Windows user experience. In this section, we'll briefly discuss both collections so that you can decide whether you might want to take advantage of them.

## Windows Live Essentials

You can download these free programs to your computer from www.windowslive.com/ desktop/, and then install the ones you want to use. You can download all the Windows Live Essentials programs at once or download individual programs.

*Point to any program to display information about ways to access and interact with it.*

The Windows Live Essentials collection consists of the following:

- **Windows Live Mail** You can quickly and easily configure Windows Live Mail to connect to any HTTP, IMAP, or POP3 e-mail account, so you can manage all of your e-mail accounts from one location. In addition to sending e-mail messages, you can send text messages to Windows Live Messenger contacts. You can also access your messages and contacts while offline.

  **See Also** For more information, visit www.windowslive.com/Desktop/Mail/.

- **Windows Live Messenger** You can use this instant messaging (IM) program to "chat" with contacts by typing in a window on your computer screen. If you have a microphone, speakers, a webcam, and high-speed Internet access, you can also use Messenger to set up video calls with contacts.

  **See Also** For more information, visit www.windowslive.com/Desktop/Messenger/.

- **Windows Live Family Safety** Designed to enhance the parental controls included with Windows 7, Windows Live Family Safety provides superior monitoring and control of family online viewing and other activities. You can control who can be contacted using Hotmail and Windows Live Messenger, monitor activity and change settings remotely, and identify safety issues from easy-to-read reports.

  **See Also** For more information, visit www.windowslive.com/Desktop/FamilySafety/.

- **Windows Live Movie Maker** If your video card supports DirectX 9, you can create a movie from a video clip or a collection of pictures. You can import videos and photographs directly from your camera or from Photo Gallery, and you can add effects such as titles, transitions, and sound. You can preview your movies, catalog them, send them to friends, or share them online.

  **See Also** For more information, visit www.windowslive.com/Desktop/MovieMaker/.

- **Windows Live Photo Gallery** Designed for use with digital pictures from cameras and scanners, this program allows you to view, manipulate, and save image files. You can create and manage image collections; view and edit file properties (including keywords); adjust photo exposure, color settings, and red eye effects; rotate images; precisely crop images to standard or custom proportions; print pictures or order prints from a professional printing vendor; and send pictures via e-mail or burn them to a disc.

  **See Also** For more information, visit www.windowslive.com/Desktop/PhotoGallery/.

- **Windows Live Toolbar** With this toolbar displayed in the Internet Explorer window, you can easily access many Windows Live services from your Web browser. You can add buttons and RSS feeds to the toolbar to provide quick access to news and other items you refer to often.

  **See Also** For more information, visit www.windowslive.com/Desktop/Toolbar/.

- **Windows Live Writer** This handy program is designed to put all the tools you need to create compelling blog posts at your fingertips. You can quickly create a blog post that includes formatting, graphics, and links; preview the post; and then publish it to most common blog services. You can also use Writer to quickly publish your videos.

  **See Also** For more information, visit www.windowslive.com/Desktop/Writer/.

## Windows Online Services

Your Windows Live ID unlocks the door to several services that are available over the Internet from your mobile devices, as well as from your desktop computer. You can visit www.windowslive.com/Online/ to learn about these services and to start using those that will enhance your Windows 7 user experience.

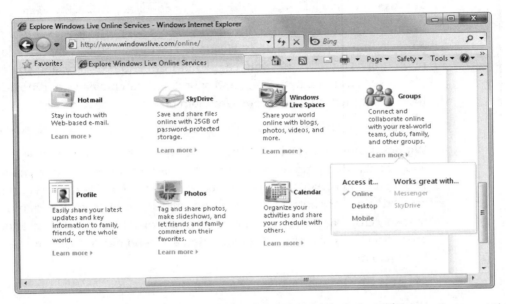

*You can access Windows Live Online Services from any mobile device with Internet access, not only from your computer.*

When you log on to Windows Live, you can display your Windows Live home page. This customizable page provides a central access point to all the Windows Live Online Services you use, which can be any of the following:

- **Windows Live Calendar** This electronic calendar makes it easy to stay on schedule. You can share your calendar with others and allow people to see when you are free or busy.

- **Windows Live Events** You can plan parties and other events in this custom workspace, including creating and sending invitations, tracking guest responses, and sharing memories.

- **Windows Live Groups** Up to 20 people can be designated as a group so that you can communicate with them all at once via e-mail, IM, or a discussion board.

- **Windows Live Hotmail** Not only does Hotmail provide a full-featured Internet-based e-mail service, but it also includes a calendar and contact list.

- **Windows Live Mobile**  With this service, you can receive e-mail messages and chat with your colleagues and friends from your mobile device.

- **Windows Live Photos**  This service provides an online storage space for your photographs. In addition to storing and displaying photos, you can catalog them, create albums, and contribute to group albums, as well as share them with others and send them via e-mail.

- **Windows Live Profile**  You can maintain your personal profile in one place and make it available in all Windows Live services, for you only or also for other people you designate.

- **Windows Live SkyDrive**  This password-protected storage site gives you 25 GB of free space in which to store documents, photographs, and other files that you want to share with colleagues, friends, and family.

- **Windows Live Spaces**  If you have ever thought about creating your own blog, you'll want to check out this service. After creating your space, you can easily post text, photographs, and videos and then share them only with the people to whom you give access.

# Installing and Removing Programs

With so many programs available to help save you time, increase your productivity, broaden your knowledge base, or simply entertain you, one of your first tasks with a new computer system is usually installing programs. When you upgrade your computer from a previous version of Windows, your installed programs remain available. If you regularly use several different programs, not having to reinstall them when you upgrade can save you a lot of time.

When you purchase a new computer, it might come with preinstalled programs that you are not interested in using. If you don't intend to use a program, you can remove it to free up disk space.

## Installing Programs

You can install programs from a variety of sources, including physical media that you can hold in your hand—such as a CD or DVD—and intangible sources such as files stored on your computer, on your network, or on a Web site. Regardless of the source of the installation files, you install almost all programs by running an executable file, which is often named *Setup.exe*. However, the precise installation process varies from program to program.

Here is what you might expect to encounter when installing programs from various sources:

- **CD or DVD installation** Many software manufacturers use an autorun file, which is located in the root directory of the CD or DVD. The autorun file either runs an executable file or asks whether you want to run it, and that file either leads you through a setup process or simply starts the program stored on the CD or DVD. Autorun files take the guesswork out of the setup process, because they don't require you to browse to a specific location, find a specific file, run a specific program, or make decisions about how to install the program.

  In earlier versions of Windows, when an autorun file was available, Windows would run it automatically. In Windows 7, inserting a disc into the disc drive displays the AutoPlay dialog box. From this dialog box, you can choose to run a default file, display the disc contents in Windows Explorer, or perform another action that is appropriate to the disc contents.

*The AutoPlay dialog box displays your options for interacting with the disc.*

- **Internet installation** Many companies sell or distribute software or software upgrades through their Web sites. To install a program from a Web site, you click the link that is provided. If your Web browser security settings allow file downloads and are set to prompt you for permission, you have two options: to run the installation file from its current location on the Internet; or to download the installation file to your computer and run it from there. If you have a high-speed Internet connection and the installation file is small, it's simplest to run the installation file from the Internet. If you have a slower or less reliable connection, or the installation file is large, it's a good idea to download the file and run it locally.

- **Network installation**  If you work for a company that keeps the most current versions of its licensed software on one or more servers rather than distributing software media to its employees, you will likely install programs directly from a network server. Your network administrator will give you instructions for locating and installing these programs.

Depending on the program you are installing, you might have to enter a unique registration code, sometimes called a *product key*, during the setup process.

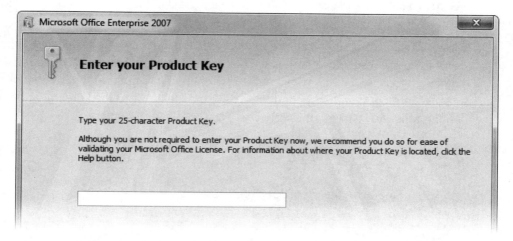

*Your product key proves that you are a legitimate owner of the product.*

Product keys are issued by the software manufacturer, either physically or electronically.

- If you are installing the program from a CD or DVD, the product key is usually located on a sticker on the back of the jewel case.

- If you are installing the program from the Internet, the software owner will supply you with a product key when you pay for it. Free software might not require a product key, but the software supplier might request or require you to register with the company before installing the software. The information you provide might be used to register your interest in the product for support purposes, for statistical purposes, or so that the supplier can follow up with marketing materials and other information.

  **Tip**  In the United States, the E-mail User Protection Act (HR 1910) requires that companies provide you with a means to remove yourself from mailing lists, and you can generally find a removal link or instructions at the bottom of the e-mail messages you receive from the company if you would prefer not to receive further messages.

- If you are installing the program from a network server, your network administrator will be able to supply the product key.

Product keys are one of the methods software manufacturers use to try to prevent software piracy. A program that requires a product key for installation can't be installed without it. (Some products can be installed but then lose or limit functionality if you don't supply a product key within a specific amount of time.) If you lose your product key, you won't be able to reinstall the program in the future, unless you can successfully appeal to the software manufacturer for a replacement product key. In such circumstances, you'll have better luck if you registered the software the first time you installed it.

**See Also** For information about software piracy, see the sidebar "The Perils of Piracy" in "Introducing Windows 7" at the beginning of this book.

Most software companies require that you read and acknowledge a license agreement before you can install their software. You might be tempted to quickly agree to the license agreement terms so that you can move on, but bear in mind that the license agreement is a legal contract. As with any contract, it's a good idea to read the agreement before consenting to it and installing the software.

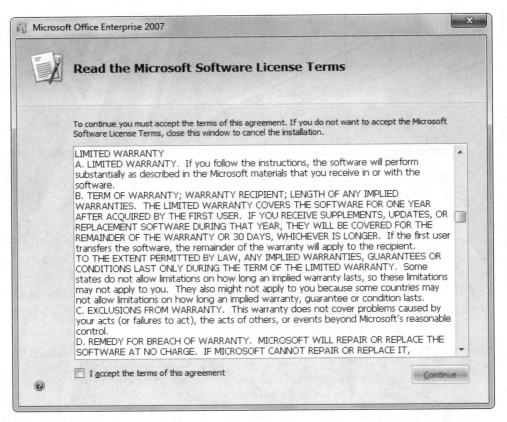

*You must agree to the terms of the license agreement to continue installing the program.*

**Tip** Depending on your User Account Control settings and whether a program you install tries to make changes to your computer settings, Windows might prompt you to provide administrator credentials to continue with a program installation process. If you do not enter the administrator password or give the program permission to proceed within a certain amount of time, the installation process will end with no visible result.

Many programs offer multiple installation options, such as *typical*, *complete*, or *custom*. Some programs that you install from a CD or DVD offer the option of copying large files to your computer or accessing them from the CD or DVD when needed. To save space on your hard disk for the features you will use most, you might have the option of waiting to install rarely used program features until the first time you need them. When choosing your installation type, consider the way in which you will use the program, the amount of space it requires, and how much space is available on your hard disk. Also think about whether the installation source will be available to you later, in case you need to reinstall the program or access features that weren't installed initially. In most cases, the default (typical) installation fits the needs of the average user and is the best choice.

When you start the installation process, some programs offer you the opportunity to accept or change the default installation location, which is usually a product-specific subfolder within the Program Files folder on drive C. Unless you have a reason for doing so, there is no need to change this default location. Accepting it guarantees that the program and Windows know where to find program files. Some programs require that their files be stored in a specific location and don't offer you the opportunity to change it.

While actively installing files, the installation program might display a progress bar to keep you informed about what is going on during the installation process, and you might be informed of specific actions as they occur.

When the installation process is complete, you might be required to restart your computer. Restarting the computer allows the installation program to replace older versions of files that are in use and to clean up after itself. If you would prefer not to restart your computer after installing a program, you can continue without restarting by clicking Restart Later or closing the message box. The final setup tasks will then be completed the next time you start or restart the computer.

**Tip** If you have trouble running an older program on Windows 7, you can use the Program Compatibility wizard to identify and repair problems. The wizard prompts you to select the program you're having difficulty with and then runs the program by using either a set of recommended compatibility settings or a set of compatibility settings that you choose based on your experience with the software. To start the Program Compatibility wizard, display the Program window of Control Panel and then, under Programs And Features, click Run Programs Made For Previous Versions Of Windows.

## Removing Programs

Most commercial programs have many components, such as executable files, reference files, theme or graphic files, shortcuts, and registry settings. Each component must reside in a specific location for the program to work correctly. If you want to remove a program from your hard disk, it would be tedious—and with some large programs, virtually impossible—to track down and delete all of its components. To ensure that a program is removed completely, and to avoid removing important components of Windows or other programs, you should always uninstall the program through Control Panel instead of deleting the program's files and folders directly.

To uninstall a program:

1. Display Control Panel, and then under Programs, click Uninstall A Program.

    The Programs And Features window opens.

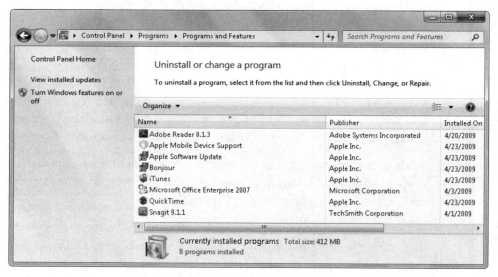

*In the Programs And Features window, you can uninstall, change, or repair a selected program.*

2. In the list of installed programs, click the one you want to remove.

    An Uninstall button appears on the toolbar. Change or Repair buttons may also appear, if these options are available for the selected program.

3. On the toolbar, click the Uninstall button.

    A message box asks you to confirm that you want to proceed.

4. In the message box, click Yes.

Simple programs might be deleted immediately, and you can then simply close Control Panel. For programs with multiple components, the process is a little more complicated. The uninstall program gathers information from your computer, including information about any shared components (those used by the program you are removing that might be required by other programs). Then it deletes the files, shortcuts, and registry entries associated with the program.

**Tip** The uninstall program should not remove any documents or other personal files you created while using the program; for example, uninstalling Microsoft Word does not remove the documents you created with Word. Nevertheless, it is a good idea to back up any information you don't want to lose, before you uninstall the program you created it with.

If the program you are removing uses any shared components, it might be necessary to restart your computer to complete the uninstall process.

5. If a message box prompts you to restart your computer, save and close any open files and then click Yes to restart your computer now, or click No to complete the uninstall process when you next start or restart your computer.

**Tip** The Change and Repair buttons re-run the setup program for an installed program, by using files stored on your computer during the initial setup process. The Change button enables you to change the installed program options; for example, you might click this button to install parts of the program that weren't included in the original installation. The Repair button re-runs the setup program with the currently installed options; for example, you might need to restore the program's functionality to its original condition if you inadvertently deleted a necessary file.

# Starting Programs Automatically

If you use a program every day, you can have Windows 7 start it for you whenever you log on to your account. For example, you might start your e-mail program first thing in the morning; or you might open your organization's Web site to look for announcements or a news Web site to stay up to date on the headlines.

**Keyboard Shortcut** You can start a new instance of a program that is already running by holding down Shift+Windows logo key and then pressing the number key representing the application's position on the taskbar. For example, if Internet Explorer is the first program pinned to the taskbar (immediately to the right of the Start button), pressing Shift+Windows logo key+1 opens a new Internet Explorer window.

When you install a program on your computer, one of the installation options might be for that program to start automatically when you log on to Windows. When you choose that option, the program may place a shortcut in your Startup folder. You can automatically start other programs, open specific locations in Windows Explorer, or even open specific files, by placing shortcuts to those items in your Startup folder. Each user has his or her own Startup folder, and there is also a Startup folder that applies to all users of your computer. So you can choose to make a program start automatically for just yourself or for everyone.

**Tip** If the program you're starting requires a user account name and password, you will be prompted to enter that information when Windows starts the program, exactly as you would be if you started the program manually.

You can access your personal Startup folder or the general Startup folder that belongs to all users through the Start menu or through Windows Explorer. Only administrators can access another user's personal Startup folder.

In this exercise, you'll set up a program to start automatically when anyone logs on to your computer, and then change it to start automatically only when you log on. This example uses the Calculator program, but you can substitute any other program.

 **SET UP** You don't need any practice files to complete this exercise; just follow the steps.

1. On the **Start** menu, click **All Programs**, and then click the **Startup** folder.

   The folder expands in the Start pane to display the programs, if any, that start automatically when you log on to Windows. Programs that appear in this list might be set up to start automatically for all users or only for you.

2. In the **All Programs** list, right-click the **Startup** folder, and then click **Open All Users**.

   Windows Explorer opens with the contents of the general Startup folder displayed in the Content pane. Any items that appear in the Startup folder on your Start menu but do not appear in this list are set up to start automatically only when *you* log on to Windows, rather than when *anyone* logs on.

3. In the **Address** bar, click the arrow to the right of **Programs**, and then click **Accessories**.

   The contents of the Accessories folder are displayed in the Content pane.

4. From the **Content** pane, right-drag the **Calculator** shortcut first to the **Start** button, pausing until the **Start** menu expands; then to the **All Programs** button, pausing until the menu expands; then to the **Startup** folder, pausing until the folder expands; and finally into the folder.

A thick black line indicates the destination of the Calculator shortcut.

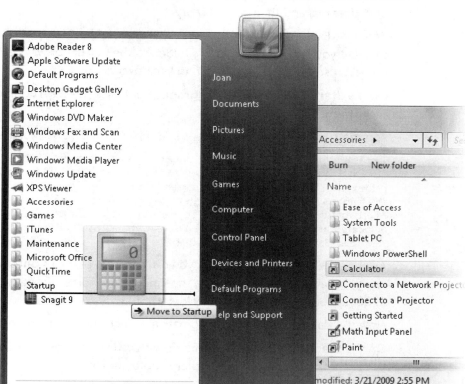

*You can right-drag programs, folders, and files into the general Startup folder.*

**5.** When the insertion line indicates that the shortcut is in the folder, release the mouse button, and then on the shortcut menu that appears, click **Copy Here**.

**Troubleshooting** The shortcut menu appears when you use the right mouse button to drag the file, rather than the left mouse button. If you use the left mouse button instead, the Calculator shortcut simply moves to the Startup folder. In that case, you will need to copy the file back into the Accessories folder.

The Calculator shortcut appears in the Start menu Startup folder.

6. In the **Address** bar of the **Accessories** folder window, click the arrow to the right of **Programs**, and then click **Startup**.

   Windows Explorer displays the general Startup folder. The copy of the Calculator shortcut you just created is in this folder, so the Calculator will start automatically for each user as she or he logs on to Windows 7.

7. On the **Start** menu, click **All Programs**, right-click the **Startup** folder, and then click **Open**.

   Your personal Startup folder opens in a separate Windows Explorer.

   **Tip** It might not be obvious from the Address bar contents which folder is your personal Startup folder and which is the general Startup folder. To identify the folder, click the folder icon that appears at the left end of the Address bar to display the folder's absolute path. The general Startup folder is located at C:\ProgramData\ Microsoft\Windows\Start Menu\Programs\Startup. Your personal Startup folder is located at C:\Users\<your user account name>\AppData\Roaming\ Microsoft\ Windows\Start Menu\Programs\Startup.

8. Arrange the two windows so that you can see both of their **Content** panes. Then using the left mouse button, drag the **Calculator** shortcut from the general **Startup** folder to your personal **Startup** folder.

   Now the Calculator will start automatically only when you log on to Windows.

9. On the **Start** menu, click the **Shut-down Options** button, and click **Log off**. When the logoff process is complete, log on again.

   After Windows completes the logon process, the Calculator starts.

**CLEAN UP** Close the Calculator program window, and then delete the Calculator shortcut from the Start menu Startup folder by right-clicking it and then clicking Delete.

# Specifying Default Programs

Usually you have only one program of a particular type installed on your computer—one word processor, one spreadsheet program, one database program, and so on. In each program, you create files of one or more specific types, identified by the file name extensions appended to their file names. For example, documents that you create and save in Word 2007 have the .docx extension. By default, these extensions are hidden from view, and you never have to type them when you assign a name to a file. But they are there nevertheless.

**See Also** For information about displaying file name extensions, see "Viewing Folders and Files in Different Ways" in Chapter 5, "Manage Folders and Files."

One of the functions of the file name extension is to identify the program that can open the file. If you double-click a file in Windows Explorer and the default program associated with that file name extension is installed on your computer, Windows 7 starts the program, and that program then opens the file. This system works well as long as each file name extension is associated with only one program. However, sometimes a file name extension represents a format that more than one installed program can work with.

A classic example of file-type competition arises with image files. File name extensions for images, including computer-generated graphics and photographs, represent the format of the images rather than the program that created them. Most image-processing programs can open and create files in several different image formats, because different formats are suited for different types of output. For example, one format might produce superior results in print, and another might be ideal for on-screen viewing. Of the file types suited to viewing on a computer, some produce high-quality images but also large file sizes; whereas others produce acceptable-quality images in smaller files that are faster to download from the Web.

Windows 7 comes with several programs that you can use to work with files of specific types. For example, until you install an image-processing program on your computer, most image files open by default in Windows Photo Viewer. When you install an image-processing program, it might configure itself as the default program for one or more file types. From that point on, when you open a file of one of those types, Windows 7 instructs that program to open the file, regardless of whether you want to use that program.

By default, the Windows 7 programs are set to work with the following file types (until you install additional programs):

- **Internet Explorer** Opens files with .htm, .html, .mht, .mhtml, and .url extensions.
- **Notepad** Opens files with .txt extensions.
- **Paint** Opens files with .emf, .jpg, .rle, and .wmf extensions.
- **Windows Contacts** Opens files with .contact, .group, .p7c, and .vcf extensions.
- **Windows Disc Image Burner** Opens files with .img and .iso extensions.

- **Windows Media Center** Opens files with .dvr, .dvr-ms, and .wtv extensions.

- **Windows Media Player** Opens audio, video, and movie file types (too numerous to list here).

- **Windows Photo Viewer** Opens files with .bmp, .dib, .jfif, .jpe, .jpeg, .png, .tif, .tiff, and .wdp extensions.

- **WordPad** Opens files with .docx, .odt, .rtf, and .txt extensions.

Your computer's manufacturer might have installed programs that work with some of these same file types.

To specify the default program for opening files of a particular type, you can work either with a file of that type, with the program, or with Windows.

- In Windows Explorer, you can right-click a file of the type for which you want to set the default program and click Open With on the shortcut menu to display a list of the installed programs that can open the file. You can then click one of those programs to open the selected file with that program this time only, or you can click Choose Default Program to display the Open With dialog box, from which you can select the program you want to use to open this type of file from now on.

  **Tip** When you double-click a file with an extension for which Windows has no program association, or if the associated program is not installed on your computer, Windows displays a message box so that you can indicate either that Windows should find the correct program or that you want to choose the program to use. If you select the latter option, Windows displays the Open With dialog box.

- In Windows Explorer, you can right-click a file, display its Properties dialog box, and on the General tab, click Change to display the Open With dialog box.

- You can open the Set Associations window from Control Panel, select a file name extension, and then change the program that should open files of that type by default.

- You can open the Set Default Programs window from Control Panel, select the program, and then choose which file types that program should open by default.

In this exercise, you'll change the default program for bitmap graphics from Windows Photo Viewer to Paint and for text files from Notepad to WordPad. You'll then reverse the changes by using a different method.

 **SET UP**  You need the MusicBox graphic located in your Documents\Microsoft Press\ Windows7SBS\Programs folder to complete this exercise. Open the Programs folder window, and then follow the steps.

1. In the **Content** pane, double-click the **MusicBox** image file.

   Unless the default program for opening bitmap files has been changed from the Windows 7 default, the image opens in Windows Photo Viewer.

2. Close the **MusicBox** image. Then in the **Content** pane, right-click the **MusicBox** image file, and click **Open with**.

   The Open With menu displays the programs installed on your computer that are most commonly used to open this type of file.

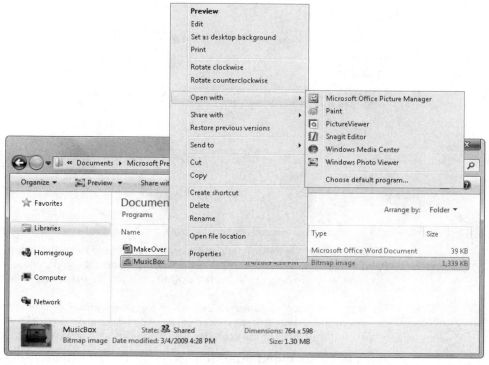

*From this menu, you can open the selected file with a specific program or change the default program.*

3. On the **Open with** menu, click **Choose Default Program**.

4. In the Open With dialog box that opens, click the downward-pointing arrow at the right end of the **Other Programs** heading, .

The Other Programs section expands.

*The programs in the Recommended Programs section are the same programs shown on the Open With menu. The programs in the Other Programs section are those installed on your computer that can be assigned as the default program for the selected file type.*

**Tip** If the program you want to use doesn't appear in the Recommended Programs section or the Other Programs section, click Browse, navigate to the Program Files folder, and then find the executable file of the program you want to use.

5. In the **Recommended Programs** section, click **Paint**. Then, with the **Always use the selected program to open this kind of file** check box selected, click **OK**.

The icon representing the MusicBox image changes from a Windows Photo Viewer icon to a Paint icon. Paint starts and opens the MusicBox image. Double-clicking any file with the .bmp extension will open the file in Paint.

6. Close the **Paint** program window and the **Programs** folder window.

7. In the right pane of the **Start** menu, click **Default Programs**. Then in the **Default Programs** window, click **Associate a file type or protocol with a program**.

   The Set Associations window opens.

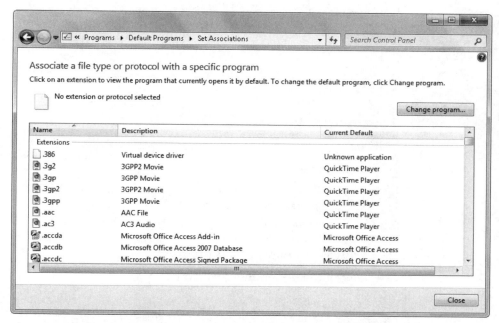

*The Set Associations window of Control Panel lists the file name extensions to which you can assign a default program.*

8. In the **Set Associations** window, scroll to the **.txt** extension.

   The Description for this file name extension is Text Document, and the Current Default setting is Notepad.

9. Click anywhere in the **.txt** row, and then click **Change program**.

10. When the **Open with** dialog box opens, click **WordPad**, and then click **OK**.

    The Current Default setting in the Set Associations window changes to reflect your selection.

11. In the **Set Associations** window, click **Close**.

12. In the **Default Programs** window, click **Set your default programs**. Then in the **Set Default Programs** window, click **Windows Photo Viewer**.

    A description of the selected program appears.

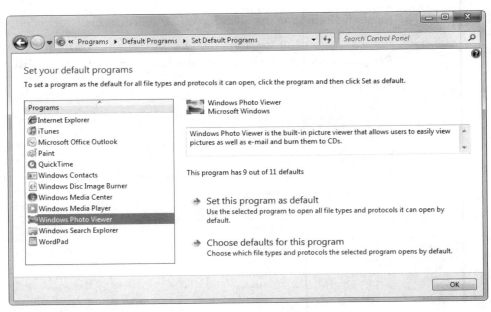

*The selected program is the default for 9 of the 11 file types it can open.*

**13.** Click **Choose defaults for this program**.

The Set Program Associations window opens.

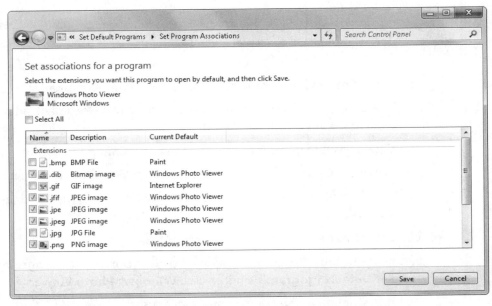

*Check boxes indicate which file types are assigned to the selected program.*

14. In the **Set Program Associations** window, select the **.bmp** check box, and then click **Save**.

   Although you can associate file types with programs in the Set Program Associations window, you cannot disassociate them, except by setting them for another program. You need to work from the Set Associations window shown earlier to restore Notepad as the default program for .txt files.

15. In the **Address** bar, click **Default Programs**. Then in the **Default Programs** window, click **Associate a file type or protocol with a program**.

16. In the **Set Associations** window, click the **.txt** entry, and click **Change program**. When the **Open with** dialog box opens, click **Notepad**, and then click **OK**.

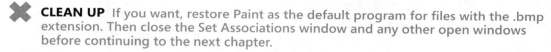 **CLEAN UP** If you want, restore Paint as the default program for files with the .bmp extension. Then close the Set Associations window and any other open windows before continuing to the next chapter.

# Key Points

- It's worth taking the time to explore the programs that come with Windows 7, such as the Calculator, Sticky Notes, and the Snipping Tool.

- Gadgets are useful tools that display real-time information on your Windows 7 desktop.

- You might want to check out the programs and services available for free on the Windows Live Web site to see whether they might be useful in your work.

- When installing new programs, Windows 7 asks you to confirm basic installation information and then handles the rest of the installation process. Similarly, Windows 7 provides a safe way of completely removing programs you no longer use.

- You can instruct Windows 7 to automatically start a program when any user logs on to the computer or only when you log on.

- You can choose the program Windows 7 starts when you double-click a file of a particular type.

# Chapter at a Glance

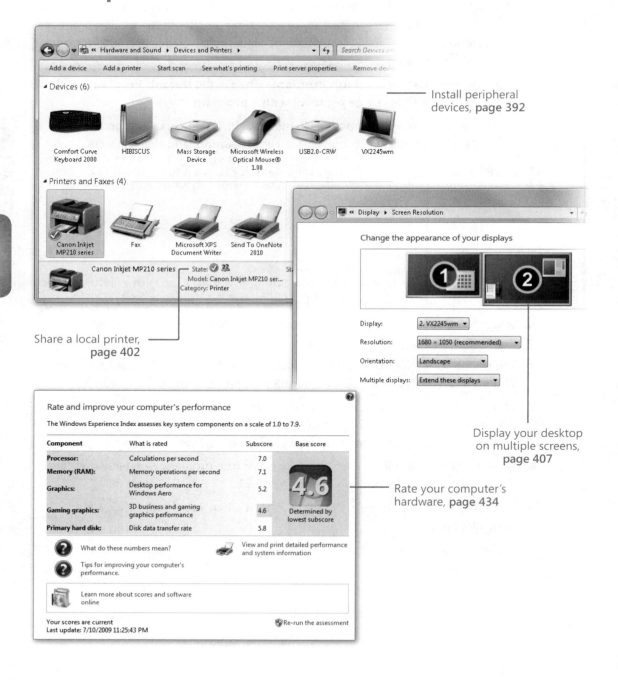

Install peripheral devices, **page 392**

Share a local printer, **page 402**

Display your desktop on multiple screens, **page 407**

Rate your computer's hardware, **page 434**

# 12 Set Up Hardware Devices

---

**In this chapter, you will learn how to**

- ✔ Install peripheral devices.
- ✔ Share a local printer.
- ✔ Connect to a remote printer.
- ✔ Display your desktop on multiple screens.
- ✔ Set up sound devices.
- ✔ Change the way your mouse and keyboard work.
- ✔ Rate your computer's hardware.
- ✔ Locate device information.

---

We discuss computers in terms of hardware and software. Physical items such as computers and monitors are collectively known as *hardware*, and all the programs that you use to do things with that hardware are collectively known as *software*. The Windows 7 operating system is the interface through which the software communicates with the hardware.

If your computer is a desktop computer, you'll need to connect peripheral hardware devices such as a monitor, a keyboard, and a mouse to it before you can use it. If your computer is a portable computer, such as a notebook or netbook, those devices are built in, but you might want to connect peripheral hardware devices such as a printer or a USB flash drive. Other common external devices are speakers, scanners, fax machines, external storage drives, and external media drives such as CD and DVD drives. Depending on your interests and how you use your computer, you might also use devices such as a microphone, video camera (commonly referred to as a *webcam*), fingerprint reader, joystick, touchpad, or drawing tablet. The point of all these devices, of course, is to make your computing experience more productive, more enjoyable, and (hopefully) simpler.

In this chapter, you'll work with a computer's most common external devices—the monitor, keyboard, mouse, printer, speakers, and microphone. In the process, you'll learn about plug-and-play devices, device drivers, and ports. Finally, you'll explore Device Manager, where you can set device properties and identify any devices that are not functioning properly.

> **Practice Files** You won't need any practice files to complete the exercises in this chapter. See "Using the Practice Files" at the beginning of this book for more information.

# Installing Peripheral Devices

*Peripheral devices* are devices that are not essential to a computer's operation, meaning that the computer can compute without them. However, some peripheral devices are essential if you are going to do meaningful work with your computer. There are two types of peripheral devices:

- **Internal** You install these inside your computer's case and are likely to consider them part of the computer. Internal devices can come in the form of an expansion card, or a new hard disk drive or DVD drive. For example, you might install an additional video card to improve your computer's graphics capabilities or support multiple monitors, or you might install a TV tuner card so that you can watch network television on your computer.

- **External** You attach these to your computer by connecting them to ports on the outside of your computer's case. Some external devices are essential to our computing experiences, such as a monitor, keyboard, and mouse; others are considered essential by some users but optional by others, such as speakers and a printer; and still others are more specialty items, such as a scanner or external hard drive.

  **See Also** For information about adding monitors to your computer system, see "Displaying Your Desktop on Multiple Screens" later in this chapter.

*Ports* are outlets in your computer's case through which various types of information can pass. Ports come in many shapes and sizes, each designed for a specific purpose. A typical computer has a VGA or DVI port to which you can connect a monitor, PS/2 ports to which you can connect a keyboard and a mouse, a parallel port to which you can connect a printer, an Ethernet port to which you can connect a network cable, an IEEE 1394 port to which you can connect high-speed devices such as digital video cameras, and several USB ports to which you can connect a variety of devices.

If you find that you don't have enough ports to connect all the devices you want to use with your computer, you don't have to limit your device choices. Here are two options for expanding your connection capacity:

- **Install extra ports**  You can purchase a card with more ports in almost any computer store. After turning off your desktop computer and removing its cover, you insert the card into one of the available expansion slots. When you turn the power back on, Windows 7 detects and installs the new ports without further ado.

- **Use a hub**  You can connect a single multiport hub to your computer and then connect multiple devices to the hub, enabling all the devices to share that single connection. Hubs are available for network, parallel, and USB connections.

A USB connection provides both power and data-transfer capabilities to a device. Many external devices that connect to your computer through a USB port (or through an IEEE 1394 port, although these devices are less common) fall into a category called *plug and play*, which quite literally means that you can plug them in and use them. Plug-and-play devices include printers, external hard drives, flash drives, fingerprint readers, smart card readers, cameras, and many others. When you connect a plug-and-play device to your computer, Windows 7 communicates with it by using a built-in device driver and configures the necessary settings. Other external devices might require a special device driver in order to work properly.

*You can connect many types of devices to your computer through a USB port.*

*Device drivers* are files containing information that Windows needs to communicate with your printer, fax machine, scanner, camera, or other device. Drivers can be specific to an individual device or to a family of devices (such as all HP LaserJet printers), and they are often specific to a particular version of Windows.

**Tip** If you want to use one USB device with two computers, you can connect the device to a multiport, USB-sharing hub and connect the hub to a USB port in each computer.

Some devices come with software you can install to take full advantage of their capabilities. For example, you might connect an all-in-one printer/scanner/fax/copy machine to your computer and be able to print, fax, and copy without installing additional software. However, to be able to scan documents to electronic files, you'll need to install the software provided with the device.

Installing a new printer or other type of device is usually easy and intuitive, because most of these devices are now plug and play. (Some older printers might connect through a parallel port; these printers are not plug and play, so you'll have to install drivers for them.) A plug-and-play device that connects through a USB connection might have a USB logo on its packaging.

When you connect a printer or other device to your computer and, if necessary, turn on the device, Windows 7 identifies the device and searches through its database of drivers to locate the appropriate driver for the device. If Windows 7 doesn't have a current driver for your particular device, it asks you to provide the driver. You might have the driver on an installation CD provided by the device manufacturer. Alternatively, Windows can search the Internet for the driver, or you can visit the device manufacturer's Web site.

**Tip** For some devices, the order in which you plug things in and turn things on affects the ability of Windows 7 to install the device correctly. Be sure to follow the instructions that come with the device.

After you install a device, you can take advantage of a technology called *Device Stage*. This new Windows 7 feature enables you to work efficiently with devices by presenting a wide variety of device-specific options in the device window. For example, the device window for a printer includes an image of the printer, its current status, and links to manage the printer. The device window for a Device Stage–supported printer might also include links to check how much ink is left in the ink cartridge and to purchase ink cartridges from an online store, as well as a link to the user manual and to the manufacturer's Web site. The

Device Stage content is provided by device manufacturers so that up-to-date information is available to customers directly through Windows rather than on a CD that ships with the device. At the time of this writing, it is expected that manufacturers such as Brother, Epson, HP, Motorola, Nikon, Sansa, Canon, Sony, and Nokia will take advantage of Device Stage for their latest products.

When you connect a new device that supports Device Stage, a device icon might appear on the Windows Taskbar. Right-clicking the icon displays a shortcut menu with a list of tasks associated with the device. Double-clicking the icon displays a device-specific window with basic information, as well as the most common tasks performed with that device. Whether or not a device icon appears on the taskbar, you can display information about and controls for your device by double-clicking it in the Devices And Printers window. Depending on the device, this displays either a device window or a dialog box.

**Tip** Don't be concerned if the device window for a particular device seems to change from time to time. Some of the information available in the window is supplied by the device's manufacturer and can be updated dynamically from the Web.

In this exercise, you'll install a printer and test the installation by printing a test page.

 **SET UP** You don't need any practice files to complete this exercise. With a printer that connects through a USB cable and the appropriate connection cable available, follow the steps.

1. Connect the printer to the appropriate port on your computer.

2. If necessary, connect the printer to a power outlet, and then turn it on.

   Windows 7 searches for the appropriate device driver.

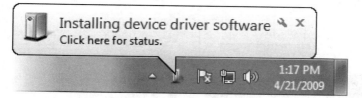

*If your computer connects to the printer through a USB port, Windows 7 recognizes the device and displays an alert while it configures the necessary settings and drivers.*

3. If Windows 7 displays an alert notifying you that it is installing the device driver software, click the alert. If no alert appears, skip to step 5.

   Clicking the alert opens the Driver Software Installation window displaying information about the drivers Windows is installing.

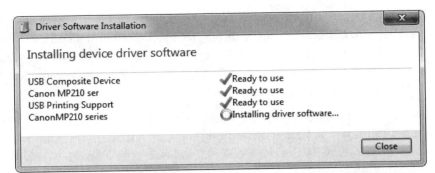

*The Driver Software Installation window displays the progress of the printer installation.*

4. After Windows announces that the printer is ready to use, close the **Driver Software Installation** window.

   If Windows doesn't automatically install the printer driver, you can install it manually as described in steps 7 through 17.

5. In the right pane of the **Start** menu, click **Devices and Printers**.

   The Devices And Printers window opens.

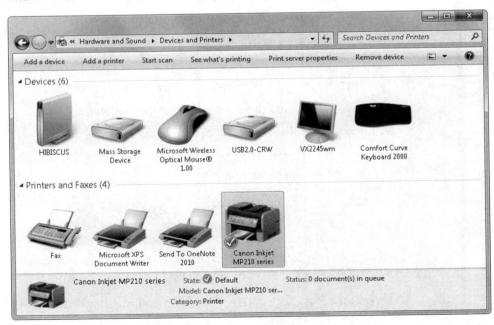

*Physical printers, virtual printers (those that print to a file rather than on paper), print services, and fax services appear in the Printers And Faxes area of the Devices And Printers window.*

**Tip** The green check mark identifies the default printer. You can change your default printer at any time. To do so, display the Devices And Printers window, right-click the printer you want to set as the default, and click Set As Default Printer.

6. If the printer appears in the **Printers and Faxes** area of the **Devices and Printers** window and no warning or error icon appears on the printer icon, your printer is installed and ready to use. Skip to step 18.

   Otherwise, follow the next steps to complete the installation.

7. At the top of the **Devices and Printers** window, click **Add a printer**.

   The Add Printer wizard starts.

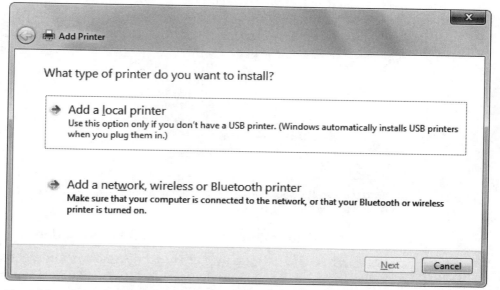

*The Add Printer wizard guides you through the process of installing a local or remote printer.*

**Tip** While working through the wizard, you can return to a previous page by clicking the Back button in the upper-left corner.

8. On the first page of the **Add Printer** wizard, click **Add a local printer**.

   **Tip** A printer that is connected directly to your computer is called a *local printer*. A printer that is available to you through your network is called a *remote printer*.

   The Choose A Printer Port page of the Add Printer wizard appears.

9. On the **Choose a printer port** page, select the port to which your printer is connected from the **Use an existing port** list. If the printer is connected to a USB port but did not automatically install, choose **USB001 (Virtual printer port for USB)**. Then click **Next**.

**Troubleshooting** It's likely that the correct port will already be selected. If not, the installation instructions from your printer manufacturer will tell you which port you should use. Some manufacturers supply helpful drawings to guide you.

The Install The Printer Driver page of the Add Printer wizard appears. The Manufacturer list includes the most common brands of printers.

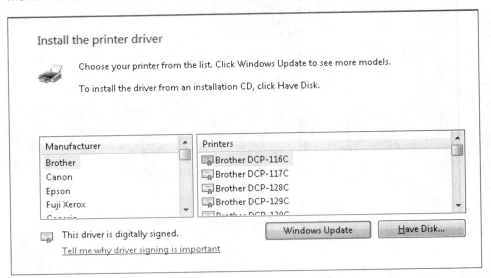

With the Add Printer wizard, you can choose a non–plug-and-play printer from a list or install it from the manufacturer's CD or DVD.

**10.** On the **Install the printer driver** page, click **Windows Update**.

Windows Update retrieves the current set of Windows 7 printer drivers from its online database and updates the Manufacturer and Printers lists in the wizard to include all the available printer drivers.

**See Also** For information about the Have Disk option, see the sidebar "Installing Printer Drivers from a CD or DVD" at the end of this topic.

**11.** In the **Manufacturer** list, click the brand name of your printer.

The Printers list changes to reflect a list of the printers available from the selected manufacturer.

**12.** In the **Printers** list, click the model of your printer (which you can usually find printed on the top or front of the printer). Then click **Next**.

If the selected driver is already installed on your computer, you can use the driver that is already installed or replace it with the driver from the Printers list.

**Troubleshooting** The Printers list is actually a list of drivers rather than printers. Many printer drivers support multiple printers, and the supported printers may not all be in the Printers list. If the list doesn't include your specific printer model, select a model with a similar name. Alternatively, download the necessary drivers from the manufacturer's Web site, return to the Install The Printer Driver page, and click Have Disk to install the printer manually.

**13.** If the **Add Printer** wizard prompts you to use or replace the current driver, click **Use the driver that is currently installed**, and then click **Next**.

The Type A Printer Name page appears. The Add Printer wizard suggests the printer driver description as the printer name.

**14.** On the **Type a printer name** page, change the printer name if you want to, or accept the suggested name. Then click **Next**.

A progress bar indicates the status of the driver installation. When the installation is complete, the Printer Sharing page appears.

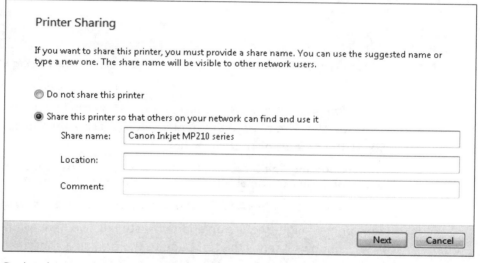

*During the setup process, the Add Printer wizard gives you the option of sharing the printer.*

**15.** We'll manually share the printer in the exercise that accompanies the next topic, "Sharing a Local Printer," so unless you plan to skip that exercise, click **Do not share this printer**. Then click **Next**.

**Tip** To share a printer with other network computer users, the Network Discovery and File And Printer Sharing settings must be turned on for the current network profile. For information, see "Sharing Files on Your Network" in Chapter 3, "Manage Your Network."

The Add Printer wizard confirms that you've successfully added the printer. If you chose to share the printer, it is now available to other network computer users.

By default, the wizard assumes you want to use this printer as your default printer. If other printers are installed on your computer, you can opt to retain your current default printer.

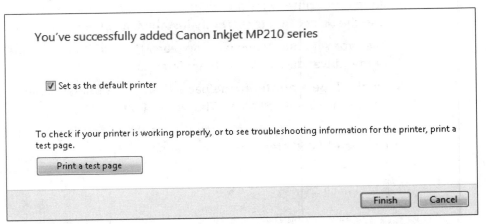

You've successfully added Canon Inkjet MP210 series

☑ Set as the default printer

To check if your printer is working properly, or to see troubleshooting information for the printer, print a test page.

[ Print a test page ]

[ Finish ]    [ Cancel ]

*If another printer is installed on your computer, you can change the default printer to the one you're installing.*

16. If you don't want Windows and any programs you run on your computer, such as Microsoft Word, to print to this printer when you click the **Print** button, clear the **Set as the default printer** check box.

   **Troubleshooting** The Set As The Default Printer check box appears only if you have active connections to other printers. If this is the only active printer, it is the default.

17. On the last page of the **Add Printer** wizard, click **Print a test page**.

   Your printer might require an additional step or two here to print the page. After Windows 7 sends the test page to the printer, a confirmation message box appears.

18. In the confirmation message box, click **Close**. Then in the **Add Printer** wizard, click **Finish**.

   An icon for the newly installed, local printer appears in the Printers And Faxes area of the Devices And Printers window.

19. In the **Devices and Printers** window, double-click the icon for your new printer.

   The device window for the printer displays information about the printer status and related tasks.

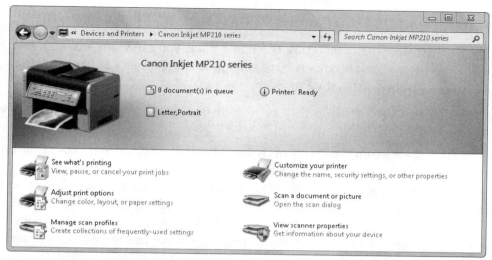

*The device window provides an efficient way to interact with the installed printer.*

**Troubleshooting** This window is available only on computers that support Aero.

**CLEAN UP** If you're continuing directly to the next exercise, click the Back button in the upper-left corner of the window to return to the Devices And Printers window. Otherwise, close the device window.

**Tip** To safely remove a printer from the Devices And Printers window, right-click the printer, and click Remove Device. You can then physically disconnect the printer from your computer or from the network without leaving any stray information or open ports behind.

---

## Installing Printer Drivers from a CD or DVD

If you have an installation CD or DVD for your printer, when you reach the Install The Printer Driver page of the Add Printer wizard, you can click Have Disk and then follow the instructions on the screen to install the printer drivers from the disc. However, the installation disc might contain:

- Out-of-date drivers that are not compatible with Windows 7. If your printer was manufactured before the release of Windows 7, the installation disc probably doesn't include Windows 7 drivers. You need to visit Windows Update or the manufacturer's Web site to download the latest drivers.

- Unnecessary printer management software programs.

Using the installation disc can actually require more time and effort than simply using the Add Printer wizard. Using the Add Printer wizard also guarantees that Windows 7 has any available enhanced information for printers that support Device Stage.

# Sharing a Local Printer

If your computer is part of a homegroup, you can share your local printer with other homegroup members by selecting the Printers check box in the Select What You Want To Share list in the HomeGroup window.

**See Also** For information about sharing local resources with a homegroup, see "Sharing Files on Your Network" in Chapter 3, "Manage Your Network."

If your computer is connected to a network, you can make your local printer available to other computers connected to the network, by sharing the printer in the Add Printer wizard when you install the printer, or at any time after you install it. When you share your printer, you assign it a name. This name might be based on the manufacturer or model of the printer (such as *HP LaserJet*), on some special feature (such as *Color Printer*), or on the physical location of the printer (such as *Front Office*). Be sure that the name you choose clearly identifies the printer you're sharing.

You can restrict the network users who can connect to your computer by turning on password-protected sharing. Then only people who have a user account on your computer can connect to the shared printer from another network computer.

In this exercise, you'll share a printer connected to your computer so that it can be used by other people.

**Important** You do not need to be connected to a network to share your printer; you can share it even if no one but you will ever use it.

 **SET UP** You don't need any practice files to complete this exercise. Open the Devices And Printers window, and then follow the steps.

1. In the **Devices and Printers** window, right-click the icon representing the printer that is connected to your computer, and then click **Printer properties**.

   The printer's Properties dialog box opens.

2. Click the **Sharing** tab.

3. Select the **Share this printer** check box.

   **Troubleshooting** If the Share This Printer check box is unavailable and a Change Sharing Options button appears above it, click the button.

   In the Share Name box, Windows automatically enters the printer name that is stored with the printer properties.

4. If you want to change the name that will identify your shared printer on your network but don't want to change the name that identifies the printer in the Devices And Printers window, replace the name in the **Share name** box with the name you want. For example, you might specify the printer's location or capabilities.

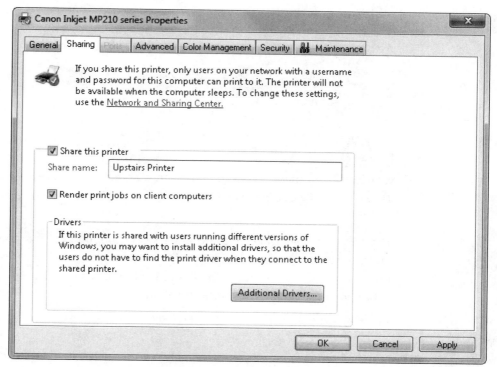

*The tabs available in the Properties dialog box vary based on the features of the printer you're sharing.*

5. If your network includes computers that are running versions of Windows other than Windows 7, and it is likely that those computers will connect to the printer you're sharing, click **Additional Drivers**. In the **Additional Drivers** window that opens, select the check boxes for the other drivers you want to install, and then click **OK**.

**Tip** To make your printer accessible to all network users, regardless of whether they have an account on your computer, you need to turn off password-protected sharing. For information, see "Sharing Files on Your Network" in Chapter 3, "Manage Your Network."

6. In the **Properties** dialog box, click **OK**.

   In the Devices And Printers window, the Details pane now indicates that the selected printer is shared.

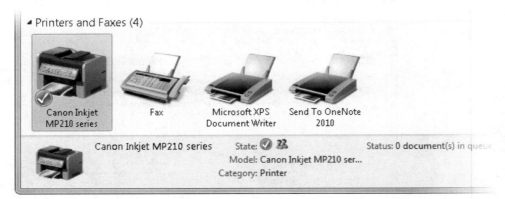

*The head-and-shoulders icon in the State field of the Details pane identifies the selected printer as shared.*

The printer is now available to other network computer users in the Devices And Printers window, in the Printers list of the Print dialog box that opens when they print from a program, and in the Printers folder of your computer when they view your computer over the network (for example, in the Network window).

**See Also**  For information about viewing network resources, see "Connecting to a Network" in Chapter 3, "Manage Your Network."

 **CLEAN UP**  If you're not continuing directly to the next exercise, close the Devices And Printers window.

# Connecting to a Remote Printer

Any remote printer made available by a user of a computer on your network, either by including it as a shared homegroup resource or by sharing the printer, is available for your use. You can simply connect and print to the printer from your computer.

If password-protected sharing is turned on for the host computer (the computer to which a shared printer is connected), the printer will be available only to computer users who have logon credentials for the host computer.

**See Also**  For information about viewing network resources and about password-protected sharing, see "Connecting to a Network," in Chapter 3, "Manage Your Network."

Your network might also include printers that are connected directly to the network through a wired or wireless network connection. These printers, which are remote printers to every computer on the network, are called *network printers*. Network printers aren't connected to any computer and are available whenever they are turned on.

In this exercise, you'll add a shared printer or network printer to the list of printers you can print to from your computer.

 **SET UP** You don't need any practice files to complete this exercise. Ensure that your computer is connected to a network that includes one or more shared or network printers. Open the Devices And Printers window, and then follow the steps.

1. On the toolbar of the **Devices and Printers** window, click **Add a printer**.

   The Add Printer wizard starts.

2. On the first page of the **Add Printer** wizard, click **Add a network, wireless, or Bluetooth printer**.

   The Add Printer wizard searches your network and displays a list of available printers. The list includes any local printers shared from your computer.

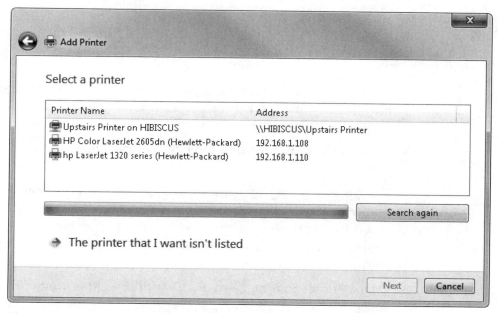

*The Add Printer wizard displays network printers and shared printers on your network.*

**Troubleshooting** If your computer isn't connected to a network, the Add Printer wizard won't find any printers; not even the one you shared earlier in this chapter.

3. On the **Select a printer** page, click the printer you want to connect to, and then click **Next**.

   **Troubleshooting** If the printer you want to connect to isn't in the list, click The Printer That I Want Isn't Listed. Then on the Find A Printer By Name Or TCP/IP Address page, in the Select A Shared Printer By Name box, type \\ (two backslashes) followed by the name of the computer to which the printer is attached, followed by the printer name, in the format shown below the box. Then click Next. If not everyone on your network is allowed to use this printer, you might be prompted to enter your user account name and password to complete the connection.

   The wizard connects to the selected printer, finds out what printer driver is required, and checks your computer for that driver. If the required driver is already installed on your computer, the wizard asks whether you want to use or replace the current driver. If the required driver isn't already installed on your computer but is available from the host computer of the shared printer, the wizard installs the driver from the host computer. (You might be prompted to give permission for this action.) If you're connecting to a network printer and the driver is not available, the wizard prompts you to locate the driver.

   **Troubleshooting** The printer installation process may vary depending on your computer hardware and the printer you're installing.

4. If the wizard prompts you to use or replace the current driver, click **Next** to use the existing driver. If the wizard prompts you to locate the driver, follow the instructions in the wizard to do so.

   The Type A Printer Name page appears. The Add Printer wizard suggests the printer name stored with the printer properties, which might not match the name shown in the Add Printer wizard.

5. On the **Type a printer name** page, change the suggested name if you want. Then click **Next**.

   The Printer Sharing page appears, giving you have the option of sharing the printer from your computer with other network users. This enables you to give access to the printer to someone with whom the printer has not been shared directly. It is a good idea to get the printer owner's permission before taking advantage of this option.

6. On the **Printer Sharing** page, click **Do not share this printer**. Then click **Next**.

   The Add Printer wizard confirms that you've successfully added the printer. By default, the wizard assumes that you want to use this newly added printer as your default printer.

7. If you don't want Windows and any programs you run on your computer to print to this printer when you click the **Print** button, clear the **Set as the default printer** check box.

8. If you want to verify that your connection to the printer is working, click **Print a test page**, and then close the message box that appears.

9. In the **Add Printer** wizard, click **Finish**.

   The remote printer appears in the Devices And Printers window, and you can now print to it as you would to a local printer.

**X** **CLEAN UP** Close the Devices And Printers window.

# Displaying Your Desktop on Multiple Screens

A basic computer system includes one monitor that displays your Windows desktop. This is sufficient for many computing experiences. However, in some situations, you might find it convenient, or even necessary, to extend your desktop across multiple monitors or duplicate your desktop on a secondary display (such as a monitor or video projector screen). You can easily add one, two, or more monitors or other display devices to your computer system.

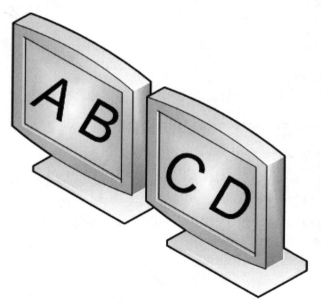

*Extending the desktop increases its width.*

Extending your desktop is convenient when:

- You want to display more columns of a spreadsheet than can be shown on one screen.
- You need to monitor your e-mail while working in another program.
- You're dragging text, graphics, or clippings from one program window to another.
- You're displaying a presentation on a projector screen and want to privately view your presentation notes on your computer screen.

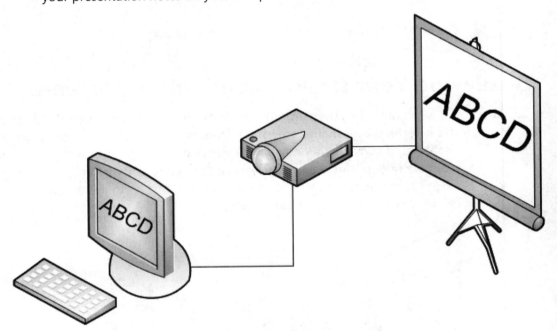

*Duplicating the desktop displays the same content on two screens.*

Duplicating your desktop is convenient when:

- You're demonstrating a process to several colleagues and it's more convenient for them to view it on a separate display.
- You're displaying information on a video projector screen and need to see the information up close to interact with it.

To connect multiple monitors to your Windows 7 computer system, your computer must have one of the following:

- A multiport video card. The ports might be of the same type (such as two VGA ports) or of multiple types (such as one VGA port, one DVI port, and one HDMI port).

- Multiple video cards.

- A dual monitor adaptor. These devices convert an existing USB port to a video port.

You can connect as many display devices as you have ports available. You connect the display to the computer by using a cable with the appropriate port connectors on it. If you don't have a cable with connectors that match the available ports, you can use an adapter to match the cable connector type to the port type.

When you connect a secondary display device to your computer, Windows 7 detects the device and, if your computer system already has the necessary drivers, automatically extends the desktop onto the newly connected display device.

**Tip** Most video projectors connect to your computer through the VGA port and use standard display drivers that don't require additional software drivers.

After connecting the display device, you can change the way Windows displays information on the devices. Options include:

- **Duplicate these displays** The same content appears on both displays. This is useful when you are giving a presentation and are not facing the screen (for example, when standing at a podium facing an audience) or want to have a closer view of the content you're displaying.

- **Extend these displays** Your desktop expands to cover both displays. The Windows Taskbar appears only on the screen you designate as the primary display.

- **Show desktop only on** Content appears only on the selected display. This is useful if you are working on a portable computer connected to a second, larger display.

To change the way your computer displays information on multiple monitors:

1. Right-click an empty area of the desktop, and then click Screen Resolution.
   The Screen Resolution window of Control Panel opens.

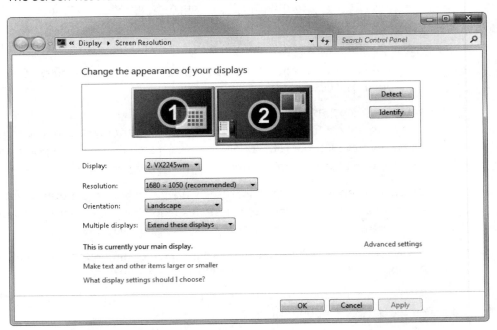

*The Screen Resolution window identifies the monitors attached to your computer.*

If a monitor is connected to your computer but not active, it appears in the preview area at the top of the window, but it is dimmed.

2. In the preview area, click Detect.
   A large number appears in the center of each monitor, corresponding to the monitor icon that represents it in the Screen Resolution window.

3. In the preview area, drag the monitors to reflect their physical arrangement (so the icon representing the left monitor appears on the left side of the preview area).

4. In the Multiple Displays list, click Duplicate These Displays or Extend These Displays. Then click Apply.

## Working with Hidden Windows

If a connection problem occurs while your desktop is extended across multiple monitors, open windows might be hidden on an inactive monitor. To retrieve a hidden window, first press Alt+Tab to display icons of the open windows, and then, holding down the Alt key, press Tab until the icon of the window you want to move is selected. Then use one of these handy tricks:

● Press Windows logo key+Left Arrow to move the active window to the left monitor, or Windows logo key+Right Arrow to move it to the right monitor.

● Press Alt+Spacebar+M, and then press an Arrow key to move the window in the direction of the active monitor.

When working on a computer connected to two display devices, Windows designates one as the primary display and the other as the secondary display. The Welcome screen and taskbar always appear on the primary display, as do most application windows when they first open. You can then drag selected windows to the secondary screen.

**Troubleshooting** You can't drag a maximized window between screens; you must first reduce the size of the window either by clicking the Restore Down button on the window's title bar or by double-clicking the title bar.

To ascertain which monitor or other display device is the primary display, point to either monitor representation in the Screen Resolution window. A ScreenTip appears, displaying the monitor's role (primary or secondary) and in the case of the secondary monitor, its position in relation to the primary monitor.

To change which monitor is designated as primary:

1. In the preview area of the Screen Resolution window, click the secondary display.

2. Select the This Is My Main Monitor check box, and then click Apply.

By default, Monitor 2 appears immediately to the right of Monitor 1. When you move the mouse pointer horizontally from screen to screen, it should leave the right edge of the left screen and enter the left edge of the right screen at vertically the same point. If your monitors are not physically the same size, are set to different screen resolutions, or are not placed level with each other, you can change the alignment of the displays so that the pointer moves cleanly between them.

## Expanding Your Portable Computer with Peripheral Devices

Portable computers (such as laptops, notebooks, and netbooks) are useful when you want to be able to move around with your computer—from room to room, from work to home, or from city to city. However, you usually have to deal with a smaller monitor, a smaller keyboard, and a touchpad or pointing stick instead of a standard mouse, and many "ultra-portable" computers don't have internal CD or DVD drives.

In addition to the frustration caused by these basic differences between mobile and desktop computing, you might find that your wrists become tired because you can't rest them on the keyboard. Or you might accidentally tap the touchpad when you're typing and enter inadvertent errors in your documents.

Although carrying a full-size monitor, keyboard, and mouse when you travel with your portable computer is not convenient, expanding it with full-size devices will improve your computing experience when you're using it in your office or at home. If you use a portable computer both at work and at home, you can set up a monitor, keyboard, and mouse at each location for a relatively small sum of money. You then have the best of both worlds—mobile computing and a full-size setup.

You connect hardware devices to your portable computer the same way you would connect them to a standard desktop computer. Notebook computers have a video port to which you can connect a monitor, but some don't have keyboard or mouse ports, so you need to use USB versions of these devices. Alternatively, you can connect the devices to a docking station, and then connect your computer to the docking station whenever you want to use the devices. This is the most convenient option, because you need to connect and disconnect only one cable rather than three.

When you attach an external monitor to your portable computer, you might at first see the same display on both monitors, or the display might appear only on the portable computer's monitor. To change which monitor displays your desktop, look at the function keys at the top of the keyboard—one of them (usually F5, sometimes F4) should include a graphic representation of a monitor. Hold down the key that activates the alternative function key behavior (usually the Alt key or a special "function" key near the lower-left corner of the keyboard), and then press the monitor-switching key to switch among three options: portable-computer display and external display, external display only, and portable-computer display only.

**Tip** If the monitor-switching key is not obvious, consult your computer's manual or the manufacturer's Web site for further information.

To adjust the relative position of the displays:

1.  In the preview area of the Screen Resolution window, drag the Monitor 2 icon to the location you want it to be in relation to the Monitor 1 icon.

    As you move the icon, a ScreenTip displays its position (in pixels) in relation to the other monitor.

*The preview area of the Screen Resolution window.*

2.  When the monitor is in the position you want, release the mouse button. Then in the Screen Resolution window, click Apply or OK.

    **Tip** After rearranging the monitor icons, you can judge whether the monitors are appropriately aligned by moving the pointer between the screens. Ideally, the pointer should remain on the same horizontal plane.

# Setting Up Sound Devices

Computers are no longer devices used primarily to produce traditional business documents such as letters, reports, and spreadsheets. You can use your computer for multimedia activities such as listening to music, watching movies, or playing games, and you can create sound-enhanced documents such as presentations and videos. Even if you're not likely to work with these types of files, your productivity might be diminished if you cannot hear the sound effects used by Windows 7 to alert to you to events such as the arrival of e-mail messages. And you'll need speakers and a microphone if you want to participate in video conferences or use your computer to place telephone calls.

## Setting Up Speakers

These days, most computer systems are equipped with sound cards and come with a set of external speakers so that you can listen to music and other audio files. Some monitors have built-in speakers that take the place of external speakers. If you're a real audiophile, you might want to purchase fancy surround-sound speakers for your computer. Or if you want to listen to audio output privately, you can connect headphones directly to your computer or (if your speakers have a headphone jack) through the external speakers.

Most standard speaker systems consist of two speakers with one cord that connects them to each other, another that connects them to the computer, and a power cord that connects them to the power source. One speaker might have a volume control (independent of the computer's volume control) and a headphone jack.

Your desktop computer has an audio output jack (usually found on the back of the computer case) and may also have a dedicated headphone jack (either on the front or on the back of the case). On a desktop computer case that features standard component color-coding, the audio output jack is indicated by pale-green coloring and the headphone jack by pale-orange coloring.

## Setting Up a Microphone

With the rapid evolution of Internet-based communications, digital video, and speech-to-text technologies, microphones are being used more commonly with business and home computer systems. Microphones come in a variety of types, such as the following:

- Freestanding microphones
- Microphones that attach to your computer
- Headset microphones with built-in headphones that allow more private communication and consistent recording quality
- Boom microphones with a single headset speaker

If you intend to record a lot of speech or to use the Speech Recognition feature, it is worth investing in a good-quality microphone. Buy anything less than the best you can afford, and you're likely to find yourself making a return trip to the store. To get the highest quality, it's critical that you choose the type of microphone that fits your needs. Headset and boom microphones maintain a constant distance between the microphone and your mouth, which helps to maintain a more consistent sound level than a stationary microphone.

Some microphones connect to your computer via an audio input jack; others connect via a USB port. On a desktop computer that features standard component color-coding, the audio input jack is indicated by pink coloring.

In this exercise, you'll connect speakers to your computer and adjust their audio output level. Then you'll connect a microphone and adjust its audio input level.

 **SET UP** You don't need any practice files to complete this exercise. Have a set of computer speakers and a microphone available and remove them from their packaging. Display Control Panel in Category view, and then follow the steps.

1. Position the speakers on either side of your monitor to provide stereo sound quality. If necessary, link the speakers by using the connector cable or wire provided.

   **Tip** If you are using an alternate audio configuration, such as a headset microphone, connect the input and output cables to your computer, and then skip to step 4.

2. Connect the speakers to the audio output jack on your computer by using the connector cable provided.

   **Tip** The audio output jack might be indicated by a small speaker icon, an arrow symbol, or the words *Audio* or *Audio/Out*.

3. Connect the speakers to a power outlet by using the AC adapter cord provided.

4. In **Control Panel**, click **Hardware and Sound**, and then click **Sound**.

   The Sound dialog box opens.

*On the Playback tab, you can configure your speakers.*

5. In the list box, click the icon for your speakers, and then click **Configure**.

The Speaker Setup wizard starts.

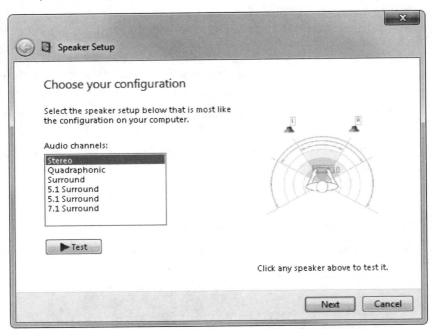

*A configuration will appear twice in the Audio Channels list if the audio channel has multiple speaker-arrangement options.*

6. On the **Choose your configuration** page, select the appropriate audio channel, and click **Test**. Then click each speaker in the speaker setup diagram.

An image representing sound waves appears next to each speaker as the wizard plays a sound through that speaker. If a sound is not audible each time the sound waves appear, or if the sound plays through a speaker other than the one indicated in the wizard, verify that the speakers are properly connected and test again.

7. On the **Choose your configuration** page, click **Next**.

The Select Full Range Speakers page appears. In some configurations, the front left and right speakers, or the surround speakers, are full-range speakers that produce the entire audio range and include a subwoofer unit to enhance bass output.

8. If your speaker configuration includes full-range speakers, select the check box for those speakers. Then click **Next**.

9. On the **Configuration complete** page, click **Finish**.

10. Plug the microphone connector cable into the audio input jack on your computer, or into a USB port, depending on the connection type.

    **Tip**  The audio input jack might be indicated by a microphone icon or the word *Mic* or *Microphone*.

11. In the **Sound** dialog box, click the **Recording** tab.

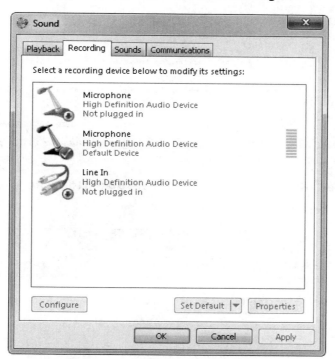

*The Recording tab displays any sound input devices connected to your computer.*

12. On the **Recording** tab, click the microphone that you plugged in. Then click **Configure**.

    The Speech Recognition window of Control Panel opens.

    **See Also**  You can change the sound scheme associated with computer events on the Sounds tab of the Sound dialog box. For information about sound schemes, see "Modifying a Theme" in Chapter 9, "Change Visual Elements."

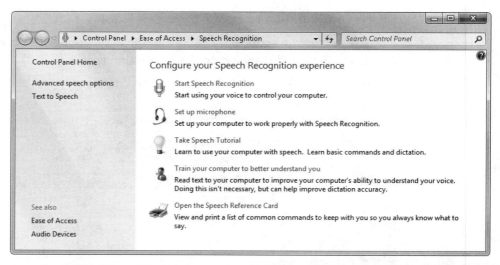

*From the Speech Recognition window, you can configure Windows 7 to accept and recognize audio input.*

**13.** In the **Speech Recognition** window, click **Set up microphone**.

The Microphone Setup wizard starts.

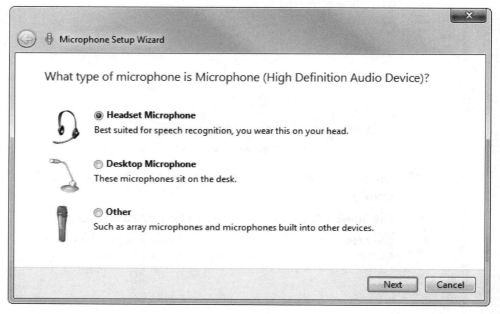

*The Microphone Setup wizard guides you through the microphone setup process.*

**14.** Select the type of microphone you are using, and then click **Next**.

**15.** On the **Set up your microphone** page, follow the instructions to correctly position the microphone, and then click **Next**.

The Adjust The Volume page appears.

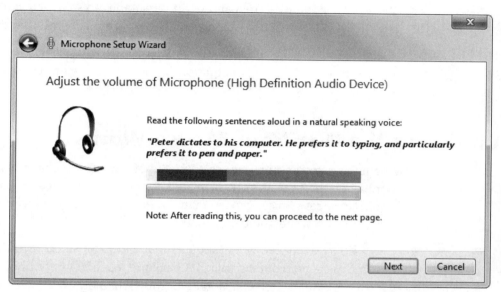

On the Adjust The Volume page, you dictate a paragraph to adjust the microphone settings to your natural speaking volume.

**16.** On the **Adjust the volume** page, read the microphone test paragraph aloud in your normal speaking voice. Or, just for fun, you might try singing a couple of lines from your favorite song! Any audio input delivered at the volume you'll use when talking into the microphone will work.

As you speak (or sing), the volume gauge moves in response to your voice.

**Troubleshooting** If the volume gauge does not move, your microphone might be incorrectly connected, malfunctioning, or incompatible with your computer. If this happens, hold the microphone close to your mouth and speak loudly—if the recording meter moves slightly, the connection is good, and the problem is compatibility between your microphone and your computer. You might be able to solve this problem by down-loading new device drivers from the microphone manufacturer's Web site, or it might be simpler to replace the microphone.

**17.** When you finish reading the paragraph, click **Next**.

If the wizard didn't gauge the input to be of the quality necessary for regular use, it displays a message and gives you the opportunity to return to the Adjust The Volume page and repeat the test paragraph.

**18.** If it seems necessary to repeat the test paragraph, do so. When you're satisfied with the results, click **Next** on each page until the wizard confirms that the microphone is set up. On the last page of the wizard, click **Finish**.

✖ **CLEAN UP** Close the Speech Recognition window. If you're not continuing directly to the next exercise, close the Hardware And Sound window.

# Changing the Way Your Mouse Works

In the beginning, a computer mouse consisted of a shell with one clickable button and a rubber ball on the bottom that correlated your mouse movements with a pointer on the screen. Nowadays, mice come in many shapes and sizes, employing a variety of functions, buttons, wheels, and connection methods.

Windows 7 offers enhanced wheel support that allows for smooth vertical scrolling and on some mice, horizontal scrolling. Check the manufacturer's documentation to see if your mouse can take advantage of this technology. Even if it can't, you can still customize your mouse settings in various ways to optimize the way it works with Windows. You can switch the functions performed by the primary and secondary buttons. This setting is useful if you are left-handed, if you have injured your right hand, or if you want to switch mousing hands to decrease wrist strain. You can also change the appearance of the pointer in its various states, and its functionality. If you want, you can allow the appearance of the mouse pointer Windows 7 to be controlled by the visual theme.

To change the way the mouse buttons work:

**1.** In the Hardware And Sound window of Control Panel, under Devices And Printers, click Mouse.

The Mouse Properties dialog box opens.

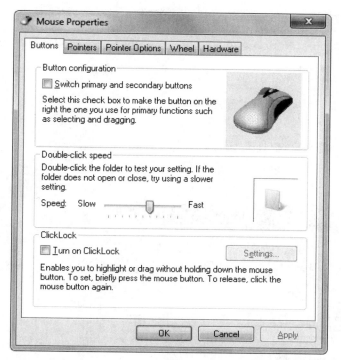

*On the Buttons tab, you can change the primary mouse button and its functionality.*

2. On the Buttons tab, make any of the following changes:

   ○ To change the default primary button from left to right, in the Button Configuration area, select the Switch Primary And Secondary Buttons check box.

   ○ Test the speed at which Windows registers a double-click. Then if necessary, in the Double-click Speed area, drag the slider to adjust the speed. (Use the right mouse button to double-click the test folder and to drag the slider if you have changed the default primary button.)

   ○ To drag without holding down the mouse button, in the ClickLock area, select the Turn On ClickLock check box. (Use the right mouse button if you have changed the default primary button.)

3. Click Apply or OK.

To change how the mouse pointer looks and works:

1. Open the Mouse Properties dialog box, and then click the Pointers tab.

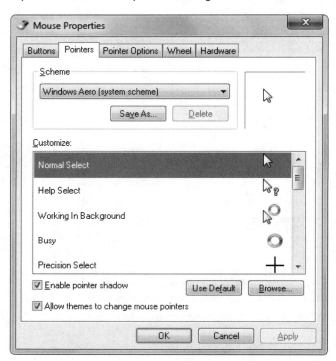

*On the Pointers tab, you can change the pointer scheme, as well as the pointer icon used to indicate individual functions.*

2. To change the entire set of pointers to one of the built-in pointer schemes, in the Scheme list, click the scheme you want.

   The Customize list displays the pointer icons associated with the scheme you've chosen. Windows 7 includes many pointer schemes designed to make the pointer easier to see.

3. To change an individual pointer icon:

   a. In the Customize list, click any pointer icon, and then click Browse.

      The Browse dialog box opens with the contents of the Cursors folder displayed. (The *cursor* is another name for the pointer.)

   b. In the Browse dialog box, double-click any pointer icon to replace the one you selected in the Customize list.

4. Click the Pointer Options tab.

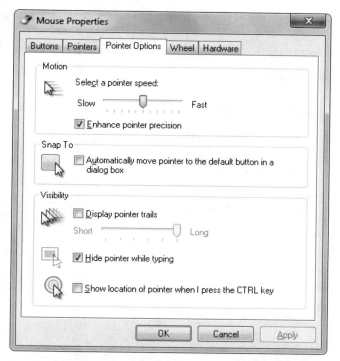

*On the Pointer Options tab, you can set the speed, movement, and visibility of the pointer.*

5. Make any of the following changes:

   ○ To change the pointer speed, in the Motion area, drag the slider.

   ○ To speed up dialog-box operations, in the Snap To area, select the Automatically Move Pointer To The Default Button In A Dialog Box check box.

   ○ To make the pointer more visible on the screen, in the Visibility area, select or clear any of the three check boxes.

6. Click Apply or OK.

   **Tip** You can restore the pointers to the original theme defaults at any time by clicking Use Default on the Pointers tab of the Mouse Properties dialog box.

To change how the mouse wheel works:

1. Open the Mouse Properties dialog box, and then click the Wheel tab.

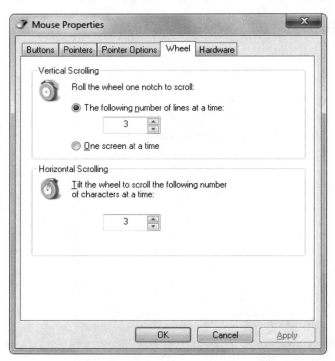

*On the Wheel tab, you can adjust vertical and horizontal scrolling.*

2. To control how much of the screen scrolls with each click of the mouse wheel, in the Vertical Scrolling area, either click The Following Number Of Lines At A Time and then type or select (by clicking the arrows) the number of lines you want to scroll, or click One Screen At A Time.

The default setting is to scroll three lines at a time, but if you frequently use the mouse to scroll through lengthy documents or Web pages, you might find it more convenient to scroll by screen rather than by line. Windows 7 sets the scrolling distance based on the size of the window you are scrolling in.

**Tip** You can move forward and backward between visited Web pages by holding down the Shift key and scrolling the wheel vertically.

3. If your mouse supports horizontal scrolling, in the Tilt The Wheel To Scroll The Following Number Of Characters At A Time box, type or select the number of characters you want to scroll horizontally when you tilt the mouse wheel to the left or right.

4. Click Apply or OK.

---

### Father of the Mouse

The mouse was invented in 1964 by Dr. Douglas C. Engelbart, a forward-thinking inventor from Portland, Oregon, while working at Stanford Research Institute.

The first mouse was a carved wooden case with two metal wheels; one turning vertically and the other horizontally. Dr. Engelbart's invention, described in the patent application as an "X-Y position indicator for a display system," was referred to as a mouse because of the cord "tail" that came out the back end. While creating the prototype of the mouse, Dr. Engelbart and his team also experimented with other pointing devices, including a knee-operated device and a helmet-mounted device.

Dr. Engelbart was also involved with the development of the Advanced Research Projects Agency's Network (ARPANET), a precursor to the Internet that consisted of four computers connected through modems to leased data-transmission lines.

# Changing the Way Your Keyboard Works

Regardless of the type of keyboard you have, they all work in the same general way: Pressing each key or key combination generates a unique key code that tells the computer what to do. Just as you can change the speed (responsiveness) of your mouse, you can change the speed at which you must press and release a key on your keyboard to input a single character.

To change the key repeat rate:

1. In the Start menu Search Box, type *keyboard*.

2. Under Control Panel in the search results, click Keyboard.

   The Keyboard Properties dialog box opens.

*On the Speed tab, you can adjust settings related to keyboard input.*

3. To adjust how long you can hold down a key before Windows repeats its character, drag the Repeat Delay slider.

4. To adjust the rate at which Windows repeats a character while you hold down its key, drag the Repeat Rate slider.

**Tip** You can test these settings in the box at the bottom of the Character Repeat area.

5.  To adjust how fast the cursor blinks, drag the Cursor Blink Rate slider.

6.  Click Apply or OK.

Pressing a key or keyboard combination that gives a command always carries out that command. (Some keyboards have programmable keys for which you can specify the command.) However, pressing a key that inputs a letter, number, or symbol can produce different results depending on a variety of settings, such as the font, the character set, and the language.

When you first set up your Windows 7 computer, you choose an input language that matches your keyboard. Under some circumstances, you might want to use a keyboard configured for a different language, or you might want to instruct Windows to treat your keystrokes on your existing keyboard as if you were using a different-language keyboard. For example, if your computer is set up to recognize a U.S. English keyboard and you frequently correspond with customers in a language—such as French, German, or Swedish—that uses characters not included in the English alphabet—such as ç, ä, or å—you will need to enter letters that don't exist on the U.S. English keyboard. You can enter those characters in most programs by pressing Alt and then a specific number combination on the numeric keypad, if you have one. (The character is inserted when you release the Alt key.) In Microsoft Word, you can enter those characters and other symbols in a document by selecting them from the Symbol dialog box.

**Tip** You can find out the Alt keyboard combination for a character by clicking the character in Character Map.

If you frequently create documents in another language, you can save yourself the trouble of inserting foreign characters by connecting a language-specific keyboard to your computer. All the letters of that language appear on the keyboard, and you simply press the keys to enter them.

**Tip** When you connect an external keyboard to a laptop, both keyboards are available to you.

If you are familiar with the layout of a language-specific keyboard but don't want to physically switch keyboards to type in that language, you can configure your computer to recognize keystrokes as though you were using the different-language keyboard. You can then switch between input languages by using the tools on the Language bar that appears on the Windows Taskbar.

## Fonts and Character Sets

If you want to see the many characters that can be generated by your keyboard, you can use the Character Map utility.

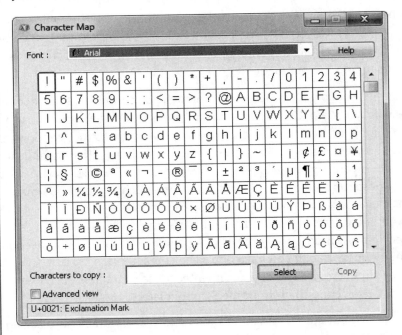

*Character Map displays the entire set of characters for each available font.*

To display Character Map:

● On the Start menu, click All Programs, click Accessories, click System Tools, and then click Character Map.

You can then select a font from the Font list to see the available characters.

To copy a character into a document:

1. Locate and click the character you want.

2. When an enlarged view of the character appears, click Select.

   The character is added to the Characters To Copy box. You can repeat steps 1 and 2 to add other characters from the same or different fonts to the box.

3. Click Copy.

   The content of the Characters To Copy box is copied to the Clipboard. From there, you can paste it into any document.

In this exercise, you'll configure your computer to recognize keystrokes as though you're typing on a Swedish keyboard. (If you're already using a Swedish keyboard, substitute another language.)

**SET UP** You don't need any practice files to complete this exercise. Display Control Panel in Category view, and then follow the steps.

1. In **Control Panel**, under **Clock, Language, and Region**, click **Change keyboards or other input methods**.

   The Region And Language dialog box opens.

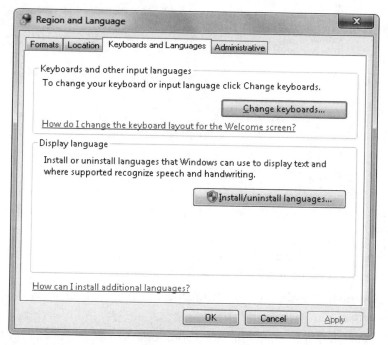

*On the Keyboard And Languages tab, you can change the keyboard or input language and the display language.*

2. On the **Keyboards and Languages** tab, click **Change keyboards**.

   The Text Services And Input Languages dialog box opens.

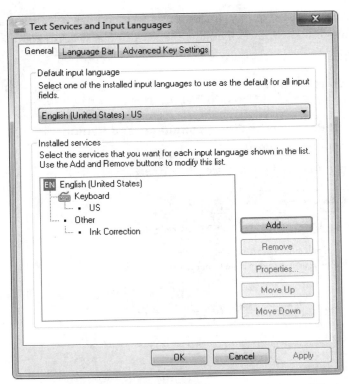

*The General tab displays your current input language and the input devices configured for that language.*

3. On the **General** tab, in the **Default input language** area, click the current input language to display a list of available languages.

4. If **Swedish (Sweden)** (or the language you want to use) appears in the **Installed Services** area, skip to step 10.

   If you haven't previously installed additional language packs, only the original input language appears in the list. To accept input from another language-specific keyboard, you must first install the language.

5. In the **Installed services** area, click **Add**.

   The Add Input Language dialog box opens.

6. Browse through this dialog box, noting the available languages. Expand a few of the languages and their **Keyboard** and **Other** lists.

   The list under each keyboard indicates the languages you can enter by using a keyboard designed for that language.

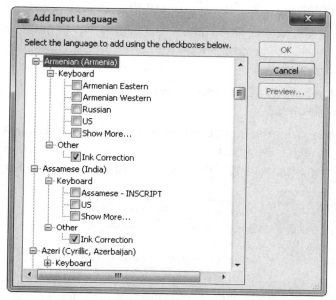

*Not all languages have an associated keyboard, but some have more than one.*

**7.** In the list, expand **Swedish (Sweden)**, and then expand **Keyboard**.

The standard keyboard options for this language are Swedish and US.

**8.** In the **Keyboard** list, select the **Swedish** check box. Then click **Preview**.

The Keyboard Layout Preview window displays the keys that appear on a Swedish keyboard.

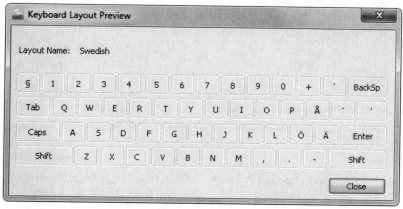

*A preview of a standard Swedish keyboard.*

Notice the three Swedish letters near the right end of the second and third rows of the diagram: Å, Ä, and Ö. These are the last three letters of the Swedish alphabet. The characters in these three positions on your own keyboard have been rearranged to make room for them.

9. Close the **Keyboard Layout Preview** window, and then click **OK** in the **Add Input Language** dialog box.

In the Text Services And Input Languages dialog box, your original language is still selected as the default, as indicated in the Default Input Language list. However, the Swedish input language option now appears in the Installed Services list.

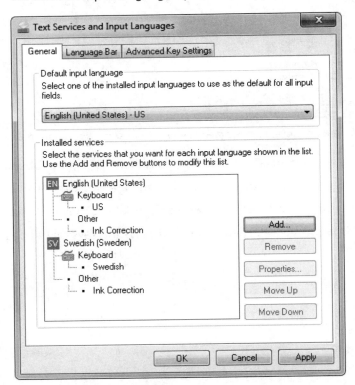

The Installed Services list now includes both your original keyboard language and Swedish.

10. Click **OK**.

The Language bar appears on the Windows Taskbar, to the left of the notification area. When minimized, the Language bar is represented by the two-letter abbreviation of the current input language.

**11.** On the taskbar, click the **Language bar** button.

The Language Bar menu appears.

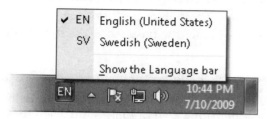

*Clicking Show The Language Bar displays the Language bar as a floating toolbar.*

**Tip** Right-clicking the Language Bar button displays a shortcut menu of options for working with the Language bar. The contents of the Language bar vary depending on what language-specific capabilities are configured. You can change the location and appearance of the Language bar from the Language Bar tab of the Text Services And Input Languages dialog box.

**12.** In the input language list on the **Language Bar** menu, click **Swedish (Sweden)**.

The Language Bar button label changes to SV (the two-letter abbreviation for *Svensk*, which is *Swedish* in Swedish).

**13.** To confirm that the input language has changed, click the **Start** button, and then with the cursor in the **Search** box, press the apostrophe (') key to the left of the **Enter** key.

The letter *ä*, which appears to the left of the Enter key on the Swedish keyboard, appears in the Search box.

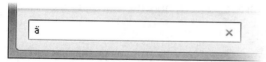

*On the Swedish keyboard, the letter ä is the equivalent of the English apostrophe.*

**14.** Press **Esc** to close the **Start** menu.

 **CLEAN UP** On the Keyboards And Languages tab of the Regional And Language Options dialog box, click Change Keyboards. In the Installed Services area of the Text Services And Input Languages dialog box, click Swedish (Sweden), and click Remove. Then close the Text Services And Input Languages dialog box and the Regional And Language Options dialog box. If you're not continuing directly to the next exercise, close Control Panel.

# Rating Your Computer's Hardware

Windows 7 rates your hardware, and gives you information about ways in which you might be able to improve your computer's performance, through the Windows Experience Index base score. The higher the base score, the better your computer's overall performance.

The base score that is necessary for a good computing experience depends a lot on what you intend to do with the computer. For example, you might receive a base score of 2 because you don't have a high-powered graphics card, even though you receive subscores of 5 or 6 in the processor, memory, and hard disk categories. Your computer would be more than adequate to run programs such as word processing and spread-sheet programs, but it wouldn't be powerful enough to adequately display Aero or sophisticated video games. To optimize your computer for those purposes, you would need to upgrade your graphics card. When you make changes to your computer's hardware, you can update the Windows Experience Index to see the effect of the change on the individual subscores and on your base score.

You can use the base score as an indicator of programs that will run well on your computer. Avoiding programs that require a higher base score than your computer's Windows Experience Index will help you avoid disappointing performance.

**Tip** When you're shopping for a new computer in a store, you can judge the relative merits of two or more computers by displaying the Windows Experience Index for any model you are considering buying.

In this exercise, you'll establish the Windows Experience Index for your computer, or update the index if one already exists, and then display a detailed report of the rating criteria.

**SET UP** You don't need any practice files to complete this exercise. Display Control Panel in Category view, and then follow the steps.

1. In **Control Panel**, click **System and Security**. In the **System and Security** window, under **System**, click **Check the Windows Experience Index**.

The Performance Information And Tools window opens.

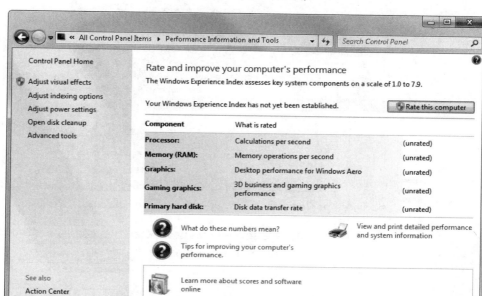

*On a new computer system, Windows might not yet have calculated your Windows Experience Index.*

2. If *(unrated)* appears to the right of each component, click **Rate this computer**. If subscores and a base score appear on the right side of the Component table, click **Re-run the assessment** in the lower-right corner of the window.

   **Troubleshooting** The Re-run The Assessment link appears only if the Windows Experience Index has already been established.

   The Windows Experience Index window opens and displays the progress of the rating process.

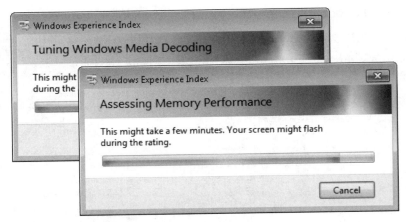

*A progress bar indicates the status of the assessment.*

The process may take several minutes. When the assessment is complete, your computer's subscores and base score are displayed.

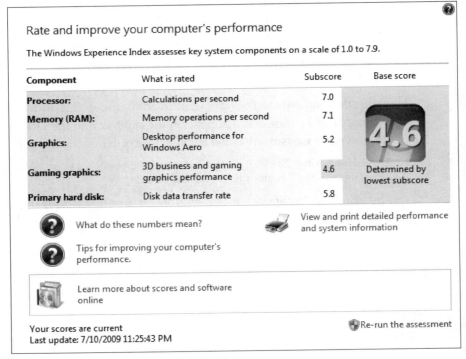

*Your base score is the lowest of the five subscores.*

**3.** On the right side of the **Performance Information and Tools** window, click **View and print detailed performance and system information**.

A second Performance Information And Tools window opens, displaying information in a format designed for printing.

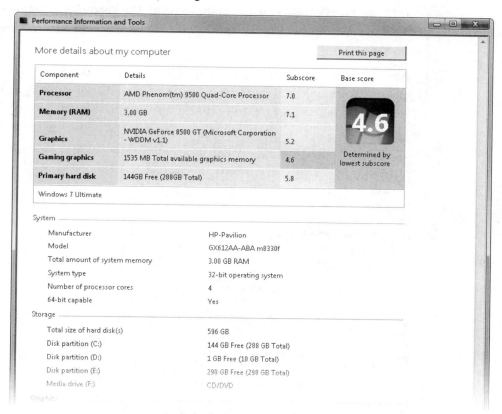

A print-ready report displays detailed information about each component.

**4.** Peruse the detailed report to gain an understanding of the component assessments.

> **Tip** To print the report, click Print This Page at the top or bottom of the window. Then in the Print dialog box, click Print.

**CLEAN UP** Close the two Performance Information And Tools windows.

## ReadyBoost

If the Windows Experience Index memory subscore indicates that you would do well to upgrade your computer's memory, you don't necessarily have to physically install additional RAM in your computer case. The ReadyBoost feature enables your Windows 7 computer to use a qualifying USB flash drive as a memory-expansion device.

When you insert a supported flash drive in a USB port, the AutoPlay dialog box that opens includes a Speed Up My System option. Clicking this option displays the ReadyBoost tab of the Properties dialog box for your flash drive.

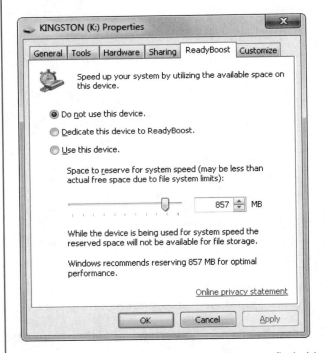

*The Properties dialog box tells you whether your flash drive can be used to supplement your computer's memory.*

If your flash drive can be used to expand memory, you can select how much of the drive capacity you want to use for this purpose. At the bottom of the ReadyBoost tab, Windows suggests an amount that is appropriate based on the flash drive's available capacity.

# Locating Device Information

The System window of Control Panel displays information about some of your computer hardware, but you can get information about all the hardware devices installed on your computer, in one place, from the System Information window. In this window, you can display a System Summary of general information, or more detailed information in three categories: Hardware Resources, Components, and Software Environment.

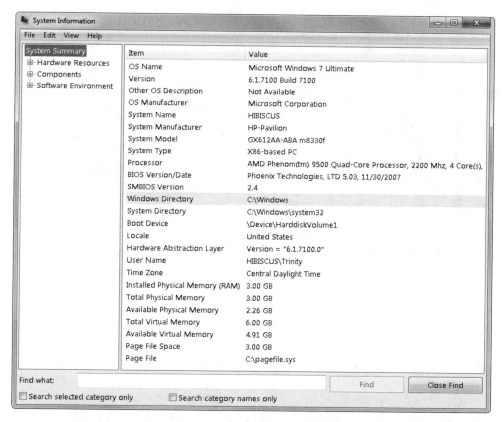

*You can view details about your computer in the System Information window.*

**See Also**  For information about the System window, see "Finding Information About Your Computer System" in Chapter 1, "Explore Windows 7."

At the bottom of the window is a Find What box in which you can type a keyword to find specific information. You can hide this area by clicking Close Find, and you can display it again by clicking Hide Find on the Edit menu to remove the check mark that indicates it's selected.

To make changes to any of your installed devices, you need to open Device Manager. There you can view and set properties for each device.

*Information about the internal and external devices installed on your computer is available from the Device Manager window.*

In this exercise, you'll locate information about your computer's internal and external devices.

 **SET UP** You don't need any practice files to complete this exercise; just follow the steps.

**Important** Don't change any system settings unless you have the experience necessary to anticipate the consequences of the change.

1. In the **Start** menu **Search** box, type **system**, and then under **Programs** in the search results, click **System Information**.

   The System Information window opens.

2. In the **System Information** window, expand **Components**, expand **Storage**, and then click **Drives**.

   The System Information window displays information about each of the drives installed on your computer.

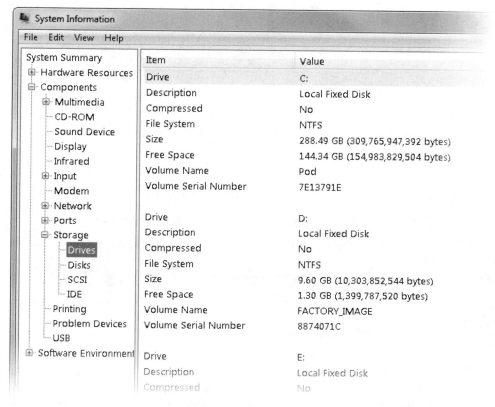

*The Drives category includes fixed disk drives, removable disk drives, and media drives.*

3. Explore the available information, and then close the **System Information** window.

   **Tip** You can print any subcategory by displaying it and then clicking Print on the File menu.

4. In the **Start** menu **Search** box, type **device**, and then under **Control Panel** in the search results, click **Device Manager**.

   The Device Manager window opens.

5. Click the arrow to the left of **Display adapters** to expand the category.

   The graphics card on which your Windows Experience Index Graphics subscore is based is shown here.

   **See Also** For information about the Windows Experience Index, see "Rating Your Computer's Hardware" earlier in this chapter.

*If your computer has multiple graphics cards, they are all shown here.*

6. Right-click the display adapter, and click **Properties**.

The Properties dialog box for the display adapter opens.

*You can explore detailed information about any device in its Properties dialog box.*

7. Explore the tabs of the **Properties** dialog box, and then click **Cancel**.

8. In the Device Manager window, expand various other categories to view the devices installed on your machine, and then view the properties of the devices.

 **CLEAN UP** Close the Device Manager window.

# Key Points

- Windows 7 automatically locates the drivers necessary to install USB printers and other USB, Bluetooth, or WiFi devices. Usually, you can connect a device and start using it without further effort.

- You can share printers and other hardware devices that are physically connected to your computer with other users on your network. You can also connect to printers and devices shared by others.

- Adding extra monitors to your computer configuration effectively increases the size of your desktop.

- You can increase the quality of audio output and input by connecting external speakers and a high-quality microphone to your computer.

- You can tailor the behavior of your mouse to suit the way you work and tailor the behavior of your keyboard to send keystrokes as if it were a different-language keyboard.

- Windows 7 makes it easy to view information about the devices installed on your computer.

# Glossary

**absolute path**  A path that defines the exact position of a file or folder. For example, C:\Program Files\Microsoft Games\FreeCell defines the path from any location on a computer to the FreeCell game code, and \\HIBISCUS\Users\Public\Documents defines the path from any location on a network to the Public Documents folder on a computer named HIBISCUS. See also *path* and *relative path*.

**Accelerator**  A type of Windows Internet Explorer add-on that enables you to work with Web page content directly from the page. Accelerators were first introduced in Internet Explorer 8.

**Action Center**  A Windows feature enabling the central monitoring and management of security and maintenance tasks. Action Center was first introduced in Windows 7.

**ActiveX control**  A reusable software component that performs a specific function or set of functions in the Windows operating system, in a program that runs on Windows, or in the Internet Explorer environment.

**Address bar**  In Windows Explorer, a text box containing the navigation path to the current folder. Clicking the arrow after each folder name displays a list of its subfolders. In Internet Explorer, a text box containing the Web address of the currently displayed Web page. In both programs, the Address bar is located at the top of the window, under the title bar.

**administrator account**  A type of Windows user account with access to all system files and settings, and with permission to perform all operations. Every computer must have at least one administrator account. This account type is not recommended for daily use. See also *standard user account*.

**Aero Peek**  When you point to a Windows Taskbar button, the technology that displays a pane containing thumbnails of open windows of the button's type. From the thumbnail pane, you can display and close the windows. Aero Peek was first introduced in Windows 7.

**All Programs menu**  The area of the Start menu, displayed when you click All Programs and hidden when you click Back, from which you can access most of the programs and utilities installed on your computer.

**Anytime Upgrade**  See *Windows Anytime Upgrade*.

**aspect ratio**  The proportional relationship of the width of an image, screen, or other visual element to its height.

**autorun file**  A file that automatically starts an installation program when you insert a disc in a drive or browse to the autorun file in a folder.

**bandwidth**  The transmission capacity of an electronic communications device or its rate of data transfer, usually expressed in bits per second.

**bitmap (.bmp)**  A patent-free digital image file format. A bitmap image consists of pixels in a grid. Each pixel is a specific color; the colors within the color palette are governed by the specific bitmap format. Common formats include Monochrome Bitmap, 16 Color Bitmap, 256 Color Bitmap, and 24-bit Bitmap. The bitmap file format does not support transparency.

*blog* Short for *web log*. An online journal or news/opinion column. Contributors post entries consisting of text, graphics, or video clips. When permitted by the blog owner, readers can post comments responding to the entries or to other people's comments. Blogs are often used to publish personal or company information in an informal way.

*.bmp* See *bitmap*.

*broadband connection* A high-speed Internet connection such as those provided by DSL or cable modem services. Broadband connections typically transfer data at 256 kilobytes per second (KBps) or faster.

*browse* To search for a folder or file by navigating through the hierarchical storage structure of a computer. Alternatively, to search for information on the Web by following links between Web pages.

*browser* See *Web browser*.

*byte* A unit of measurement for data; a byte typically holds a single character, such as a letter, digit, or punctuation mark. Some single characters can take up more than 1 byte.

*CD key* See *product key*.

*central processing unit (CPU)* The main circuit chip in a computer. It performs most of the calculations necessary to run the computer. Also called a *processor*.

*click* To point to an interface element and then press the primary mouse button one time, usually for the purpose of selecting an item or positioning a cursor.

*command* An instruction you give to a computer program.

*Command bar* An Internet Explorer, a toolbar located above the Content pane that provides buttons for common tasks associated with the home page, Web Slices and RSS feeds, printing, Web content display, and safety, as well as tools for managing Internet Explorer.

*Compatibility view* An Internet Explorer feature that displays a Web site as though you were using an earlier version of the Web browser. Compatibility view was first introduced with Internet Explorer 8.

*compress* To reduce the size of a set of data, such as a file or group of files, inside a compressed folder that can be stored in less space or transmitted with less bandwidth.

*compressed folder* A folder containing a file or files whose contents have been compressed.

*Content pane* In Windows Explorer, the pane that displays files and folders stored in the currently selected folder or storage device. See also *Details pane*, *Navigation pane*, and *Preview pane*.

*context menu* See *shortcut menu*.

*Control Panel* A Windows program that contains items through which you can control system-level features of the computer and perform related tasks, including hardware and software setup and configuration.

*CPU* See *central processing unit*.

*credentials* Information that provides proof of identification that is used to gain access to local and network resources. Examples of credentials are user names and passwords, smart cards, and certificates.

*cursor* The point at which text or graphics will be inserted. The cursor usually appears on screen as a blinking vertical line.

*desktop* The work area on a computer screen, on which you can arrange windows, gadgets, icons, and shortcuts to programs, folders, and data files. The contents of the Desktop folder of your user profile appear on the desktop. You can control the appearance of the desktop by changing the theme or the desktop background.

**desktop computer**  A computer designed for use at one location. A typical desktop computer system includes the computer case containing the actual computer components, a monitor, a keyboard, a mouse, and speakers. See also *portable computer*.

**Desktop Gadget Gallery**  A gallery from which you can choose gadgets that display a variety of dynamic information directly on your desktop. The Desktop Gadget Gallery was first introduced in Windows 7 as a replacement for the Windows Sidebar.

**desktop shortcut**  See *shortcut*.

**Details pane**  In Windows Explorer, the pane at the bottom of a folder window that displays details about the folder or selected items. See also *Content pane*, *Navigation pane*, and *Preview pane*.

**device driver**  See *driver*.

**DHCP**  See *Dynamic Host Configuration Protocol*.

**dialog box**  A window that appears when you give a command that requires additional information. Also used to provide information or feedback about progress.

**dial-up connection**  The connection to a network through a device that uses the telephone network. Includes modems with standard telephone lines and ISDN cards with high-speed ISDN lines.

**digital signature**  An electronic signature that is composed of a secret code and a private key. Digital signatures are used to help verify file authenticity. Also called a *digital ID*.

**digital subscriber line (DSL)**  A type of high-speed Internet connection that uses standard telephone wires.

**DLL**  See *dynamic-link library*.

**DNS**  See *Domain Name System*.

**domain**  In Windows, a logical (rather than physical) group of resources—computers, servers, and other hardware devices—on a network, that is centrally administered through Windows Server. On the Internet, a name used as the base of Web site addresses and e-mail addresses that identifies the entity owning the address.

**Domain Name System (DNS)**  A technology that translates Internet address names into numerical addresses (IP addresses) so that the address can be found over the Internet. For example, if you type www.microsoft.com into a Web browser, the name is translated into a numerical address and that address is used to connect you to the server hosting the Microsoft Web site.

**double-click**  To point to an interface element and press the primary mouse button two times in rapid succession, usually for the purpose of starting a program or opening a window, folder, or file.

**drag**  To move an item to another location on the screen by pointing to it, holding down the primary mouse button, and then moving the mouse.

**driver**  A program that enables Windows to communicate with a software program or hardware device (such as a printer, mouse, or keyboard) that is attached to your computer. Every device needs a driver in order for it to work. Many drivers, such as the keyboard driver, are built into Windows.

**DSL**  See *digital subscriber line*.

**dynamic**  Changing in response to external factors.

**Dynamic Host Configuration Protocol (DHCP) server**  A server that manages a pool of IP addresses and client confirmation parameters and assigns IP addresses to computers and devices on a network.

**dynamic-link library (DLL)**  An operating system feature that allows executable routines (each generally serving a specific function or set of functions) to be stored separately as files with .dll extensions. These routines are loaded only when needed by the program that calls them.

**Ethernet**  A system for exchanging data between computers on a local area network by using coaxial, fiber optic, or twisted-pair cables.

**Ethernet cable**  A twisted pair cable, generally a CAT-3, CAT-5, or CAT-6 cable, through which you establish a wired connection to a network. Depending on the type, Ethernet cables allow data to travel at a rate of 10 Mbps, 100 Mbps, or 1000 Mbps (1 Gbps). The data transfer rate is determined by the network router.

**executable file**  A computer file that starts a program, such as a word processor, game, or Windows utility. Executable files can often be identified by the file name extension .exe.

**expansion card**  A printed circuit board that, when inserted into an expansion slot of a computer, provides additional functionality. There are many types of expansion cards, including audio cards, modems, network cards, security device cards, TV tuner cards, video cards, and video processing expansion cards.

**expansion slot**  A socket on a computer's motherboard, designed to establish the electrical contact between the electronics on an expansion card and on the motherboard. Many form factors (physical dimensions) and standards for expansion slots are available, including AGP, PC Card, PCI, and PCI Express. An expansion slot accepts only expansion cards of the same form factor.

**Extensible Markup Language (XML)**  A text markup language, similar to HTML, used to define the structure of data independently of its formatting so that the data can be used for multiple purposes and by multiple programs.

**extension**  See *file name extension*.

**external peripheral**  A peripheral device installed by connecting it to a port from outside the computer. Examples are a monitor, keyboard, mouse, and speakers. See also *internal peripheral* and *peripheral device*.

**Favorites bar**  In Internet Explorer, a toolbar located below the Address bar that provides buttons for storing Web locations for easy future access, obtaining add-ons, and accessing sites that match your browsing history.

**Favorites Center**  In Internet Explorer, a pane with three tabs: Favorites, on which you can save and organize links to Web sites and Web pages; Feeds, on which you can save and organize RSS feeds; and History, on which you can view your browsing history.

**feed**  Information streams that contain frequently updated content published by a Web site. Feeds are often associated with news sites and blogs, but are also used for distributing other types of digital content, including photos, music, and video. See also *Really Simple Syndication*.

**file name extension**  Characters appended to the name of a file by the program that created it and separated from the file name by a period. Some file name extensions identify the program that can open the file, such as .xlsx for Microsoft Office Excel 2007 files; and some represent formats that more than one program can work with, such as .jpg graphics files.

**filter**  To display only items that match specified criteria.

**FireWire port**  FireWire is the brand name given to the IEEE 1394 port by Apple, Inc., one of the patent holders of IEEE 1394 technology. See also *IEEE 1394 port*.

**flash drive**  See *USB flash drive*.

**frame**  The outer border of a window.

**gadget**  A customizable program that displays information, such as time, weather, and news, on your Windows desktop.

**GB** See *gigabyte*.

**Gbps** Gigabits per second; a unit of data transfer equal to 1000 Mbps (megabits per second).

**.gif** See *Graphics Interchange Format*.

**gigabyte (GB)** 1024 megabytes of data storage; often interpreted as approximately 1 billion bytes.

**graphical user interface (GUI)** A user interface that incorporates visual elements such as a desktop, icons, and menus, so that you can perform operations by interacting with the visual interface rather than by typing commands.

**Graphics Interchange Format (.gif)** A digital image file format developed by CompuServe that is used for transmitting raster images on the Internet. An image in this format may contain up to 256 colors, including a transparent color. The size of the file depends on the number of colors actually used.

**Guest account** A built-in Windows user account that allows limited use of the computer. When logged on to a computer with the Guest account, a user can't install software or hardware, change settings, or create a password. The Guest account is turned off (unavailable) by default; you can turn it on from the User Accounts window of Control Panel.

**GUI** See *graphical user interface*.

**hardware** Physical items such as computers and monitors. See also *software*.

**Hibernate mode** A shut-down option similar to Sleep mode, except that it saves any open files and the state of any running programs on your hard disk instead of in memory and then completely turns off the computer. When you turn on your computer to resume working, Windows retrieves information from the hard disk and restores your previous computing session.

**home network** A network to which you connect with the Home Network connection type.

**home page** In Internet Explorer, the page or pages that open automatically when you start your Web browser, and that open when you click the Home button. For Web sites, the first page displayed when you connect to a site.

**homegroup** A password-protected connection among a group of computers through which you can share files and printers. A homegroup can exist only on a home network. A home network doesn't require a homegroup, and it is not necessary to join a homegroup to use the home network. Homegroups were first introduced in Windows 7.

**homegroup member** A computer that is joined to a homegroup.

**HTML** See *Hypertext Markup Language*.

**hub** A device used to connect multiple devices of one type. See also *network hub* and *USB hub*.

**hyperlink** A link from a text, graphic, audio, or video element to a target location in the same document, another document, or a Web page.

**hypertext** See *hyperlink*.

**Hypertext Markup Language (HTML)** A text markup language used to create documents for the Web. HTML defines the structure and layout of a Web document by using a variety of tags and attributes.

**icon** A visual representation of a program, folder, file, or other object or function.

**IEEE 1394 port** A port for the high-speed transfer of audio and video data. See also *FireWire port*.

**IM** See *instant messaging*.

**IMAP** See *Internet Message Access Protocol*.

**Information bar** In Internet Explorer, a gold-colored bar that appears below the Favorites bar to notify you that there is a security issue or that a pop-up window has been blocked. You can click the bar to display a menu of actions appropriate to the situation.

**information technology (IT)** The development, installation, and implementation of computer systems and applications.

*InPrivate Browsing*  A browsing mode that opens a separate Internet Explorer window in which the places you visit are not tracked. The pages and sites do not appear on the History tab, and temporary files and cookies are not saved on your computer.

*insertion point*  See *cursor*.

*instant messaging (IM)*  A real-time electronic communication system that you can use to "chat" and interact in other ways with other people by typing in a window on your computer screen.

*integrated services digital network (ISDN)*  A high-speed digital technology that uses existing telephone lines to provide Internet access.

*interface*  See *user interface*.

*internal peripheral*  A device installed inside the computer's case, such as an expansion card, a hard disk drive, or a DVD drive. See also *external peripheral* and *peripheral device*.

*Internet Message Access Protocol (IMAP)*  A method computers use to send and receive e-mail messages. It allows you to access e-mail without downloading it to your computer.

*Internet Protocol (IP) address*  An address that identifies a computer that is connected to the Internet or a network. There are two types of IP addresses: IP version 4 (IPv4) and IP version 6 (IPv6). An IPv4 address usually consists of four groups of numbers separated by periods, such as 192.200.44.69. An IPv6 address has eight groups of hexadecimal characters (the numbers 0–9 and the letters A–H) separated by colons—for example, 3ffe:ffff:0000:2f3b: 02aa:00ff:fe28:9c5a.

*Internet service provider (ISP)*  A company that provides Internet access to individuals or companies. An ISP provides the connection information necessary for users to access the Internet through the ISP's computers. An ISP typically charges a monthly or hourly connection fee.

*IP address*  See *Internet Protocol address*.

*ISDN*  See *integrated services digital network*.

*ISP*  See *Internet service provider*.

*IT*  See *information technology*.

*JPEG (.jpg) file format*  A digital image file format designed for compressing either full-color or grayscale still images. It works well on photographs, naturalistic artwork, and similar material. Images saved in this format have .jpg or .jpeg file extensions.

*jump list*  In the recently opened programs list or pinned items area of the Start menu, an efficient method of accessing the features and files you are most likely to use with a program. Pointing to a right-pointing arrow associated with the program in either location displays a list of tasks and recently opened files.

*KB*  See *kilobyte*.

*Kbps*  Kilobits per second; a unit of data transfer equal to 1000 bits per second or 125 bytes per second.

*keyword*  A word or phrase assigned to a file or Web page so that it can be located in searches for that word or phrase.

*kilobyte (KB)*  1024 bytes of data storage. In reference to data transfer rates, 1000 bytes.

*LAN*  See *local area network*.

*laptop*  An outdated term for a portable computer, referring to the fact that portable computers are small enough to set on your lap. See also *netbook*, *notebook*, and *portable computer*.

*library*  A virtual folder that isn't physically present on the hard disk but that displays the contents of multiple folders as though the files were stored together in one location.

*local*  Located on or attached to your computer.

*local area network (LAN)*  A computer network covering a small physical area, like a home or office, with a central connection point such as a network router and a shared Internet connection. See also *network*.

*local printer* A printer that is directly connected to one of the ports on a computer. See also *remote printer.*

*lock* To make your Windows computing session unavailable to other people. Locking is most effective when your user account is protected by a password.

*log off* To stop your computing session without affecting other users' sessions.

*log on* To start a computing session.

*malware* Software designed to deliberately harm your computer. For example, viruses, worms, and Trojan horses are malicious software. Also called *malicious software.*

*map a drive* To assign an available drive letter to a specific computer or shared folder; usually a folder located on another computer on the network. This is commonly done to create a constant connection to a network share but can also be used to maintain a connection to an Internet location.

*maximize* To increase the size of a window so that it completely fills the screen. A maximized window cannot be moved or resized by dragging its frame.

*MB* See *megabyte.*

*Mbps* Megabits per second; a unit of data transfer equal to 1,000 Kbps (kilobits per second).

*media* Materials on which data is recorded or stored, such as CDs, DVDs, floppy disks, or USB flash drives.

*megabyte (MB)* 1024 kilobytes or 1,048,576 bytes of data storage; often interpreted as approximately 1 million bytes. In reference to data transfer rates, 1000 kilobytes.

*menu* A list from which you can give an instruction by clicking a command.

*menu bar* A toolbar from which you can access menus of commands.

*metadata* Descriptive information, including keywords and properties, about a file or Web page. Title, subject, author, and size are examples of a file's metadata.

*minimize* To reduce a window to a button on the taskbar.

*modem* A device that allows computer information to be transmitted and received over a telephone line or through a broadband service such as cable or DSL.

*mouse pointer* See *pointer.*

*Navigation pane* In Windows Explorer, the left pane of a folder window. It displays favorite links, libraries, and an expandable list of drives and folders. See also *Content pane*, *Details pane*, and *Preview pane.*

*.NET Passport* See *Windows Live ID.*

*netbook* A small, lightweight portable computer designed primarily for Web browsing and simple computing. Most netbooks have a 1.6 GHz processor and a screen size of less than 11 inches.

*network* In Windows, a group of computers connected to each other through a wired or wireless connection. A network may be as small as two computers connected directly to each other or as large as the Internet. In Windows Live, a group of people you communicate and share with on Windows Live. Your network includes people you add to your Windows Live profile, to your Windows Live Messenger contacts, or both. People in your network can see information about your latest activities in the What's New listing, and may see other information, depending on permissions settings. See Also *local area network.*

*network domain* A network whose security and settings are centrally administered through Windows Server computer and user accounts.

*network drive* A shared folder or drive on your network that you assign a drive letter to so that it appears in the Computer window as a named drive.

*network hub*　A device used to connect computers on a network. The computers are connected to the hub with cables. The hub sends information received from one computer to all other computers on the network.

*network printer*　A printer that is connected directly to a network through a wired (Ethernet) or wireless network connection, or through a print server or printer hub.

*network profile*　Information about a specific network connection, such as the network name, type, and settings.

*network router*　A hardware device connecting computers on a network or connecting multiple networks (for example, connecting a LAN to an ISP).

*network share*　A shared folder on a computer on your network (not your local computer).

*notebook*　A standard portable computer designed for all types of computing. Notebooks have technical specifications that are comparable to those of desktop computers. Most notebooks have a screen size ranging from 11 to 17 inches.

*notification area*　The area at the right end of the Windows Taskbar. It contains shortcuts to programs and important status information.

*OEM*　See *original equipment manufacturer.*

*offline*　Not connected to a network or to the Internet. Also used to describe time that you will be away from your computer.

*online*　Connected to a network or to the Internet. Also used to describe time that you will be working on your computer.

*operating system*　The underlying programs that tell your computer what to do and how to do it. The operating system coordinates interactions among the computer system components, acts as the interface between you and your computer, enables your computer to communicate with other computers and peripheral devices, and interacts with programs installed on your computer.

*option*　One of a group of mutually exclusive values for a setting, usually in a dialog box.

*option button*　A standard Windows control that you use to select one of a set of options.

*original equipment manufacturer (OEM)*　A company that assembles a computer from components, brands the computer, and then sells the computer to the public. The OEM might also preinstall an operating system and other software on the computer.

*parallel port*　The input/output connector for a parallel interface device. Some types of printers connect to the computer through a parallel port.

*password*　A security measure used to restrict access to user accounts, computer systems, and resources. A password is a unique string of characters that you must provide before access is authorized.

*password hint*　An entry you record when you create or change your password to remind you what the password is. Windows displays the password hint if you enter an incorrect password.

*password reset disk*　A file you create on a flash drive or floppy disk to enable you to reset your password if you forget it.

*path*　A sequence of names of drives, directories, or folders, separated by backslashes (\), that leads to a specific file or folder. See also *absolute path* and *relative path*.

*peer-to-peer*　A network, such as a workgroup, where computers and resources are connected directly and are not centrally managed by a server.

*peripheral device*　A device, such as a disk drive, printer, modem, or joystick, that is connected to a computer and is controlled by the computer's microprocessor, but is not necessary to the computer's operation. See also *external peripheral* and *internal peripheral*.

**personal folder** In Windows, a storage folder created by Windows for each user account and containing subfolders and information that is specific to the user profile, such as Documents and Pictures. The personal folder is labeled with the name used to log on to the computer.

**PID** See *product key*.

**pinned items area** An area at the top of the left pane of the Start menu to which you can drag links to programs and files so that they are easily accessible.

**pinned taskbar button** A button representing a program, which appears permanently at the left end of the taskbar. A button that is not pinned appears only when its program is running.

**pinning** Attaching a program, folder, or file shortcut to a user interface element such as the Start menu or taskbar.

**pixel** The smallest element used to form an image on a computer monitor. Computer monitors display images by drawing thousands of pixels arranged in columns and rows. Each pixel displays one color. See also *screen resolution*.

**plug and play** A technology that enables the computer to automatically discover and configure settings for a device connected to the computer through a USB or IEEE 1394 connection.

**.png** See *Portable Network Graphic*.

**point** To position the pointer over an element. Also called *hover* or *mouse-over*.

**pointer** The onscreen image that moves around the screen when you move your mouse. Depending on the current action, the pointer might resemble an arrow, a hand, an I-beam, or another shape.

**pointing device** A device such as a mouse that controls a pointer with which you can interact with items displayed on the screen.

**POP3** A standard method that computers use to send and receive e-mail messages. POP3 messages are typically held on an e-mail server until you download them to your computer, and then they are deleted from the server. With other e-mail protocols, such as IMAP, e-mail messages are held on the server until you delete them.

**pop-up window (pop-up)** A small Web browser window that opens on top of (or sometimes below) the Web browser window when you display a Web site or click an advertising link.

**port** An interface through which data is transferred between a computer and other devices, a network, or a direct connection to another computer.

**portable computer** A computer, such as a notebook or netbook, with a built-in monitor, keyboard, and pointing device, designed to be used in multiple locations. See also *desktop computer*.

**Portable Network Graphic (.png)** A digital image file format that uses lossless compression (compression that doesn't lose data) and was created as a patent-free alternative to the .gif file format.

**Power button** The button in the lower-right corner of the Windows Start menu that carries out the default shut-down option. Clicking the Shut-down Options button (the arrow to the right of the Power button) displays a menu from which you can choose a non-default shut-down action. See also *shut-down options*.

**Preview pane** In Windows Explorer, a pane used to show a preview of a file selected in the Content pane. See also *Content pane*, *Details pane*, and *Navigation pane*.

**primary display** In a multiple-monitor system, the monitor that displays the Welcome screen and taskbar. Most program windows appear on the primary display when they first open. See also *secondary display*.

**printer driver**  See *driver*.

**product key**  A unique registration code issued by the manufacturer of a program. The key must be supplied during the setup process to verify that you have a valid license to install and use the program. Also called a *product ID*, *PID*, *registration key*, or *CD key*.

**program icon**  See *icon*.

**property**  Identifying information about a file, folder, drive, device, or other computer system element. Some properties are supplied automatically and others are supplied by you. For example, the properties of a file include information such as its file name, size, modification date, title, tags, and comments. You can view an item's properties by right-clicking the item in an interface such as Windows Explorer or Device Manager, and then clicking Properties.

**public folder**  In Windows, a storage folder system created by Windows and accessible to all user accounts on the computer. The public folder contains information and settings that are shared by all user accounts. The public folder can be shared with other network users.

**public network**  A network to which you connect with the Public Network connection type.

**random access memory (RAM)**  A data storage area a computer uses to run programs and temporarily store current information. Information stored in RAM is erased when the computer is switched off.

**ReadyBoost**  A Windows feature that makes it possible to increase the available system memory by using a USB flash drive as a memory-expansion device.

**Really Simple Syndication (RSS)**  A method of distributing information from a Web site or blog to subscribers for display in an RSS reader or aggregator.

**recently opened programs list**  A list on the Start menu of the last several programs you have started.

**Recycle Bin**  The folder on your hard disk where Windows temporarily stores files you delete. By default, the Recycle Bin is represented by an icon on the desktop. You can recover deleted files from the Recycle Bin until you empty it.

**registration key**  See *product key*.

**registry**  A repository for information about the computer's configuration. The registry stores settings related to the hardware and software installed on the computer. Registry settings are typically updated through the proper install and uninstall procedures and programs. You can manually update the registry, but only experienced users should undertake this task because mistakes can be disastrous.

**relative path**  A path that defines the position of a file or folder in relation to the current location. For example, ..\Images\MyPicture.png defines a path up one level to the parent folder of the current location, down one level into the Images folder, to the MyPicture image. Relative paths are frequently used in Web site navigational code. See also *absolute path* and *path*.

**remote printer**  A printer that is not connected directly to your computer. See also *network printer* and *shared printer*.

**resolution**  See *screen resolution*.

**restore down**  To return a window from a maximized state to its previous size.

**restore point**  A snapshot of your computer system settings taken by Windows at a scheduled time as well as before any major change, such as installing a program or updating system files. If you experience problems with your system, you can restore it to any saved restore point without undoing changes to your personal files.

**right-click**  To point to an interface element and press the secondary mouse button one time.

**right-drag**  To move an item on the screen by pointing to its title bar or handle, holding down the secondary mouse button, and then moving the mouse. A shortcut menu displaying possible actions appears when you release the mouse button.

**root**  Short for *root folder* or *root directory*. The highest or uppermost level in a hierarchically organized set of information. The root is the folder or directory from which all other folders or directories branch.

**router**  See *network router*.

**RSS**  See *Really Simple Syndication*.

**RSS feed**  See *feed* and *Really Simple Syndication*.

**screen resolution**  The fineness or coarseness of detail attained by a monitor in producing an image, measured in pixels, expressed as the number of pixels wide by the number of pixels high. For example, 1024 × 768. See also *pixel*.

**screen saver**  A blank screen, picture, or moving images that Windows displays after a specified period of inactivity. A screen saver can be used to save power or to hide information while you are away from your desk.

**ScreenTip**  Information that appears when you point to an item.

**scroll bar**  A vertical or horizontal bar that you move to change the position of content within a window.

**search provider**  A company that provides a search engine, which you can use to find information on the Web.

**search term**  The term you type in the Search box of the Start menu or any folder window. Windows then filters the contents of the available storage locations or of the folder window's Content pane to include only the items that contain the search term.

**secondary display**  In a multiple-monitor system, the monitor on to which you can expand programs so that you can increase your work area. See also *primary display*.

**shared component**  A component, such as a DLL file, that is used by multiple programs. When uninstalling a program that uses a shared component, Windows requests confirmation before removing the component.

**shared drive**  A drive that has been made available for other people on a network to access.

**shared folder**  A folder that has been made available for other people on a network to access.

**shared printer**  A printer connected to a computer and made available from that computer for use by other computers on a network.

**share**  To make local files or resources available to other users of the same computer or other computers on a network.

**shortcut**  A link, usually represented by an icon, that opens a program, data file, or device. For example, clicking a shortcut to Microsoft Word starts Word.

**shortcut menu**  A menu displayed when you right-click an object, showing a list of commands relevant to that object.

**shut down**  To initiate the process that closes all your open programs and files, ends your computing session, closes network connections, stops system processes, stops the hard disk, and turns off the computer.

**shut-down options**  Ways in which you can disconnect from the current computing session. You can shut down the computer, switch to a different user account, log off from the computer, lock the computer, restart the computer, or put the computer into Sleep mode or Hibernate mode.

**signature**  See *digital signature*.

**Simple Mail Transfer Protocol (SMTP)** A protocol for sending messages from one computer to another on a network. This protocol is used on the Internet to route e-mail.

**Sleep mode** A Windows feature that saves any open files and the state of any running programs to memory and then puts your computer into a power-saving state.

**SMTP** See *Simple Mail Transfer Protocol*.

**software** Programs that you use to do things with hardware. See also *hardware*.

**software piracy** The illegal reproduction and distribution of software applications.

**sound card** Hardware that enables audio information and music to be recorded, played back, and heard on a computer.

**spyware** Software that can display advertisements (such as pop-up ads), collect information about you, or change settings on your computer, generally without appropriately obtaining your consent.

**standard user account** A type of Windows user account that allows the user to install software and change system settings that do not affect other users or the security of the computer. This account type is recommended for daily use. See also *administrator account*.

**Start menu** A list of options displayed when you click the Start button. The Start menu is your central link to all the programs installed on your computer, as well as to all the tasks you can perform in Windows.

**Start menu Search** A feature of the Start menu that enables you to type any characters in the Search box to immediately display a list of programs, Control Panel items, documents, music, videos, and e-mail messages containing that string of characters, grouped by category.

**Suggested Sites** An Internet Explorer feature that tracks your Internet site visits and recommends other sites that are relevant to your personal browsing history. Suggested Sites was first introduced in Internet Explorer 8.

**surf the Web** To browse information on the Internet.

**syndicated content** See *feed*.

**system cache** An area in the computer memory where Windows stores information it might need to access quickly, for the duration of the current computing session.

**system disk** The hard disk on which the operating system is installed.

**system folder** A folder created on the system disk that contains files required by the Windows operating system.

**tab** In a dialog box, tabs indicate separate pages of settings within the dialog box window; the tab title indicates the nature of the group. You can display the settings by clicking the tab. In Internet Explorer, when tabbed browsing is turned on, tabs indicate separate Web pages displayed within one browser window. You can display a page by clicking its tab, or display a shortcut menu of options for working with a page by right-clicking its tab.

**tabbed browsing** An Internet Explorer feature that enables you to open and view multiple Web pages or files by displaying them on different tabs. You can easily switch between pages or files by clicking the tabs.

**tag** In Windows Explorer, a keyword assigned to a file. See also *keyword*.

**task pane** A fixed pane that appears on one side of a program window, containing options related to the completion of a specific task.

**taskbar** See *Windows Taskbar*.

**taskbar button** A button on the taskbar representing an open window, file, or program. See also *pinned taskbar button*.

**theme** A set of visual elements and sounds that applies a unified look to the computer user interface. A theme can include a desktop background, screen saver, window colors, and sounds. Some themes might also include icons and mouse pointers.

*title bar* The horizontal area at the top of a window that displays the title of the program or file displayed in the window, as well as buttons for controlling the display of the window.

*toolbar* A horizontal or vertical bar that displays buttons representing commands that can be used with the content of the current window. When more commands are available than can fit on the toolbar, a chevron (>>) appears at the right end of the toolbar; clicking the chevron displays the additional commands.

*troubleshooter* A Windows utility for diagnosing and fixing problems. Windows 7 includes more than 20 specific troubleshooters. Troubleshooter categories include programs; hardware and sound; network and Internet; appearance and personalization; and system and security.

*UAC* See *User Account Control*.

*UNC* See *Universal Naming Convention*.

*Uniform Resource Locator (URL)* An address that uniquely identifies the location of a Web site or page. A URL is usually preceded by http://, as in http://www.microsoft.com. URLs are used by Web browsers to locate Internet resources.

*Universal Naming Convention (UNC)* A system for identifying the location on a network of shared resources such as computers, drives, and folders. A UNC address is in the form of \\ComputerName\SharedFolder.

*Universal Serial Bus (USB)* A connection that provides data transfer capabilities and power to a peripheral device. See also *USB hub* and *USB port*.

*upgrade* To replace older hardware with newer hardware or an earlier version of a program with the current version.

*URL* See *Uniform Resource Locator*.

*USB* See *Universal Serial Bus*.

*USB flash drive* A portable flash memory card that plugs into a computer's USB port. You can store data on a USB flash drive or, if the USB flash drive supports ReadyBoost, use all or part of the available drive space to increase the operating system speed. See also *ReadyBoost*.

*USB hub* A device used to connect multiple USB devices to a single USB port, or to connect one or more USB devices to USB ports on multiple computers. The latter type of USB hub, called a *sharing hub*, operates as a switch box to give control of the hub-connected devices to one computer at a time.

*USB port* A connection that provides both power and data transfer capabilities to a hardware device.

*user account* On a Windows computer, a uniquely named account that allows an individual to gain access to the system and to specific resources and settings. Each user account includes a collection of information that describes the way the computer environment looks and operates for that particular user, as well as a private folder not accessible by other people using the computer, in which personal documents, pictures, media, and other files can be stored. See also *administrator account, standard user account*.

*User Account Control (UAC)* A Windows security feature that allows or restricts actions by the user and the system to prevent malicious programs from damaging the computer. Windows 7 has multiple UAC levels.

*user account name* A unique name identifying a user account to Windows.

*user account picture* An image representing a user account. User account pictures are available only for computer-specific user accounts and not on computers that are members of a network domain.

*user credentials* See *credentials*.

*user interface (UI)*  The portion of a program with which a user interacts. Types of user interfaces include command-line interfaces, menu-driven interfaces, and graphical user interfaces.

*video projector*  A device that projects a video signal from a computer onto a projection screen by using a lens system.

*virtual*  A software system that acts as if it were a hardware system. Examples are virtual folders (called *libraries*) and virtual printers.

*virtual printer*  A program that "prints" content to a file rather than on paper. When viewed in the file, the content looks as it would if it were printed.

*Visual Search*  An Internet Explorer feature that displays additional information, including images, in the search results list generated by certain search engines. Visual Search was first introduced in Internet Explorer 8.

*Web*  An abbreviation of *World Wide Web*. A worldwide network consisting of millions of smaller networks that exchange data.

*Web browser*  A software program that displays Web page content and enables you to interact with Web page content and navigate the Internet. Internet Explorer is a Web browser.

*Web feed*  See *feed*.

*Web log*  See *blog*.

*Web Slice*  An Internet Explorer feature that displays up-to-date information from feed-enabled sites on the Favorites bar, without leaving the current Web page. Web Slices were first introduced in Internet Explorer 8.

*Welcome screen*  The screen that appears when you start your computer, containing a link to each active user account and to accessibility tools.

*WEP*  See *Wired Equivalent Privacy*.

*Wi-Fi Protected Access (WPA)*  A security method used by wireless networks. WPA encrypts the information that is sent between computers on a wireless network and authenticates users to help ensure that only authorized people can access the network. WPA2 is a more secure form of WPA.

*wildcard character*  In a search operation, a keyboard character, such as an asterisk (*), a question mark (?), or a pound sign (#), that represents one or more characters in a search term.

*window*  A frame within which your computer runs a program or displays a folder or file. Several windows can be open simultaneously. Windows can be sized, moved, minimized to a taskbar button, maximized to take up the entire screen, or closed.

*Windows Anytime Upgrade*  A Windows feature that you can use to perform an online upgrade of the edition of Windows currently installed on your computer.

*Windows Experience Index*  A Windows utility that assesses a computer system and assigns a base score that reflects the lowest of a set of subscores for the processor, memory, graphics card, and hard disk.

*Windows Live ID*  An e-mail address, registered with the Windows Live ID authentication service, that identifies you to sites and services that use Windows Live ID authentication.

*Windows Sidebar*  See *Desktop Gadget Gallery*.

*Windows Taskbar*  A bar on the desktop that displays buttons you can click to run programs, utilities, and commands, as well as buttons representing the windows of open programs and files.

*Windows Update*  A Windows feature through which you can manually or automatically ensure that your computer operating system is up to date. Windows Update catalogs your computer's hardware and software components, communicates with the Microsoft Update online database, and identifies any updates that are available for your operating system, software, or hardware drivers.

*Wired Equivalent Privacy (WEP)*  An algorithm-based security protocol designed for use with wireless networks. WEP was the original wireless network security protocol and, although not as secure as the more recent Wi-Fi Protected Access (WPA) protocol, is still an option in most wireless router configurations.

*wizard*  A tool that walks you through the steps necessary to accomplish a particular task.

*work network*  A network to which you connect with the Work Network connection type.

*workgroup*  A peer-to-peer computer network through which computers can share resources, such as files, printers, and Internet connections.

*WPA*  See *Wi-Fi Protected Access*.

*XML*  See *Extensible Markup Language (XML)*.

*XML feed*  See *feed*.

*XML Paper Specification (XPS)*  A digital file format for saving documents. XPS is based on XML, preserves document formatting, and enables file sharing. XPS was developed by Microsoft but is platform-independent and royalty-free.

*XPS*  See *XML Paper Specification*.

*zip file*  See *compressed folder*.

*zipped folder*  See *compressed folder*.

# Index

## Symbols and Numbers

# C

# S

# W

# X

# Z

# What do you think of this book?

We want to hear from you!

To participate in a brief online survey, please visit:

**microsoft.com/learning/booksurvey**

Tell us how well this book meets your needs—what works effectively, and what we can do better. Your feedback will help us continually improve our books and learning resources for you.

Thank you in advance for your input!

**Microsoft**® *Press*

## Stay in touch!